'In this important book, Guy Standing, always an original and impassioned thinker, looks at the despoliation of the oceans by overfishing, mining, waste and rising temperatures. The crisis he outlines persuasively and in detail is the result of our short-sighted and largely uncontrolled exploitation. Standing offers radical ideas for creating new forms of common property'
Martin Wolf, *Financial Times*, Books of the Year

'A landmark book . . . *The Blue Commons* is at once a brilliant synthesis, a searing analysis, and an inspiring call to action'
David Bollier

'Standing makes an urgent case for a new politics of the ocean . . . For anyone who has watched a David Attenborough documentary and wished it made a clearer appeal for a change in ocean governance, this is the book for you'
India Bourke, *New Statesman*

'Guy Standing writes with remarkable erudition, but also with passion and lyricism about the Blue Commons. He commands the reader to wake up to the threat posed by *rentier* capitalism's violent policies for extraction, exploitation and depletion of that which is both common to us all, but also vital to our survival: the sea and all within it. He offers radical and hopeful alternatives to the dominant economics for "making a killing" from the commodification of nature'
Ann Pettifor

'As capital sets its sights on the seas, our planet's final frontier, the struggle for the comm[on]
is a powerful, visionary boo[k]
for a better world'
Jason Hickel

About the Author

Guy Standing has held professorships at Bath, London and Monash universities, was a programme director in the UN's International Labour Organization and has advised many international bodies and governments on social and economic policies. He co-founded the Basic Income Earth Network and is now its co-president. He is author of the bestselling *The Precariat: The New Dangerous Class* (2011), *Basic Income: And How We Can Make It Happen* (2017) and *Plunder of the Commons: A Manifesto for Sharing Public Wealth* (2019).

GUY STANDING

The Blue Commons
Rescuing the Economy of the Sea

A PELICAN BOOK

PELICAN
an imprint of
PENGUIN BOOKS

PELICAN BOOKS

UK | USA | Canada | Ireland | Australia
India | New Zealand | South Africa

Penguin Books is part of the Penguin Random
House group of companies whose addresses can
be found at global.penguinrandomhouse.com.

Penguin
Random House
UK

First published 2022
Published in paperback 2023
001

Text copyright © Guy Standing, 2022

The moral right of the author has been asserted

Book design by Matthew Young
Set in 10/14.664pt FreightText Pro
Typeset by Jouve (UK), Milton Keynes
Printed and bound in Great Britain by
Clays Ltd, Elcograf S.p.A.

The authorized representative in the EEA is
Penguin Random House Ireland, Morrison
Chambers, 32 Nassau Street, Dublin D02 YH68

A CIP catalogue record for this book is available
from the British Library

ISBN: 978-0-241-47588-1

MIX
Paper from
responsible sources
FSC® C018179

Penguin Random House is committed to a
sustainable future for our business, our readers
and our planet. This book is made from Forest
Stewardship Council® certified paper.

www.greenpenguin.co.uk

For Andre,
Blue-Green Commoner
Carpe diem!

Contents

Preface

The oceans have a special place in human culture. From the beginning of history, the seas have shaped our human destiny[1] and excited our imaginations, from the fantastical sea creatures in the myths and legends of the ancient world to the underwater civilizations of modern-day science fiction. The sea and its imagery infuse the plays of Shakespeare and star in later classics of English literature, in the works of Joseph Conrad (*Lord Jim*, *Typhoon*), Herman Melville's *Moby Dick*, Ernest Hemingway's *The Old Man and the Sea*, through to Yann Martel's *Life of Pi*, to name but a few.

Alongside tales of pirates and great naval battles, we celebrate the adventures and discoveries of the courageous navigators and explorers: the Polynesians, Vikings and Phoenicians who braved vast ocean expanses in canoes and barques to trade and settle; Zheng He, the fifteenth-century Chinese admiral and explorer, who mounted expeditions as far afield as India and East Africa; Ferdinand Magellan and Francis Drake, the first to circumnavigate the globe in the sixteenth century; the search for the Northwest Passage through the Arctic Ocean, which claimed many British lives before the first navigation by Roald Amundsen of Norway in 1903–6; and Britain's Robin Knox-Johnston, who in 1968–9 became the first person to sail single-handed and non-stop around the world.

And, in rich countries at least, we have a romantic and sentimental regard for fishers and their communities, reinforced by reality TV programmes such as *Deadliest Catch* (about Alaskan crab fishing), with fishers depicted as heroic figures struggling against the elements. How else to explain how fishing rights became a make-or-break issue in the Brexit talks on Britain's exit from the European Union, although fisheries contribute just 0.1% of UK GDP and 0.2% of the EU's?

The immense and uncontrollable forces of the ocean inspire awe and also respect. As we interact with it, we recognize that we are an integral part of nature, and that the seascape in all its glories and power defines our limitations as well as our sense of adventure and love of life. Yet in modern times awe and respect have given way to a hubristic arrogance, grounded in the view that the oceans, the seabeds, coastal wetlands, the seashore, the sandy or rocky beaches and the estuaries where rivers flow into the sea are ours to exploit, for our 'food security', for our pleasure and, increasingly, as our future wealth.

Already, ocean ecosystems are threatened with collapse as a result of humanity's activities on land and sea. Rising water temperatures and acidification from global warming, pollution from industry and agriculture, urban coastal development and overexploitation of fish and other marine life have put at risk the 'life support system of our planet', in the words of António Guterres, UN Secretary-General.[2]

Alexander von Humboldt (1769–1859), the pioneering

explorer and polymath who inspired Charles Darwin and the science of evolution, was perhaps the first to recognize the interconnectedness of ecosystems and warn of the dangers from human attempts to subdue and control nature, such as clearing forests and damming rivers, which he saw in South America. But in recent years these dangers have become existential threats. The destruction of natural habitats and biodiversity has contributed to the growing risk of pandemics such as COVID-19, by bringing people and wild creatures into close proximity and causing viruses deprived of wild hosts to seek an alternative host in humans.[3]

The oceans too are striking back, as warming seas create ever fiercer storms, change weather patterns by shifting global currents and aid the survival and spread of tropical diseases.[4] Rising sea levels lead to coastal erosion, inundations, contamination of freshwater sources and food crops, loss of nesting beaches and displacement of coastal communities as their lands succumb to the invading waters. Moreover, the ocean's ability to act as a carbon sink is weakening, after absorbing as much as half of all anthropogenic carbon emissions over the past two centuries.

Planet Earth is much more blue than green. About 70% of its surface is covered by the seas and oceans, which provide half of the oxygen we breathe and contain about three-quarters of all life. Nearly 40% of the global population live in coastal communities and depend on ocean, coastal and marine resources for their livelihoods and wellbeing. Yet green issues, not blue, have hitherto dominated environmental politics and political movements.

For example, in its 2020 report *State of Nature in the EU*, assessing the status of species and habitats in the European Union, the European Environment Agency had very little to say about the sea, even though the sea area under EU jurisdiction is nearly five times its land area. In a colourful graphic entitled 'The state of nature report in a nutshell', a compressed blue area at the bottom of the page shows a little trawler, a leaping dolphin and a small whale, with the caption 'Status and trends of marine species and habitats remain largely unknown'.[5] At least it deserved marks for honesty.

This inattention is despite the substantial coverage given to the oceans in international debates on the environment in recent years. The awakening of interest was almost certainly due in part to the BBC's *Blue Planet* series, released at the end of 2001 and narrated by Sir David Attenborough. This, and the sequel in 2017, brought the plight of the oceans to global attention. It is even called the 'Blue Planet effect'.[6] Outside the USA, the *Blue Planet* series is one of the most widely viewed documentaries in history.[7] The finale of the second instalment, which saw Attenborough speaking passionately about plastics in the oceans, is regularly cited as a reason for the higher priority given by the international community to ocean pollution since then. In February 2018, Theresa May, then British prime minister, presented the *Blue Planet* box set to Chinese President Xi Jinping while trying to negotiate a post-Brexit trade agreement, a gift to symbolize partnership to protect the oceans.[8]

More controversially, in 2020 Netflix released *Seaspiracy*, a polemical documentary watched by millions that draws attention to the loss of fish species and degradation of ocean habitats caused by a rapacious seafood industry. Though criticized for some inaccuracies and misrepresentation, the film will have convinced many to demand drastic correct- ive action. In a later survey of 8,000 people in England and Wales, 94% said the fate of the oceans and that of humanity were inextricably linked, 85% said safeguarding marine life was personally important to them, and more than half rated global ocean health as 'poor' or 'very poor'.[9]

The desire to save the oceans has led to an astonishing number of international conferences and initiatives, though whether these have achieved much is another matter. And whereas the UN Millennium Development Goals launched by world leaders in 2000 touched only briefly on the oceans, their successor, the UN's Sustainable Development Goals, finalized in 2015, gave the oceans more prominence. Sustain- able Development Goal 14 'life below water' sets ambitious targets for governments, including ending overfishing, mas- sively scaling up marine protected areas, removing plastics from the seas and phasing out all harmful fishing subsidies by the end of 2020. Yet, despite the Blue Planet effect, all these ambitious pledges remain unfulfilled.

This book argues that failure to protect the oceans is an inevitable consequence of the system of 'rentier capitalism' that now dominates human activity in the sea, based on pri- vate property, the drive for profit, the increasing role of fi- nancial institutions and the accumulation of ocean 'assets' by giant conglomerates. The survival of the oceans as a thriv- ing ecosystem, with all the benefits humankind receives from it, depends not only on reversing these trends but on recog- nizing and managing the seas as a commons that we all have an interest in protecting and sustaining.

In the case of fishing, the emphasis should often be on giving, or giving back, management powers to local communities, ideally organized as commons, as many fishing communities were in past times. The key features of a commons community can be summarized as democratic decision-making, shared activity ('commoning'), shared benefits and a concern to sustain and reproduce the source of those benefits to ensure the continued strength of the community.

However, the book goes further in advocating that commons principles should be applied to the oceans in their entirety, including everything in and under the water. And it proposes that every littoral nation should establish a Blue Commons Fund, financed by levies on commercial exploitation of ocean resources, that could be used to redistribute the benefits of exploitation in the form of an equal common dividend, or basic income, to every individual.

The book is not an attempt to provide a comprehensive assessment of the 'blue economy', or the state of the blue environment. It is a call for action to build a 'blue commons' alternative to the 'rentier capitalism' model. Continuation of this model will lead inexorably towards a frightening dystopia, a sorry tale of extinction, as the search for new and short-term sources of profit and wealth depletes marine life and disrupts ecosystems, with irreversible consequences for life on earth, including ours. Instead of trying to maximize growth of GDP, as almost all governments do, we should aim to preserve and enhance our common-wealth, recognizing that the inherent reciprocities between nature and humanity make the benefits of nature a part of that wealth.

*

'They are not fishermen. They are killers.' This was said with some vehemence by a local fisher, Baisha Salim, as we were out on his rod-and-line fishing boat four miles from the East African coast. Shortly before, he had himself killed a dorado, an elegant luminous fish, which at first made his statement seem incongruous. But he had a point. He was looking across the sea at a 15-metre open boat where twenty men were casting a large 'ring-net', about 160 metres in length and several metres in depth, scooping up everything in its wake, big or small, edible or not. The boat, he said, was from the neighbouring country, fishing illegally in his country's waters.

Baisha said he had swum across to cut their net a few weeks before, preventing them from fishing for the day. That evening he had been visited by some local police, accompanied by a man from the boat, who said he should go with them to the police station. He refused. Several people who had gone off with 'police' never came back. But there are wider questions, too. Was the ring-net fishing illegal? It is common for the skippers of such boats to pay local bureaucrats or police for a 'permit', allowing them to operate unmolested by the authorities.

This episode encapsulates many aspects of a story this book tries to tell: the competition for resources that results in overfishing and depletion of fish populations; the struggle to preserve fish populations for the benefit of local communities; the 'crimogenic' nature of fisheries; and the shortcomings of fisheries management and enforcement that have allowed the plunder of the blue commons to continue unabated.

While the book is not only about fisheries, its inspiration

came from the work and activism of my son, André, in support of small-scale fisheries and their organizations in Africa and elsewhere. The book draws on his work, duly cited, and on themes developed in an earlier book of mine, *Plunder of the Commons*.[10] André has read the text and made excellent comments, though of course, all views and conclusions should be attributed to me, not to him.

In the background is the legacy of three remarkable women whose work has shaped a counter-narrative to the mainstream. The first is Rachel Carson (1907–64), a brave and principled trailblazer in the 1950s and early 1960s. In a prophetic television interview in April 1963, Carson stated that 'man's endeavours to control nature by his powers to alter and to destroy would inevitably evolve into a war against himself, a war he would lose unless he came to terms with nature.'[11] Sadly, we have not yet done so.

Carson's view of the sea was lyrically expressed in her seminal book of 1951, *The Sea Around Us*:

> For the sea lies all about us. The commerce of all lands must cross it. The very winds that move over the lands have been cradled on its broad expanse and seek ever to return to it. The continents themselves dissolve and pass to the sea, in grain after grain of eroded land. So, the rains that rose from it return again in rivers. In its mysterious past it encompasses all the dim origins of life and receives in the end, after, it may be many transmutations, the dead husks of that same life. For all at last return to the sea to Oceanus, the ocean river, like the ever-flowing stream of time, the beginning and the end.[12]

The second is Elisabeth Mann Borgese (1918–2002), dubbed 'the mother of the oceans', who fought to change human behaviour towards the oceans and ensure a fair and equitable distribution of their resources to benefit current and future generations. Alongside Arvid Pardo (1914–99), regarded as 'the father of the Law of the Sea', she wrote a proposed constitution for the world's oceans and instigated the first international conference on the law of the sea, held in Malta in 1970, under the title of *Pacem in Maribus* ('Peace in the Oceans').

And the third is Elinor Ostrom (1933–2012), who received the Nobel Prize in Economics in 2009 for her lifetime work on management of the commons for the common good. This put to rest the influential but erroneous claim that only private property could avoid 'the tragedy of the commons', in which a free-for-all resulted in resource depletion and exhaustion.

In addition, I am indebted to the many scholars, particularly marine biologists, whose work on blue issues has informed this book, while personal thanks go to Peter Barnes, Rahul Basu, Maria Bedford, David Bollier, Pete and Sean Darnborough, Pete Linebaugh, Rob Naysmith and Frances Williams. Finally, a special thanks to all those who have taken me out on their boats over the years, off the coasts of Australia, Canada, England, the Faroe Islands, France, Greece, Iceland, Ireland, Italy, Jamaica, Kenya, Mozambique, New Zealand, South Africa, the USA and Zanzibar. Blue commoners all!

Who Owns the Sea?

> The sea is common to all, because it is so limitless that it
> cannot become a possession of any one, and because it is
> adapted for the use of all, whether we consider it from the
> point of view of navigation or of fisheries.
> — Hugo Grotius, 1609.

Who owns the sea? For most of human history the question
would have seemed absurd. By their very nature, like the air
we breathe, the vast expanses of the oceans were considered
common to all and free for all to navigate and fish. No individual or nation could claim ownership or jurisdiction, or deprive others of use of the sea. Yet by the end of the twentieth
century, nations had done precisely that, establishing property rights in the sea that have turned much of the blue commons into zones of exclusion and private profit. The world's
failure to manage and protect the oceans as a commons belonging to us all is wreaking havoc on ocean ecosystems that
support life on earth.

The commons as a legal concept stems from ancient
Roman law, and specifically the Justinian Codex of AD 529–34.
A Byzantine by birth, Justinian became Roman Emperor in
AD 527 and, finding the laws confusing and incoherent, set

up a commission of jurists to codify them. The AD 529 Codex has been lost, but a version from AD 534 has shaped common law for nearly 1,500 years. Among its achievements was the definition of four types of property – *res privatae* (private thing/matter), *res publicae* (public thing/matter), *res nullius* (nobody's thing/matter) and *res communis* (common thing/matter). The last category is often expressed as *res communes omnium* (things belonging to all).

Alongside the Codex, a textbook for law students produced in AD 533 contained the following much-cited passage that was articulated hundreds of years earlier by the classical jurist Marcian in the early second century AD. As a result, Marcian has often been called the founder of the common law of the sea:

> For certain things are common to all by the law of nature, certain things are public, certain belong to an entire body [of the people], certain to no one, many things to individuals, which are acquired by each person in different ways . . . And, in fact, the following items are common to all persons through natural law: the air, and flowing water, and the sea, and through this the shores of the sea.[1]

Fourteen centuries later, in his *Mare Liberum* (*The Free Sea*, sometimes translated as *The Freedom of the Seas*), which became a standard reference for debates on property rights in the sea, Dutch lawyer Hugo Grotius echoed this theme in stating emphatically, 'Nature knows no sovereigns.' He was writing in 1609, at a time of mercantilist states that, led by his own country, the Netherlands, and Great Britain, Spain and Portugal, were battling for supremacy of the sea routes and for the spoils to be gained from them. The seas, he wrote, are inappropriable and inexhaustible, therefore they are not property.

Drawing on theological and legal theory, Grotius wrote his tract in response to what was known as the *mare clausum* (closed sea) policy. In the Treaty of Tordesillas of 1494, Spain and Portugal, then the two Catholic superpowers, had agreed to divide up newly discovered lands and the seas of the known world between them. In effect, this and a later treaty gave Portugal control of the Indian Ocean and most of the South Atlantic east of a defined North-South meridian line, while Spain claimed the Pacific and the Atlantic waters west of the same meridian and so almost the entire land mass of the Americas from South to North. (The one exception was Brazil, whose lands extended east of the meridian, which was duly granted to Portugal.) The carve-up was ratified by Pope Alexander VI (Rodrigo Borgia, who was Spanish by origin) and his successors in a series of papal bulls. Grotius made the obvious point, among others, that the Pope had no right to divide up ownership of the seas, since papal authority surely could not extend to members of other churches or to 'infidels'.

Some have claimed that Grotius was merely trying to defend freedom of the seas for Dutch fishing and trading monopolies. The subtitle to his book was 'The right that belongs to the Dutch to take part in the East Indian trade'. And there was tension between Portugal and the Netherlands at the time, sparked by a blatant act of piracy by a Dutch ship in 1603 when it seized a valuable cargo from a Portuguese ship near Singapore.

However, *Mare Liberum* made the more general case that the seas could not be turned into national property. Naturally, this proposition was opposed by Spain and Portugal, but there were dissenting views in Britain too. The most notable was the riposte by English jurist John Selden, whose *Mare Clausum* of 1635 asserted that England had sovereign rights over the adjacent seas. Earlier, soon after the publication of *Mare Liberum*, a Scottish lawyer, William Welwood, argued that Scottish fishermen had the right to unchallenged use of their own waters. In a published response to Welwood, Grotius noted that he was referring to what we typically call the open sea, where 'the use of that which belongs to no one must necessarily be open to all, and among the uses of the sea is fishing'.

For aeons, the seas, rivers and lakes of the world teemed with life. The idea that there could be a shortage of water or of fish would have seemed ridiculous. They were free 'states of nature', accessible to all and free for use by all. The rights to have water to drink and to fish – the right of piscary – were later enshrined in one of the twin foundational documents of the British constitution, the Charter of the Forest of 1217, which accompanied the Magna Carta. The Charter, which subsequently became law, aimed to prevent the monarch and landholders from depriving local people – commoners – of their rights to access their traditional commons and make use of their resources.

But property ownership bred ambition. The powerful annexed more and more of the land for their exclusive use, mainly through enclosure – the erection of physical barriers to access, such as hedges, ditches, fences and walls. This enabled them to wrest control of the resources and amenities of the commons that could be used for production, including sources of water. Lakes and streams where commoners previously fished could be dammed to power watermills. Fish could be taken by or with permission of the landowner and sold in the market at a profit.

In 1804, the eighth Earl of Lauderdale, an amateur political economist, wrote a perceptive essay in which he observed that as private riches increased, public wealth declined. This has been dubbed the Lauderdale Paradox. As the rich enriched themselves by taking ever more from what had been the commons, they effectively restricted supply and created 'contrived scarcity' of what had previously been abundant, free and accessible to all. Restricting supply pushed up prices of these newly generated commodities, which could then be sold for private gain.

Those living in the commons were depicted as holding back 'progress'. What commoners had for centuries regarded as nature's bounties, to be conserved and reproduced, to be cherished and nourished, were seen as resources for economic growth, for progress. Nature could only be harnessed to progress and economic growth if it could be exploited, which required private ownership ready to sacrifice reproduction for profit. Thus emerged the rationalization for private property rights.

For generations, this view, which drove the Industrial Revolution of the eighteenth and nineteenth centuries and the formation of industrial capitalism, seemed relevant primarily to exploitation of the land-based natural world. But there was a more turbulent economic frontier waiting for capitalism and the 'free market' economy: the sea, and the globe's great oceans.

Following Grotius, the seas were considered to be a 'state

of nature', with open access for all. This was anathema to societies wedded to the idea of economic progress. Mercantilist powers set out to 'rule the seas', to protect their commercial interests. In the sixteenth century, the main goal was to secure commodity trading routes on the high seas; fishing was mostly confined to the near shore. However, the Dutch developed an export-led fishing industry in the seventeenth century, building bigger vessels and salting their catches on board. They also became a dominant maritime trading nation, largely based on trade with the Far East, including Japan, before losing primacy to the British in the eighteenth century. Later, in the nineteenth century, at the height of empire, Britain imposed the *Pax Britannica*, using its unrivalled sea power to control most of the world's most important maritime trade routes.

Meanwhile, the seas' resources, which until the twentieth century basically meant fish and other sea creatures, were treated as *res nullius*, belonging to nobody, and so could be taken at will and become somebody's property. In 1851, Herman Melville's classic novel *Moby Dick*, about the obsessive pursuit of a giant white whale, described the difference between 'fast fish' and 'loose fish'. 'Fast fish' were those made 'fast' to the boat and, via possession, became the private property of the fisher or whaler. 'Loose fish' were for anyone to take if they could. This broadly accepted rule of thumb, observed by fishing and whaling communities, was to influence jurisprudence in fisheries, particularly in the USA.[2]

The nineteenth century saw US courts rationalizing private property rights in nature by citing the so-called 'law of nature' derived from the philosophical father of private property rights, John Locke. Writing in the seventeenth century as capitalism took shape, he had argued that the earth – 'God's Commons' – was given to man with the obligation to appropriate it for the fulfilment of his needs and desires. *Ferae naturae* (wild nature) became the property of man if he exerted labour to obtain it. Henceforth, 'possession' became synonymous with private property.

The nineteenth century also saw transformative structural changes in the fishing industry. Instead of swarms of small boats, larger industrial fisheries took over as mechanization ushered in the era of steam trawlers. In 1882 in Grimsby, then the biggest English fishing port, there were 623 sail-powered fishing boats and just two steamers. In 1909, there were 29 sailing vessels and 608 steamers. This reflected a shift to distant-water fishing. As a correlate, seas that had hitherto been 'states of nature', inaccessible to most fishers, became zones of conflict over access to 'resources'.

Market competition became two struggles, between commercial, profit-oriented fisheries and artisanal or commoner fisher communities, and between the fishing industries of rival countries, sometimes spilling over into skirmishes and shows of military force. And these struggles intensified further with the second industrialization of fisheries, the so-called Great Acceleration, between the 1950s and the late 1970s.[3] Large-scale fishery corporations emerged, alongside global commodity chains providing high-value fish to wealthy customers all over the world.

In the post-1945 era, under the influence of then-orthodox economic development theory, the main policy model was state-led industrialization, involving public-private investment in fishing fleets, infrastructure, processing plants and research. In developing countries, the UN's Economic Commission for Latin America and the Caribbean (ECLAC) was the leading advocate of this strategy. One lasting consequence was that some coastal states came to have huge industrial fisheries. In Chile and Peru, fishing capacity increased by about 1,300% between 1955 and 1970.[4]

The adverse impact of this huge global expansion of industrial fisheries on fish populations and on small-scale fisheries lent new urgency to the need for global regulation of what nations and their fishing industries could do in the open sea. The issue of who owns the sea became the subject of protracted international negotiations that concluded with the 1982 UN Convention on the Law of the Sea (UNCLOS).

The 'Great Enclosure' of the sea

Without trying to trace the full history of UNCLOS, it is worth recalling two conflicts over fishing, between the USA and Japan and between Britain and Iceland, because they had a profound effect on the negotiations and the subsequent commercialization of the sea.

The first conflict began in July 1937 when thirty Japanese commercial fishery vessels, several weighing over 10,000 tonnes with onboard canning and processing facilities, moved into Bristol Bay in the Bering Sea off the coast of Alaska to catch prized wild salmon traditionally reserved for American consumers. Although the US and Japanese governments reached an agreement in 1938 to stop the incursions, it ceased to be honoured by Japan following its attack on the US naval base at Pearl Harbor, Hawaii, in December 1941.

After Japan was crushed militarily, the US administration promptly issued what became known as the Truman Proclamation in September 1945, which unilaterally declared that all the resources of the seabed on the US 'continental shelf' belonged to the United States. The continental shelf was defined as extending out to a depth of 200 metres. A concurrent proclamation extended US jurisdiction to fishing in areas of the high seas off the US coast that were important, actually or potentially, to US fishers.

Although ostensibly aimed at establishing conservation areas, this was an act of imperial power. The proclamations were the first modern assertion of exclusive jurisdiction over marine resources beyond a country's territorial sea (usually regarded as twelve nautical miles). And they set a precedent.

In June 1947, Chile and then Peru went further and declared that 200 nautical miles beyond their coasts were henceforth their exclusive territory. The reason for the selection of 200 miles seems to have been Chile's use of a map drawn up by the USA and Britain in 1939 to block the resupplying of Axis ships from South American ports. This was formalized in the Santiago Declaration of 1952 between Chile, Ecuador and Peru, by which time a number of Arab states had made similar moves.

The Santiago Declaration was the first international instrument asserting a 200-mile limit, and deserves to be quoted:

> owing to the geological and biological factors affecting the existence, conservation and development of the marine fauna and flora of the waters adjacent to the coasts of the declarant countries, the former extent of the territorial

sea and contiguous zone is insufficient to permit of the conservation, development and use of those resources, to which the coastal countries are entitled.

Accordingly, the three governments proclaimed 'as a principle of their international maritime policy that each of them possesses sole sovereignty and jurisdiction over the area of sea adjacent to the coast of its own country and extending not less than 200 nautical miles from the said coast'.

The Declaration also provided for sole sovereignty and jurisdiction over the sea floor and subsoil, and maintained the principle of 'innocent passage' through the zone but not, as in Chilean and Peruvian legislation, freedom of navigation.

The UN Convention on the Continental Shelf of April 1958 enshrined national sovereignty over the continental shelf in international law. However, for a while, many coastal countries continued to operate with modest enclosure of the sea around them, usually imposing strict sovereignty for three nautical miles from the coastline and less stringent rules up to twelve miles. These distances were also arbitrary in origin. The three-mile limit was first proposed in 1702 by Dutch jurist Cornelius van Bynkershoek, this being then considered the limit of the range of coastal cannon.

The global enclosure of the seas was further accelerated by the conflict between Britain and Iceland over fishing rights. Iceland has always depended on its fishing industry, especially on the export of cod. But as cod stocks in the North Atlantic came under stress, more British vessels began fishing in traditional Icelandic waters. Three defining 'cod wars' between Iceland and Britain occurred between 1958 and 1976; each resulted in victory for Iceland after clashes at sea involving the Royal Navy and the Icelandic Coast Guard in which the nets of British fishing boats were cut and both sides mounted ramming attacks. The first, between 1958 and 1961, began when Iceland extended its exclusive fishing zone from four to twelve nautical miles. The second, between 1972 and 1973, followed Iceland's extension of its fishing zone to fifty miles, and cost one life and considerable damage to boats. It ended when Iceland threatened to leave NATO, the North Atlantic Treaty Organization, at which point Britain conceded the extension in return for some limited fishing rights.

The third cod war began in July 1975 when, following calls at the third United Nations Conference on the Law of the Sea for a 100-nautical-mile limit to territorial waters, Iceland followed the Chilean precedent in extending its fishing zone to 200 nautical miles. After more expensive and dangerous engagements at sea, and further threats by Iceland to withdraw from NATO, the UK again conceded. This led to the loss of several thousand jobs in British fishing ports.[5]

The third cod war gave further impetus to global acceptance of the principle of national sovereignty over an Exclusive Economic Zone (EEZ) extending 200 nautical miles from the coast. Enshrined in the United Nations Convention on the Law of the Sea (UNCLOS) in 1982, this can be described as the greatest single act of enclosure in the history of the world, covering about a third of the world's oceans.

According to UNCLOS, an Exclusive Economic Zone is defined as:

an area beyond and adjacent to the territorial sea [in which] the coastal State has (a) sovereign rights for the purpose of exploring and exploiting, conserving and managing the natural resources, whether living or non-living, of the waters super-jacent to the seabed and of the seabed and its subsoil, and with regard to other activities for the economic exploitation and exploration of the zone, such as the production of energy from the water, currents and winds ... [6]

UNCLOS also granted states rights to the seabed of the continental shelf if it extended beyond their EEZ, up to 350 nautical miles from the coast. And it solidified the notion of 'territorial seas' up to twelve nautical miles, which have sometimes been reserved for small-scale fisheries.

There were dissenting voices opposed to the EEZ concept, and one above all others. Arvid Pardo, a Maltese-Swedish diplomat described as 'the father of the Law of the Sea Conference', used a passionate speech at the UN General Assembly in November 1967 to argue that all the sea beyond immediate territorial waters should be regarded as the 'common heritage of mankind'.[7] He warned of the dangers of allowing a few technologically and militarily strong countries to dominate the oceans for their own benefit. His warnings were to no avail.

The global legitimization of EEZs was in effect an act of neo-colonization. Countries with long coastlines, such as Australia and Russia, gained most, as did those with large archipelagos of islands, such as Indonesia and Japan. The USA, France and Britain also won huge tracts of blue territory for their exclusive exploitation and profit, thanks to colonial possessions far from their own countries. As a result, France today is the world's biggest sea-holder, with 11.7 million square kilometres, followed by the USA, with 11.4 million km², and then Australia (8.5 million km²), Russia (7.5 million km²), the UK (6.8 million km²), Indonesia (6.2 million km²), Canada (5.6 million km²), Japan (4.5 million km²), New Zealand (4.1 million km²) and Brazil (3.8 million km²).[8]

It is noteworthy that the two largest countries in terms of population, China and India, do not figure in the top ten. China's EEZ under UNCLOS is only 900,000 km², so it is scarcely surprising that it has a sense of grievance now that it has emerged as a world superpower. In defiance of UNCLOS demarcations and a ruling in 2016 by an international tribunal, it is backing its claims to ownership of small islands and reefs in the South China Sea, and the marine resources that go with them, with construction of military bases and naval patrols. While its actions threaten to become serious military flashpoints, they are also a reflection of the inherent unfairness of the UNCLOS division of the seas.

Moreover, about 90% of all marine catch is taken inside EEZs, and those wanting to fish in EEZs must pay for the privilege. This favours industrial fisheries for which licence payments are a minor cost, while squeezing out small-scale artisanal fisheries. It is scarcely an exaggeration to say that the establishment of EEZs also spawned what decades later became known as IUU (illegal, unreported and unregulated) fishing, since it effectively criminalized those fisheries unable or unwilling to pay for access.

The vast enclosure of the sea unleashed by UNCLOS in effect turned it from an 'open access' unmanaged zone – a 'state of nature' – into a commons managed by the state for its citizens. Yet governments have mostly ignored their acquired responsibility to protect the sea as a commons, from which all their citizens are entitled to benefit. Just as the owners of landed property used enclosure to deprive commoners of access to resources, claiming them instead for private profit, so the legitimation of sovereignty over the continental shelf and the Exclusive Economic Zones established the basis for governments to hand the exploitation of marine resources to private, often multinational, corporations whose primary interest is making money for their owners and shareholders, wherever they may be in the world.

The following chapters show how treating the seas as private property and a source of profit has set a disastrous course that has not only severely damaged ocean ecosystems and the livelihoods and cultures of coastal communities but will inevitably continue to do so, whatever the environmental rhetoric of governments and companies. The rest of this chapter gives a brief overview of the present dire state of the oceans and their coastal hinterlands, the result of treating the commons not as *res communis* that belong to us all but as *res nullius*, available for private appropriation but nobody's responsibility to preserve and protect.

The state of fisheries

The oceans are home to about 28,000 identified species of fish, alongside a bewildering diversity of other marine life that has evolved over millions of years. But over the past century, and particularly in the past three decades, humanity has devastated ocean ecosystems at an increasing pace, most conspicuously though not exclusively by overfishing. By early in the twenty-first century, the majority of major fish species were under threat. Some species have already become too scarce to regenerate and risk extinction. And many of the most beautiful and most prized fish are disappearing. For instance, bluefin tuna, the preferred delicacy of the world's finest sushi chefs, sank to 3% of its historical population by the mid-noughties and was set to become as rare as the Bengal tiger before tougher restrictions on catches of Atlantic bluefin led to a modest and still fragile recovery.

The depletion of the world's fish began in pre-industrial times as the expansion of agriculture, deforestation, draining of marshlands, and dams to power grain mills fouled fresh water, reducing stocks of migratory freshwater fish. Then commercial fleets of whalers and sealers killed off much of the marine mammal life.

Once steamers emerged, destruction spread to many kinds of saltwater fish. This was worsened by subsequent technological changes, including the shift from coal to oil for fuel after the First World War, refrigeration and the building of government-financed industrial long-distance trawlers after the Second World War, and energy-intensive deep-sea fishing. All these developments have been facilitated by state subsidies through the ages and in various guises, starting with funding by monarchs and rich merchants.

The share of the world's fish populations being fished unsustainably rose from an estimated 10% in 1974 to 34% in 2020.[9] About 88% of all designated fish stocks around the world are either fully exploited or are overexploited. In 2020, an international study concluded that of 1,300 species of fish and marine invertebrates examined, 82% are being removed faster than they can repopulate.[10]

Overfishing – taking too many fish, so reducing the ability of fish stocks to reproduce in sufficient numbers – is not the only reason for depletion of fish populations across the world. Other causes include 'unbalanced' fishing that breaks the food chain, for example, by ravaging sardine stocks, which deprives larger species of adequate diets, and industrial fishing methods that destroy fish habitats and breeding grounds, notably by 'bottom trawling' with huge weighted nets that scrape the seabed.

Then there is the impact of other human activities: ocean warming and acidification caused by global heating; the devastation caused by millions of tonnes of plastic, unchecked oil spills and the pumping of diesel fuel into the sea; the damage and destruction from mining and related activity in the sea, such as the drilling for oil and gas by BP in the world's largest deep-sea coral reef (see Chapter 8); and the weakening and displacement of 'blue commoners', communities of fisherfolk whose practices reproduce and preserve local ecosystems.

Among other concerns, plunging fish populations threaten economic development. About 80% of all seafood is produced in developing countries, while more than 90% of fishers and fish farmers are in Africa and Asia. Ocean warming alone is predicted to reduce wild fish catches by 8% between 2000 and 2050, affecting the livelihoods of over 650 million people globally and threatening the food security of many more. Catch potential in tropical waters may decline by 40% or more.[11]

The word 'production' seems odd in the case of fish, but it is the word used in most official reports. It covers the capture of what are called 'wild' fish and fish bred and produced on fish farms. According to the UN Food and Agriculture Organization (FAO), fish production amounted to about 180 million tonnes in 2018, taking saltwater and freshwater species together, and is now about five times as large as in the 1950s.[12]

Much of this growth reflects soaring aquaculture production, from virtually nothing in the 1950s to nearly half of total production in 2018. Meanwhile, humans' annual fish consumption has risen by more than five times since the 1950s to over 20 kilos per person, as production has outpaced population growth, the increase being most dramatic in developing countries. Aquaculture provided just 7% of fish for human consumption in 1974. Three decades later that share was 39%, and since 2016 aquaculture has become the main source of fish for human consumption, providing just over half in 2018.

As far as marine catches are concerned, however, we know that official FAO statistics are substantial underestimates. According to one study, using a 'catch reconstruction' method, total marine catch peaked at 130 million tonnes in the late 1990s rather than the 86 million tonnes estimated by the FAO, meaning reconstructed catches are 53% above reported data.[13] And whereas the FAO figures suggest only a slight decline after that, the reconstructed figures suggest a much steeper decline.

One reason for the discrepancy is that the catch by small-scale fisheries is substantially under-reported in many countries. It also reflects the omission in the FAO figures of discarded bycatch, recreational fishing and illegal and unreported catch. FAO data refer to 'landings' and explicitly exclude discarded catches, estimated at over ten ten million tonnes every year. Moreover, neither the FAO data nor the reconstructed data include estimates of so-called 'underwater discards', fish kills due to fishing gear, or what is known as 'ghost fishing' when fish are caught in lost or abandoned fishing gear.

Blame for marine destruction rests predominantly with industrial fishing, which took off in the twentieth century. Before that, seas 'seethed with life'.[14] Only 10% of the historical populations of big fish remain.[15] About 100 million sharks are killed every year, many just for their fins to make shark-fin soup, a popular Chinese dish. The number of sharks around the world has shrunk by about three-quarters in the past fifty years or so.[16] But the destruction goes all the way down the food chain. For instance, stocks of krill, on which whales in particular depend, have declined by 80% since the 1970s.[17] Sadly for those who love to eat them, we have lost 85% of all wild oyster reefs in the world.[18] Even above the sea, the destruction continues. Seabird numbers have declined by 70%.[19]

Every year, 100,000 small whales, dolphins and porpoises are slaughtered for meat, bait or body parts.[20] Some are processed into pet food for export. Others go into flourishing illegal markets. Many are caught and killed simply because they are regarded as competitors for the remaining fish.[21] Others are dying from ingesting heavy metals, chlorinated organic compounds and other toxic substances that shorten lifespans and their fertility. North Atlantic whales are one step away from extinction, hit by shipping or weakened by entanglement in fishing gear.[22]

Depletion has been so great that 'in every ocean basin,

hotspots of life are only relics of what was once there'.[23] By the late 1980s, the capacity of the world's fishing fleets was already one-third more than needed to catch all the available fish in the world's oceans.[24] As the saying goes, too many boats are chasing too few fish. This is due partly to technological advances that have enabled bigger boats to catch and process more fish, and partly to mercantilist trends unleashed by globalization, in which every country has been urged to become 'more competitive'.

It is not just the number and variety of fish that have been shrinking, but also the size of those that remain. For instance, the average size of swordfish today is less than half what it was a hundred years ago.[25] Global warming is one factor; overfishing is another. And another trend threatening artisanal fisheries is that catching fish is moving deeper. The average depth for industrial fishing is 350 metres below the average in 1950, which is increasingly removing low-productivity species that live at greater depths and cannot quickly recover.[26]

Fish are the staple diet for much of the world. Over three billion people rely on fish for 20% of their average animal protein intake, and in some countries, such as Bangladesh, Ghana and Cambodia, it can be 50% or more.[27] High demand for fish has raised prices and made fish production extremely profitable for commercial companies and their financiers. It has also driven international trade in fish, which has grown enormously in recent decades. In 2018, the overall trade value of seafood reached $184 billion, making it one of the most valuable non-petroleum products traded internationally. The growth of trade has been both a cause and consequence of the increase in fish consumption, and thus also of overfishing.

Out of sight of almost all of humanity, supersized fishing trawlers, many longer than a football pitch, have been plundering the oceans. They use longlining – long lines with thousands of baited hooks – or huge circular nets known as purse-seine nets that close like a purse around whole shoals of fish. Meanwhile, the seas are dotted with hundreds of thousands of buoys called fish aggregating devices, often equipped with sonar and GPS, that draw huge numbers of fish into one place to be swept up.[28] It is a fishing-industrial complex with a high-tech slaughterhouse out in the open, only made possible by state enclosure of EEZs. The industrial fisheries effectively buy, through state licensing, an exclusive area where they are permitted to place the fish aggregating devices, in an unheralded extension of private property rights to the ocean.

These trawlers are not only catching too many fish to sell. They gather huge bycatches of unwanted species that are thrown back dead. And their industrial methods shatter habitats on which marine life depends to survive and reproduce. In a few hours, trawlers can devastate vast areas that nature took thousands of years to create. According to one study, 'Each year the world's fleet of bottom trawlers disturbs a seabed area twice the size of the contiguous United States.'[29] Industrial fishing is undoubtedly the main cause of marine biodiversity destruction.[30]

A number of countries, including members of the European Union, have belatedly taken steps to ban or restrict bottom trawling in parts of the sea they control. However, only Hong Kong, Indonesia, Palau and Belize have banned the practice altogether. (In 2021 Indonesia reimposed its ban after lifting it just months earlier under pressure from its large-scale fisheries.) Even where prohibitions exist, they are barely enforced. Checks, inspections and sanctions are rare. And it is hard to imagine the coastguard of tiny Palau (population 18,000) confronting the mighty trawler fleet of China.

Moreover, in 2006 fishing nations led by Iceland, Russia, China and South Korea stymied a proposed United Nations ban on bottom trawling on the high seas, the seas beyond national jurisdiction. Except off Antarctica, industrial fisheries can operate on the high seas with few restraints, and New Zealand, Japan, the Cook Islands, Spain, South Korea and the Faroe Islands all permit their flagged vessels to bottom trawl in international waters.

While fish populations in the seas and oceans are in crisis, river and lake fish, which account for over half the world's known fish species and provide the main source of protein for 200 million people, are in even worse trouble. The main causes of plunging populations are man-made – the hundreds of thousands of dams, habitat destruction, overfishing, global warming, and water pollution and extraction. Nearly a third of freshwater fish species face extinction.[31]

Migratory river fish, such as salmon, trout and giant catfish, have declined by over three-quarters since 1970.[32] In Europe they have fallen by over 90%, with sturgeon and eels virtually disappearing. This has had a devastating impact on river ecosystems, affecting many species inland that rely on migratory fish and the nutrients they bring upriver, including land animals such as bears, wolves and birds of prey. About 1,100 freshwater species must migrate in order to survive.[33] Human actions are blocking them from doing so. In a few places, management and restoration plans, including the removal of dams no longer needed, have curbed losses and stimulated recovery, but such projects remain few and far between.

The extinction threat: blue pollution, global warming and ocean acidification

Pollution of the sea is accelerating the damage caused by industrialized fishing. The deep sea has been used as a dumping ground for radioactive waste, sewage, toxic chemicals and much else. Oil production and transportation has been a major culprit, the two worst cases being the Exxon Valdez disaster in Alaska in 1989 and the Deepwater Horizon explosion in 2010, which spewed 4.9 million barrels (210 million US gallons) of crude oil into the Gulf of Mexico. To compound the damage, the chemicals used to disperse the spill are also toxic for marine life.

Oil and other discharges from ships are a regular occurrence. Industrial fishing is a major polluter as well as a threat to fish populations. The ratio of oil used to fish caught is extraordinary – fifty billion litres of oil to land just over eighty million tonnes of fish. Fisheries account for nearly 2% of global oil consumption, and most of that is accounted for by large industrial trawlers.[34] Industrial fishing is the most energy-intensive food production method in the world.[35] And the energy efficiency of fishing has actually declined, because vessels need to search longer for fish and to fish deeper in offshore waters as coastal stocks decline.

Commercial activities on land are another major source of ocean pollution. Excess fertilizer dumped or leached into rivers goes to the sea where cyanobacteria (blue-green algae) feed on the nutrients and proliferate. As they die, they feed bacteria which suck oxygen from the water, asphyxiating sea creatures. Industrial agriculture is responsible for an increasing incidence of toxic algae blooms around the world, with 300 reported incidents in 2018. But pollution from industry and raw sewage are also factors.

To mention just a few egregious incidents in recent years, in 2007 mysterious algae spread for hundreds of miles along China's eastern seaboard, including near the port city of Qingdao, which was due to host the sailing events in the 2008 Olympics. Chinese environmentalists attributed the algae to industrial pollution and fish farming.[36] In South Africa, an algae bloom killed 200 tonnes of rock lobster in 2015. A 'red tide' off Florida lasted fourteen months into 2019, killing manatees, dolphins and sea turtles, and hundreds of tonnes of fish. And in 2021 a plague of slimy 'sea snot' (marine mucilage) blanketed harbours, shorelines and swathes of sea south of Istanbul in Turkey's Sea of Marmara, choking aquatic life including vulnerable corals; this was blamed on industrial waste and untreated sewage from coastal cities and ships.

Toxic algae blooms have made water supplies in some parts of the USA temporarily unfit to drink or use for washing.[37] A bloom in Lake Erie covered over 600 square miles. And the blooms pump brevetoxins into the air, which are harmful to humans as well as marine and aquatic life. Eating fish poisoned by toxins can kill marine mammals and seabirds, but it is also dangerous for human health, forcing the temporary closure of affected fisheries.[38]

Although oxygen-depleted 'dead zones' can arise naturally, pollution from agricultural effluent and untreated sewage has increased their frequency and longevity. This is exacerbated by rising water temperatures due to global warming, because warmer water itself holds less oxygen. Some dead zones cover vast expanses of the ocean. One dead zone in the vital Bay of Bengal, a cradle of fish serving the eight countries adjoining it and their export markets, extends over 60,000 square kilometres.[39] And even where oxygen depletion is not enough to stifle marine life, it still has a deleterious effect, for example, in reducing the maximum size of fish species.

Ocean temperatures have risen sharply since the late 1950s, and the five years 2017–21 were the hottest on record. Warmer water expands, causing sea levels to rise. By the end of the twenty-first century, the sea level is expected to rise by about a metre, sufficient to displace an estimated 150 million people living in coastal regions.[40] And atmospheric changes above the warming water are causing more frequent and more destructive storms and floods, which have already wiped out some small-scale fishing communities by destroying boats, equipment and infrastructure, made fishing everywhere more dangerous, and cost lives and livelihoods in coastal communities.

Ocean warming is also producing new phenomena that are killing marine life up and down the food chain. In 2016, a giant 'hot blob' spanning 380,000 square miles (one million square kilometres) off the north-west coast of the United States caused the death of about a million seabirds, apparently from starvation. The warmer water boosted the metabolism of fish such as salmon and halibut, increasing competition for a limited supply of smaller fish.[41]

Up to now, the oceans have been a buffer against climate

change, soaking up over 90% of the excess heat linked to rising greenhouse gases produced by humans since 1970, and absorbing a quarter of the carbon dioxide emitted by vehicles, power stations and factories.[42] But there is huge uncertainty as to how much CO_2 they will absorb in the future, partly because global heating is disrupting the oceanic carbon cycle and partly because human activity is weakening the oceans' storage capacity.

For example, industrial fishing for Antarctic krill threatens to deplete this tiny crustacean that plays a vital role in oceanic carbon capture.[43] Meanwhile, industrial trawling and pollution are destroying seagrass meadows which, besides being important fish breeding habitats and a vital support for other marine ecosystems, are one of the world's most efficient carbon sinks;[44] they alone account for 10% of the ocean's carbon sequestration.[45] Moreover, recent studies suggest that, because the oceans naturally equilibrate with the atmosphere, if we succeed in reducing atmospheric CO_2 concentrations, the oceans will correspondingly reduce absorption, making tackling climate change more difficult.[46]

The absorption of so much carbon dioxide is also making the oceans more acidic, which destroys corals, a vital habitat for marine species.[47] Acidification disrupts fish shoal behaviour important for acquiring food and protecting against predators, increases fish mortality and reduces reproduction.[48] Shellfish are being affected in similar ways, particularly in European waters.[49]

Global warming is thus threatening fisheries through habitat destruction, pollution, deoxygenation and ocean acidification.[50] Although total production has continued to expand, catch-per-unit-of-effort worldwide has approximately halved since the 1950s.[51] According to the authoritative Intergovernmental Panel on Climate Change, the impact of global warming alone could reduce fish catches by a quarter by the end of the twenty-first century, relative to the average between 1986 and 2005.[52]

While overfishing is considered an even greater threat to fish populations than climate change,[53] drastic reductions in global CO_2 emissions will be needed to prevent falling global catches and revenues, concentrated in the tropics.[54] The decline in revenue is expected to be much greater than the fall in total catch, because of a bigger drop in catches of high-value fish. And the fall in catches is likely to have the most adverse impact on countries nutritionally dependent on fish, primarily in West Africa.[55] Data already suggest that higher ocean acidity and falling fish consumption have increased neonatal mortality in coastal low-income communities.[56]

Another consequence of rising ocean temperatures is the melting of sea ice in the Arctic. This has opened up prospective trading routes for shipping as well as drilling for oil and gas, with all their pollution risks for this fragile ecosystem. For China, a 'polar silk road' could cut ten to twelve days from the time now taken to send goods to Europe by sea.[57] But an increasingly ice-free Arctic Ocean is fuelling global tensions as well as pollution risks. Both the USA and Russia have security concerns about China's plans, and the eight-nation Arctic Council, set up in 1996 as a forum for regional cooperation, has no mandate to resolve security issues.

How plastics shame us all

Plastic waste has ravaged the blue commons for decades, but only recently have its disastrous effects been recognized. It comes down rivers in horrifying quantities, and a growing proportion is dumped in the sea from boats,[58] with no respect for nations, local communities or the fisherfolk who rely on the sea.

Plastic, especially microplastic, kills birds, turtles, mammals and fish, destroys the marine environment and is ingested by land creatures that eat fish, including humans. Carried on ocean currents, plastic 'rafts' transport alien and invasive species, including toxic microalgae, across the world, reaching some of the planet's most sensitive and unique environments such as Antarctica and the Galapagos Islands.[59]

The scale is staggering. Every year about eleven million tonnes of plastic reach the oceans and, while the plastic debris washed up on beaches and coastlines around the world is only too visible, the vast bulk of plastic in the oceans degrades into microparticles that float below the surface or sink to the bottom, doing untold damage out of sight.[60] In 2020, the UK's National Oceanography Centre reported that the amount of plastic in the Atlantic was ten times greater than previously thought, with an estimated 200 million tonnes of microscopic particles near the surface.[61] Another study predicted that, on current trends, the amount of plastic entering the oceans could triple by 2040 to 29 million tonnes a year, the equivalent of fifty kilos for every metre of coastline in the world.[62]

The scale of the destruction of marine life is extraordinary. Over a million seabirds, 100,000 mammals and uncountable numbers of fish die each year in the North Pacific alone from eating plastic or being ensnared in it.[63] One young whale that drifted onshore and died in the Philippines in 2019 was found to have forty kilos of plastic bags, nylon rope and netting in its belly. Another that was found just afterwards, beached in Sardinia, had nearly 22 kilos of plastic dishes and tubing inside it. And irresponsibility in one part of the world does damage to distant places. Marine rubbish collected on a Scottish reserve was found to come from the USA, Ireland, Sweden and Spain.[64] Plastic has been found in the sea ice of Antarctica and in the depths of the Mariana Trench.

Moreover, having identified microplastics in abundance, scientists are identifying even smaller particles, nanoplastics, that are absorbed into the bloodstream of many species, including humans, with toxic effects that include neurological damage and reproductive abnormalities.

An international agreement to limit the dumping of hazardous materials, which now includes plastics – the Basel Convention on the Control of Transboundary Movements of Hazardous Wastes and their Disposal of 1989 – has been weakened by the absence of the USA, the world's second biggest producer of plastic after China and a large exporter of plastic waste, which never joined the 188-member Convention. And as of 2021, there was no US legislation pending to help in the struggle, largely reflecting the political power exerted by the plastics industry, aided by the many millions of dollars it spends on political lobbying.[65]

In March 2022, over 170 countries agreed to conclude by 2024 a legally binding treaty on plastics covering their full lifecycle from production to disposal. This was despite a strong push by the US plastics industry to restrict the treaty's scope to waste alone. Rising production of oil-based plastics threatens attempts to reduce carbon emissions as well as directly endangering human health and the environment. But any treaty will only be effective if the big polluters sign up.

Reefs, seashores . . . and sand

Reefs, seashores, beaches and estuaries are also part of the blue commons, and all are in trouble.

Coral reefs, a glorious part of the blue commons, range from coral-covered seabeds close to the ocean surface, such as the iconic Great Barrier Reef off Queensland, Australia (which is roughly the size of Italy) to the world's biggest deep-water coral reef off Mauritania and Senegal. Nobody who has had the privilege of snorkelling or scuba diving over coral reefs can fail to appreciate not only their beauty but the vital role they play in the global cycle of marine life. According to Callum Roberts, a world expert on reefs, we live at a time when hundreds of millions of years of evolution of coral reefs have reached their zenith, in terms of diversity and productivity.[66]

The reefs harbour a quarter of all marine diversity in just 0.2% of the ocean floor. But they are under extreme stress – from warming seas, overfishing, pollution and illegal activities such as dynamite fishing – and could collapse within decades. Mass 'bleaching' of coral reefs due to rising sea temperatures has become a recurrent hazard. The Intergovernmental Panel on Climate Change has forecast that within the next twenty years most of the world's tropical coral reefs will have died.[67] In some places, it is too late. Already, only 10% of the original coral reef habitat in the Caribbean is left.[68]

A few dedicated activists and marine scientists are working to protect those reefs that remain, but they have a daunting task ahead.[69]

Economic and political vested interests hinder action to stem coastal run-off from raw sewage, farm effluent, sediment from beach-front building sites, and plastic and other debris from land that spread hostile bacteria. A new threat to the Great Barrier Reef, for example, is the extension of inland coal mining and the associated expansion of port facilities and sea transport on the Queensland coast. After several decades of regulatory denial, the Australian federal and state governments admitted in late 2019 that the reef is suffering from excessive levels of several agricultural pesticides that are banned in other countries, including those of the European Union.[70] Meanwhile, drilling for oil and gas threatens the Mauritania/Senegal reef, described in more detail in Chapter 8.

Coral reefs are particularly important for local low-income fishing communities. About an eighth of the world's population lives within 100 kilometres of a reef; 130 million people rely on reefs for food and their livelihoods. And corals protect 150,000 kilometres of shoreline in over a hundred countries from buffeting by the sea, as well as generating billions of dollars in revenue from tourism.[71]

Unlike coral reefs, we generally take the seashore for granted. There seems so much of it. Yet there is a growing scarcity of sea sand. In a world experiencing creeping desertification, particularly in Africa, a shortage of sand may seem strange. But desert sand is too fine to be used as a filler for concrete, for which the world has an insatiable commercial appetite. After water, sand and gravel are the most used natural materials in the world, and a looming global shortage of suitable sand has even produced a 'sand mafia', supplying the construction industry with illegally dredged sand.[72] Malaysia is just one country that has banned the sale and export of its sand.

The global market demand for sand and gravel is about 40–50 billion tonnes annually. The industry is rife with criminality, regulations are minimal and labour conditions are often dangerous and ill-paid.[73] Sand extraction is also having harmful environmental effects, including land loss and riverbank instability, while the production of concrete accounts for a substantial chunk – 8% – of global carbon dioxide emissions.

To think that common beach sand could become scarce is extraordinary. In most parts of the world the sand we see is 'free', or at least it used to be. Children build sandcastles, holidaymakers jog and sunbathe on it. But now, in an illustration of the Lauderdale Paradox mentioned earlier, it is subject to 'contrived scarcity' and treated as a commodity. Deals have been done, dredging is extensive, and vast quantities are transported across the world for buildings, bridges, roads and dams. Construction and property companies make profits from 'free' sand, but no compensation is paid to the communities that experience erosion of their traditional habitats.

In Myanmar, riverbed farmers are losing their land as sand mining intensifies, and across the Mekong Delta, the noise of sand dredging is affecting fish and diminishing fish catches, as homes and roads crumble into rivers. In Ghana, years of illegal sand mining have accelerated beach erosion, now averaging two metres a year. The authorities have built rocky sea defences along the shore to curb erosion and protect homes from rising sea levels, but these block easy access to the sea for both fishers and tourists, and so hurt livelihoods.[74]

Global coastal ecosystems, including wetlands and mangrove forests, are among the most rapidly disappearing natural ecosystems, and one-third of the world's coastal ecosystems have already been lost over recent decades.[75] For example, in the US state of Indiana, nine-tenths of its wetlands have been filled, farmed or used for building.[76] Quite apart from the valuable habitat wetlands provide for creatures great and small, wetlands play a vital role in flood prevention, slowing the release of rainwater into rivers and providing natural flood overspills. They have also been called 'the kidneys of the landscape' because they tend to clean pollutants and prevent contamination of rivers. Indiana's Wabash river, which flows into the Mississippi, now hosts an algae bloom each summer, fed by nitrates from farm waste, that finally washes into the Gulf of Mexico and contributes to its annual deoxygenated dead zone. In 2019 the hypoxic zone measured 18,000 square kilometres.

Noise

Barely recognized until recently is the damage caused to ocean life by the noise from human activity. In some areas, ocean noise levels have doubled every decade since the 1950s. The main culprits are shipping and airguns used in seismic mapping for offshore oil and gas exploration, the reverberations from which can be heard up to 4,000 kilometres from the source.[77] But noise threatens the very survival of marine mammals, fish and other ocean wildlife.

It has long been known that marine animals hear over

much greater distances than they can see or smell. Mammals such as whales and dolphins use sound to navigate, find food, locate mates, avoid predators and communicate with each other. Anthropogenic noise masks these sounds, disrupting migration routes and breeding patterns, and causing physical harm. Fish are similarly affected by masking. Noise has been shown to interfere with the reproduction of Atlantic cod and haddock, which also use sound for communication during the spawning season.[78]

A further threat comes from plans to massively increase the use of sonar in the oceans, until now deployed exclusively for military purposes, originally to detect submarines. Underwater sonar, which generates deafening sound waves that can travel hundreds of miles, can be deadly for whales. To escape it they will swim huge distances, rapidly change their depth (sometimes leading to bleeding from the eyes and ears), and even beach themselves.[79] Yet plans are being developed by a number of countries to create a subsea data network, dubbed 'the internet of underwater things (IoUT)', that would involve installing laser and sonar transmitters across vast undersea expanses.[80] These transmitters would send signals to transponders on the ocean surface, which would then send them on to communications satellites. The consequences for marine life could be devastating.

The shipping industry: systemic corruption, dirty tactics

International trade has grown dramatically in the past four decades, due in part to globalized supply chains that split goods assembly and component production between countries. And about 90% of all trade in goods is transported by sea. Shipping is a rogue industry that has been allowed to flout rules and conventions with impunity, while polluting the seas, damaging seashores and making a substantial contribution to global warming. Oil and chemical spills are frequent.

A burning container ship off the coast of Sri Lanka in May 2021, with nearly 1,500 containers on board, including hazardous chemicals, polluted fishing grounds that support thousands of artisan fishers, as well as popular beach resorts that, before the COVID pandemic, attracted tourists from all over the world.[81] Worse still, according to a United Nations report, was the spillage of eighty-seven containers full of lentil-sized plastic pellets known as 'nurdles', the largest plastic spill in history, that will continue to circulate in ocean currents and wash ashore for decades.[82]

In 2020, the world fleet of vessels of 100 tonnes or more comprised over 95,000 ships. Each ship is required to carry a country flag, which determines the national law it must obey. In principle, the owner must be domiciled in the flag state. But a few countries operate 'open registries', allowing ships to fly their flag on payment of a registration fee. And UNCLOS explicitly gives nation states the freedom to 'fix the conditions for the grant of its nationality to ships, for the registration of ships in its territory, and for the right to fly its flag'.

These 'flags of convenience' give ship owners several advantages: tax avoidance, since most of the countries providing flags of convenience are tax havens; no obligation to comply with their true country's domestic regulations; the ability to conceal real ownership; and little or no enforcement of international conventions on safety, labour standards and pollution control. Ships have become commodities in a global market for ship nationality.

According to the International Transport Workers' Federation, thirty-three countries and territories offer flags of convenience, of which twenty-three are developing countries and three are landlocked. The leading open registries are Belize, Honduras, Panama, and St Vincent and the Grenadines. Registration can often be completed without any need for physical inspection of the vessel. And many of the flags of convenience states are small and have no resources to make ships comply with regulations. Nor do they want to. They have consistently refused to require the owner or skipper to adopt the nationality of the registry state,[83] or to accept registration of beneficial owners only if they are able to exercise effective control of their activities.

Unsurprisingly, the majority of cargo ships fly flags of convenience. They also dodge liabilities – responsibility for damage, oil spills and so on – by differentiating between types of ownership. The legal owner is the 'registered owner'; the one ultimately benefiting from the income derived from ownership is the 'beneficial owner', who may or may not be the registered one; and the ship may be operated by a third party, the 'operator'. In addition, firms owning ships have increasingly used the core of modern capitalism, the limited liability company, to evade liability or to limit the risks they face.[84] Large corporate groups have turned each of their ships into a subsidiary company, thereby ensuring that if, for instance, the ship spills fuel or cargo into the sea and pollutes the local seashore, only the subsidiary company can be sued for damages. So now most registered owners are one-ship owners. It is a global scam.

Moreover, international law permits ship owners to limit their own responsibility to a fixed value, depending on the ship's tonnage, regardless of the value of the damages. The ultimate owner is protected, while more and more of the risk has been transferred to the citizens of countries where the damage is done.

This is aided by a differentiation in types of flags of convenience. When new, ships are more likely to be registered in the country of origin or where the ultimate owner is based. One reason is that these countries are more likely to abide by international standards, reducing the risk that a ship will be subject to inspection in a foreign port under Port State Control rules. Ships found not to comply with international standards can be detained in port until fixed, at high cost to the company. As the ship ages, however, it is more likely to be put under a flag of convenience, the principal countries involved being Liberia, the Marshall Islands and Panama.

This has led to a phenomenon known as the 'last voyage flag'. When a ship is old or in poor condition, the beneficial-owner company transfers the ship's flag and legal ownership to a company that takes the boat and either sinks it or, more often, 'beaches' it in a selected location. The ship is deliberately driven ashore onto a beach, where local workers dismantle it for raw materials, rewarding the beaching company. The three main places for beaching are said to be Chittagong (Bangladesh), Alang (India) and Galani (Pakistan). The crew of beached ships are often left with unpaid wages, workers are handling toxic materials including heavy metals without protective equipment, and pollution is spread around the beaches and into the sea. In 2019, China, the world's fourth largest ship-breaker, banned the import of foreign-flagged ships for dismantling because of the environmental damage it causes. But the beaching practice carries on.

Shipping is clearly what can be termed a 'crimogenic' industry, where lax regulation and enforcement permit socially, economically and ecologically irresponsible behaviour to flourish. It is not just rogue elements. The mainstream shipping companies too have deliberately minimized their liability risks and so the need to take preventive action to avoid disasters; they have deliberately acted to avoid complying with regulatory standards; and they have deliberately chosen to maximize short-term profits at the expense of workers and the blue commons environment.

As shipping grows, ports grow

Think of any port or harbour. Some are huge, many are minuscule, unable to cater for more than a few ships. Historically, it would have seemed strange to think of a harbour being owned by one person or even one company. Most harbours and ports were forged over many generations, integrated into the surrounding community, and managed by the community or by the local government on its behalf. Yet today, many ports have been turned into global commodities that can be bought and sold and used to generate tidy incomes for their owners far away. Multilateral financial institutions, such as the World Bank, have pushed for port privatization, even though some of their technical reports suggest privately owned ports do not necessarily perform better than state-owned ones.[85]

The development of massive container ships, supertrawlers, five-decker luxury cruise liners and giant oil tankers has fuelled a global expansion in the size of ports. To accommodate these much bigger ships, port owners have dredged vast 'bluefield' sites and extended port infrastructure out to sea, destroying pristine marine areas. Other environmental concerns include oily ballast water discharge from ships, air and water pollution, noise, transfer of alien marine species – the list goes on.

Almost all the world's shipping trade goes through 835 major ports, which have seen a conglomeration of ownership and control in recent years, as well as increasing involvement of financial institutions. In terms of tonnage handled, the biggest operator is Hutchison Port Holdings, a Hong Kong private holding company incorporated in the tax haven of the British Virgin Islands, which owns container terminals in over fifty ports in twenty-seven countries in every continent. Singapore-based PSA International comes second with fifty locations in twenty-six countries. Third in tonnage is Dubai-based DP World, which owns the largest number of ports, eighty-two at the last count, scattered across the world in thirty-four countries, from Southampton in England to Maputo in Mozambique. Under political pressure from the US Congress, DP World sold its US interests to the asset management arm of American International Group (AIG). Another financial institution, Canada-based Brookfield Asset Management, owns thirty-seven ports.[86]

One relatively new factor has been the building and expansion of ports as part of China's $900 billion 'New Silk Road' project, the Belt and Road Initiative, designed to serve Chinese trade with Asia, Europe, Africa and the Pacific. China has lent huge amounts of money to developing countries to build new ports or expand old ones, saddling these countries with large amounts of debt, which they are struggling to repay. These projects also pose important environmental risks and threaten vulnerable communities.[87] In Sri Lanka, a sea reclamation project will create a new city, Colombo Port City, with planned luxury developments targeted at corporate investors. Local fishers fear the extended sand excavation will alter the coastline and harm fish breeding areas. There have also been violent protests against another Chinese-financed port development in Sri Lanka, at Hambantota, which will turn local villages and farmland into a related industrial zone for Chinese companies. The multiplication of ports is a little-noted environmental calamity.

Tourism and the curse of cruise liners

The seaside has been a popular destination for relaxation since antiquity. But in recent decades marine tourism, including cruises, has seen explosive growth, to become the second largest generator of income and profits in the blue economy after ocean energy, and the second-largest generator of jobs. At the same time, it has become a serious and visible threat to the health of the oceans and the wellbeing of local communities.

The commercializing trends of global tourism involve a steady erosion of the blue commons, taking land and resources for the entertainment of those able to afford holidays. Private developments may shut off access to beaches and the sea to locals, while urbanization destroys habitats, creates waste and pollution, and strains clean water supplies and sewage systems. The majority of local inhabitants often gain little or nothing from the increasingly corporatist ventures that pre-dominate.[88] Tourism jobs for locals tend to be seasonal and poorly paid, essentials cost more for them to buy, and the social and cultural life of the community is disrupted.

Cruise liners, meanwhile, have become a global menace. These monster multistorey vessels, carrying many thousands of passengers, generate short-term revenue for corporations and public agencies, but degrade both the environment and the social and cultural heritage of their favoured destinations, from Alaska to Zanzibar. Some European port cities, such as Dubrovnik in Croatia and Palma in Mallorca, have now re-stricted cruise ship visits to limit visitor crowds, but have stopped well short of a ban. And, after years of campaigning, it was only in August 2021 that cruise liners were permanent-ly prohibited from docking alongside the historic centre of Venice, after UNESCO, the UN Educational, Scientific and Cultural Organization, threatened to put the World Heritage Site on its endangered list.[89] Already under threat from rising sea levels, the city was suffering severe further damage from liner backwash and oil pollution, not to mention intolerable overcrowding and the ruin of the skyline by ships that towered above the churches and palaces lining the canals.

Cruise ships are also a major source of air pollution. Each ocean liner uses as much fuel as whole towns while in port, since they keep their engines running, and they use dirty 'bunker fuel', the most polluting form of diesel, which con-tains high levels of sulphur and other pollutants. In the Eng-lish port of Southampton, the resultant air quality is so poor that it breaches international guidelines.[90] In Marseille on France's Mediterranean coast, the increase in luxury cruise liners has been linked to a rise in the incidence of throat cancer.[91] In Civitavecchia, Italy, where passengers disembark for the sights of Rome and Florence, people living within 500 metres of the port have a significantly higher risk of dying from lung cancer or contracting neurological diseases.[92] And other research suggests that about 50,000 people in Europe die prematurely each year due to pollution from ships.

In 2020, the International Maritime Organization (IMO) agreed new rules to cap the sulphur content of bunker fuel, but this would still leave levels more than 100 times higher than diesel used in cars. Later the same year, the IMO set a legally binding target for reducing the 'carbon intensity' of shipping by 2030, which will effectively allow total shipping emissions to rise as activity increases, even as ships become more energy efficient. The industry claims that shipping is exempt from the Paris Agreement on Climate Change, which commits countries to reducing emissions. Yet ships now emit about one billion tonnes of carbon dioxide each year, 2.6% of the global total and more than twice the UK's annual carbon footprint. Noting that shipping industry bodies had helped craft the agreement that was reached, environmental groups blamed 'corporate capture of the IMO'.[93]

At the UN Climate Change Conference in November 2021 (COP26), a group of countries including the UK, USA, Panama and the Marshall Islands signed a declaration pledging to 'strengthen global efforts' to reach net zero on shipping emissions by 2050, while twenty-two countries said they would aim to create 'green shipping corridors' – zero-emission maritime routes between two or more ports. But these will depend on 'willing ports' and 'voluntary participation' by ship operators. For the foreseeable future, those luxury cruise liners can continue to go on with their dirty business.

Where do we go from here?

> All that is left of the common heritage of mankind is
> a few fish and a little seaweed.
> — Arvid Pardo, 1973[94]

For most of world history, the seas were considered a 'state of nature' common to all and open to all without restriction. Once the seas were subject to state enclosure, nation states assumed responsibility for managing the blue commons under their jurisdiction for the benefit of their citizens. They have not lived up to that responsibility. It is clear beyond any doubt that the state of the oceans is disastrous and unsustainable, and that current and past policies supposedly designed to halt the devastation have failed.

As subsequent chapters aim to show, the roots of this failure lie in the weakening of commons communities, privatization of the seas, the handing of exploitation rights to multinational corporations, and the pursuit by governments of endless GDP growth. While global warming must be tackled at an international level, this book argues that the only hope of restoring a healthy ocean ecosystem for the benefit and wellbeing of all lies in managing the seas according to commons principles and supporting and encouraging local communities to do so.

In his famous article of 1968, 'The tragedy of the commons', Garrett Hardin claimed that the commons were doomed to depletion because every user had an incentive to maximize what they could take out of it.[95] This profoundly misunderstood the essence of a commons – that is, agreed rules and practices for managing a shared resource. At the same time, we should be wary of calling marine life 'common pool resources', the term devised for limited shared resources by Elinor Ostrom, who won the 2009 Nobel Prize in Economics for her work on the commons. Part of the tragedy of the blue commons is that humanity has lost respect for the natural world, treating it purely as 'resources' to use for its benefit.

Human ownership of the sea has been institutionalized, by enclosing part of it in the form of Exclusive Economic Zones and by declaring common ownership of the high seas outside them. Some have called the oceans 'the last commons to be enclosed'.[96] Meanwhile, fish have become commodities to be managed. In 1976 one analyst wrote that 'The goal of fisheries management is to optimize society's total benefit from the use of natural resources.'[97] As Eileen Crist aptly put it, 'The intent of "fisheries management" is not to restore such living waters, but to make maximal taking from the ocean pantry sustainable.'[98]

Symbolizing the commercialized nature of global fishing, the names of some fish have been changed to make them more commodifiable. Fish that for generations were known as 'slimeheads' when caught around Australia and New Zealand have been renamed 'orange roughy', and 'toothfish' have been renamed 'Chilean sea bass'.[99] A result has been serious overfishing of orange roughy, long-lived, slow-growing fish that live on seamounts in the deep sea. These fish have been driven towards extinction, the fishing methods destroying in the process the seamount coral 'forests' that shelter a host of other marine life.

Thinking about the blue commons should embrace the full cycle of nature with which humans interact. 'Commoning' is not just a matter of sharing activities and resources between people; it also involves respect for the total environment. Physical closeness is also relevant. Commoners live adjacent to and among their 'resources', watching their recreation, their infancy, their maturing, their dying and rebirth, and often their beauty and power. The natural world that surrounds them becomes an integral part of the commoners' culture and ways of thinking, living and working, respecting the reciprocities and interdependence of life. By contrast, industrialized fishing distances both the catching of fish and the eating of fish from where the fishermen come and from where the consumers live. Thus vernacular knowledge fades and disappears with commercialization.

CHAPTER 2

The Sirens of 'Blue Growth'

> The evidence is very clear; even the ocean is not too big to fail.
> — Sylvia Earle, deep-sea explorer

The marine part of our world is clearly in a state of disarray and decay. As subsequent chapters will show, much of this is due to the way in which the seas and seashores, and everything in and under them, have been incorporated into the global economy and treated as economic resources for exploitation by private corporations and financial capital. And this market-driven economic model has come to dominate thinking about environmental protection, first on land and later in the sea.

Governments have attempted to turn the restoration and preservation of ocean ecosystems into profitable ventures, claiming that only the private sector can provide the huge sums of money supposedly required, which means giving business financial incentives to stump up. As Chapter 1 has indicated, this approach has been a dismal failure. The state of the oceans is worse than it has ever been. Whatever the rhetoric of 'sustainable growth', 'green growth' or 'blue growth', claiming to deliver a triple win for economic expansion, environmental protection and poverty reduction, the pursuit of endless growth and profit is simply not compatible with saving the oceans from further degradation and species extinction. This will impoverish many coastal communities and accelerate global warming and ecosystem destruction, threatening the wellbeing of all humanity.

The historical context is important. By the time UNCLOS was signed in 1982, giving countries jurisdiction over large swathes of the sea, globalization had taken off, shaped by the newly hegemonic doctrine known today as 'neoliberalism'. Summarized in what was dubbed the Washington Consensus, this doctrine advocated a 'free market' economic system and a development strategy based on maximizing economic growth, that is, increasing output or GDP as fast as possible.

The Chicago school of law and economics, the hub of neo-liberalism, argued that maximizing growth was best achieved by increasing private property rights, so as to boost incentives for entrepreneurs and property owners to increase investment and the use of productive resources. In its economic model, which required liberalization of all markets, protective and other regulations were justifiable only if they did not impede economic growth. The language of deregulation, liberalization and privatization became predominant. As Britain's Prime Minister Margaret Thatcher infamously said, 'There is no alternative', soon to become the acronym TINA.

This was a recipe for rapid resource depletion, ecological destruction, excessive consumerism and existential folly, as countries pursued economic growth at all costs. The apologists for the economic orthodoxy responded with equanimity. They would turn the challenge of environmental sustainability and conservation into a profitable industry, by putting a market value on 'natural capital'. Companies could make money by doing good, embracing the notion of Corporate Social Responsibility (CSR), and forming public-private partnerships with government agencies and non-governmental organizations (NGOs). Elites could become the world's philanthropists, benevolently doling out some of their billions of dollars to worthy causes.

The neoliberal emphasis on privatization went with a determination to 'shrink the state' by cutting public spending and reducing the capacity of state institutions to regulate, monitor and police economic activities. This was to have enormous implications, particularly in developing countries where so-called 'structural adjustment' policies were enforced by the international financial agencies, and later in countries making the transition from communism to a market economy under the variant of neoliberalism known as 'shock therapy'.

However, the neoliberal consensus paved the way for the emergence of a profoundly different global economic system than was promised by its early advocates. It is best described as 'rentier capitalism', in which an ever-larger chunk of the revenue generated by productive activities flows to those owning assets or property – physical, financial or intellectual – rather than to workers and others generating that revenue.[1] There is thus no free-market economy but merely a rigged one favouring asset owners, who can exert pressure on governments and international agencies to stymie competition and oppose policies that would reduce their 'rentier' income.

It is in this context that oceans and marine ecosystems have become the new frontier for exploitation by rentier capitalism, supported by an international architecture of institutions and regulations that have aided and abetted privatization and the plunder of the blue commons that belongs to us all.

The legacy of Rachel Carson

Concern over the impact of human activity on land-based ecosystems dates back at least to the early nineteenth century, when Alexander von Humboldt noted the environmental destruction wrought by colonization in South America. In Britain, writers such as William Blake lamented the 'satanic mills' that were blighting 'England's green and pleasant land'. But, like Grotius, few believed the abundant oceans to be at risk until the alarm was raised by American marine biologist Rachel Carson in her book *The Sea Around Us*, published in 1951. Mixing science with lyrical prose, it introduced the wonders and complexity of the oceans to a lay public, while warning of the damage to sensitive ecosystems from rising sea levels and a warming climate. It was the best-selling book in America for several months, and gave its name to what was to become one of the world's most prestigious and productive marine research programmes, at the University of British Columbia in Canada.

Carson's 1962 book, *Silent Spring*, which exposed the adverse health and environmental effects of pesticides and chemicals widely used in industrialized agriculture, was even more influential. It focused international attention on the contamination of the natural world by American agrochemical giants in the pursuit of short-term profits, and provided the spark that ignited nascent environmental movements in America and Europe. In 1963 Carson and her book were the subject of an hour-long CBS television documentary watched by an estimated 10–15 million people, and she subsequently testified in US Senate hearings on pesticide use. Very importantly, she attacked the growing influence of agrochemical corporations on democratic governance and regulatory policy. Until her early death in 1964 at the age of fifty-seven, she campaigned for the public's right to know the damage that industry was doing to the planet, and decried the appointment of politicians to senior posts in regulatory agencies. It was to become an all-too-familiar failing of the governance of nature.

The US agrochemical industry, most notably Monsanto, financed a vicious slander campaign against Carson, who was hounded by the media, threatened with lawsuits and branded a communist. As the *New York Times* wrote in 2012, in a fiftieth-anniversary celebration of her book, one of the most disturbing legacies of *Silent Spring* was the advent of industry disinformation campaigns against environmental critics: 'The well-financed counter-reaction to Carson's book was a prototype for the brand of attack now regularly made by super-PACs in everything from debates about carbon emissions to new energy sources.'[2]

Subsequently, a neo-Malthusian interpretation of the newly recognized ecological crisis-in-the-making gained political influence. In 1968, echoing the doom-laden predictions of British economist Thomas Malthus in the early nineteenth century, Paul Ehrlich depicted population growth as a time-bomb that would bring about worldwide famine,[3] and Garrett Hardin raised the spectre of growing numbers of people competing for limited resources in his highly influential article, 'The tragedy of the commons'.[4] In 1972 the Club of Rome, founded by European and American scientists, issued a prophetic report, *The Limits to Growth*, which questioned the ability of economies to continue growing in a world with finite resources.[5] Such was its claim to scientific objectivity, and so dramatic was its central message, that it sold twelve million copies and was translated into thirty languages. In testimony on the report to the US Congress in 1973, the US economist Kenneth Boulding famously said, 'Anyone who believes that exponential growth can go on forever in a finite world is either a madman or an economist.'[6]

The legacy of Maurice Strong

The year 1972 also saw the convening of the United Nations Conference on the Human Environment (Stockholm Conference), the first ever global conference on environmental issues, which was attended by delegations from 114 countries. The conference formally recognized the links between economic activity and environmental degradation, but its 109 recommendations were exhortatory and chiefly concerned with monitoring and international cooperation. Of greater significance for our story, however, the Stockholm Conference led to the establishment of the United Nations Environment Programme (UNEP) in December 1972, and marked the entrance onto the world stage of a figure who was to be pivotal in the evolution of the euphemism of 'sustainable development' and promotion of a leading role for private business in environmental protection.

This was Canadian Maurice Strong, principal organizer of the Stockholm Conference, who at the age of 43 was named the first Executive Director of UNEP. It was ironic that Strong, who had made his fortune in the North American oil and gas industry, was put in charge of cleaning up the global environment which the oil and gas industry had done so much to imperil. And he remained involved in the oil industry and other business enterprises for the rest of his long life, while flitting back and forth from a succession of UN appointments and commissions.

The 1970s, when Strong first arrived on the UN scene, were a time of Cold War tension between the declining Soviet Union and an increasingly muscular United States, which also saw the ascendancy of the US-dominated World Bank as the leading agency orchestrating 'development'. A summit in Nairobi in 1982 was a flop, largely because of that geopolitical tension and a lack of US interest. However, throughout the 1980s a growing number of critical studies of the capitalist model of development espoused by the World Bank and others revealed its damaging environmental impact, both locally in disruption of ecosystems and the livelihoods of peasant and indigenous communities, and globally in generating more greenhouse gas emissions.[7]

In 1987, the World Commission on Environment and Development (WCED), chaired by Gro Harlem Brundtland, a former (and future) prime minister of Norway, issued its final report entitled *Our Common Future*. The report, which Maurice Strong as a prominent member of the Commission had helped draw up, marked the international legitimation of the concept of sustainable development, with its three pillars – 'green' growth, protection of ecosystems and poverty reduction. Essentially, this is the comfortable notion that with the right interventions the world can have its cake and eat it – growth and economic development can coexist with safeguarding the planet.

The Brundtland report set the scene for the first Earth Summit, the UN Conference on Environment and Development held in Rio de Janeiro in 1992, for which Maurice Strong was appointed secretary-general. The Rio summit was attended by delegates from more than 170 countries and by 108 heads of state, the largest UN conference in its history at that time. A parallel Global Forum for civil society, organized by NGOs and private business bodies, attracted 17,000 registered participants and an attendance of well over 100,000 people.

Maurice Strong opened the conference by declaring that it would 'define the state of political will to save our planet'. He was to be proved right, but surely not in the way he hoped. The conference sought to forge a new sense of partnership between very different interests, capitalizing on hopes for a 'peace dividend' following the collapse of the Soviet Union and the end of the Cold War. But that was wishful thinking. Indeed, the Rio Earth Summit set the tone for US engagement on multilateral environmental initiatives. President George H. W. Bush refused to endorse two of the three binding conventions agreed by heads of state, the Convention on Biological Diversity (CBD) and the Convention to Combat Desertification.[8] And in signing up to the Framework Convention on Climate Change, already weakened in ambition by US negotiators, President Bush took care to declare that 'The American way of life is not up for negotiations. Period.'

The core premise underpinning the 1992 Earth Summit

was that underdevelopment, poverty and environmental decay were primarily due to a lack of capital and modern technology, which could be remedied by mobilizing sufficient funds, from private as well as public sources. The tensions between economic development, environmental protection and reducing poverty were minimized. Economic growth was seen as the key to improving environmental management, while the solution to unsustainable development was to be found in harnessing the innovative power of competition and markets.[9] Multilateral development banks would catalyse private capital for sustainable development, notably through the Global Environment Facility set up in 1989 and run by the World Bank.

As Wolfgang Sachs, one of the most insightful critics of this way of thinking, put it,

> Environmental problems in the South are framed as the result of insufficient capital, outdated technology, lack of expertise and slackening economic growth. How much better off would the planet be, one hears these voices say, if those down there had only additional resources, efficient power plants, better management skills and more growth![10]

Not everybody was convinced. Shortly before the summit was due to begin, the Brazilian Secretary for the Environment, José Lutzenberger, made the dissenting comment that:

> I am scared of big money, which has always meant big destruction, big social disruption and inevitable corruption. What we need instead is a change in attitude – with the right attitudes, we could be needing less money, not more.[11]

He was hastily removed from his post before the summit began, later becoming head of the Gaia Foundation.[12] But one of the most cogent critical outlets, *The Ecologist*, backed him:

> For the poor, the landless, those whose livelihoods are under threat, 'new and additional funds' hold no attractions. The solutions they seek are not financial, but political and cultural ... It does not cost money to reduce consumption in the North, to reclaim large plantations for peasant agriculture or to plant trees that will restore their ravaged homelands. But it does require addressing the questions of who owns the land, who controls decision-making, who should manage the commons and in whose interest.[13]

These questions were not addressed, of course. Instead, the summit institutionalized the role of multinational corporations in international environmental deliberations. In 1990, as part of preparations for the summit, Strong had appointed Stephan Schmidheiny, a Swiss industrialist, to act as his special adviser on business and the environment.[14] Schmidheiny went on to convene a Business Council for Sustainable Development, established in 1991 to ensure the business voice was heard.

Schmidheiny had made his views plain in several publications, including *Changing Course*, published in 1992,[15] promoting the neoliberal view that market mechanisms, not regulations, were the way to address damage to the environment caused by company operations. This view was obviously welcomed by big business; the original forty-eight members of the Business Council included Chevron Oil, Volkswagen,

Coca-Cola, Mitsubishi, Nissan, Nippon Steel, S. C. Johnson and Son, Dow Chemical, Browning-Ferris Industries, Alcoa, Dupont and Royal Dutch Shell.

In the final summit recommendations, known as Agenda 21, the Business Council, alongside the International Chamber of Commerce, mounted an intensive lobbying campaign behind the scenes to remove criticism of business activities and drop proposals for corporate regulation. As Pratap Chatterjee and Matthias Finger said later in their remarkable exposé *The Earth Brokers*, 'The only mention of corporations in Agenda 21 was to promote their role in sustainable development. No mention was made of their role in the pollution of the planet.'[16]

For his part, Maurice Strong described the Business Council as 'a cadre of the world's leading practitioners of sustainable development', which had become 'happy partners with our own secretariat in the process'.[17] Meanwhile, many of the social movements and environmental not-for-profit organizations that had participated in the summit felt their unprecedented inclusion in the negotiating process had been little more than a public relations stunt. As one of the authors of *The Earth Brokers* wrote at the time, Rio 'divided, co-opted, and weakened the green movement . . . NGOs are now trapped in a farce by which they have lent support to governments in return for some small concessions on language and thus legitimized the process of increased industrial development.'[18]

Though pilloried as the 'corporatisation of activism',[19] some big US- and UK-based environmental organizations took what they believed was the 'realistic' option to work with development banks, big business and private investors.

In the years that followed Rio 1992, large environmental NGOs entered a proliferation of business partnerships, appointed prominent CEOs to their governing boards, and became dependent on World Bank financed projects and corporate donations. The idea of 'market-based mechanisms' for saving the planet, generating business profits while making ecological gains, became mainstreamed, evident in voluntary eco-labelling schemes, carbon trading systems and 'eco-tourism'.

Maurice Strong had helped to forge a powerful alliance of governments, business and a part of civil society, but on terms suited to corporate and financial capital. He went on to receive a string of honours and advisory roles in international organizations and corporations. When he died aged eighty-six in November 2015, tributes came from the great and good of the multilateral system, with James Wolfensohn, former president of the World Bank, among those giving eulogies at his funeral. A former employee and protégé of Strong, Wolfensohn had made him a special adviser after being appointed to head the World Bank in 1995.

Despite the plaudits, Strong revealed an almost Malthusian pessimism in his 2001 call-to-arms, *Where on Earth Are We Going?*, projecting that in 2031 'the human tragedy' would be 'on a scale hitherto unimagined'.[20] The brightest prospect, he felt, was that two-thirds of the world's population might be gone, describing this scenario as 'a glimmer of hope for the future of our species and its potential for regeneration'. It would be unfair to treat the pessimism of a man approaching old age as his epitaph. But his courting of global capitalism to save the planet via sustainable development surely stood condemned, and this by the man who had done more than any other to put the partnership model into effect.

Partnerships for sustainable development

When Maurice Strong said that Rio 1992 would define the political will to save the planet, he was right. There was no will. The dire trends identified in Rio continued unabated. But for two decades afterwards, governments and international organizations continued to put their faith in partnerships and in leveraging private finance for sustainable development. As capitalist expansion on land and sea accelerated, its advocates claimed that failure to halt and reverse environmental degradation was due to non-implementation of the partnership model, not to its inherent contradictions. A process driven by capital and finance is inevitably oriented to short-term profit maximization, at the cost of resource depletion and equitable sharing of the gains from rapid growth.

Among the most controversial environmental programmes in this period were 'debt-for-nature swaps'. NGOs such as WWF, Conservation International and The Nature Conservancy brokered deals between their home governments, commercial banks and governments of highly indebted countries, under which the NGO bought some of the high-risk debt that was trading at a discount in the secondary market. The debtor country could then buy the debt back from the NGO, reducing the country's debt servicing charges and releasing funds for the NGO's conservation projects.

These market-based mechanisms sidestepped criticism that 'odious' debt and unfair trade arrangements had undermined poor countries' own resources for development and natural resource management. Later, several reports into debt-for-nature swaps revealed they did little to reduce debt, while generating large profits for commercial banks and transferring control of local environmental projects to Washington DC, New York and London.[21] For this and other reasons, including the advent of more effective debt restructuring and forgiveness schemes, the number of new debt-for-nature swaps has dwindled since their heyday in the 1990s. However, they are still being promoted in other guises, as we shall see.

The UN moved in a similar direction, launching a grandiose project in 2000 called the Global Compact. This is a voluntary corporate social responsibility programme that, in return for pledges to act ethically and responsibly, allows companies to use the blue UN logo for corporate branding purposes. Some of the thousands of companies that have since signed up are among the most polluting in the world.[22] There is no formal monitoring mechanism.

There were some positives from Rio 1992, such as recognition of the 'polluter pays' principle – polluters must pay for preventing and remedying harm – and the precautionary principle – the need to adopt precautionary measures to reduce possible environmental or health risks in the face of scientific uncertainty. Following Rio, the 'polluter pays' principle is the basis of most pollution regulation, requiring companies to finance prevention or clean-up measures, or imposing taxes to incentivize them to do so. The precautionary principle has also been widely adopted as a guide to policy, for example by the European Union, though interpretation in practice has varied widely. Another of the Rio

Principles affirmed the right of the public to access information about environmental decisions made by their governments, to participate in decision-making processes and to have access to justice. In 1998 this was formalized in the UN Convention on Access to Information, Public Participation in Decision-Making and Access to Justice in Environmental Matters, known as the Aarhus Convention.

In 2002, the second Earth Summit, formally named the World Summit on Sustainable Development, was held in Johannesburg, South Africa. It was almost universally described as a disaster. US President George W. Bush declined to attend, and the US delegation turned up with instructions to block any agreement on renewable energy and quash any anti-corporate misgivings.[23] The most ambitious goal of the summit was a new partnership between governments, civil society and business corporations to implement the ten-year-old Agenda 21 in pursuit of sustainable development.

However, the 2002 summit gave the oceans much more attention than they had received in Rio a decade earlier. This was partly because ocean protection was less controversial than other major topics such as fossil fuels and corporate accountability, where the USA refused to engage. At Rio 1992, governments had pledged to support 'the conservation and sustainable use of marine living resources on the high seas' but stopped short of specific targets. In Johannesburg, delegates made a formal commitment to end overfishing and restore fish stocks to sustainable levels by 2015. There were also commitments to end illegal, unreported and unregulated (IUU) fishing, eliminate harmful fishing subsidies, expand marine protected areas and encourage small-scale fisheries, as well as a pledge of donor assistance to help developing countries implement an ecosystem approach to coastal management to enhance marine biodiversity.

Unsurprisingly, by the time of the third Earth Summit (Rio+20), held in Rio de Janeiro in June 2012, none of these goals had materialized or come close to being realized. The organizers, primarily UNEP, had a hard job to explain why, after twenty years of happy partnership with business, almost every environmental indicator signalled that matters were worse than in 1992.

Green growth and blue growth

The focus of Rio+20 was the concept of the green economy. It was presented as a paradigm shift, with a plea for world leaders to reject business as usual. But the claim that 'green growth' was a new idea was unconvincing. The 1987 Brundtland Report had already argued that economic development could be ecologically sustainable and that an environmentally friendly path to economic development would be more prosperous. It amounted to a firm rejection of the idea that there were limits to growth.

UNEP decided that the summit would affirm this crucial position. The aftermath of the 2008 global financial crisis seemed to present an opportunity. Various organizations, including UNEP, saw the post-crisis rebuilding of the economy as an opening to promote green investment. With the roll-out of post-crisis stimulus packages worldwide, UNEP and others argued that not only could the global economy seize the chance to decouple economic development from resource depletion, but that greening the economy would produce more growth and jobs. UNEP argued in its concept paper for the summit that the 'greening of economies is not generally a drag on growth but rather a new engine of growth'.[24]

UNEP's proposed Global Green New Deal hinged on a combination of technological improvements (producing more from less) and a shift to cleaner energy production, supported by the mobilization of large amounts of investment finance. The vexed question of whether economic growth, or accelerated growth as set out by UNEP, could be sustainable was brushed aside. UNEP was so convinced that it dismissed the idea of limits to growth as a 'dangerous myth', a threat to the sustainable development ideal. American economist and Nobel Prize winner Paul Krugman echoed this sentiment; he referred in the *New York Times* to critics of green growth as 'prophets of despair'.[25]

Many accounts of the surge in 'blue growth' initiatives trace it to Rio+20, although 'blue growth' as such was not mentioned in the pre-summit documents, one of which, produced by UNEP, was entitled *The Green Economy in a Blue World*.[26] Governments of small island developing states, dependent on fishing and marine tourism, had pressed for recognition of a distinct 'blue economy', but UN agencies and some governments claimed it would create confusion. UNEP had distinguished the 'brown' from the 'green' economy and there was unease about having too many colours.

Nevertheless, although the final official document of Rio+20 did not refer to the blue economy, the idea took hold. The European Commission launched a Blue Growth Strategy for Europe just after the conference.[27] UNEP, despite its position in Rio+20, rushed out a communiqué on the 'blue economy', claiming that one of its appealing features was that it was 'a developing world initiative pioneered by small island developing states'.[28] This lent legitimacy; it was a development concept not forced on developing countries, but one emanating from them.

In 2016, the World Bank launched a $6.4 billion Blue Growth Portfolio, taking the lead from the EU's Blue Growth Strategy and the UN Food and Agriculture Organization's Blue Growth Initiative, launched in 2013.[29] A host of other bodies have joined the chorus, including UNEP, the UN Development Programme, the Global Environment Facility, organizations representing commercial fisheries such as the International Coalition of Fishing Associations and the Maritime Stewardship Council, and WWF. Almost all the main multinational donors have launched blue growth or blue economy initiatives, and many governments and intergovernmental organizations, including the European Commission and the African Union, have followed suit. Scores of countries have renamed or created ministries to promote blue growth or the blue economy. The concepts have become critical to debates on the future of the oceans and coastal communities.

Those coordinating the FAO's Blue Growth Initiative have stressed that none of the partners would take the lead.[30] Nevertheless, the two global movements representing small-scale fishers – the World Forum of Fisher Peoples and the World Forum of Fish Harvesters and Fish Workers – have felt marginalized. Implicit in the blue growth way of thinking is that small-scale fishing communities should be helped to become participants in industrial fisheries, which they reject.

'Meetings, meetings'

For many years, people devoted to the conservation of marine ecosystems and fisheries complained that the issues were largely overlooked. That was valid but is no longer true. A pivotal year was 2012, largely due to Rio+20, since when the number of international conferences has proliferated.

Just before the summit, the World Bank launched the Global Partnership for Oceans, which brought together governments, intergovernmental organizations, many of the world's largest environmental NGOs and a long list of multinational businesses, including the world's biggest seafood and oil and gas companies. This was quietly disbanded in 2015 after the Norwegian government, its main funder, withdrew support following criticism of the Partnership for encouraging privatization of fishing rights.

However, 2012 also saw the launch of the World Ocean Summit, organized by the Economist Intelligence Unit. This is now an exclusive annual gathering that brings together heads of state, business leaders, private investors and civil society. It resembles Davos for the oceans; the venues chosen are among the world's most beautiful and lavish oceanfront hotels, with tickets to attend costing thousands of dollars. And since 2017, the UN has also started hosting an annual UN Ocean Conference, the first drawing an attendance of 6,000 people from 200 countries.

Although the bandwagon of support has rumbled on, some prominent organizations have resisted the blue growth bandwagon. Greenpeace, for example, despite being at the forefront of global campaigns to save the oceans, has avoided branding its work with the blue growth slogan. Greenpeace has not been among speakers at the World Ocean Summit and similar occasions, nor was it invited to be part of the Global Partnership for Oceans. And social movements representing the interests of millions of small-scale fishers, such as Via Campesina, the World Forum of Fisher People, Bread for the World and the International Collective for Small-Scale Fishers, have denounced it. They too have been conspicuously absent from many blue growth conferences. Indeed, at perhaps the largest single event promoting blue growth, the Sustainable Blue Economy Conference, hosted by Kenya in 2018, not one representative from small-scale fishing organizations was included in any of the main panel events.

The sheer number of international meetings and partnerships dealing with the oceans might give some cause for optimism. But the simple fact is that global events on environmental issues have been strikingly unproductive in terms of ecological achievements. Thus, of the twenty pledges on biodiversity made by governments at the UN summit on biodiversity in Nagoya, Japan, in 2010, not one had been met when world leaders met virtually at the UK-hosted biodiversity summit ten years later.[31] Similarly, the UN's Sustainable Development Goal 14 on 'life below water' included targets to end overfishing, scale up marine protected areas, curb plastic pollution of the oceans and phase out harmful fishing subsidies by 2020. These have not been met either. The problem is compounded because meetings give the appearance of something being done, but lure people into passivity, when far more robust action is required.

What is the ocean 'worth'?

In recent years, a plethora of terms have shaped the debate – 'blue economy', 'blue growth', 'blue revolution', 'blue transition', 'blue carbon', even 'blue finance' and 'blue bonds'. The idea of the 'blue economy' is simply a way of promoting economic growth based on marine life and resources.[32] The 'blue revolution' is supposed to be analogous to the 'green revolution', which is based on new crop varieties, and is mainly about how aquaculture can supposedly displace wild-capture fisheries. 'Blue carbon' is linked to the important role coastal ecosystems play in carbon sequestration and storage, providing a 'service' in the fight against climate change.[33] All these terms reflect a perception of the marine world as a new economic frontier ripe for exploitation in the quest for sustainable development.

While the crisis of ocean conservation and the role of marine ecosystems in ameliorating climate change have been factors behind the interest in blue growth, economic factors have been significant too. The European Commission's Blue Growth Strategy, set out in 2012, said candidly that the oceans around Europe presented an enormous opportunity for economic growth and new jobs to help kick-start European economies after the financial crash.[34] Its strategy focused on five sectors for increased investment and support from the Commission: shipping, energy, mining, tourism and aquaculture (fishing was excluded as already fully exploited). Later iterations have emphasized emerging potential growth sectors, including deep-sea mining and carbon storage. As critics have pointed out, the inclusion of sustainability in the Commission's Blue Growth Strategy has been secondary to its desire to increase growth, while the third pillar of sustainable development, poverty reduction or 'inclusive growth', remains even more marginal.

According to the World Bank, what it calls the Ocean Economy – which includes marine energy (oil, gas, offshore wind), deep-sea mining, bioprospecting, shipping, aquaculture and tourism as well as fisheries – already accounts for 3–5% of global GDP,[35] and in 2016 the Organisation for Economic Co-operation and Development estimated that it would more than double in size between 2010 and 2030 to $3 trillion.[36] In 2010, by far the most valuable industry according to the OECD was offshore oil and gas, accounting for 32% of total global value added. The next most lucrative were maritime and coastal tourism (accounting for 26%) and the production of maritime equipment and port activities (13%). Industrial fisheries, including processing, accounted for only 6%, and small-scale and recreational fisheries were not included at all due to the absence of reliable data.

By 2030, the share of oil and gas was predicted to decline, given commitments for meeting climate change targets, while coastal and maritime tourism would expand to become the largest single sector. Growth of port activities was likely to triple due to the expansion of global shipping. The OECD envisaged zero growth in wild-capture fisheries, but annual growth for fish farming at sea, already the fastest growing food production system in the world, of about 5%.

Shortly before the OECD published its analysis, WWF

produced its own report on the value of the global ocean economy, estimating its contribution to global GDP (what it called the Gross Marine Product) at $2.5 trillion, with a 'natural asset base' worth $24 trillion.[37] The report claimed that if the ocean economy were a country, it would rank seventh in size, just behind the UK. The estimates were described as conservative because, in contrast to the OECD's, they excluded the energy sector (as not generated by the sea), as well as 'valuable intangibles' such as the ocean's role in climate regulation and what the WWF called 'spiritual and cultural services'. However, its estimates did include a notional valuation of ecosystem services, such as carbon sequestration and the protective role of mangroves, as well as putting a value on shipping lanes as an 'ecosystem service'.

Among numerous other studies, the UN Conference on Trade and Development (UNCTAD) put the total value of the ocean industries at $4 trillion in 2014,[38] while a shoal of industry studies have pointed to specific growth areas. For instance, the global market value of marine biotechnology was forecast by Smithers, a US-based market research company, to rise from an estimated value of just over $4 billion in 2015 to $6.4 billion by 2025.[39]

Based on such forecasts, the idea that blue growth has massive potential to generate economic wealth has become a dominant narrative. Thus, in its Africa Vision 2063 document – a 50-year plan for sustainable development on the continent, subtitled The Africa We Want – the African Union characterized the blue economy as the source of a new 'African Renaissance'.[40] Its Africa Blue Economy Strategy, published in 2019, identified the main growth engines as tourism, offshore oil and gas, deep-sea mining, shipping and port building, and aquaculture. Deep-sea mining, for example, was claimed to have the potential to grow from almost nothing in 2019 to be worth $70 billion a year for African countries by 2030, almost four times as much as the marine fisheries sector.[41]

In the light of all these reports of vast economic growth potential, the balance with environmental sustainability has been hard to maintain. Nevertheless, the promise – if not the reality – of decoupling growth in the ocean from the destruction of marine habitats and greenhouse gas emissions is central to all blue growth strategies, including those of the EU and the African Union.

As with the 'green' economy, the emphasis has been on technological progress and efficiency, and a shift towards less environmentally harmful modes of production. In practice, many of these initiatives have run afoul of the 'Jevons paradox', the proposition that increasing the efficiency with which a resource is used increases, rather than decreases, the rate of depletion of that resource.[42] This applies with a vengeance to industrial fishing, but also to other technological advances aimed at improving efficiency of operations in the sea.

Blue growth has another dimension that distinguishes it from the green economy. The blue economy is seen as a way of reducing the ecological impact of land-based industries. The oceans are being promoted as a new development space for cleaner and more efficient production of energy and food, taking the strain off the land. For example, the shift from fossil fuels to electricity to power vehicles depends on storage batteries that require cobalt. There is a cobalt shortage on land, so corporations and financial capital are eyeing deep-sea deposits. Lessening ecological damage in one direction threatens to increase it in another.

Similarly, blue growth scenarios often depict 'sustainable aquaculture' as a low-carbon, relatively cheap source of healthy food. Farmed fish already make up about half the fish humans consume, and advocates of fish farming argue that further investment would provide substantial extra protein, reducing pressure on wild-capture fisheries and land-based animal products. The Global Aquaculture Alliance, for example, claims that, in comparison to livestock rearing, fish farming has a much lower carbon footprint and so is a cleaner and safer option.[43] Others claim the opposite, as we shall see.

Blue growth strategies, such as the European Commission's, also identify shipping as a less environmentally destructive mode of transport than land-based modes or air freight. So, it is argued, a transition to 'clean' shipping technologies, including low-sulphur fuels, would allow the industry to continue to expand while contributing to climate change objectives. The European Commission has set a target for shipping of a 75% reduction in the 'greenhouse gas intensity' of fuels by 2050, which is neither net zero nor an absolute reduction. However, the EU has since joined the USA, UK and several other countries in urging the International Maritime Organization to agree a global net zero goal for 2050.

Offshore energy production, via wind, floating solar systems and tidal energy, is another sector where blue growth is seen as reducing greenhouse gas emissions. Likewise, while mining for minerals and metals on land is destroying habitats, polluting land and water courses and disrupting communities, proponents of offshore and deep-sea mining claim it will sustain production with less ecological damage. This has been an argument advanced by Pacific island states for expanding deep-sea mining in their waters. 'Seabed mining is a far more "greener" option for our region and the world and should be embraced by everyone who cares about the climate future of our planet,' states an official press release from Nauru, Tonga and the Cook Islands.[44] These claims are hotly disputed.

The green credentials of blue growth are also found in proposals related to blue carbon. According to one study, seagrass meadows, tidal marshes and mangrove forests sequester 30–50 times the organic carbon in their sediments as terrestrial forests.[45] So, preserving or expanding coastal habitats is now recognized as having a major role in mitigating climate change, spurring a plethora of initiatives by governments, international bodies and NGOs.

Most blue carbon projects have focused on plants. However, in 2019 the International Monetary Fund (IMF) published a remarkable study proposing a 'financial mechanism' to restore the whale population to pre-whaling numbers as 'nature's solution to climate change'.[46] It turns out that whales play an important role in the reproduction and flourishing of phytoplankton, essential to life on earth, which release oxygen into the atmosphere and sequester carbon by a process of photosynthesis. Whales also act as enormous carbon sinks, accumulating on average thirty-three tonnes of carbon during their lifetime. On their death this sequestered carbon settles on the ocean floor where it remains for centuries, unlike carbon stored in trees that is released into the atmosphere quickly when they die.

The IMF study described the collapse of whale populations as an example of Hardin's 'tragedy of the commons', because 'no individual who benefits from them is sufficiently motivated to pay their fair share to support them'. It claimed that all the whales living today would have a market value of about $1 trillion and that, if everyone on the planet contributed to paying for their 'ecosystem services', we would all have to pay $13 a year! 'Luckily', the report continued, 'economists know how these types of problems can be solved.'

It proposed a fund to provide financial incentives to industries responsible for whale deaths, such as fisheries and shipping, to kill fewer whales. The paper left it uncertain whether whales could become credits in carbon offset markets, or whether all this would be paid for through other means. Fortunately, there is no market or global facility established yet for any living mammalian blue carbon. But for those who see madness in the commodification of nature, this is surely one of the most shameful examples.

Private property rights and dispossession

Accompanying the drive for blue growth has been the refrain that sustainable marine development requires stronger private property rights. Ragnar Arnason, for decades a senior adviser to both the FAO and the World Bank, stated in a much-quoted paper:

> Fisheries, as so many natural resource extraction activities, are among the economic activities where property rights are poorly defined or even non-existent. This generally results in huge inefficiencies, frequently referred to as 'the fisheries

problem'. Since the fisheries problem fundamentally stems from lack of property rights, the obvious solution is to introduce those rights. It follows immediately that the fisheries problem would disappear if only the appropriate property rights could be defined, imposed and enforced.[47]

This reiterates the conventional view first outlined in a seminal paper of 1954 by Scott Gordon, and in a slightly later one by Anthony Scott, which long predated Hardin's much more famous 1968 paper. They all asserted that the commons comprise an 'open access' resource, and that as such they will be used excessively and driven to extinction.[48]

Gordon put it most succinctly, in stating that 'most of the problems associated with the words "conservation" or "depletion" or "overexploitation" in the fishery are, in reality, manifestations of the fact that the natural resources of the sea yield no economic rent.'[49] This was due, in his view, to the absence of property rights over the resources. Because fish swimming around in the sea belonged to nobody, there was no incentive for fishers to leave them there, resulting in 'the race to fish'. Since the 1950s, this view has been perpetuated again and again, as reiterated by Arnason and colleagues in calling for 'enclosure and privatization of the common resources of the ocean'.[50]

The World Bank too has long blamed the growing problem of overfishing and fish stock depletion on weak governance and lack of private property rights.[51] According to the Bank, 'Most marine wild fisheries are considered to be property of nations. Governments are generally entrusted with the stewardship of these national assets, and their accepted role is to ensure that these assets are used as productively as possible, for both current and future generations.'[52] For the Bank, strengthening property rights was an important step in that direction.

Earlier, in a report on agricultural development, it had made its premise very clear, stating, 'Secure and unambiguous property rights also allow markets to transfer land to more productive uses and users.'[53] This stems from an accounting framework that measures productivity by market costs and prices, and financial profitability, not the intrinsic value to local communities, let alone the natural environment in which they live and work.

In 2010, the World Bank's International Finance Corporation (IFC), the arm charged explicitly with spreading capitalism across the world, corralled a powerful group of international banks known as the Equator banks, and then drew in the International Fund for Agricultural Development (IFAD), UNCTAD and the FAO to agree a set of Principles for Responsible Agricultural Investment that Respects Rights, Livelihoods and Resources.[54] Despite its title, this document formalized a strategy for commodifying all land in developing countries.

The IFC had long promoted the registration of all land, thereby establishing private property rights. The Principles extended this by linking financial aid to the conversion of agricultural land into potential financial assets. Of course, some of the most commodifiable land targeted in this way adjoins the sea and is needed most by those who make their living from the sea. Their needs, and their historical claims to such land, were to be sacrificed in the name of economic growth and 'efficiency'.

The UN Special Rapporteur on the Right to Food decried the Principles as 'a checklist of how to destroy the global peasantry responsibly'.[55] A group of prominent civil society organizations called them greenwashing and 'a move to try to legitimize what is absolutely unacceptable: the long-term corporate (foreign and domestic) takeover of rural people's farmlands'.[56] For farmlands, also read fishing communities. Though the FAO later issued Voluntary Guidelines on the Responsible Governance of Tenure, reminding governments of their human rights obligations and the need to respect customary tenure rights, land grabbing has continued apace.[57]

The IFC has induced developing-country governments to create and extend land titling, that is, to create private property rights where none existed before, on land that hitherto was presumed to belong to the state or to the communities that had occupied it for generations. The World Bank's programmes of titling land have promoted only individual property rights when traditionally, in many communities, there had been communal land or commons.

By this means, the IFC has been responsible for converting farmers, herders and fishers into propertyless squatters. The World Bank has even had the audacity, through a scoping exercise using satellite imagery and proxy indicators of population density, to 'find' farmland available for commercial investment around the world, coming up with an estimate of 446 million hectares.[58]

Land titling has facilitated financialization of the environment. Once a private property right is established, it becomes a commodity to be bought and sold, and is easily turned into an asset class for speculative investment. Much of the surge in land grabbing in the twenty-first century has involved multinational corporations backed by global finance, often aided by the international financial agencies. By 2020, just 1% of agricultural companies operated more than 70% of the world's farmland, with substantial investment from private equity firms and some of the world's biggest asset-managed funds.[59]

In the marine world too, private property rights have been strengthened over several decades, and yet this has co-incided with an acceleration of marine destruction. It is like medieval quackery. If a person was ill, apply the leeches; if they did not recover, suck more blood. In the case of fish-eries, the answer was to privatize; when the problem grew worse, the answer was more privatization. In both cases, the prescription risks premature death.

Financialization and commodification

Financial markets and institutions are pivotal to driving the ocean sustainability agenda.[60]

Blue growth thinking has evolved in the context of the finan-cialization of the global economy, and the emergence of ren-tier capitalism, which has seen owners of financial and other assets gaining a disproportionate share of the income gener-ated. A widely quoted definition of financialization is 'the in-creasing role of financial motives, financial markets, financial actors and financial institutions in the operation of the do-mestic and international economies.'[61] Financial institutions increasingly determine what is done, how it is done, by whom it is done and for whose benefit, and also determine what is not done and who cannot do what they might wish to do.

Financialization took off in the 1980s, when US President Ronald Reagan and UK Prime Minister Margaret Thatcher liberalized their financial markets. From then on, finance has risen from being a servant of productive capital to being the primary force of a globalizing economic system. Today, the value of financial assets held by financial corporations in the UK is over 1,000% of GDP, and in other industrialized countries it ranges from 400% to 700%.[62] Finance dwarfs the rest of the economy.

Financialization is linked to what has been aptly called 'accumulation by dispossession'. Picture a coastal commons – a coastland, with a small harbour, a few shared fishing boats, and a sea teeming with fish. The commons has value for the community, providing livelihoods, a sense of social solidarity, a shared culture and a mostly unspoken desire to reproduce itself. To those ends, none of the key assets is for sale. The commons has no 'exchange value', no price. But for neoliberal economists, those assets must be converted into a form of property, owned by somebody in a position to sell to those who can make most 'efficient' use of them. Finance thrives on turning nature into property and then creating a market for it. Given likely economies of scale – larger entities can take advantage of advanced technologies, access to wider markets and so on – local people may be easily persuaded or bribed to sell or give up their niche.

As the financial sector expands, it can dictate to production capital by its sheer presence and size, threatening to switch investment unless firms or governments maximize profits and efficiency, often under its direction. Neoliberal economists claim that private property rights foster long-term investment and are thus a responsible form of capitalism respecting the need to preserve resources. Global finance mocks this pretension. The old notion that shareholders were there to assure long-term investment strategies was never convincing. But finance, and particularly private equity capital and hedge funds, aims to maximize short-term profits. Finance is rootless: move in, move on, move out.

The financialization of commodity markets has led to speculation in 'futures' (buying in advance to take advantage of a price difference at the time of delivery) by financial institutions and funds that have no intrinsic interest in the future availability of the commodity. Financial speculation has been linked to rising food prices and food price riots in developing countries.[63] Finance thrives on high trading volume and volatile prices, whereas small-scale producers want stable and predictable prices.

Fish and fish products are among the most heavily traded commodities, with an estimated 45% of the world catch now traded internationally. Unsurprisingly, finance is eyeing fish as yet another potential vehicle for speculation. Salmon futures are already traded on a Norway-based international exchange, Fish Pool, whose contracts are cleared by the US stock exchange Nasdaq. Crustaceans such as lobster and shrimp are also seen as promising candidates,[64] while China has reportedly studied the creation of a domestic seafood futures market.

Extensive financialization also necessitates pursuit of rapid economic growth. Finance depends on a system of widespread credit that puts corporations, households and communities in quasi-permanent debt. Their capacity to service debt depends on future economic growth. So if economic growth potential on land is judged to be limited, more investors will turn to the perceived high-growth potential of the blue economy to save financialization from unravelling.

Finance facilitates vertical and horizontal conglomeration of corporations to gain economies of scale and scope, often aided by government subsidies. As a result, the blue economy is increasingly controlled by global giants. For instance, the world fishing industry is dominated by a handful of huge multinationals, led by two Japanese conglomerates – Maruha Nichiro and Nippon Suisan Kaisha – followed by Thai Union, Mowi (a conglomerate originally based in Norway), and Mitsubishi (more famous for cars, shipyards and Zeros – long-distance fighter aircraft). Mitsubishi's fishing arm is whimsically called Zero; it also owns Cermaq, formerly Norway's state-owned salmon farmer. The Red Chamber Group, the leading US seafood group, is the world's seventh largest by revenue, after Dongwon, a South Korean conglomerate. What stands out in this list is not just the capitalization values of these behemoths, but also the enormous range and global reach of the top few corporate groups.

Putting a price on nature

Financialization has coincided, not coincidentally, with an extraordinary movement to measure nature in money terms, to put a dollar value on species, habitats and pollutants, including greenhouse gases. This has led to the spread of various market mechanisms that essentially operate on trade-offs between different forms of 'capital', now expressed in the common denominator of money. Thus companies can buy permits to emit carbon, or buy carbon offsets that finance tree planting, as long as the total stock of 'capital' is unchanged or increased. Another example is the use by rich countries of environmental projects in poor ones to meet climate change targets. One US-based company has even introduced an 'international marine mitigation bank',[65] which offers credits to companies that damage ocean habitats, such as mining companies, that are then used to finance the building of artificial coral reefs elsewhere.

These initiatives reflect the ascendancy of neoliberal economics, where price is the only measure of value, coupled with the recognition from the 1970s onwards that economic growth was depleting natural resources and imposing unsustainable costs on the environment. From that stemmed a belief that putting a value on 'natural capital' would somehow lead to greater emphasis on conservation and greener investment and growth. If governments and investors appreciated the economic value of nature (and the cost of losing it) they could preserve 'natural capital' by taking that value into account in decision-making. According to this argument, governments and business destroy nature because it is undervalued, or its value is simply ignored; the answer is to 'put a price on nature to save it'.[66]

Conventional measures of GDP growth tend to treat nature as a free factor of production and do not take account of its degradation or destruction. As Partha Dasgupta, author of a report commissioned by the UK government on the economics of biodiversity,[67] put it in an earlier article:

Contemporary models of economic growth and development regard nature to be a fixed, indestructible factor of production. The problem with the assumption is that it is wrong. Nature is a mosaic of degradable assets. Agricultural land, forests, watersheds, fisheries, freshwater sources, estuaries, wetlands, the atmosphere – more generally, ecosystems – are assets that are self-regenerative, but can suffer from deterioration or depletion through human use.[68]

So, if a wetland is drained for agricultural use, the farm production would add to GDP; but loss of the wetland, and its role in providing services for humans such as flood prevention, as well as a habitat for wildlife and so on, would not be counted. If change were measured in terms of net social wealth rather than GDP, we would see that much of what contributes to increases in GDP *reduces* net social wealth. Maximizing economic growth today could minimize public wealth tomorrow. Having a measure of natural capital has thus seemed a good idea. But it has had perverse consequences.

The World Bank has not helped. Since the 1990s, it has set out to measure natural capital as part of a comprehensive measure of the wealth of nations.[69] But, at least in its early attempts, far from highlighting the value of nature, it actually belittled it. In its original major report in 2011, one conclusion was that as a country grows 'richer', the value of its natural capital inevitably declines because it converts natural capital into other types of capital. This result emerged partly because no *intrinsic* value was given to nature. A beautiful landscape or unspoilt seashore has no price and thus has no value.

Meanwhile, the value of land was measured by how much it would sell for as farmland. Forest land was valued by how much the trees would sell for as timber. Water and fish were not given any value, apparently because of lack of data. Worse, the Bank gave a very high value to so-called 'intangible capital' such as 'human capital' and 'institutional capital'. Overall, in rich countries, it concluded that natural capital amounted to merely 2% of total wealth, while intangible capital comprised 81% and produced capital 17%.[70] For the whole world, the figures were 5%, 77% and 18%.

Since 2011, the Bank has attempted to refine its measure of natural capital. But it cannot escape from its false premise that nature can be valued by its selling price. 'Natural capital is measured as the discounted sum of the value of rents generated over the lifetime of the asset,' the Bank states in its 2018 report, which estimated that natural capital had risen to 47% of total capital in low-income countries, from 30% in 2005.[71] Here again, the valuations seem arbitrary. The Bank includes in its estimates of natural capital land-based energy, minerals, agricultural land, forests and terrestrial protected areas, but excludes marine fisheries and marine protected areas, 'ecosystem services' and the costs of air pollution, for lack of data.

The World Bank aside, most attempts to measure natural capital have tried to include some valuation of so-called 'ecosystem services'. The Millennium Ecosystem Assessment (MEA) provided one of the most general definitions of ecosystem services: these are the benefits people obtain from ecosystems, including *provisioning* services such as food, water, timber and fibre; *regulating* services that affect climate, floods, disease, wastes, and water quality; *cultural* services that provide recreational, aesthetic and spiritual benefits; and *supporting* services such as soil formation, photosynthesis and nutrient cycling.[72]

In this definition, there appears to be no limit on what can be called services so long as they are connected in some way to human welfare. And despite being one of the most open definitions of ecosystem services, the MEA still assumes (like most in this school of thinking) that ecosystem services are only classifiable as services if they are of benefit to humans. Obviously, that gives zero value to all the 'services' nature provides to other species and parts of nature, some of which have beneficial effects on other services that might be of benefit to us humans. And it makes no allowance for scientific and other knowledge. What is not of service today may turn out to be the basis of a service tomorrow.

Moreover, it gives no weight at all to the value of community. What value could economists put on the culture, social solidarity and shared activity of a community based around a threatened coral reef, fishing ground or mangrove forest? It is another example of the damaging calculus that implicitly assigns zero value to things that cannot be priced.

Still, ascribing a money value to ecosystem services has prompted hundreds of mostly small-scale projects in which local people are paid to conserve nature, usually by agreeing not to engage in destructive practices but sometimes by participating in regeneration activities such as tree planting. The idea behind 'payment for ecosystem services' (PES) is to 'translate external, non-market values of the environment into real financial incentives for local actors to provide such services'.[73] But although PES has been described as win-win, for the environment and for poverty reduction, in practice the results have been disappointing on both counts.[74]

Scheme designs have often favoured entrenched interests rather than maximizing environmental or poverty-reduction benefits (as in the prevention of deforestation in Costa Rica). Payments are often too low to compensate for forgoing income from resource extraction (as with the prevention of forest clearing for palm oil plantations in Indonesia). Also, monetary incentives can weaken intrinsic collective motivations to conserve nature, and disrupt local notions of rights in communities with strong traditions of cooperation and altruism.

Putting a price on nature has enabled financial capital to design and profit from new financial instruments. But it has not had a noticeable impact on ecosystem preservation. On the contrary, by putting all forms of capital, natural and otherwise, on the same monetary basis, it has allowed trade-offs that weaken or nullify commitments to environmental protection. Meanwhile, much of nature cannot be valued, nor can a simple cost-benefit analysis cope with irreversible environmental destruction. This sort of economic analysis may remind governments of the extent to which all human activity is dependent on functioning ecosystems, but it does little to exact the urgent and determined policy response that is desperately needed.

Financial capital and blue bonds

Green/blue growth strategies have consolidated the idea that transition to a sustainable and equitable economy requires enormous investment of capital, which only multinationals and financial institutions can provide. This view was cemented at Rio 1992, when it was estimated that implementing the activities laid out in its Agenda 21 would require at least $600 billion a year. Twenty years later, in its background report for Rio+20, *Towards a Green Economy*, UNEP estimated that the annual financing to 'green' the global economy was in the rather broad range of $1.05–2.59 trillion.[75] As a target, UNEP settled on the sum of $1.3 trillion, representing 2% of global GDP.

Similar estimates of trillions of dollars have been made for the delivery of the UN's Sustainable Development Goals. A UN report in 2014, led by American economist Jeffrey Sachs, estimated that the Sustainable Development Goals would require between $5 trillion and $7 trillion of investment.[76] Such figures far surpass official aid for development and the charity of philanthropists. So, the argument goes, the shortfall, frequently referred to as the 'funding gap', requires mechanisms to bring in private capital.

An influential 2014 study published by Credit Suisse, WWF and the global consultancy McKinsey estimated that the amount needed to finance global conservation was about $300–400 billion annually.[77] Existing funding for conservation, combining government budgets, official development assistance (ODA) and philanthropic spending, only came to about $50 billion a year. And the study used a very conservative estimate of conservation financing needs (for example, it did not include the restoration of degraded ecosystems, only the conservation of what remains, primarily terrestrial). Indeed, in 2011 UNEP estimated that the transition to sustainable fisheries alone required an upfront cost of about $240 billion.[78]

The perceived need to massively scale up private finance for conservation and development activities has become a prominent theme promoted by the world's largest environmental NGOs. This is one reason why, since the 1990s, they have often touted their pro-business credentials. Repeated in many of their strategic documents is the story that relying on traditional sources of aid has limited their impact. Thus, saving the planet requires conservation NGOs to befriend the capitalists, not only to steer them towards a greener path, but also to access their money.

One outcome has been a proliferation of partnerships, designed to leverage new private funds, between corporatized NGOs, multilateral development banks, UN agencies and an array of private banks, investment funds and consultancy firms. Some NGOs have gone further and developed specialist finance departments, often employing people with a work history in banking or securities trading, to design projects specifically intended to attract private investors. An example of this type of partnership was the launch in 2015 of NatureVest, an NGO created by The Nature Conservancy and the US bank JP Morgan, which has several blue growth projects on its books.

The presumption is that transitioning to a sustainable and just economy is an extremely expensive endeavour, which only the private sector can afford. This means investment in sustainability must be profitable, providing rates of return that are competitive with those being offered in the 'brown' economy.[79] While this would seem a daunting challenge, those promoting conservation financing remain upbeat. The 'funding gap' could easily be closed, they argue, if funds, institutions and, especially, 'ultra-high-net-worth' individuals – referred to as 'impact investors' – could be persuaded to allocate the equivalent of just 1% of all new private investment each year to conservation.

Another reason for optimism, it is claimed, is that investing in the green/blue economy can be very profitable. A report by US-based Encourage Capital, co-published by Bloomberg Philanthropies and the Rockefeller Foundation, claimed that business investment in sustainable fisheries could generate returns of up to 35%.[80] Credit Suisse describes the blue economy as 'a life-supporting system filled with unprecedented economic opportunities' and 'a market in the making with growing opportunities for investors'.[81]

Insufficiently scrutinized in the push for private investment is the extent to which all this new money will do good, ecologically or socially. Conservation financing has so far focused on the challenge of convincing private investors to invest. The thorny issue of how to ensure enticing returns to investors while achieving environmental gains and benefiting poor communities has received little attention. Research published by the World Bank acknowledges that, despite billions of dollars of aid money being spent in the fisheries sector, the results have been ambiguous and often disappointing, particularly in promoting wealth for coastal communities.[82] Conservation financing mostly focuses on financial returns, and extraction yields higher profits than conservation.

In May 2019, the World Bank co-hosted a conference with the US NGO Rare and the Inter-American Development Bank, entitled 'Mobilising capital for the oceans: The new frontier in natural infrastructure investment'. A summary of the outcomes stated: 'Communities must be able to absorb capital and deliver on the impact in marine resources, and simultaneously generate revenue that provides the investment returns.' It thereby identified coastal communities less as potential beneficiaries than as potential risks for private investment.[83]

Growing financialization of development and conservation projects has also paved the way for the innovative financing mechanism known as 'green (or blue) bonds', which channel the funds raised to environmentally friendly activities. The European Investment Bank launched the first green bond in 2007, with the World Bank's 'virgin green bond' coming a year later. The Bank subsequently launched a Green Bond Programme, which by 2020 had raised over $16 billion to finance over 220 projects in developing countries. This has been copied by other multilateral development banks and has inspired a larger global market, including green bonds issued by corporations, investment banks and public authorities at national and sub-national levels. Growth is described in some reports as 'spectacular'. By 2019, nearly 1,800 green bonds labelled as such had been issued worldwide, with a combined value of $257 billion.[84] 'Unlabelled' bonds that would probably have met the green bond definitions were estimated in 2017 to be three times as large as labelled bonds.[85]

However, there are no firm rules for labelling a bond green (or blue); this is left to various voluntary standards and initiatives, of which the Green Bond Principles, established by the International Capital Market Association (ICMA) in 2015, are the most widely used.[86] The Principles do not themselves define what 'green' means, so a lucrative consultancy industry has sprung up to provide third-party assessments, all with their own definitions. These assure investors that money raised will most likely be used for green purposes, but whether it ends up doing is another matter. This is not assessed, and it is unclear how investors would respond to this information if it were produced. Nevertheless, issuing and investing in green bonds are seen by companies as useful in burnishing their credentials as good corporate citizens.

Some green bonds released in recent years have involved the blue economy. Fiji, which comprises 300 volcanic islands, raised $50 million from a sovereign green bond launched in 2017 to fund climate change resilience projects, backed by the World Bank and the Australian government. And in 2020, Mowi, one of the world's largest aquaculture multinationals, became the first seafood company to issue a green bond, raising €200 million.[87] The World Bank, rather than issuing 'blue' bonds, has issued 'sustainable development bonds for the blue economy', with two in 2019. The first, dealing with plastic pollution, is managed by Morgan Stanley; the second, which has a broader theme of promoting blue economy projects, is managed by Credit Suisse.[88]

The first specifically 'blue bond' was pioneered by NatureVest for the Seychelles in 2018. This issue, worth about $15 million, to be repaid to investors over ten years with an interest rate of 6.5%, was guaranteed by the World Bank and supported by the UN's Global Environment Facility, in effect subsidizing private investors. In 2016, The Nature Conservancy had also helped broker a deal for the Seychelles government to cut foreign aid debt in return for pledges to invest the savings in marine conservation – a debt-for-nature swap. The two sources came to about $40 million, which The Nature Conservancy is helping to spend. Little noted was the loan made by The Nature Conservancy itself to the Seychelles government to buy back the foreign debt, which was to be repaid with interest over ten years. As a result, the Seychelles government has seen little or no financial benefit while losing control of the conservation effort. Nevertheless, *The Economist* ran a story celebrating the swap deal ('debt relief for dolphins' was the sub-editor's choice) and quoted the CEO of NatureVest as predicting that over the next decade they would be handling at least a billion dollars in blue bonds.[89]

Seychelles was in effect a 'pilot' for what The Nature Conservancy later described as an 'audacious plan' to create $1.6 billion worth of blue bonds in partnership with twenty small island developing states.[90] As of late 2021, this was struggling to attract investor interest. However, in November 2021 The Nature Conservancy finalized the biggest debt-for-nature swap in history, for debt-strapped Belize, financed by a 'Belize blue bond'.[91] This involved paying off holders of the Caribbean country's existing $550 million Eurobond, already threatened with default, at fifty-five cents to the dollar with the proceeds of a $364 million loan to the Belize government in the form of a blue bond arranged by Credit Suisse. The bond is to be repaid over nineteen years at an interest rate that begins below that of the Eurobond but rises above it over time. Other deals are said to be in the pipeline for Kenya, St Lucia and Barbados, while Ecuador has said it is negotiating a debt swap even bigger than Belize's to raise funds for enlarging the marine protected area surrounding the Galapagos Islands.[92]

Governments that raise private debt to fund the transition to sustainable green/blue economies are gambling that borrowing money now, at commercial rates, will pay off later. The stakes are obviously higher with bonds than they are with traditional development aid, including soft loans that have provided the mainstay of financing for fisheries and conservation development. And what happens when the gamble fails, as in Mozambique (see Chapter 5). Who pays for the consequences?

'Let them eat cake'

The blue growth vision has obvious attractions, of the 'have cake and eat it' variety, but as the following chapters will show, in practice growth has taken precedence over the other two pillars: environmental protection and poverty reduction. In what has been dubbed the Blue Acceleration, human exploitation of the oceans has increased almost exponentially since the turn of the century, even as concern over its effects has grown.[93] This was inevitable once markets, commodification of nature and private finance became embedded in strategies for sustainable development. Business and finance will always put profit first, and the source of continuing profit is economic growth. Protection of the environment or local communities will often involve *not* doing something. This is not a path with investor appeal.

Moreover, even sustainable growth runs up against limited resources, and there are bound to be some adverse effects on the environment and to communities. In putting a price on nature, the World Bank and others imply that a reduction in natural capital in one area can be offset by an increase in another area or in a different sort of capital such as 'human capital'. This essentially allows environmental degradation to be traded for other supposed benefits, while the integrity of communities is given no weight at all.

The neoliberal agenda also sees privatization as the route to a smaller state, shrinking resources for public action and eliminating protective regulations deemed to constrain economic growth. Yet this weakens the ability of governments to check environmental destruction, including in the oceans, and enables private interests to capture the benefits of resource exploitation for themselves while avoiding the costs. As Chapter 5 also points out, lawlessness is inherent in what happens in the vastness of the sea, which only a strong state apparatus can check.

CHAPTER 3

The Blue Commons

I must down to the seas again, to the vagrant gypsy life,
To the gull's way and the whale's way where the wind's like
    a whetted knife;
And all I ask is a merry yarn from a laughing fellow-rover,
And quiet sleep and a sweet dream when the long trick's over.
— John Masefield, 'Sea Fever', 1902

The revival of both marine ecosystems and the blue economy depends in large part on the revival of the blue commons, the values of commoning, and the robustness and resilience of blue commoners. They stand in opposition to the dictates of blue growth and the neoliberal framework identified above.

But what are the commons, commoners and commoning? In medieval times, most people would have had no difficulty in defining them. But more recently, particularly in the neoliberal era, these words – and the concepts behind them – have fallen into desuetude. It is a struggle to put them back in circulation. If you try to type the word 'commoning' in a Word document, the word processor presumes you have made a spelling error and converts it into 'communing'. Clearly, there is some explaining to do.

A succinct definition of the commons comes from

Greenpeace: 'They are dynamic, living systems created to meet shared needs. A commons requires three components: a resource, an associated community, and the rules the community uses to govern the resource. Commoning, as the practice is known, is an enduring, historical and essential survival strategy, offering fairer ways to meet our needs, especially in challenging times.'[1]

For our purposes, a commons may be defined as an environment that, actually or potentially, provides amenities and resources for a defined community to access, use and – vitally – preserve and reproduce. It does not have to be *owned* by the community, and usually is not. In Europe, historically, much of the land and its contents was deemed to belong to the monarch or ruler, who might then assign stewardship of parts of the territory to loyal followers. Within that territory, the commons were areas where common folk, or people who had little if any land of their own, were afforded specific rights – the right to graze their animals, the right to take a certain amount of firewood, the right to fish (piscary), and so on. In other parts of the world, before conquest and colonization, communities gained their subsistence in commons that had once been created from 'states of nature'.

Commons have always existed on sufferance, in tension with powerful external forces. They are fragile societal arrangements, depending on moral principles such as sharing and co-operation that must be constantly refreshed. Cultural rituals have often been crucial for maintaining the commons ethos. Yet they have not been sufficient to withstand the pressures of privatization and colonization. The extent of the commons and the permitted activities within them have diminished almost everywhere. Commons have been sold off to individuals and corporations to exploit as their private property, and the subsistence rights of peasants, indigenous communities and fishers have been restricted and even criminalized. This has been a key form of land grabbing or, in the case of the blue commons, ocean grabbing and coastal grabbing.

What of commoners? In Europe in medieval times, to be a commoner was a worthy status. It signified a claim on local resources and to be treated as an equal in the community and before the law. Only when capitalism started to take shape, when the presumptions of private property were strengthened, did a more pejorative interpretation take hold. We need to rescue the original meaning.

We are all commoners in at least one sense of the idea. If the world and what could be converted into resources in it belong to anybody, they belong to everybody, and the only moral meaning of that is that they belong to everybody *equally*. It is presumptuous to claim that any species on the planet, or any natural creation, belongs to us as humans. But to the extent we lay claim to make use of them, each and every one of us has an equal claim to the proceeds.

To this generic claim can be added more parochial claims. There are localized commons, and there are social, civil, cultural and knowledge commons. What characterizes each of these is a sense of common-ness, a sense that a certain definable community of commoners has access to and use of them, and the notion of heritage – that is, they have been accepted as a commons for a prolonged period.

The commons challenge the fundamental presumption, the bedrock, of neoliberal capitalism: the alleged sanctity of private property rights. This applies to the blue commons as much as to any other. Advocates of private property rights like to depict the commons as a simple state of nature in which there is automatically 'open access'. For instance, Madsen Pirie, president of the right-wing Adam Smith Institute in London, began a paper on British fishing policy with the following:

> The tragedy of the commons is that if a resource is not owned by anyone, there is no one to protect it, to preserve it, to enhance it, to maintain it or to renew it. Someone who owns property has an interest in preserving its value so that they may enjoy it in the future, be able to exchange it for something they value even more, or to pass it on to enrich their heirs and successors. Unowned assets have no guardians to care for them.[2]

If this were true, it would be depressing. But it is ideology dressed up as logic. There is nothing to stop the state, or other bodies, setting up mechanisms to protect natural resources in the commons. And it profoundly misrepresents the character of modern global capitalism, in which financial capital aims to maximize short-term profits, before selling depleted assets or switching into more lucrative avenues of profit-making.

Another right-wing author, from the Institute of Economic Affairs, made a similar point at around the same time:

> The essential problem with sea fisheries is that there are often no well-defined property rights. Many fisheries are huge 'commons' that can, in principle, be exploited and ultimately destroyed by trawler owners . . . The solution is

to establish property rights in sea fisheries . . . because we are the beneficiaries of our efforts.[3]

The libertarians' deliberate mistake is to pose a dichotomy between private property rights and 'open access'. A commons consists of a community, with rules of governance and traditions of sharing, preservation and reproduction. Unlike capitalist private property, a managed commons does not allow the deliberate depletion of resources. Only a commons perspective can make the preservation and reproduction of resources a formal social commitment, grounded in real local communities.

Blue common-wealth

The opening paragraphs of this book recalled that early Roman law categorized four types of property – private, public, belonging to nobody and belonging to all in common (*res communes omnium*). This was the first legal expression of the idea of the commons, which in Roman times encompassed 'the air, flowing water, the sea and its shores'. And it shaped the common law that still governs jurisprudence in the anglophone world, following the 1297 decision by King Edward I to adopt Magna Carta and the Charter of the Forest as the law of England. Henceforth the monarchy, as the embodiment of the state, was bound to protect the commons and commoners' rights.

This gave rise to what is known as the public trust doctrine, the duty of the state to preserve the commons and act as steward or trustee. So, common law requires that the state owning title to lands submerged under navigable waters must manage them in trust for the public to use for navigation, fishing and commerce and must not alienate them to the detriment of the public interest. This has obvious relevance to exploitation of the blue commons.

Minerals under the earth, oil and gas, wild animals and all natural things in, under or alongside the sea, only become 'wealth' when captured or mined and converted into commodities. But who has the right to mine or capture them, and who has the right to turn them into commodities and to take the proceeds? These questions have exercised philosophers and political economists through the ages.

This book takes the position that, to the extent that humankind may take nature as 'resources', they belong to everybody equally, where 'everybody' refers to the commoners in what constitutes the state, usually the nation. If the state grants to a corporation or community the right to mine or to capture, those directly engaged in the activity deserve compensation for their labour and reasonable profit. But the state has a duty to preserve the value of nature's bounty for its commoners, present and future. This is the basis of the intergenerational equity principle, which holds that future generations have as much right to the value of inherited common-wealth as today's.

In turn, the public trust doctrine requires the state to act as steward or trustee to ensure, as far as possible, that the principle of intergenerational equity is respected. This is a necessary role, for otherwise commoners may act opportunistically and behave like proto-capitalists, trying to maximize short-term profits and take excessive resources from the commons.

Nature in the form of latent wealth should be considered a common *asset*. As such it has value. But in conventional national economic accounting, the extraction of whatever is there, when sold or used for commercial purposes, is treated as *revenue*, adding to economic growth. The associated loss of common-wealth in extracting and using the asset is ignored. This book argues that everything in and under the sea, and in or on areas adjoining the sea, should be treated as common-wealth, and extraction of any part of it should be seen as a deduction from public wealth for which the commoners should be compensated. We will return to the implications of this position in the final chapter. But note that if we treat fish populations as 'fish stocks', as a form of shared inheritance, then the state should act as the primary trustee, charged with preserving and reproducing the shared public wealth. It should not allow the maximizing of short-term revenue and profits.

Where commercial interests are allowed to take from nature and own whatever they take as resources and commodities, the Lauderdale Paradox mentioned in Chapter 1 comes into play. The accumulation of those resources and commodities in private hands creates 'contrived scarcity', driving up prices and the value of private wealth while at the same time depleting common-wealth. The blue growth strategy is intensifying contrived scarcity, to an unprecedented and unsustainable extent. By contrast, a commons is based on respect for 'frugal abundance' and what has been called 'enoughness'. The idea of a commons sits comfortably with ideas of 'degrowth'.

The commons and time

A commons is, and always has been, defined in terms of time. Both the commons as a community and commoning as a set of shared activities are legitimized by having been accepted as such for some considerable time.

In medieval Britain, a commons existed if it had been that way since 'time immemorial', or 'in time out of mind of man', meaning for as long as anyone alive could remember. This informal rule gradually evolved to the definition that still applies today – being a commons, uncontested, for at least twenty years.[4] A similar rule could be applied to a blue commons. If a coastal community collectively built or paid for a local harbour, managed for use by community members, it would become a commons if accepted as such after twenty years. Crucial to the ethos of a commons and commoning is social memory – a shared recollection of how things came to be and why. Whereas a capitalistic system thrives on, and requires, constant change with little respect for traditions, a commons gives primacy to stability, durability and continuity.

However, in many parts of the world, defending a commons today can involve contending with a difficulty also faced by commoners in medieval times: that of determining how long the commons character has prevailed in the absence of written, formal documentation. Commons were frequently lost through enclosure when written records and surveying, employed to contest the existence of a commons, came to outweigh oral testimony. That threat persists in many communities in the developing world where written records are scant or non-existent, requiring local witnesses to attest to the durability of a commons.

In the case of marine commons, there is also a conceptual challenge relating to the increasing incidence of fish migration, due mainly to warming oceans. What happens if, for generations, a particular fish population is regarded as the commons resource of one country, or of one community within a country, and for climatic or other reasons the fish stock migrates to a different territory? If, for instance, a jurisdiction feels it has nurtured a fish stock to ensure its sustainability, deliberately preventing overfishing or introducing expensive nursery management, would it have a legitimate continuing claim to the commons resource if it moved into another EEZ?

Commoning and commoners

The verb 'to common' should be rescued, since the essence of commons in medieval times was the *activity* of commoning, shared self-governed activity by groups of commoners. Commoning need not be the main activity, let alone the only form of activity, in a commons. But it must be significant, playing a role in preserving the commons as a social organization. Commoning typically consists of reproductive and care activities, not only for other commoners but for nature and the environment.

This sense of commoning, first celebrated in the Charter of the Forest of 1217, is manifested nowadays as 'peer production', where modern-day commoners work together on a common project without relying on market signals or managerial commands.[5] Contemporary examples include community gardens, Wikipedia and the open-source computer operating system Linux, where people collaborate and share without outside direction or financial reward. In an idealized commons society, we could imagine shared activities being so extensive that the values of reproduction and cooperation would be pervasive, while profit-maximizing, accumulative, resource-depleting activity would be marginalized.

Many sharing activities have helped to define the blue commons, such as guarding the environment, cleaning processing areas, protecting against pollution, serving on governance committees, and giving assistance to fellow commoners in difficulty. Some activities are as familiar in the blue economy as on land. One such is foraging. The sea literally throws up much of potential human use, and common foraging through the ages, even if not essential for food security, will have been valuable for social bonding.

Traditions of commoning are still observed in many places across the blue planet. One form of collective foraging takes place in the mouth of the Alaskan Kenai River where, every July and August, all resident Alaskans are allowed to catch a certain number of sockeye salmon free of charge: twenty-five for the nominated head of household, plus ten for each family member. According to the Alaskan Department of Fish and Game, 'The fish are owned by all Alaskans equally. It's a really cool, unique benefit that Alaskan residents get. It's a way to use the resource owned by the people for the benefit of the people.'[6]

In 2020, 26,000 households applied for the dip-netting permits. An official of the Department pointed out, 'It's hugely important for Alaskans. You're talking $8 or more per pound of protein, and all these people are getting that by sticking a net in the water. The freezer of meat they'll have is worth thousands of dollars.' While there are downsides to the scheme, such as privileging those who are physically fit enough to fish, it surely strengthens a sense of commons.[7]

In another example of commoning as foraging, from British Columbia in Canada, a group of volunteers, researchers and First Nation 'knowledge holders' go out on winter nights to a beach that was once a clam garden, an ancient form of mariculture that coastal First Nation people used for millennia, and which provided them with food security.[8] Now, commoners are returning to the beaches to care for them, so that clams can again breed and grow there.

The clam gardens did more than provide food, however. As a First Nation leader said, 'I think that one of the most important things about restoring these places is that it requires that we restore people's relationships with them. It forces us to rethink humans as only having negative impacts on our ecosystem, and remember that for millennia we have had really positive and reciprocal relationships with the places we belong to, and we can have those kinds of relationships once again.'

Historically, a related form of commoning has been gleaning – gathering scraps and left-overs – as celebrated in the famous painting by Jean-François Millet of 1857, depicting three peasant women in a field bending to pick scattered stalks of wheat after the harvest. Gleaning has also been an integral part of commoning in artisanal subsistence fisheries, notably around coral reef flats and estuaries.[9] It is a shared collective activity and a way of maximizing the crop and minimizing waste. However, it is mainly, if not exclusively, done by women and children, underlining the gendered nature of many commons and warning against over-idealization.

Commons knowledge

> [Knowledge] resembles a magnificent structure that has no foundation.
> — Francis Bacon, 1622

Normally, a commons is bound together by a common body of knowledge, of what should be done, how it should be done and why it should be done. To an outsider, some of the practices and norms may appear strange or counterintuitive. But to the extent that they have stood the test of time, they may fit into a complex and sensitive set of relationships that preserves the system. A commons usually prioritizes certain types of knowledge and ways of building or changing knowledge on which actions are based. Some have called this 'situated knowledge', inseparable from the knowledge holders and the local environment.[10]

Commoning includes activities that are about adapting and reinforcing indigenous knowledge, which is important for monitoring strains on the environment. Sometimes known as 'folk knowledge', it may be vital.[11] Commons knowledge often depends on relationships and connections between living beings and non-living entities, based on understanding cycles of interdependency. Introducing an alien knowledge system, even with good intentions, in the name of 'objective science', may have destructive consequences. A commons can be dislocated, disrupted or dismantled by the import of external knowledge designed for 'improvement', especially knowledge as 'science' that focuses on efficiency.

In the 1950s and 1960s, the UN Food and Agriculture Organization (FAO) sent Western experts to developing countries, taking with them their Western ideology of 'progress', in an effort to transform agriculture and fisheries based on the best available scientifically grounded practices. One assessment dubbed those sent out 'scientist-ambassadors'.[12] They focused on helping to build large-scale, mechanized, industrial fisheries. In so doing, they weakened the blue commons, inadvertently or otherwise, turning time-honoured norms into disparaged 'old ways', so eroding the legitimacy and sustainability of traditional practices and norms. Yet in recent years, anthropologists and others have begun to show that there are different types of knowledge, and that modern science is not necessarily optimal when applied in ecosystems and communities built over many generations.

A commons knowledge system's claim to legitimacy is linked to the idea of 'consilience', the belief that there can and should be a 'jumping together' of different knowledge traditions to resolve real-world problems in all their complexity. A commons knowledge system has a natural unity, blending ideas and practices by pragmatic adaption over time, giving priority to what has worked in the past and what has been of value to the community. By contrast, modern scientific knowledge is artificially fragmented.[13]

The social sciences too have been split into ever narrower disciplines, and modern neoliberal economics laid its initial claim to be 'scientific' by aping engineering and mechanics. As it evolved, it formed a partnership with neoliberal psychology, in which attitudes and behaviour are seen as conditioned by incentives. This gave rise to so-called 'behavioural economics', the core idea of which is to find ways of nudging people to behave in ways best suited to a market economy. It is a system for manipulating people and institutions to fit the neoliberal model.

A commons knowledge system is profoundly at odds with a neoliberal knowledge system, which has no place for history, no place for social classes, no place for commons or multiple forms of property. In an era in which neoliberal incentives are predominant, a vernacular knowledge system quietly operating in the community can provide a risk-reducing barrier to profiteering. But the absence or bypassing of vernacular knowledge circuits can have deleterious consequences. For instance, if an outside donor agency funds or encourages the adoption of high-tech fishing gear, more entrepreneurial or lucky individuals may flourish, momentarily increasing economic growth, but at the cost of bankrupting or marginalizing the less adaptable or fortunate. By fragmenting the community, the intervention may damage the economic, social and cultural support structures on which maintenance of the commons depends.

For many years, indigenous or commons knowledge was disparaged, and it was relatively easy for development crusaders to brush it aside as unscientific, a barrier to 'progress'. However, anthropologists are coming to terms with the reality of multiple knowledge systems, and the need to adopt what one perceptive First Nation elder in Canada has called a 'two-eyed seeing' approach that gives equal respect to indigenous knowledge and scientific knowledge.[14] This would not mean scientists taking an unscientific view, merely that each knowledge system must be given equal respect a priori. If that is done, negotiated change geared to reproduction of the commons will be more likely, enabling folk wisdom to moderate potentially disruptive effects. For example, a dugong and marine turtle protection programme in northern Australia that integrated indigenous and scientific expertise was judged a 'stand-out success', not only in saving wildlife but in generating additional social, cultural, environmental and economic benefits for the indigenous communities managing the project.[15]

Indigenous knowledge has pointed the way to fishing techniques and technologies that can sustain otherwise declining salmon populations on Canada's west coast.[16] It has led to improvements in early warning of impending natural disasters in India.[17] And it has helped to show how to reverse declines in species and to improve collective adherence to fishery management policy, as in the Maine lobster fisheries in the USA.[18]

A commons perspective recognizes that a positivistic epistemology (that there is one knowable truth, based on experiments and objective observation) is at best risky because of inherent uncertainties. Today's scientific fact can be tomorrow's refuted fallacy – or the initiator of unintended consequences that respect for local knowledge could have predicted and prevented. In globalized capitalism, the latest knowledge can be implemented far more widely and rapidly than before. If it proves to be dysfunctional, the damage is much greater. Best practice today could become less good or even bad tomorrow. Unlike global science, commons knowledge proceeds incrementally and reversibly through trial and error in practice. There are no great breakthroughs but no disasters either.

Sustaining the blue commons

Picture two stylized extremes. In an ideal commons society, the governance of production and distribution is delegated largely but not entirely to local commoners, with layers of state actors setting the broad parameters and acting as stewards or trustees. The image of a pyramid probably applies.

In global neoliberal capitalism, the pyramid is inverted. All the power is taken from local levels, ultimately to rest in the hands of supra-national institutions that represent financial and multinational capital. Seen in this schematic way, commoners have a primary interest in preserving their own local commons and its resources, whereas in globalized rentier capitalism, those holding the power have little or no interest in preserving a local environment. Once resources are exhausted in one location, the industrial juggernaut can move to somewhere else.

An erosion of the middle layers of governance also endangers the commons as the institutions that could help protect them become corrupted or collapse through lack of funding or political commitment. In a process of what might be called 'decentration', the initial pyramid changes shape to an hourglass. The power transfers upwards and the commons are left exposed, putting the nation state in an opportunistic alliance with global commercial interests. We will see how devastating that can be.

A commons worthy of the name depends on explicit and implicit rules, norms and mechanisms of governance.[19] Every blue commons exists on a bundle of *de jure* and de facto rights, with rules roughly corresponding to the following:

- *Rules on boundaries*. It is often a teaser to ask where a commons begins and where it ends. A commons needs defined boundaries and defined resources covered by the commons, such as a particular species of fish. As these have often relied on social memory, they have been easily eroded.
- *Rules of access or use*. These may be set by conventional practices or be more formalized.[20] Rules of access define who is a commoner in the relevant commons, and the criteria to be used for inclusion, suspension and exclusion. There should also be rules of limitation, in case the number of people entitled to be included exceeds the limit of sustainability. Such rules may not exist in many blue commons. Others may tie inclusion to payment of an entry fee or being related to somebody living and sharing in the commons in the past.

Rules of access are likely to define the permissible extent of fishing, duration and timing of fishing, and respect for rules on methods, processing and storage. However, although in some countries, rights of small-scale and indigenous fishers are codified and even published, in practice problems can arise in registering individual fishers.

For example, as part of the post-apartheid restructuring of the fisheries sector, South Africa's Department of Agriculture, Forestry and Fisheries required all small-scale and subsistence fishers to apply for legal status, previously denied to most Blacks. However, the registration process proved chaotic. Fishers did not know they had to apply for permits or were unable to navigate the complex bureaucratic application procedures. Decisions were promised within ninety days, but there were long delays and the vast majority of applications were refused. Some fishers were successful in appealing decisions through the courts, with legal assistance from civil society organizations. But there were also allegations that people who were not part of traditional fishing communities, and had no history of being engaged in fishing, were nonetheless granted legal status. This example highlights the challenges that arise in the formalization of fishing rights.

- *Rules on harvesting*. These refer to who can harvest or take what and when and how. In blue commons that have existed in similar form for generations, such rules may be part of the social memory. However, modernization and globalization have been associated with the development of numerous formal rules, often introduced with objectives that have nothing to do with the preservation of fisheries as commons. These include, but are not necessarily limited to, quota rules, days-of-effort rules and anti-discard rules, most designed with conservation and sharing objectives.

Rules on harvesting can evolve as the commons adapts to its specific ecosystem. In the Lofoten Islands in the far north of Norway, a portion of the cod fishery is set aside for sail-powered boats. Factory trawler ships are prohibited. These Norwegians know that modern techniques would bring them higher yields. But they are not sure modern techniques will ensure them fish for their lifetime and that of their children and grandchildren. Despite repeated attempts by the government to emphasize revenue, the fishers' primary goal is not maximum yield or profit; it is a secure fishery. The result is a relatively 'inefficient' management regime, but one with a track record of over a century of successful management, and some 500 years of exporting cod to the Mediterranean. Similar stories can be told for long-standing small-scale inshore fisheries around the world.

- *Rules on management rights.* A commons requires management, and it should be clear who has management rights. That need not be the whole community, and rarely has been. Commoners may delegate the management role to one or several bodies, ideally to an elected body with a term limit. However, if a commons is to be sustained, the commoners must feel confident in that arrangement.

- *Rules on excludability.* Most commons, including blue coastal commons, have explicit rules of excludability that block outsiders from access. They are not 'open access' but nor does that make them private property. Shrinking the area of a commons, as is happening in fisheries, makes it easier to exclude non-commoners.[21]

- *Rules on alienation.* These refer to the ways a commoner can leave or transfer rights in the commons to existing commoners or to outsiders who thereby become commoners. These rules are particularly important in fishery management systems relying on quotas. Blue commons can be lost when powerful interests take advantage of loopholes for non-commoners to obtain commons resources. As we shall see, the way the British quota system has been implemented has largely destroyed the commons, making a radical overhaul essential.

- *Rules on inheritance.* Decisions have to be made about who may take over from a commoner who dies or leaves the commons, and about what is inherited – for example, ownership of an asset, such as a vessel, licence or quota, or use of a resource. In some cases, there may simply be a rule that no inheritance is allowed – that the right expires with the commoner who held it.

  Inheritance rules are potentially a source of structural advantage for a commons over any system of private property rights. In a fishery commons, the most frequent rule is for rights and responsibilities to be transferred to family members, and each generation sets out to preserve and reproduce the resources for the next. One reason for this rule is that at some stage the existing fisher retires and expects continued support from the children who have taken over. There is thus an inherent tendency to respect the principle of intergenerational equity. Similar respect is less likely in a system of private property rights, since a commercial fishery can maximize short-term profits and then move elsewhere, or simply reinvest the revenue in some other sector.

- *Rules on infractions.* Clearly, a well-managed commons must have rules on what should happen to commoners who break the rules on sharing, access and so on, and how they should be judged. Rules on infraction should also cover what non-commoners do, for example, if there are unauthorized incursions into commons fishing grounds.

- *Rules on credit and loans.* In blue commons, as in other commons, there are often implicit or informal rules on credit and loans provided within the commons, so that risks are shared between those playing different roles in the production process. This is done without reliance on intermediaries, acting as a partial block on financial rent-seekers such as moneylenders or banks. There is thus an integral process for retaining more of the income within the community and reinforcing trust relationships that strengthen community resilience. The typical informal credit system is illustrated in some of the *mama karanga* (meaning 'frying women' in Kiswahili) women fish-trader communities operating along the Kenyan coast.[22] In these traditional rotating savings groups called 'merry-go-rounds', each member contributes a small amount at monthly get-togethers. The total is then paid out to one of the members on a rotating basis.

Few blue commons are likely to have adequate rules covering all these aspects, which contributes to their vulnerability. But, as noted above, an important feature of a commons is the learning and reproduction of trust-based relations of production and distribution. Whatever the bundle of rights and reach in the set of rules, the learning of rules converts them into community values and then into an integrative morality that 'this is the way it is done' and 'this is our way'.

In a fishery made up of individual private property owners, who can enter or leave the sector at any time, learning trust and feeling able to rely on others to respect the rules is far less likely. Whereas a blue commons depends on trust, capitalistic concerns have at best paid cynical lip service to it.

Stewards and gatekeepers

Most commons exist within a state, which should act as the steward or trustee of the commons, in principle as an arbiter in matters of dispute between different commons and as a 'nightguard' protector of commons from external threats. However, in a globalized open economic system, commons survival depends on the existence of multiple stewards, at local, national and supra-national levels. The steward has ultimate responsibility for preserving the commons and for handing it on to future generations. Yet most states have failed to do this, often for ideological or political reasons; many have been captured by financial and corporate interests keen on dismantling the commons for private gain.

A steward may be the formal owner but does not have exclusive private property rights to use, exploit or dispose of resources in the commons. In artisanal fisheries, the primary stewardship role might be played by a local authority. But, since fish are notoriously disrespectful of watery borders, there may be competing communities trying to exploit an overlapping marine resource. There is thus a need for stewardship by the state or national government, and by supranational authorities as well. In the blue commons, this has led to the development of co-management systems as alternatives to full privatization, where co-management refers to shared responsibilities between a government body and the 'stakeholders' in a fishery community.

A useful, if rather scholastic, framework for considering multiple stewards for blue commons is the distinction between 'horizontal governance' and 'vertical governance' networks. Horizontal networks link counterpart officials of similar status and authority. Vertical networks link layers of authority over complementary aspects of a commons, which might mean at sub-national, national and supra-national levels.[23]

A steward has a quasi-juridical responsibility to preserve and reproduce the commons. But a steward may err, become slack or fail in other ways. Accordingly, to be sustainable, a commons needs one or more 'gatekeepers', that is, protective organizations with as much access to relevant information as the stewards and with the ability and designated legitimized responsibility to hold the stewards to account in the performance of their functions.

A question is whether fishery associations, of which there are a large number with varying constitutions and coverage, fulfil a stewardship role or a gatekeeper role. In the UK and the European Union, at least, producer organizations seem to be losing their gatekeeper character and are evolving into stewardship bodies, particularly with regard to the allocation of quotas and licences (see Chapter 4). A better example of a gatekeeper is British Columbia's Halibut Advisory Committee. Its elected and appointed members, intended to represent all stakeholders in the fisheries, advise the Canadian Department of Fisheries and Oceans on management and policy.

In countries such as Britain and the United States, the ultimate gatekeeper is common law, which is based on precedent and the public trust doctrine derived from Roman law. As common law developed over the centuries, air, running water, the sea and seashore were all deemed to be outside private ownership; they were regarded as open to public use. Common law was charged with protecting and maintaining the resources for that purpose. In many parts of the world, however, the laws and institutions responsible have been emasculated to the point where the civil commons (the justice system) has ceased to function equitably or efficiently. This has left many seashore communities susceptible to 'dispossession of legality' as well as 'dispossession of resources'.

In 1299, however, a legal case brought by a humble washerwoman called Juliana established a precedent that to this day has not been overturned.[24] Juliana challenged her powerful neighbour John de Tytyng, the Mayor of Winchester, demanding that he desist from cutting off her use of the local watercourse. The case went all the way up to King Edward I, a staunch believer in common law, who gave judgment in Juliana's favour. His ruling not only stated that 'water has always been common', but included prohibitions on polluting Winchester's rivers and streams, for example, with dyes, blood or excrement, that were subsequently put on the statute book. This was the first legal enunciation of the 'right to water', which has since become an internationally recognized human right. And it established that common law had a positive duty to defend common rights and so act as gatekeeper of the commons. Those aiming to uphold the historical rights of the blue commons will wish to appeal to the likes of Juliana the Washerwoman and the public trust doctrine.[25]

By remarkable coincidence, in November 2016, another

Juliana (Kelsey Juliana) headed a case brought by twenty-one youths before the District Court of Oregon against the US government on the grounds that the US administration had a positive duty under the public trust doctrine to act against dangerous climate change but was failing to do so, thereby violating their right to a safe environment. In her historic opinion and order in favour of Juliana, the district court judge wrote, 'Exercising my "reasoned judgment", I have no doubt that the right to a climate system capable of sustaining human life is fundamental to a free and ordered society.'[26] However, in January 2020, a panel of the Ninth Circuit Court of Appeals, in a split decision, 'reluctantly' ruled against Juliana, saying the plaintiffs should address the executive and legislative branches of the US government since the court system could not provide a remedy for violation of the plaintiffs' rights. This was upheld by the full appeals bench, following which the youths asked to file an amended complaint and adjust the remedy sought. This request was still pending at the time of writing. Meanwhile, eighteen Republican states, led by Alabama, filed an intervention motion seeking to obstruct settlement negotiations and have the case dismissed.

In Australia, a federal court ruled in July 2021 that the environment minister had a 'duty of care' to protect Australian children from climate harm that would be caused by the expansion of a coal-mining project.[27] Australia's greenhouse gas emissions per capita are among the world's highest, and the government has done little to curb them. Yet it immediately said it would appeal the ruling, in effect denying its duty of care under the public trust doctrine, and two months later the environment minister approved the coal-mine expansion in question.

Still, activists are not giving up. Over a thousand climate change-related cases have been brought since 2015, against both governments and corporations.[28] In the Netherlands a court ruled in 2015 that the government had a duty of care to protect citizens from climate change, obliging the government to cut emissions further than it had planned. In 2021 another Dutch court ordered Shell to cut emissions by almost half by 2030, while the German constitutional court ruled that the government's failure to protect the climate for future generations was unconstitutional. Meanwhile, in October 2021, the UN Human Rights Council declared that having a clean, healthy and sustainable environment is a human right. States are now obliged to implement this right, including protection of the natural systems such as marine ecosystems that support lives and livelihoods.[29]

How blue commons are lost

> Property is not theft, but a good deal of theft becomes property.
> — Richard Tawney[30]

We can identify seven mechanisms by which any blue commons can be lost or eroded, differentiating between internal disruption (or decay) and external corrosion.

The first is erosion by 'neglect'. This can arise from a loss of social memory – social forgetting – but is more likely to result from inadequate supporting resources from government.[31] For instance, in Britain many commons – parks, libraries and museums, social services and amenities, and cultural venues – fell victim to the austerity policies that followed the financial crash of 2007–8.[32] In developing countries, commons have been sacrificed as part of 'structural adjustment' programmes imposed by international financial institutions. Cutting resources for the maintenance and protection of commons has often been a preparatory step to privatization.

Second, commons have been lost through 'encroachment'. It has always been vital to define and defend boundaries, not just in a spatial sense but also in a functioning sense. For example, a fishing community may have rules that condition the right to fish on certain qualifications and experience. If the government introduces a separate licensing system, that encroaches on the commons.

Encroachment is likely to be gradual. It might arise from the state turning a blind eye to outsiders that abuse or ignore traditional rules, perhaps in return for a bribe or some quid pro quo. Encroachment may also be implicitly allowed when a government cuts back on protective measures, as Britain has done in the austerity era.

In medieval times, encroachment led to the tradition in England of 'beating the bounds', an annual perambulation by local commoners around the commons boundary to check for inroads. Combating acts of encroachment in the blue commons is obviously more difficult; identifying boundaries in moving water is hard, and identifying culpability may be harder. Making and enforcing boundaries is further complicated by movement of the 'resources'.

The commercialization of adjacent resources, on which certain common pool resources depend, is another form of encroachment. For instance, mining of a seabed may deplete the fish that are the primary resource of the pre-existing local commons, by noise, disruption, water pollution or the construction of infrastructure. More obvious is ocean grabbing or coastal grabbing by private interests, for agriculture, tourism or port development as well as fishing. In some cases, local commoners have aided the process, taking resources from more vulnerable groups.

There have also been instances where local commoners have 'grabbed back' marine resources.[33] In 1999, the indigenous Inuit people were granted the new territory of Nunavut in the far north of Canada, which restored their traditional lands and coastal waters. In Port Mouton Bay in Nova Scotia, government-supported commercial aquaculture disrupted traditional lobster and other fishing. Faced with ruin, the local fishers set up the Friends of Port Mouton Bay to do research, demand regulations, a role in management, and space set aside for conservation.

A third way in which the commons are lost is 'enclosure', the most frequent cause of loss of land commons, although it has also affected seashores and water spaces. As noted in Chapter 1, UNCLOS achieved the largest enclosure by area in history. Enclosure alters the property form, turning commons into private property or state property that could be privatized in the future. Privatization is usually assumed to be the direct conversion of public ownership into private property and private capitalistic production. But historically, enclosure of commons was an intermediary step on the way to private ownership.

Another form of enclosure takes place when a government decides to allocate quotas for fish or shellfish to producer organizations or individual fisheries to distribute, as in Britain and a growing number of other countries. This takes decisions on quotas away from the commons and commercializes them for private profit.

Enclosure can also combine with other forces that erode the commons. Incremental encroachment may gradually undermine the capacity of the commons to sustain production for 'enoughness', and lead to increased inequalities and social strains that contribute to a crumbling of the governance structure and the community. In many cases, the process will involve initial enclosure followed by the sale to private interests, made more likely these days by financial incentives paid to politicians and bureaucrats.

Privatization, the transfer to private property, is a fourth way of losing the commons. Turning communal fisheries into zones of private property rights has been a standard strategy since the onset of neoliberalism in the 1970s. Enclosure and privatization have been advocated on the grounds that such production is more efficient than in a commons, a claim used extensively in Africa and Latin America.[34] In its role as the leading development agency, the World Bank has given no respect to communal property rights. It has long had a target of having 70% of people with private property rights by 2030, justifying private land titling on the grounds that it boosts agricultural productivity.[35]

However, customary commoning may have lower productivity because it favours more diversified cropping and rotation practices, in contrast to the mono-production of export crops with more value in the world market. The higher productivity of privatized production may simply reflect the fact that food production is destined for other parts of the world rather than for feeding the local community.

The same may apply to a fishery. A local commons may eat what they catch, and land a wide variety of fish, many with low market value. A privatized fishery may treat the latter as bycatch, throwing them back dead, while focusing on catching mainly high-value species. The productivity difference is thus a matter of community choice.

A fifth destructive mechanism is 'commodification', when a commons resource is transformed into a market commodity, for sale, rather than for direct consumption or sharing by the commoners. Fish stocks are by nature a commons resource, owned by nobody and by everybody equally. Chapter 2 referred to the argument that fish only become private property when they are caught.[36] Even then, however, they do not become a commodity if they are not brought to market. Increasingly, it is the quotas or licences to fish that are being turned into commodities to be bought and sold, extending private property rights to fish as yet uncaught.

A sixth means by which the commons have been lost is 'colonization'. Globally, this was the main mechanism of destruction of the blue commons in the eighteenth, nineteenth and early twentieth centuries. But modern forms of colonization have continued into the twenty-first century, in the corrosion of the blue commons by foreign governments, foreign firms and foreign property companies.

'Financialization', a scourge of the modern era, is the seventh way of losing the commons. It is useful to differentiate the acquisition and destruction of a commons by financial capital from both ordinary privatization and colonization. Financial institutions, notably private equity and hedge funds, have been turning to the blue commons as a lucrative source of rental income, obliging firms in which they invest to go for high short-term profits. The development of futures markets in food, including high-value fish, is further eroding the capacity of blue commons to survive external pressures.

Different mechanisms for plundering the commons may occur in tandem. Shrimp fishing in the North-West Atlantic is an example of how state enclosure can result in a direct transition from open access to privatization and industrialized fishing. Before 1977, Scandinavian fishing companies dominated shrimp fishing off the Canadian coast. That year the Canadian government extended jurisdictional sovereignty to 200 nautical miles, dispossessing Scandinavian interests and leading to the 'Canadianization' of northern shrimp fishing.[37] Enclosure led to privatization through state issuance of licences and the imposition of a quota system.

The combination of encroachment, commercial penetration and externally driven technological change can spur a toxic cycle of destruction. In southern India, worsening drought due to climate change has hit agricultural livelihoods and impelled tens of thousands of farmers to join fishing communities in the Bay of Bengal, driving down average incomes of fishers and further depleting fish populations.[38] These communities were already suffering the consequences of misguided policies in the 1960s when Western aid agencies encouraged commercial trawling for prawns in Indian waters. This was intended to raise incomes by tapping into export markets for 'pink gold'. But the trawling nets, dragged along the sea floor, destroyed whole ecosystems on which the prawns and other fish depended. Many once abundant species have all but disappeared.

Meanwhile, diminishing catches in inshore waters have led trawlers to stray into waters further and further from traditional fishing areas, fuelling conflict between Bay of Bengal coastal countries. In 2015, Sri Lankan authorities claimed to have spotted over 40,000 Indian trawlers in their territorial waters; seventy trawlers were seized, 450 fishermen were arrested, and there were over 100 deaths. Meanwhile, Sri Lankan tuna fishermen were arrested in Indian waters. And Thai squid trawlers have been emptying some of the richest fishing grounds off Myanmar, helping to make Thailand the world's largest exporter of squid but devastating the livelihoods of local fishers in the process. These instances show what happens when the commons are encroached and subjected to a form of neo-colonial invasion.

The seashore and seabed around Britain also illustrate how the commons can be lost by a failure of stewardship and the combination of enclosure and privatization. The seashore of a country belongs to everybody as commoners, so the state should act as steward with a duty to protect, ensure access, preserve and pass on that commons to future generations. Yet of the 8,000 or so miles of coast around Britain, 45% is still 'owned' by the Crown, 45% is formally owned by the Ministry of Defence or by the National Trust, while 10% has passed into private ownership. Meanwhile, the Crown Estate has auctioned large areas of the seabed for offshore wind farms, mostly operated by multinational corporations, the benefits of which will be shared between the monarchy and the Exchequer.

There are other threats to the commons, including habitat decay, caused by global warming and other ecological stresses on the marine environment. However, this book concentrates on the impact of neoliberal globalization and the structural changes and development strategies it has engendered. Neoliberalism has operated partly as an ideological force and partly as a systematic attempt to give priority to the creation and defence of private property rights. The main structural change has been the integration of the global economy, most notably the rapid rise of China and South-East Asia, the emergence since the 1990s of Russia as a rogue state working on behalf of its industrial fishery corporations, and the opportunistic support given to their equivalents by the European Union.

This has facilitated the growth and impunity of illegal and unregulated commercial fishing, revealing the crimogenic nature of the global fishing industry. Examples will be described later, and justifiably angry observers have already listed several elsewhere, including the grotesque destruction of beluga sturgeon that now face extinction in most of their old habitats.[39] Here, consider the plight of the long-snouted (or spiny) seahorse (*Hippocampus guttulatus*), one of forty seahorse sub-species in the world, which lives in a unique saltwater lagoon of long-protected water, Mar Piccolo, near the southern Italian port of Taranto.[40]

Before globalization, it was a zone of wonderful biodiversity in which the seahorses and sea cucumbers were stars. Because most Europeans do not eat either of these, they were safe, and the modest protective system operated by the Taranto authority was adequate for conservation. In recent years, however, demand for both species from China and other parts of Asia has led to large-scale poaching, with the result that seahorses in the lagoon are now severely endangered. They have become part of an illegal global trading chain that traffics some thirty-seven million seahorses each year. The local protective regulatory system has proved inadequate for the task and the state has failed to build it up. Had a strong commons been preserved, poaching could have been stopped by collective policing by local commoners. Instead, political inaction prevailed.

Local activists reckon that the lagoon poachers receive €0.80 (£0.70) for each kilo of sea cucumbers they catch. The intermediaries who clean and process them receive about eight times as much, and the Chinese consumer pays over thirty times as much. For seahorses, the eventual retail price is a higher multiple still. Those managing the illegal global trade are making fortunes, while a gorgeous part of a commons ecosystem is slowly vanishing.

Related to this poignant example is the widespread growth of 'illegal, unreported and unregulated' fishing. The acronym IUU probably does not help analytically or politically, because it compresses dissimilar phenomena. Some unreported and unregulated fish catch is undertaken by artisanal fisheries, mostly on a small scale and sometimes driven by necessity, as was the case for some South African fishers who failed to obtain legal permits in the example mentioned earlier. Some unreported and unregulated fishing may be illegal as well, if it exceeds allowable quotas or generates revenue that is not declared for tax. It may also threaten the commons if it leads to unsustainable overfishing.

However, commercial fishing that deliberately sets out

to evade or avoid regulation is a bigger threat to the blue commons, by taking commons resources and damaging their capacity to reproduce. Had protective regulations been strengthened in the 1980s rather than derided by the neo-liberal ascendancy as impeding economic growth, IUU fishing might not have taken on the proportions it has. Aided by pressure from international financial agencies favouring deregulation, the crimogenic character of the fishing industry has prevailed.

Commonization and decommonization

The above discussion can be illustrated by two real-world examples of how commons are formed ('commonization') and dismantled ('decommonization'). The first relates to Chilika Lake, the largest lagoon in India, in the state of Odisha (formerly Orissa).[41] The fishing communities around the lagoon became commoners over generations, stretching back to the eighteenth century. The lagoon was, and still is, state property, and caste-based fisher communities were commonized through a lease system endorsed by the state government. This offered leases for specific fishing areas to fishing villages, not to individual fishers, although the leases only applied to fisher castes. The system operated well, precisely because it was not based on private property rights.

A multilayered governance structure took shape. Fishers formed village groups to set norms and rules for fishing and equitable rules for sharing the proceeds. In other words, they operated methods of access control and rules of conduct and sharing. Later the villages formed a cooperative and federation at regional level to represent them in negotiations with

Odisha government departments. The structure operated an elaborate system of leasing and sub-leasing.

However, by the early 1980s decommonization pressures were eroding the commons. The principal economic factors were globalization and the commercial riches to be made from industrial aquaculture. No doubt with potential economic growth in mind, the state government changed from a passive steward of the commons to an advocate for intensive prawn aquaculture. It supported the investment in aquaculture by outsiders, including what the local fishers termed the *Chingudi* (prawn) mafia.

Another factor in decommonization was the creation of protected areas in the lagoon. This was a form of enclosure, depriving fishers of access to their traditional fishing areas. The state government then signed a deal with the Tata holding company to hand over a large expanse of the customary fishing grounds of nine fishing villages. Tata subsequently pulled out of the deal after mass protests, but the area remained out of the control of the fishing villages and the state government changed the lease law, allocating even more of the fishing villages' customary fishing grounds to aquaculture by non-fisher caste villages and doubling the price of fishing leases.

Although the Odisha government later formally banned aquaculture following a Supreme Court order, and rescinded the lease reform, illegal prawn aquaculture remained dominant and the fisheries were decommonized. More of the villages sub-leased parts of their customary fishing areas to moneylenders, who transferred them to aquaculture farmers. Then the government created a centralized administrative agency, dismantling the old system of governance and making it inaccessible to local fishers. As resources diminished, fishing became more individualistic, while many fishers left the villages to become casual labourers, joining the urban and rural precariat.

As this example shows, commonization may take a long time and is highly sensitive to encroachment, enclosure and privatization. As so often, decommonization followed a collapse of the 'resources', which was directly linked to a capitalistic form of production. The main winners were illegal aquaculturists, who could not have thrived without the knowledge and tacit approval of the state government. This is a classic case of the state-corporate collusion, discussed in Chapter 5, that has epitomized the blue economy globally.

The sequence in the lagoon went from commonization to decommonization to almost open access as traditional fishing grounds were abandoned, leaving a free-for-all that benefited the powerful, and then to privatization.[42] Contrary to the standard neoliberal claims, private property rights coincided with the depletion of the resource base. There is now a 'contrived scarcity' of fish.

Another example of decommonization is the disintegration of a blue commons in the Tam Giang Lagoon in Vietnam.[43] Here the trajectory was from a form of state socialism to capitalism. The lagoon has provided livelihoods for about 300,000 inhabitants for generations. The coastal economy was nationalized in the 1970s, but gradually commercial aquaculture became a major export industry, and is now the country's third-largest economic sector after oil and garments.

Its growth was accompanied by steady decommonization as earth ponds, net enclosures and pen culture spread.

There was declining use of the old practice in which village authorities auctioned long-term rights to local fishers using traditional methods; private property rights were introduced and strengthened.

These examples also show how a bundle of common rights linked to a shared resource disintegrated, underlining their fragility in the face of external political, economic and ecological forces, and in the absence of corrective political action by the state. They also demonstrate the need to accommodate and integrate common rights in the property rights regime. To combat decommonization, common rights should have the same legal weight as the bundle of rights that go with private property ownership.[44]

From blue commoners to the precariat

If a commons is to survive, the commoners must be both robust and resilient, where robustness is the ability to withstand or prevent disruption and shocks, and resilience is the ability to bounce back from shocks or setbacks. This book focuses on communities of small-scale fisheries as the core group of blue commoners, although blue commoners also include all those subsisting on, in and around marine ecosystems.

According to the FAO, small-scale fishers comprise 90% – over thirty-one million – of the thirty-five million fishers recorded globally, and a further twenty million people are involved in related small-scale fish processing. In addition, millions of others who are not recorded as fishers in the official statistics are involved in seasonal or occasional fishing activities.[45] Combining the numbers of fishers and fish workers with those providing equipment and services to fishing communities, perhaps 200 million people worldwide depend in some part on small-scale fisheries for their livelihood.

The conventional image of the fishery sector is men going out in boats to catch fish. But in many places, a larger number of people are involved in the processing of landed fish, and a majority of those are often women. As with their work on land, the involvement of women in fisheries is deplorably underestimated by official data.[46]

The four types of fishery – industrial, artisanal, subsistence and recreational – are usually defined as follows:

- *Industrial* – large-scale fisheries using trawlers, purse-seiners or longliners, with high capital input, often fishing across the seabed.
- *Artisanal* – small-scale fisheries whose catch is predominantly sold and that use static or stationary ('passive') gear that does not have to be dragged, pulled or towed, such as hook and lines, traps, wires and gill nets. They operate largely in domestic waters, within their country's EEZ, or up to fifty kilometres from their coast or 200 metres in depth.[47]
- *Subsistence* – small-scale non-commercial fisheries, whose catch is mainly consumed by fishers and their families, while any sales usually bypass reporting systems.
- *Recreational* – non-commercial fishing for enjoyment and domestic consumption.

The contribution of recreational fishing is probably underestimated. A report in 2012 estimated that over 225 million people around the world participated in recreational fishing,

CHAPTER 3

spending at least $190 billion annually on permits, fishing tackle, boat hire and so on.[48] In the USA, the economic and employment impact of recreational marine fisheries is more than three times that of commercial fisheries.

Recreational anglers tend to be modest conservationists, returning alive much of what they catch.[49] They have often led protests against the ravages of industrial fishing, particularly the most destructive trawling, and have led campaigns against pollution, dredging, dumping and overfishing. They have been prominent in petitions for more and better marine reserves and against the industrial fisheries' practice of discarding low-market-value fish. Potentially, recreational fishers have an important role to play in pressuring governments and international bodies to respond to the plunder of the blue commons.

Long-sustained commons fisheries are the potential saviours of global fishing. Yet they are losing access to the means of production and to raw materials adequate to preserve a commons-based livelihood. The neoliberal blue growth paradigm and its offspring – industrial fisheries – are endangering their survival,[50] transforming many blue commoners into members of the global precariat, without corporate or community attachment.[51] This growing mass of working people around the world is obliged to endure an existence of erratic and insecure labour, volatile and low earnings, and lack of rights that reduces them to supplicants. In a way, they are the opposite of commoners, being denizens not citizens, wherever they live.

Some are being converted into what has been called an 'eco-precariat', deprived of their previous livelihoods by international aid projects intended to combat overfishing or other ecologically destructive practices.[52] In Kenya, a project for mangrove reforestation barred most mangrove pole cutting that the coastal communities combined with subsistence fishing. Instead, the project employed local people as casual labourers to carry out or monitor the project under conditions specified by the project management. Meanwhile, communities were supposed to self-enforce the protection of mangroves from 'illegal' harvesters, encouraging community members to spy on each other.

In rich countries, there is a perception of fishers, reinforced by reality TV programmes, as heroic figures struggling against the elements. Yet, as one perceptive review of a string of such programmes concluded, 'they show how the larger economic structures firmly anchor most crew members and even many captains – especially younger ones – within the precariat class.'[53] The reality is that the median twenty-first-century fisher lacks embeddedness in a commons.

Commoners in waiting

To be a commoner, and to participate in commoning, engenders feelings of connection to the community and its inheritance, and respect for norms of reproduction and tradition. We can think of a commons consciousness, as opposed to a neoliberal consciousness or a proletarian or labour consciousness. A commoner has a consciousness of being in a commons, for which we have a sense of kinship, an affinity. As Sigmund Freud recognized, kinship is linked to love, and with love we do not objectify the environment; it merges with us as humans.

A commons consciousness values the idea of community and commons over the dictates of markets and efficiency, and directs the mind and actions to the longer term rather than the short term. It understands that structured reciprocities around empathy and compassion are inherently preferable to the egotistic aggrandizement that underpins neoliberalism.

Of course, we should not romanticize commons uncritically. They have their internal contradictions, including inherited racisms and traditions of patriarchy and ageism. But a commons perspective provides a normative commitment to the ideal values of a commons. It judges trends ontologically – whether changes are moving towards or away from commons ideals. Regrettably, most of the changes in the neoliberal era have been leading the blue economy further away.

The commons and commoning are linked to ideas of deliberative democracy and republican freedom, the freedom from domination by figures having unaccountable authority. In an ideal commons community, the members are not only both producers and consumers of what they produce but are also part of the governance of reproduction. They are real partners. Commons decisions may take longer to reach than those directed from above, but they are potentially more durable because they are more likely to reflect a consensus within a community, rather than an assertion of individual or corporate power against the will of the commons.

CHAPTER 4

Fisheries: The Tragedy of Decommoning

It's not just a few bad guys. The global seafood industry
is dysfunctional.
— Donna-Mareè Cawthorn, University of Mpumalanga,
South Africa

Fishing is surely the most emotional and visible part of the
blue economy. It provides food for billions and livelihoods
for many millions of people. While it may not always be the
most significant in money terms, it is the single human activity that has had the most far-reaching impact on global
marine life and ecosystems. What has been happening to the
world's fisheries is a drama of epic proportions, with unfolding tragedies.

It is a story in which the blue commons and long traditions
of commoning have been battered by several variants of capitalism, including the colonialism of the nineteenth century,
the stuttering period of the early twentieth and the neoliberal
era of the late twentieth century. Fishing has become a frontier of globalized rentier capitalism. It is a story about power,
and the abuse of it. And it is a story of unfinished business,
with little time to rewrite the ending of predictable collapse.

The world risks running out of food from the sea, and much of the responsibility lies with how fisheries have been restructured in the pursuit of profit and rent.

The refrain from mainstream fishery economists has been that 'the fisheries problem' – by which they usually mean overfishing – stems from lack of private property rights. Such rights have been extended in several ways, accentuating already extensive privatization. Yet this has not remedied the problem; rather it has worsened a deteriorating situation. The policies used have legitimized rent-seeking at the expense of the blue commons and commoners.

There is an irony about fishing as an industry that marks it out from other spheres of economic activity. Most economists equate efficiency with economic growth. But in fisheries, greater technological efficiency has resulted in *falling* productivity in terms of catches because advanced technology is depleting the resource base. Describing fishing in UK waters, Callum Roberts, one of Britain's foremost marine scientists, noted: 'For every hour spent fishing today, in boats bristling with the latest fish-finding electronics, fishers land a mere 6% of what they did 120 years ago. Put another way, fishers today have to work seventeen times harder to get the same catch as people did in the 19th century.'[1]

Industrialized fishing epitomizes what happens when capitalism escapes societal control. It can be dated from the launch of the first coal-fired steam trawlers in the late 1880s, which led to longer fishing trips by bigger vessels with heavier equipment. Since then, the industry has become a guzzler of fossil fuels, accounting for nearly 2% of global oil consumption. As noted in Chapter 1, the ratio of fuel used to landed catch – equivalent to a tonne of oil for every two tonnes of marine life[2] – makes industrial fishing the world's most energy-intensive food production method.[3] And, despite more fuel-efficient boats, the energy efficiency of fishing overall may have declined, since vessels must search longer and fish deeper in offshore waters as coastal stocks decline.

In a more recent technological development, hundreds of thousands of fish aggregating devices (FADs), floating devices equipped with GPS and sonar to detect volumes of fish underneath, effectively convert the area of the sea surrounding them into private property for the profit of the FAD owner. In the Western and Central Pacific, the world's largest tuna fishery, 60% to 70% of all catches are taken with the aid of FADs.[4] They give a huge advantage to large-scale industrial fisheries, intensify overfishing, and contribute to the 'race to extinction' of fish populations.

The Great Acceleration

For centuries, it was presumed that fish were inexhaustible and, although there were some local restrictions, fisheries were mostly unregulated, with open access.[5] However, with the expansion of industrial fishing, overfishing was identified as an international problem even before the Second World War. Today, generations after those first warnings, the situation is much worse, with nearly 90% of designated fish stocks fished at or above a sustainable limit.

In the 1930s, landings of fish around the world rose steadily, mainly by small-scale artisanal fisheries. Landings fell sharply during the Second World War, as fishing boats were requisitioned for wartime tasks and others did not dare go out for fear of attack. But immediately after the war there occurred what has been called the Great Acceleration, due in part to use of technologies such as refrigeration, and others developed in the war for submarine hunting, such as sonar (echo sounders).[6] At the time, there was widespread fear of a global famine, which gave extra value to fish, and led to the establishment of the UN's Food and Agriculture Organization (FAO) in 1945.

While marine fisheries were seen as a source of economic growth and job creation, the post-war period was also a time when Western governments and the new international financial bodies, such as the International Monetary Fund (IMF) and the World Bank, wished to spread industrial capitalism around the world. The rebuilding of industrial fishing fleets was part of that broader project, much of it financed by large subsidies or direct investment by governments, notably those of Norway, Greenland, Iceland, the UK, the USA and Canada's province of Newfoundland.[7] Subsidies became a feature of industrial fisheries, rationalized as raising efficiency, with an emphasis on increasing capacity.

A mantra took hold that size mattered. The first super-trawler, the 264-foot *Fairtry*, was built in Aberdeen, Scotland in 1954. Promptly, the Soviet Union ordered twenty-four of them as it set out to create the world's biggest fishing fleet. By the 1970s, the Soviet Union owned more than half the world's tonnage of big fishing vessels and its fleet was four times as large as Japan's, the next biggest. Alongside US-backed Peru, these countries led the charge to supersized fishing fleets that make up what today are called long-distance fleets, or distant-water fleets. Spain followed later, and both the Soviet Union and the USA helped to build up China's capacity, assistance that they will have almost certainly come to regret as Chinese fishing fleets ravage the world's oceans in the twenty-first century.

The presumption that the seas' resources were inexhaustible fed into the controversial concept of maximum sustainable yield (MSY), a term first used by Wilbert Chapman, influential assistant to the first US Under-Secretary of State for Fisheries, in a 1949 report on US fisheries policy. He defined MSY as a measure 'to make possible the maximum production of food from the sea on a sustained basis year after year'.

Chapman's view was that too little fishing represented a waste of natural resources, adding the bizarre claim that fish populations benefited from 'thinning'. If some were removed – those somehow presumed to be ageing and no longer productive – that would stimulate growth of more virile fish. By plotting an inverted U-shaped curve, marine scientists could calculate the optimal fish take, with the top of the curve as the target.

The MSY was a way of rationalizing limited state intervention, giving the USA free rein to send its fishing boats into foreign waters. Thus Chapman argued that Pacific tuna off Latin America were underfished, whereas the Alaskan salmon fishery was overfished. It so happened that US fisheries were aggressively fishing for Pacific tuna (as Chapman had long advocated), while they were under pressure from Japanese fisheries off Alaska. As Carmel Finley has pointed out, Chapman's use of the MSY concept was politics masquerading as science, vaunting a vision of freedom of the seas.[8]

Other countries, including Chile and Peru, tried to promote

an international agreement allowing them to restrict foreign fishing in their coastal waters, taking 'their' fish. But they were outmanoeuvred by the USA and its allies. In 1955, the International Law Commission in Rome said that countries could fish until critical biological limits were reached. In 1958, the first Law of the Sea meeting made a recommendation requiring scientific evidence of overfishing before fishing could be restricted. This conveniently allowed the growing distant-water fleets to fish off the coasts of developing countries.[9] As there were no scientific studies in those places, there was no way to estimate the MSY, and so no constraint to overfishing.

Fish were 'resources' to be used maximally according to scientific guidelines. With this mindset, countries poured subsidies into ultra-efficient technologies that paid scant attention to fish preservation and allowed practices long known to be injurious. As far back as 1866, witnesses to a Royal Commission in Britain warned that bottom trawling was destroying the seabed, wiping out fish stocks and ripping up coral reefs, oyster beds and sponges. But, in a refrain that was to become all too familiar, the Commission concluded the economy could not afford to ban it.[10] After 1945, the same mentality held. Growth prevailed over everything.

The Great Acceleration established the pivotal significance of the MSY, which has continued to this day. For example, in 2013 the European Union's new Common Fisheries Policy (CFP) replaced a centralized regulatory framework with one that devolved management decisions to the fishing industry, which further enthroned the MSY concept. The CFP is still based on a political decision by ministers each year on the 'total allowable catch' for major species caught in EU waters. Although that decision is supposedly based on scientific guidance, the scientific recommendations have been consistently exceeded, under pressure from the powerful fishing lobby, which influences how governments implement their allocated quota.

Looking back at the Great Acceleration, it is clear that the reactions to the understandable need for more fish after 1945 created conditions that resulted in a plunder of commons resources over succeeding decades. One outcome was an existential threat to small-scale artisanal fisheries almost everywhere, and particularly for fishing communities in developing countries, as long-distance commercial fisheries, aided by governments and international agencies, marauded around the blue planet.

Incipient mercantilism

As the Great Acceleration proceeded, long-distance fisheries assumed a strategic importance for a few maritime nations. Partly in reaction to overfishing and declining returns in their own inshore waters, they moved into the waters of other nations, mostly in Africa, Latin America and Asia. Some bitter conflicts occurred, the most documented being the cod wars between Iceland and the UK. But the major development was the Great Enclosure established by UNCLOS.

Article 62 of UNCLOS obliged distant-water fishing countries to reach fishing access agreements if they wished to fish inside the EEZs of other nations, the stated idea being to allow foreign fleets to fish for surplus stocks. The Article presumed that maximum sustainable yields could and would be estimated, and that the total allowable catch and total actual catch could be known, none of which was likely.[11]

Moreover, inserted at the insistence of the fishing powers, the Article stated that coastal states 'shall' provide access to their waters if there were surplus fish they were unable to exploit themselves. Nowadays, it is accepted that no country could be taken to the UNCLOS tribunal for failing to provide access to foreign fishing companies. No case has ever been brought. But the political effect was important.

It is hard to imagine a similar clause in a binding international accord applying to any other natural resource – obliging nations to let others access their resource if they did not maximize its exploitation. It also reveals the anxiety of the fishing powers to guarantee their continued access to fishing grounds as developing countries staked claims to EEZs during the 1970s and 1980s.

While most developing countries had limited resources to manage their expanded fishing grounds, they hoped to benefit by charging foreign boats to fish in their waters. Some countries issue short-term licences, based on set fees for different types of fishing, that can be bought in an open market. These are known as 'free licences' ('pay, fish and go'). But most developing countries and distant-water fishing fleets have preferred to manage licensing through renewable framework agreements negotiated between governments, typically lasting five years, which set rules on access, fees and catch quantities, and may include issues such as using locals as crew, landing fish in local ports, and so on.

The outcome was to encourage a new mercantilism, in which rich countries used access agreements to gain monopolistic market advantage for themselves. In acquiring fishing resources, they denied them to potential competitors.[12] The Japanese were an early leader in combining foreign aid for developing countries with agreements to allow their fisheries to take local fish stocks. In the 1970s, with 12% of the global fishing fleet, Japan had 135 overseas investments, mostly in Asia and Oceania, but also in North America, Africa and Latin America.

Not to be outdone, between the 1950s and 1980s, fishing access agreements with developing countries became part of Moscow's strategic efforts to spread the Soviet model of development. In the 1950s, it became one of the three major long-distance fishing powers of the world, alongside Japan and Spain. In addition to its fleet of giant fishing vessels, it went on in the 1960s to pioneer the use of 'mother ships' – factory vessels that freeze and package fish at sea, allowing fishing boats to stay out for longer. In the 1970s and 1980s, the Soviet Union had bilateral agreements with a number of African countries, including Angola, Mozambique, Senegal and Sierra Leone, as well as Peru in South America.

The USSR also developed an extensive network of joint-venture agreements to partner with local fisheries, the first signed in 1959 with Guinea-Bissau. By the late 1970s, it had joint-venture agreements with forty developing countries, spanning Africa, the Middle East and Latin America. Host country governments were given financial and technical assistance in developing local fisheries, while the Soviet Union pledged half of the profits of the joint venture. The USSR was unique in using joint ventures to expand *local* markets for selling fish, which were an important source of revenue for its over-capitalized fishing fleet. Its huge vessels targeting sardines and other small pelagic fish off Africa relied largely on selling into West African markets, particularly Nigeria. From the 1950s until the 1980s, Soviet boats accounted for most of the small pelagic fishing by foreign countries off West Africa. In 1982, in West and Southern Africa, Soviet catches were reported to be over 1.8 million tonnes, nearly three times as much as the 652,000 tonnes caught by Spain, the second largest.[13]

The Soviet Union did help to construct useful local infrastructure. But a feature of both the Soviet and Japanese strategies was the deliberate marginalization of small-scale artisanal fishers. The Soviets saw them as a 'backward' zone, a zone for petty accumulation set to be taken over by the state.

Meanwhile, West European countries, led by Spain, negotiated access agreements that evolved into strategic aspects of foreign policy when the European Communities became the European Union in 1993. Since that time, the EU has negotiated agreements on behalf of all member states; where they exist, EU boats are not allowed to fish outside their remit. These agreements too have weakened small-scale fisheries, by permitting fishing on a scale that makes it impossible for artisan fishers and industrial fisheries to coexist.

Another aspect of global fisheries in the 1950s and 1960s was the emergence of Latin America as a major force.[14] The countries on its western seaboard benefit from the Humboldt Current, one of the most productive marine ecosystems on earth, that flows from Antarctica up to the Galapagos Islands near the Equator. Aided by US capital, Peru became the continent's leading industrial fishing nation, with a flourishing anchovy fishery that was massively expanded in the late

1950s, partly due to the collapse of California's sardine fishery and the transfer of US processing plants to Peru. By the 1960s, Peru accounted for 18% of marine catch and nearly half the world's fishmeal; annual catches peaked at twelve million tonnes, accounting for one-third of Peru's exports.

Ironically, Peru was set back by the intervention of a group of US marine scientists, sent to Peru with US and UN backing to advise on a maximum sustainable yield. The group, led by American Milner Schaefer, recommended that the MSY should be lowered to ten million tonnes.[15] It is unclear whether Schaefer's MSY target was respected, but three years after it was agreed, the fishery was in crisis. By the mid-1980s, annual catch had plummeted to just 22,000 tonnes.[16] The world's biggest fishery, under the oversight of the world's best fisheries scientists, had been wiped out. It took over thirty years to recover, partially.

Fishing access agreements were in effect imposed on developing countries as a means of plundering their fish populations. And matters deteriorated further in the 1980s, with the spread of neoliberal economic thinking. Developing countries were put under intense pressure to implement radical 'structural adjustment' policies, orchestrated by the World Bank. These demanded deep cuts in public spending and extensive privatization, which enfeebled regulations and mechanisms for preventing overfishing and errant behaviour by foreign fishing fleets. And, as we shall see, generous public subsidies were to be used to extend private property rights, mostly through fishing quota systems, that have allowed large corporations to 'own' much of the world's fish.

Neoliberal economics justified subsidies to leverage and

expand markets, while faith in private property rights justified quota systems. In short, access agreements, subsidies
and quotas turned global fishing into a zone of rentier capitalism, where returns to property ownership determined
incomes. Nothing resembling a free-market economy was
constructed.

Aid and development: neo-colonialism in action

In the post-1945 era, most developing countries initially adopted a development strategy focused on import-
substitution industrialization; fisheries were favoured as
providing food security, although some countries set out
to become industrial producers and exporters of fish, most
notably in Latin America. But in the 1980s, the development
orthodoxy became export-led industrialization; countries
were pressured to prioritize industrial-scale fisheries to gain
foreign currency. The international financial agencies, led by
the World Bank and rich-country donor agencies, were all
too keen to create opportunities for foreign capital.

Fisheries were also affected by what was dubbed the
'green revolution' in the 1960s, led by the USA, Europe and
the Soviet Union, which involved international efforts to
transform agriculture in developing countries, based on a
transfer of technologies for industrial farming, fertilizers and
pesticides, and new strains of seeds to create bumper crops. It
was an era of rapid growth, but also one of unscrupulous land
grabs by powerful corporations, and ecological destruction.

Unpublicized, and on a smaller scale, there was also a
roughly parallel 'blue revolution', with similar outcomes.

Foreign governments and donor agencies began to transform marine fisheries in developing countries, claiming that this would boost economic growth and increase food security. The accelerated erosion of coastal commons dates from this surge for 'development'. Fisheries historian John Kurien has summarized what happened:

> . . . the initial euphoria of increased harvests, enhanced revenues, and higher profits was followed by ecosystem changes and resource depletion. At the same time, this strategy led to economic marginalization of coastal fishing communities and reduced their autonomy for participation in the new structure of the fish economy. It ruined the commons and the commoners.[17]

Development agencies saw local fisheries, like traditional farm practices, as a barrier to progress – primitive, undeveloped and inefficient. Canada's International Development Agency described small-scale fisheries as 'a transitory feature in the evolution of modern fisheries'.[18] Aid agencies set themselves the task of transforming local fisheries into something like they had 'back home'. This mindset overlooked forms of governance that operated, quite successfully, in traditional fishing communities. According to one critical review of development programmes in Ghana, 'It is the influence of international donors and policy advisers that has perhaps had the greatest impact on how small-scale fisheries are perceived and managed within the country.'[19]

The modernizing imperative was adopted by most developing countries. In the 1960s and 1970s many introduced subsidies to speed the process, blending public resources with overseas aid to lower fuel costs, assist in marketing and upgrade technologies. For example, in 1972, the government of Senegal launched the Centre d'Assistance à la Motorisation des Pirogues, which financed the purchase and upkeep of 6,700 outboard motors for the traditional canoe-like boats used by artisan fishers.[20] That transformed the fishing industry, tripling annual catches.[21] Motorization also turned Senegal into a regional plunderer; soon, Senegalese fishing vessels were roving into Mauritanian waters and as far as Guinean waters. They were not alone in treating the seas as open access spaces before the Great Enclosure of UNCLOS.

Rich countries were also encouraging the transformation. The first fisheries improvement programme, funded by the Norwegian government in Kerala, India, started in 1952 and ran for thirty years. It was followed by many others. In 1985, the FAO estimated that spending on fisheries projects by multilateral and bilateral donors had risen from $200 million a year in the mid-1970s to $500 million a year by the mid-1980s.[22] These figures did not include the Soviet Union, then the biggest 'donor' for fisheries development. A later review for the World Bank found that between 1973 and 2001 over 4,300 schemes targeted developing-country fisheries, with a combined value of $16.3 billion.[23] Since then, funding has increased even further.

While some schemes set out to boost the supply of fish in local markets and raise the incomes of traditional fishing communities, most funds went to support export-oriented industrial fishing to capitalize on an insatiable market for seafood in the developed world.[24] According to the FAO, by the mid-1980s, at least half of all aid was for developing industrial fishing, with just 17% going to small-scale fisheries. And much of the aid came from governments keen to expand opportunities for their own companies, including through joint ventures or processing facilities. In Madagascar, for instance, French aid has underpinned commercial prawn trawling since the 1960s, with French companies the main actors and France the main export market.[25] Moreover, investment in processing grew sharply during the oil crises of the 1970s, when higher fuel costs made distant-water fishing too costly for some powerful fishing nations. Thus Japan switched to sourcing seafood from foreign suppliers, rather than relying on its own fleet.

Aid for modernization of fisheries in developing countries has had variable outcomes. In Africa, by the mid-1980s, a widespread view among aid agencies was that their spending had been a costly failure. Small-scale fisheries continued to struggle, while poverty in fishing communities persisted.[26] Elsewhere, modernization and 'structural adjustment' had a significant impact in expanding production and trade, but growth was often pursued recklessly, without heed to environmental and social costs, as the experience of countries in South and South-East Asia makes clear.

For example, in the 1960s, the Norwegian aid project in Kerala helped finance the purchase of semi-industrial trawlers targeting prawns. Although the project started with the intention of helping traditional fisherfolk, it ended up benefiting an emerging merchant class able to exploit the economic potential of fish exports, particularly to Japan. In 1962, India exported just nine tonnes of prawns a year; by the early 1980s, it was exporting over 37,000 tonnes.[27]

CHAPTER 4

The original intended beneficiaries were by then openly protesting that the trawling had caused a precipitous drop in their catches. The project had inadvertently contributed to a transformation of the fisheries sector. The much-expanded export industry relied on low-paid casual labour, mainly by young women from outside fishing communities, while profits mostly went to a wealthy elite.[28] Small-scale fishers were forced to invest in motorized boats to travel further out to sea to find fish, as the trawlers had destroyed their traditional fishing grounds.

Similar problems were linked to aid and government subsidies throughout South-East Asia.[29] In Thailand, Germany provided financial and technical assistance to expand semi-industrial trawling, while Japanese companies with government assistance launched joint ventures. Whereas ninety-nine trawlers had operated in 1960, by 1966 there were 2,700. And after depleting fish populations off the Gulf of Thailand, trawlers spread out to the waters off Vietnam, Myanmar, Sarawak, East Malaysia and Java. By 1977, the Thai trawler fleet operating across South-East Asia had grown to 6,300 vessels.

In Indonesia, between 1974 and 1983, huge grants and soft loans were provided by the Asian Development Bank, the World Bank and Japan, almost all channelled towards commercial trawlers and purse-seine fishing boats. Less than 5% was earmarked for the country's three million small-scale fishers.[30] In addition, over $64 million was invested by overseas fishing companies, mainly Japanese, to establish joint ventures. Exports of frozen prawns, mostly directed to Japan and the USA, rose from 5,600 tonnes in 1969 to 117,000 tonnes in 1980 and a remarkable 288,000 tonnes in 2002.[31]

While the modernization agenda dominated donor thinking, it was clear from an early stage that aid, including technical assistance, was geared to promoting privatization and investment of foreign capital. The FAO led the way in claiming that secure tenure rights were vital for 'catalysing private sector involvement'. Its Coastal Fisheries Initiative set up a Challenge Fund, led by the World Bank and Conservation International, an NGO, to give grants to support 'market-based solutions that help leverage improved fisheries management'.[32]

Fisheries policy in Chile became a poster child for the neoliberal model. Chile has one of the world's most productive and largest marine areas, covering 3.7 million square kilometres. It also has the world's eighth-largest fishing capacity,[33] and is the second-largest producer of fishmeal. Ironically, this has resulted in Chileans eating less fish than the global average. High-value fish such as tuna and salmon are exported for high prices that Chileans cannot afford, and low-value fish they might otherwise eat are turned into fishmeal for aquaculture.

Beginning with the Pinochet dictatorship in the 1970s, the government set about liberalizing and privatizing the fishing sector, prioritizing industrial fishing through a system of quotas that ended the open access small-scale fishers had enjoyed. Quotas were initially non-transferable, but in 2013 a new law further liberalized fisheries and aquaculture to facilitate foreign investment, making it possible to buy and sell fishing licences, fish quotas and aquaculture concessions.

This amounted to an invited colonization by foreign capital, which led to an increased concentration of ownership. Chile's 92,000 artisan fishers received 40% of the total catch, whereas the industrial fleet, owned by seven wealthy families, took 60%. Granting access rights, through quotas, to industrial fisheries in the 1970s and 1980s had already led to over-capitalization and overfishing, as it had in Mexico and Peru.[34] And, contrary to claims that private property rights in a quota system would encourage long-term sustainability, Chile's national fish, common hake (*merluza*), though still the most popular fish for eating, has been decimated. Marginalized, small-scale fisheries have turned to illegal fishing.[35]

The Chilean experience may be extreme, but almost everywhere concentrated support for large-scale producers that profit from exporting fish to the developed world has left fish populations depleted and small-scale fishing communities struggling to survive. Since the turn of the twenty-first century, some corrections have been made to encourage decentralized management and co-management of fisheries, with participation by locals. But much more than this will be needed to end and reverse the damage to the blue commons from the 'modernization' agenda.

Chinese state capitalism

Adding to the pressure on fisheries in developing countries has been the emergence of China as a major global player. In the 1960s and 1970s, its fisheries were nurtured by the Soviet Union and by Western aid. But China has since become the principal threat to global fisheries and fish populations, devastating fishing areas across the world. In 2013, President Xi Jinping urged the Chinese fishing industry to 'build bigger ships and venture even farther and catch bigger fish'.[36]

Including boats fishing in its domestic waters, China may

now account for nearly half the world's total fishing capacity.[37] In recent years, it has captured about one-fifth of all marine fish caught legally, and probably a higher share of the considerable amount caught illegally or unreported. And it has become the leading exporter of fish and fish products.

The expansion has been dramatic. In 1985, for the first time, thirteen Chinese trawlers were sent to fish off West Africa. Today, its long-distance fishing fleet is by far the world's largest, consisting of some 17,000 vessels according to a recent estimate, far greater than previously thought.[38] It may have over 2,600 supertrawlers. For comparison, the USA's distant-water fleet comprises about 300 boats. In 2017, China announced plans to cap the size of the fleet at 3,000 vessels by 2021. Clearly, even though independent estimates vary wildly, it has done nothing of the kind.

The fleet has a complex structure, with hundreds of vessels classified not as fishing vessels but as fuel providers, tender boats and reefers. Some operate at sea as fish-processing factories, supplied by others doing the fishing. Foreign observers have concluded that the fleet looks more fragmented than it is, and that it is dominated by a few huge companies.

The Chinese government heavily subsidizes fuel and ship construction, partly through tax exemptions.[39] Its subsidies have been estimated at $16.6 billion a year, or nearly half of all identified global fishing subsidies. On a pro rata basis, Chinese subsidies per boat may come to $347,000 a year, over ten times as much as the heavily subsidized EU vessels.[40] In a special form of subsidy, it has sent medical ships to distant fishing grounds to help the fleet stay at sea for longer. And it assists its

roaming fleet by using satellites and research vessels to identify where to find lucrative squid and other fish stocks.

China's global fishing activity is now an integral part of its
Belt and Road Initiative, the construction of a vast network
of trade routes on land and sea across the globe. It is building
fishing bases in developing countries across four continents,
including the construction and operation of ports and huge
fish-processing plants. Many involve secret infrastructure-
for-access deals, whereby coastal states cede fishing rights
within their waters to Chinese vessels in return for investment in port and processing infrastructure.[41]

China's presence in Africa is ubiquitous: it has fishing
agreements with, among others, Angola, Gambia, Ghana,
Guinea-Bissau, Mauritania, Mozambique and Somalia. It is
also funding and building facilities elsewhere. In 2018, it un-
veiled plans to build a port west of Montevideo, including
processing facilities to accommodate the 500 Chinese vessels now fishing off Uruguay. The plan secured the support of
Uruguay's president, but had to be withdrawn in the face of
fierce local opposition. It is unlikely to be the last such plan.

Quota systems: state-sponsored rent-seeking

As fish populations came under increasing stress in the
twentieth century, a number of countries introduced quota
systems as a way of sharing out a restricted total catch of
particular types of fish. In principle, a quota system could be
a commons, if designed and implemented by a community
to support sustainable fishing and equitable distribution of
access or reward. In practice, most quota systems have been
imposed by governments or international bodies influenced

by commercial interests, and used to create private property rights as the way of limiting entry to fishing grounds. They have been a means of enclosure, commodification, conglomeration and rent-seeking by corporate fisheries.

Although still comprising a minority of marine fisheries, there are now over 200 of these rights-based fisheries operating in forty countries and covering over 500 species of fish.[42] The most usual systems in commercial fishing are based on dividing the total allowable catch into catch shares or quotas allocated to individual vessels or companies, giving them an individual property right to access and take a certain quantity of fish. Other right-based systems are possible, however. In some cases, a fishery might divide and sell shares of total fish caught, specify the number of lobster pots or boats that can be used, or provide shares in areas of the sea or even individual reefs.

Proponents of quota systems argue that they support conservation objectives. By creating a link between long-term fish-stock productivity and future income, they motivate fishers to act as stewards and look to long-term sustainability.[43] Quotas are also said to improve crew safety by reducing the competitive pressure to 'race for fish'.[44] Giving individual fisheries a set amount of fish they can take each year means they will be less tempted to take boats out in dangerous conditions. And they guarantee higher returns for fisheries. By limiting entry to fishing grounds to those with quotas, fisheries can earn economic rent from possession of a limited resource (the quota).

The most widespread variant is the 'individual transferable quota' (ITQ), pioneered in the 1980s in Australia, New

Zealand and Iceland. Known in the USA as 'harvesting rights schemes' or 'limited access privilege programs', ITQs are based on the idea that enabling fisheries to sell or lease their quota will encourage good management and conservation; both will increase the value of their share, which they can realize by trading the quota rather than selling the fish. A central state body gives or sells permissible quotas of fish that a fishery is allowed to catch in a specified period, usually a year, but the holder can sell or lease their quota to others.

ITQs are said to have the advantage over non-transferable quotas because the most efficient producers will accumulate the quota while the inefficient are phased out.[45] Ragnar Arnason, a leading advocate of private property rights in fisheries, has praised the ITQ systems developed in Iceland and New Zealand as coming closest to 'the perfect property right'. His reasoning is that they incorporate exclusivity (ensuring only a limited number of users), durability (facilitating long-term planning), transferability (ensuring economic efficiency) and security (property rights are protected by the state).[46]

One US study claimed that ITQs had halted the collapse of fisheries, and that those managed by ITQs were half as likely to collapse as those that were not.[47] This has been interpreted as showing that 'privatising fishing stocks can avert disaster'.[48] Favourably reviewing ITQs in 2008, *The Economist* cited the Alaskan halibut fisheries:

> After a decade of using ITQs in the halibut fishery, the average fishing season now lasts for eight months [rather than a few days as before]. The number of search-and-rescue missions that are launched is down by more than 70% and

deaths by 15%. And fish can be sold at the most lucrative time of year – and fresh, so that they fetch a better price.[49]

Making quotas tradable meant that fisheries wishing to catch more could buy rights from others, avoiding the 'race to fish'. To indicate the dangers of the latter, *The Economist* cited the king crab fishery in the Atlantic, vividly illustrated in the TV series *The Deadliest Catch*.

Others have rebutted the claimed positive effect of ITQs on fish conservation.[50] The evidence is at least equivocal. One review concluded that 'while in the short-run ITQs may avert ecological collapse . . . the long-term ecological conditions are yet to be evaluated.'[51] By contrast, it is now widely acknowledged that ITQs lead to an inequitable distribution of benefits and increased inequality of ownership, and loss of intergenerational access to fisheries.[52] ITQs have unleashed 'social tragedies' by promoting fishery consolidation that has strengthened large-scale fisheries, encouraging more capital-intensive production geared towards global commodity chains, and engendering losses to small-scale fisheries.[53] These have been shown in coastal communities as far apart as Denmark and South Africa.[54]

Most quota systems have started inequitably, by giving out quotas based on past records. For instance, Iceland's ITQ system was based on giving free quotas to vessel owners in proportion to their historical catch in the period 1981–3, obviously penalizing newcomers and small-scale fisheries. The EU's Common Fisheries Policy started in a similar way, and individual member countries did so of their own accord. However, these initial inequities are magnified when quotas can be traded as commodities. Larger fisheries, typically with political connections and power in the industry as well as more effective technology, tend to buy up the quotas of smaller-scale fisheries. Moreover, the prospect of income from leasing out quotas, or turning a profit from trading them, has attracted non-fishing investors and created a market for financial speculation. In Iceland, speculative activity derived from the quota system reached such a spate that it contributed to the country's financial crisis in 2008.[55]

Halibut fishing in British Columbia provides an illustration of how ITQs squeeze out small-scale fishers and reward investors.[56] Until 1991, when an ITQ system was introduced, this was traditionally the domain of owner-operators, who caught over 80% of the halibut. Although they acquired 90% of the initial quota, by 2016 owner-operators were catching only 45% of the halibut and owned only 15% of the quota. Some of the original quota owners sold their quotas to other boats, but others became 'slipper skippers', leasing out their quotas, alongside new investors with no fishing history. The newcomers did not add value to the fishery by investing in infrastructure, vessels or processing; instead, they sucked out rent from owning the licences and quotas. Moreover, the shift from owner-operators to rentier investors weakened stewardship, resulting in more pressure on fishers to maximize their catch at lowest cost, thereby eroding safety standards. The study's author concluded: 'Investors represent the flight of wealth out of the fishery and out of fishery-dependent coastal communities.'[57]

Another example of the iniquities of ITQs relates to squid fishing in California, where a bizarre law passed in

1933 keeps confidential the identity of fishery owners as well as 'receipts, reports and other records' of commercial fishing.[58] There is no such law barring public knowledge of land ownership. In 1998, faced with overfishing, the authorities closed the squid fishery to new boats, and in 2005 issued just seventy-five transferable permits to selected vessels, giving quotas free of charge based on fishing capacity. Subsequently, some of the seventy-five sold their quota for millions of dollars to unknown insiders, creating a fishery cartel.

Thus, while the jury is out on whether ITQs help conservation, they indisputably intensify inequality and marginalize blue commoners. And quotas, transferable or not, have become forms of privatized property, often guaranteed for permanent ownership if the holder wishes. Why should a company be given permanent ownership of part of the sea's bounty?

The scourge of subsidies

> If we wait another 20 years, there may be no marine fisheries left to subsidise – or artisanal fishing communities to support.
> — Ngozi Okonjo-Iweala, Director-General of the
> World Trade Organization

Another cause of the plunder of fish populations and erosion of the blue commons has been the edifice of distortionary subsidies, partly stemming from attempts by governments to give their fishing industry a competitive advantage over others. Most countries have given subsidies to their fishing industries, as they have to other industries, all the while claiming that free markets based on private property rights would solve 'the fisheries problem'. Estimating fishery subsidies is not straightforward and depends on what is counted. However, the World Trade Organization (WTO) cites a commonly accepted figure that governments hand out some $35 billion in fisheries subsidies each year, two-thirds of which go to commercial fishers, enabling them to send out boats that would not be economically viable without the subsidies.[59]

Fishing subsidies have long been blamed for fish-stock depletion.[60] Amid mounting concern, trade ministers meeting in Doha, Qatar, in 2001 issued a Ministerial Declaration committing governments to 'negotiate and improve WTO disciplines' on fishing subsidies. A year later, heads of state at the Johannesburg World Summit on Sustainable Development called for the elimination of harmful fishing subsidies. And in 2015, the UN General Assembly adopted the Sustainable Development Goals, Target 14.6 of which set a 2020 goal of prohibiting subsidies that induce overfishing, such as subsidies that increase capacity, or that foster illegal, unreported and unregulated (IUU) fishing. Readers will note that 2020 has been and gone; subsidies are more durable, as are the business lobbies.

The WTO's failure to reach agreement after more than twenty years reflects a classic collective action problem. If one country cuts subsidies unilaterally, this would disadvantage its fisheries relative to those of others. And countries that have used subsidies to gain an unfair advantage are less likely to want their abolition, even if globally that would be beneficial, for human welfare, fish welfare and ocean conservation. Industrial fisheries are eager for more subsidies, and politicians are eager to oblige. So, subsidies persist.

The OECD has estimated that, from 2008 to 2017, China accounted for 41% of global fishing subsidies, followed by Japan (12%), Brazil (9%), the USA (8%) and Canada (7%).[61] The European Union taken as a bloc would fall between the USA and Canada. But the type of subsidy is also relevant. Of the $35 billion spent on subsidies each year, some $22 billion is estimated to contribute to overfishing by increasing capacity and lowering costs.[62]

A simple taxonomy is 'good', 'bad' and 'ugly'.[63] The main 'good' subsidy, one of few deserving that label, is for 'management and services', including spending on surveillance of fishing practices. Another that might be classified as 'good' is investment in marine protected areas (MPAs).[64] But if this is a subsidy, there has been woefully inadequate spending on it, amounting to less than 3% of all subsidies to fisheries.

The primary 'bad' subsidy, and the single largest form of subsidy, relates to fuel costs, accounting for a fifth of all subsidy spending. Cheapening fuel leads to lack of care, excessive fuel use, less maintenance of motors, and pollution. It also enables boats to go further afield and stay out longer. Without fuel subsidies, it is estimated that over half the world's long-distance fisheries would go out of business, which would be a boon to fish populations.[65] Almost all China's subsidy spending goes to reduce fuel costs.[66] In the USA, fuel subsidies represent 44% of all federal and state subsidies for the fishing industry.[67]

A primary 'ugly' subsidy is vessel buyback. Designed to encourage the decommissioning of old, inefficient boats, reducing the size of the fishing fleet and so overfishing, this seems to have had the opposite effect. Boosting the incomes of the remaining fishers, who gain a bigger share of the catch, it has encouraged them to invest in more efficient boats and technologies, and increase capital utilization by fishing longer. One study of Danish fisheries found that vessel buy-back had no positive effect on fish catches.[68] Based on experience with North Atlantic fisheries, researchers calculated that even if a fishery were reduced to a single monopolistic producer, that owner could still maximize long-term revenue by exhausting the fish stocks.[69]

Subsidies for vessel modernization should probably be put in the same 'ugly' category, though there can be positive by-products, such as more knowledge of how to target desired fish and how to limit bycatch, making the subsidy potentially 'good'.[70]

Another perverse subsidy has been unemployment insurance, intended to give income security to fisherfolk. As applied in Canada, for instance, this has encouraged more fishers to enter or stay in fisheries, lowering average income. Thus, unemployment insurance reduced the duration of the fishing season in Newfoundland but increased the time spent fishing to qualify for benefits.[71]

What about the impact of subsidies on small-scale fisheries and the blue commons? Only a sixth of global fishery subsidies go to small-scale fisheries.[72] And 90% of capacity-enhancing subsidies, which do most to exacerbate overfishing, go to large-scale fisheries, intensifying their advantage. Construction of large-scale vessels is aided by big subsidies, while small-scale boats receive none. And 90% of fuel subsidies go to industrial fisheries. According to one assessment, the average industrial fishery receives 187 times more fuel subsidy each year than the average small-scale fishery, although small-scale fisheries catch four times more fish per litre of fuel.[73] This grossly unequal provision is undermining the viability of small-scale fisheries.[74] Put more strongly, it is destroying the blue commons, its resources, its ecosystems and its communities.

For years, overcapacity and overfishing have meant that gross costs of fishing have exceeded gross revenue. This should have led to an exodus from fisheries. But subsidies have reduced costs and made fishing economically if not ecologically viable. For instance, subsidies for new and modernized vessels increased the capacity of Canada's North-West Atlantic fleet eighteenfold between 1954 and 1968.[75] Despite the subsequent collapse of cod stocks off Newfoundland, the government funded a new round of subsidies for vessel construction and improvement in the late 1970s and 1980s to compete with EU distant-water fleets. By 1989, this had increased capacity to five times what was needed to catch the annual quota. Another collapse of cod stocks followed, the industry faced financial ruin and the Canadian government had to intervene with yet more subsidies and support, this time for downsizing.

Similarly, in the EU, between 1970 and 1987, subsidies for modernization resulted in a doubling of registered tonnage and a tripling of engine power, which precipitated drastic declines in major fish populations in EU waters, including cod, hake, herring and, in the Mediterranean, anchovies.

Areas of the blue economy that could be classified as an open-access commons are the high seas outside EEZs, which cover 64% of the world's seaspace. In 2020, *The Economist*

began an article on the stalled WTO fishery subsidy negotiations with a familiar statement: 'Overfishing is a tragedy
of the commons, with individuals and countries motivated
by short-term self-interest to over-consume a limited resource.'[76] This is nonsense. Even in the high seas, the problems are not due to open access but to state support for
capitalistic fisheries. Although it still accounts for under 6%
of global catch and only 8% of global fishing revenue, the
catch from the high seas has risen sharply.

High-seas fishing depends on subsidies, which bars countries that cannot afford them. Thus it is dominated by fisheries from just a few countries able to subsidize fuel costs and
transhipment at sea. As of 2016, six – China, Taiwan, Japan,
Indonesia, Spain and South Korea – accounted for 77% of the
global high-seas fleet, and fourteen countries took 90% of
the catch, with China taking over a third. In 2014, subsidies
to high-seas fisheries were estimated at $4.2 billion, while
profits came to $1.4 billion. Without subsidies, the fishing
would not be economically viable.

Ecologically too, the subsidies are unjustifiable. High-
seas fishing is based on bottom trawling, described by Enric
Sala as 'one of the most destructive practices on the planet.
[Trawlers] have nets so large they can hold a dozen 747 jets.
These huge nets destroy everything in their path, including
deep sea corals. And it is not profitable without subsidies.'
Sala posed the rhetorical question, 'If it is ecologically destructive and economically unprofitable, why don't we end
all high-seas fishing?'[77]

Another factor is the gross exploitation of workers. Commercial fishing on the high seas has a history of slave and

underpaid labour. It persists despite the FAO's code of conduct on fishing on the high seas, which is barely enforced, while vessels rarely reveal information on costs, ostensibly for competitive reasons.

The most comprehensive study of high-seas fishing found that 54% of fleets would be unprofitable without subsidies and low-paid labour, and that even with them, 19% of the currently fished high seas could not be exploited profitably.[78] But secrecy around high-seas fishing may be concealing the extent of catches. According to one study, global marine catches have been 30% larger than reported to the FAO.[79] Would extra monitoring and inspection be uneconomic, or is feeble monitoring contrived by complicit governments?

Furthermore, most analysts have ignored implicit subsidies, so relevant to a commons perspective. These arise from government *inaction*, a failure to recover resource rents. One commentator has argued that, as the WTO's subsidies accord requires governments to collect 'adequate remuneration' for trees harvested from public lands, then 'why don't we require governments to collect "adequate remuneration" for fish that are harvested from public waters?'[80] Quite so. Indeed, the non-collection of resource rents should be considered as 'revenue that is otherwise due' and so a subsidy as defined by the WTO agreement.

Besides subsidies, there is also the impact of taxes.[81] Taxation can mobilize funds for investment in fisheries, and licences can limit fishing. But there is a danger of prioritizing short-term budgetary needs over longer-term sustainability. In Morocco the tax system has led to under-declaring of catch and more sales in informal markets. Another example is the 1982 Nauru Agreement between eight Pacific island states, which introduced licences to try to stop illegal fishing by foreign fleets. While this has raised revenue, since boats must pay at least $8,000 a day, it has penalized small-scale fisheries.

'Ecological fiscal transfers' (EFTs) are a third prong of tax and subsidy policies relating to fisheries. These compensate communities, or administrations, for implementing fishery management systems that have benefits that go beyond their communities. For example, fishing communities may be compensated for being required to limit production, by accepting no-take zones or marine protected areas. In Bangladesh, the hilsa fishery is the largest single-species fishery, providing income for three million people, but overfishing and population growth prompted the government to ban fishing during the reproductive season. As compensation, it provided over 210,000 affected households with forty kilos of rice and offered alternative economic activities. It seems fish catch levels have begun to rise.[82]

Subsidies are a transfer from the public (commoners) to private interests. If it could be shown that they did incentivize recipients in the way intended, if they were distributed equitably, and if the public received the equivalent to the subsidies, one might say that they were socially just. Whether the subsidies were ecologically just would depend on whether they produced ecological decay or regeneration. But fishing subsidies, and subsidies in the blue economy in general, fail in terms of both social and ecological justice. They constitute rental income, largely gained by financial and corporate capital. Subsidies have accelerated decommoning, increased inequalities and accelerated the erosion of the blue commons.

Nobody seriously disputes that fish populations are in crisis. Nobody seriously questions that subsidies lead to overfishing. But powerful corporate lobbies and complicit governments have managed to prevent international agreement to scrap them.

Fishing access agreements and arrangements

Fish have become a globalized commodity; nearly half of all fish landed is sold in international trade, increasingly caught off one continent and sold in another. Foreign and export-oriented domestic industrial fleets are fishing in the waters of developing countries, largely based on the bilateral access agreements that spread in the post-1945 era, and later with the EU.[83] Although there have been over thirty EU agreements, as of 2021 only thirteen were operational, eleven of them with African countries. They include nine tuna agreements allowing EU boats to pursue migrating tuna stocks through the country's waters and four 'mixed' agreements permitting fishing in its EEZ for a wide range of species.

Fishing access agreements and joint ventures have turned the waters off West Africa into a 'fish basket' for Europe that now comprises a quarter of all fish caught by EU boats.[84] They have contributed to the displacement of numerous blue commons communities. For instance, in Mauritania, with which the EU has its biggest mixed agreement in terms of both payment and allowed catches, overexploitation of stocks has devastated local artisanal fisheries. No longer able to make a living by fishing, many former fishers have turned to mining or agriculture, or set out on the perilous journey to Europe.

The EU calls its agreements, rather misleadingly, Sustainable Fisheries Partnership Agreements, in which 'the EU gives financial and technical support in exchange for fishing rights'. But Brussels has not been very generous. Thus, its six-year agreement expiring in 2026 commits the EU to pay the Seychelles just €5.3 million a year for the right to catch tuna in its EEZ, of which €2.8 million is earmarked for support of the fisheries sector. EU boats pay fees in addition, but the tuna they catch are worth many times more than the Seychelles receives.

The EU's agreements with Senegal, the first of which dates back to the 1980s, have involved even more derisory sums and have had similar devastating effects on artisanal fishing communities as in Mauritania. Annual catches more than halved between 1994 and 2005,[85] while the number of locally owned boats fishing Senegal's waters shrank by 48% between 1998 and 2008. In 2006, the agreement was cancelled after Senegal demanded more compensation. But another five-year agreement was reached in 2014 and renewed in 2019, with payment of €1.7 million a year, of which half is for fisheries support.

Payments in other EU access agreements vary but are way below giving African countries a fair share of the value of the fish taken from their waters. The EU agreements also involve big subsidies to its own industrial fisheries. On average, the EU pays 75% of the amount provided to the host government, with the remainder paid by the fisheries. As a result, the fees paid by the industry often come to less than 2% of their gross revenue from the fishing.[86] And the EU's payments for support of the fishing sector, such as monitoring and surveillance, have tended to benefit its own distant-water vessels by lowering their management costs – a hidden subsidy – rather than developing local small-scale fisheries.[87]

The murky sphere of fishing access agreements is scarcely known.[88] Deals are made between governments of rich countries and governments of developing countries, between fishing corporations and governments, and between the EU and governments. We, the public, do not know how many agreements exist or, the EU accords apart, what they contain. Bilateral access agreements invariably involve confidentiality clauses. The contracts and protocols setting out the rules and obligations of foreign vessels are often treated as quasi-private documents, with local governments prohibited from sharing them. As a result, information on fishing access agreements is based largely on investigative work, while knowledge of their contents often comes from leaked contracts.

The EU's Sustainable Fisheries Partnership Agreements are touted as the world's most transparent, a benchmark for other fishing nations to follow. However, gains in public accountability and participation have been won only after years of protracted advocacy and legal actions. The contracts were only made public in the mid-2000s. Even then the agreements were published after they had been concluded, and before being presented for debate by the European Parliament's Committee on Fisheries, which is tasked with oversight of EU fishing in foreign waters. And the negotiations were devoid of local consultation or publicity.

The European Commission continues to resist open-
ness in other ways. DG-MARE, the directorate responsible
for fisheries, commissions environmental and ecological assessments of EU agreements; these show the extent of fishing opportunities available to European companies and the
agreement's impact on host states, including small-scale
fisheries. The directorate also publishes accounts of how
host governments have used EU funds.[89] For decades these
reports were treated as internal intelligence reports, rarely
shared with the European Parliament. Isabella Lövin, a
Swedish Green Party MEP, who was a member of the Committee on Fisheries from 2009 to 2014, recalls being granted
access to evaluations in a closed room, under a strict directive not to copy or share the contents.[90]

In 2012, a request for access to these documents was
made by two European NGOs, the Coalition for Fair Fisheries Arrangements (CFFA) and Client Earth. DG-MARE refused, claiming that the documents contained commercially
sensitive information and that publication would endanger
the economic interests of the EU fishing fleets. It was put
to the Commission that they were acting in contradiction
to the Aarhus Convention, ratified by the EU in 2001, which
gives citizens a legal right to access environmental information held by governments, in the public interest. Eventually, the European Commission capitulated. Heavily redacted
reports were released, and since then new evaluations have
been posted on the DG-MARE website. Predictably, those
prepared for public access are far less revealing or critical
than their confidential counterparts used to be.

In sum, access agreements have been a mechanism for

rent-seeking. Rich countries pay well below the market value of the fish and pay little towards infrastructural costs or to compensate for resource depletion. They are institutionalized 'unequal exchange'. Distant-water industrial fisheries, mostly flagged to richer countries, now account for over 80% of industrial fish capture in low-income countries.[91] They are literally crowding out local fishers and accelerating the decommonization of developing-country fisheries. All distant-water fishing powers have claimed that access agreements are a form of development aid. In reality, they are publicly funded subsidies to facilitate overseas business and trade. It is scarcely consolation for European consciences that, as we shall see, Russian and Chinese access agreements have been even more exploitative.

The financialization of fisheries

The extension of private property rights in fisheries, through catch shares in the USA and transferable quota schemes elsewhere, has greatly extended the opportunity for financialization. These rights have become assets that, used as security, allow their owners to access loans and credit, enabling them to buy up others or purchase complementary assets and rights. In this way, finance has gained control of capitalized assets in the sea. For instance, the catch share system enabled a British investment firm to acquire a quarter of all US clam-based products.[92]

International finance has contributed to the expansion of industrial fisheries and global overfishing. Thus, international banks have invested billions of dollars in companies plundering at-risk species of tuna.[93] Led by Citi, followed by Morgan Stanley and HSBC, the banks have lent to – or underwritten bonds issued by – companies targeting these species and ranching young tuna caught in the wild. Between 2010 and 2020, Citi loaned an incredible $2 billion to those companies.

Banks such as Citi cannot legitimately claim they are following sustainability principles if, while they are lending to one part of a huge fishery company that is abiding by environmental rules, it is known that another part is not. For instance, one of Citi's clients is Mitsubishi Corporation, Japan's largest trading company and biggest purchaser of endangered bluefin tuna. Over a decade, Citi provided it with $7 billion.

Yellowfin tuna in the Indian Ocean, described as the 'worst managed yellowfin stock in the world', is close to collapse.[94] Over a ten-year period, the giant seafood corporation Thai Union sold huge amounts of yellowfin caught in the Indian Ocean to Europe, aided by $485 million from HSBC. The British-based bank says it 'actively engages with clients to understand and improve their environmental and sustainability strategies' and is 'committed to engaging with scientific advice'.[95] Meanwhile, overfishing has increased.

One related trend reflecting financialization is the increasing domination of the global seafood industry by the horizontal and vertical integration of corporations controlling the fish trade, where horizontal integration means linking firms doing specific activities, such as fishing or processing or wholesaling, and vertical integration means linking firms in all stages of fish and seafood production and sale. As a result 'Most of the big companies involved in the fishing industry don't actually do any fishing.'[96] Finance makes this possible.

Part of the fraudulent nature of global capitalism in the seas is the 'limited liability company' concept. Shareholders living thousands of miles from a company's investments, from which they are gaining dividends, are not affected by the costs imposed on local communities, and may not know of them, or care to know. So, they exert no pressure on the company and can turn a blind eye. The technical term for the market failure is 'tort irresponsibility', or really 'no liability'.

This situation amounts to an implicit subsidy. As Katharina Pistor, Columbia Law School professor, has put it, 'Property rights, every economist knows, are meant to increase efficiency by ensuring that owners internalize the costs associated with the assets they own. But limited liability insulates investors from the externalities created by the companies they own; heads, they win – and tails, they win too.'[97]

This is why finance has helped in the construction of complex conglomerates of vertically and horizontally integrated seafood structures in which the components are legally separate limited liability companies. Thus, the giant Thai Union has activities in various countries that, because they are run by supposedly independent firms, enable it to do deals between them to minimize tax obligations, a practice known as transfer pricing.

As in all parts of the global economy, neoliberal economic policies are morphing into rentier capitalism, increasingly shaped by private equity capital. Large funds, led by the biggest, such as Blackstone, are looking to buy up industrial fisheries and put together huge vertical and horizontal mergers through acquiring linked corporations.[98] Other private equity funds are following suit on a smaller scale, as in Mauritania where a European private equity firm has helped a Spanish seafood conglomerate to implement its vertical integration strategy by taking a stake in a local fishing company.[99]

Consolidated fisheries gain from economies of scale and, by broadening the range of their fish-based products, also 'economies of scope' which exploit synergies between different parts of the business. By acquiring wholesale and retail companies, and by merging them with fisheries, they gain further economies of scope. The result is a trend towards monopolization and more rentier income. As with all sectors penetrated by private equity, this drives out small-scale producers, processors and distributors.

Private equity groups could not do this if the blue economy was a genuine commons. They can do it because fisheries have been enclosed and regulated in the interest of private property rights. The impending threat to global fisheries cannot be overemphasized. Financial capital is moving into action. According to one US-based financial adviser: 'The industry dynamics are attractive and seafood, compared to other protein sectors, is a very attractive asset class for both debt and equity investors. The obstacle for investors has been that the seafood industry is complex, fragmented, and quite regulated.'[100]

Private equity is being drawn to fishery firms that own valuable quota, that is, private property rights, as a basis for fishery consolidation. As that financial adviser put it: 'Large global seafood companies with ownership of resources have come to the realization in recent years that in order to gain market access in the US they have to invest in, or acquire, a well-established distributor in the US, as it takes a lifetime to build market share and get closer to the customer, essentially tying together the resource access and the market access.'

Lavish subsidies are another attraction for international finance. In 2018 the manager of one impact investment fund investing in fisheries said: 'At this point, almost every fishery-management investment has been accompanied by some kind of subsidy, suggesting that blended finance strategies may be more successful in the short run than purely privately funded investments.'[101]

In other words, finance can rely on governments to bear at least part of the risk, enabling financial institutions to make more profits. It completes a picture of an economic sphere set up for rent-seeking and short-term speculative activity, with no concern for the long-term sustainability of fish populations.

For all the above reasons, there has been a surge in investment by financial institutions in fisheries and seafood companies. It has been suggested that this will give finance greater leverage to support 'blue growth', by demanding that the firms it invests in conform to environmental sustainability principles. As mentioned in Chapter 2, there is also much talk of the potential of 'blue bonds' to mobilize private investment in 'sustainable' fisheries. However, the Principles for Investment in Sustainable Wild-Caught Fisheries, launched at the World Ocean Summit in March 2018, are a voluntary framework and do not appear to have had any effect so far.

In addition, financial investments have been scattered across numerous firms, rather than concentrated in selected companies.[102] That gives financial institutions less leverage

CHAPTER 4

in pressuring managements to respect sustainable principles. Without a stronger enforceable set of principles, the
financialization of fisheries will merely accentuate short-
term profiteering, with predictably disastrous effects.

Unresolved challenges of industrial fishing

Three further issues underline the threat posed by industrial
fishing to the blue commons and blue commoners: the treatment of bycatch, the reaction to 'straddling fish stocks' and
the reality of marine protected areas.

Bycatch, the capture of species that are not the fishing
target, is a major contributor to the destruction of marine
life, including species important for artisanal fisheries. The
ultra-efficient technologies deployed by industrial fisheries,
such as purse-seine nets and longlines, guarantee extensive
bycatch, some of which may be retained and sold but most of
which is discarded. By all accounts, the tendency to discard
fish has grown dramatically as fishing fleets have expanded
their capacity and targeted the most profitable species.

There is little cost imposed on fisheries that ensnare and
kill turtles, dolphins, sharks or other 'unwanted' species.
There is no cost if they catch juveniles and throw the dead
fish overboard or use them for bait. On one estimate, for
every pound weight of wild shrimp caught, over six pounds
of sea life are thrown overboard, while commercial shrimp
trawls in the Gulf of Mexico result in thousands of turtles
being killed every year.[103]

Within the EU, discarding became pervasive when boats
exceeded their total allowable catch; rather than risk a fine
on returning to port, they threw overboard lower-value fish,

amounting to anything between 20% and 60% of the total catch by volume.[104] In 2019, the EU finally banned discarding for its domestic fisheries, requiring all fish caught to be landed and tallied. Monitoring every boat is nevertheless impossible, so discards are likely to have continued. And skippers are allowed to discard fish deemed 'diseased or damaged', effectively a let-out clause.

Straddling fish stocks are another threat to blue commons communities, especially in the tropics. Fish and other marine animals are moving from warming waters in and close to the tropics in the direction of the Arctic and Antarctic, at a rate of about 70 km a decade, which is accelerating.[105] Because warmer seas hold less oxygen, effectively the fish are swimming for their lives. This threatens to empty tropical waters of valuable fish stocks, hitting many fishery commons. And it is increasing the potential for conflict between states. Many important national fish populations now straddle EEZ borders. One study concluded that without checks on ocean warming a third of all EEZs in the world, mostly in temperate and cold waters, could host new transboundary fish populations by 2060.[106]

International rules require states to cooperate on fish populations that straddle two or more EEZs – but the agreements mostly focus on historically straddling stocks, few have clear rules on new inflows, and enforcement is weak. This leaves the fish unprotected and vulnerable to overfishing, with over 36% of migratory species already at risk of extinction.[107] It also raises the risk of acrimonious disputes between fishing nations. Some EEZs in East Asia are projected to host up to ten new populations in the coming years, in a region already rife with territorial disputes, overlapping

EEZ claims and illegal fishing. A study of all militarized disputes between 1945 and 1992 found that a quarter of them were over fisheries and fishing boundaries.[108]

Countries that pride themselves on conserving fish stocks, only to see them departing for the waters of other countries, have a cause of resentment. Will that lead them to abandon conservation efforts? Will it lead them to send their fishers into foreign waters? Will competition for straddling fish populations lead to proxy conflicts, or to the near extinction of those fish populations, or both? Wise statesmanship, sorely lacking at present, will be needed to avoid these distinct possibilities.

An example of the impact of fish migration relates to the capelin, a small foraging fish that has long thrived in Icelandic waters. Capelin is eaten as an alternative to herring, is a major food for cod, and is used to make fishmeal. But these essential fish are moving. One fisherman told the *New York Times*, 'For the first time last winter, we didn't fish because the fish moved.'[109] Blue whiting, another fish traditionally found in Icelandic waters, is moving north towards Greenland. The cod are shifting too, partly because they feed on capelin. Meanwhile, mackerel and monkfish have moved north into Icelandic waters, creating tension with the EU, Norway and the Faroe Islands, which themselves spent years wrangling over quota shares in the North-East Atlantic before coming to an agreement in 2014.

Iceland has set a national annual quota for mackerel, which it raised by 30% in 2019 to 140,000 tonnes. This gave rise to an angry response from the EU, Norway and the Faroe Islands, which regard Iceland as enforcing property rights over 'their' fish. In a joint statement, they declared, 'Such action, which has no scientific justification, undermines the efforts made by the EU, Norway and the Faroe Islands to promote long-term sustainability of the stock.'[110] They promptly raised the 2020 quota for themselves by 41%.

The blue commons have been eroded by the migration of fish stocks. Local communities have been built up over many generations around one or a few types of fish. If they move en masse, the resource base of the local commons is destroyed. Another threat is the temptation for locals, faced with fish stocks moving out of managed national waters, to break their own sustainability rules. When Dan Pauly, one of the world's leading experts on fisheries, told officials in Dakar, Senegal, that their fish were moving north to Mauritanian waters, the response was, 'Let's catch them, let's catch them before they get there.'[111] He said this was a typical response elsewhere as well.

The movement of fish has also affected fishing in British waters, with fisheries reporting that they are catching more warm-water species. And the growth of straddling fish stocks is complicating the already tortuous international governance of fisheries. The legal framework built around UNCLOS does not cover fluctuating or moving distributions. Under UNCLOS, countries must ensure that fisheries in their EEZs are not endangered by overexploitation. National regulations are the focus. In the case of straddling stocks, UNCLOS obliges states to cooperate to establish necessary conservation and management rules. But this is ineffectual.

At the UN Conference on Straddling Stocks and Highly Migratory Fish Stocks in 1993, developing-country coastal states tried unsuccessfully to extend their jurisdiction beyond the 200-mile limit. Predictably, they were opposed by countries with long-distance fishing fleets. Two years later, the UN Fish Stocks Agreement was adopted, coming into force in 2001. Article 6(6), which specifically applies to straddling and migratory stocks, states:

> For new and exploratory fisheries, States shall adopt as soon as possible cautious conservation and management measures, including, inter alia, catch limits and effort limits. Such measures shall remain in force until there are sufficient data to allow assessment of the impact of the fisheries on the long-term sustainability of the stocks, whereupon conservation and management measures based on that assessment shall be implemented. The latter measures shall, if appropriate, allow for the gradual development of the fisheries.

The UN Fish Stocks Agreement reinforced national obligations to cooperate and to apply a precautionary approach, but it has not forced countries to focus on fish populations that move from their traditional waters.[112] It vests the right to manage fish populations of the high seas in regional fisheries management organizations (RFMOs), which remain the main vehicle for managing fish stocks that straddle several EEZs. They are demonstrably unfit for this task.

Many RFMOs address single species, such as tuna or salmon, so the influx of other species lies outside their remit, delaying needed action. Moreover, RFMOs do not have the power to exclude vessels from fishing the high seas, and have no jurisdictional power to enforce any rules they do set.[113] Membership of RFMOs is voluntary, so if they did set and implement conservation rules successfully, states outside the regional club could enter to take the enlarged fish stock.

There has been little progress in developing pre-emptive mechanisms of cooperation.[114] There is an urgent need to increase global resources for fact-finding in new and exploratory fishing areas. Time lost could mean disastrous destruction of fish populations. Often the moving fish go into regions where relevant scientific knowledge is limited, making it hard to design appropriate governance rules. The role model for these circumstances is held to be the Commission for the Conservation of Antarctic Marine Living Resources, in force since 1982.

Two proposals on straddling and migratory fish stocks are under discussion. One is to institute regular updating of national allocations of catch and/or effort (for systems based on measures of fishing activity such as time spent fishing or size of nets used) to take account of fish-stock redistributions. The other is to make fisheries permits tradable across political boundaries. The permit option would probably give large-scale fisheries a new advantage. But neither proposal offers an effective response to an unfolding tragedy in the sea.

In response to the crisis in fish populations, most countries with marine coastlines have established *marine protected areas* (MPAs) designated for conservation, where fishing and exploitative marine activities are banned or restricted. From covering less than 1% of the ocean area in 2000, they have since spread rapidly. In 2015 more than 11,000 MPAs covered about 3.5% of the oceans,[115] and by 2020, there were over 15,000, covering 27 million square kilometres (10.6 million square miles), equivalent to about 7.5% of the oceans. Great hopes have been placed in MPAs, for preserving fish populations and as incubators for sustainable fishing outside them.

However, despite the impressive numbers, the reality is more sobering. The word 'protection' seems to have a disturbing range of meanings. The Marine Conservation Institute reckons that only 5% of the oceans comprises 'true' MPAs (implemented and offering some degree of protection), which seems generous and would still be only half the 10% UN target for 2020.[116] And less than half the area covered by 'true' MPAs is defined as 'fully or highly protected'.[117] The target of 30% of the oceans protected by MPAs by 2030, to which almost all countries have paid lip service, looks dismally far off.

As the impetus for MPAs has come from overfishing, they can be held up as a solution to overfishing rather than a needed response to humankind's destruction of the marine environment. Many appear to have been designed as little more than an incubator for fish 'stocks', ignoring the protection needs of often highly mobile marine mammals and birds.[118] Often, they are set up in response to overfishing by long-distance fisheries to protect the remaining fish populations, offering the fisheries the prospect of more fish in the future. The author recalls going over an MPA off the coast of the Seychelles and seeing six Chinese fishing trawlers just outside the boundary, as if waiting for the fish to swim their way. In this form, MPAs constitute an implicit subsidy for industrial fisheries, providing breeding grounds for them to continue their plunder outside the protected area.

This is an aspect of so-called 'fortress conservation': in protecting a small area, MPAs may fail to protect everything around them. Moreover, the MPAs are often set up in zones where local blue commoners have traditionally made their living. They thus encroach on the blue commons and reduce the resources available to local fishing communities by the enclosure of seaspace. The resultant impoverishment is another implicit subsidy, since the industrial fishery does not bear the cost of that socio-economic 'externality'.

Many marine protection schemes have been disappointing in conservation terms too. In 2000, New Zealand established its first national sea park, the Hauraki Gulf Marine Park, covering 13,900 square kilometres. It has failed to prevent ecosystem collapse, largely because it remained legal to trawl the sea floor. New Zealand could not meet its commitment under the UN's Sustainable Development Goals to conserve at least 10% of coastal and marine areas by 2020, and is unlikely to contribute much towards the global push to protect 30% of the world's oceans by 2030.[119]

Peru is planning to establish a marine reserve, the Nazca Ridge, containing a submerged mountain range 4 kilometres down which is a refuge for endangered species such as the loggerhead turtle, sharks, orcas and the blue whale, as well as yellowfin tuna and swordfish.[120] The plan divides the protected area horizontally, allowing commercial fishing in the first kilometre below the surface and banning it below that. However, there is one exception to the ban. A family with six boats will be allowed to continue deep-sea longlining for Patagonian toothfish, as it has done for years, because in Peruvian law prior rights trump conservation. So, destruction of the mountain ecosystem will continue.

MPAs have also been linked uncomfortably with plans to expand blue tourism, including eco-tourism. A result has been the displacement of many artisanal fishing communities. One well-known case concerns the Mafia Islands Marine Park, Africa's largest marine park, off Tanzania. Its creation led to investment by foreign-owned tourist corporations and the enclosure of sites, including coral reefs, mangrove forests and the best beaches, previously occupied by traditional communities. Similarly, in the Indian state of Maharashtra, the Malvan Marine Wildlife Sanctuary curtailed local fishing activities in the interest of boosting tourism. Again and again, the interests of local commoners are sacrificed on the altar of growth.

Another example is South Africa's Operation 'Phakisa' (Hurry Up!), a plan to increase returns from oil and gas, tourism, commercial aquaculture and MPAs. In 2006 the government created a marine protected area and issued transferable quotas that overnight excluded nearly 50,000 small-scale fishers. They took to the streets, appealed to the courts and eventually won, though the current permit system is also far from ideal.

MPAs in general are dogged by a pervasive dissonance in the marine world between formal laws and policies and their enforcement. This is worse than on land, mainly because much of the abuse and lawbreaking takes place out of human sight. Another factor is complicity between lawbreakers and politicians and agents appointed to monitor the application of the laws. Both factors highlight the need to put the relevant commoners in charge of monitoring compliance, backed with adequate funding to make that possible and a mandate to bring government agents in charge of enforcement to legal account.

Marine protected areas in the UK, which cover nearly a quarter of its territorial waters, exemplify this lamentable situation. Confusingly called marine conservation zones (MCZs) in England, Wales and Northern Ireland, and marine protected areas (MPAs) in Scotland, they are intended to protect ecosystems and species, including dolphins and harbour porpoises, and are described as part of the government's 'world leading' boast to be on course to meet the target of protecting 30% of ocean biodiversity by 2030. The prime minister presumably included them in his claim at the virtual UN Summit on Biodiversity in September 2020 that 26% of the country was already protected for the recovery of nature.[121]

But the seas are not protected. In 2019 Oceana, a non-governmental conservation organization, found that bottom trawling and dredging, the most destructive fishing methods, were being deployed in seventy-one of the seventy-three offshore MPAs around the UK. Marine scientist Callum Roberts called MPAs 'paper parks', and accused the government of 'misleading the public, wasting resources, protecting nothing'.[122]

Recall that supertrawlers are over 100 metres in length and can catch hundreds of tonnes of fish in a day, using nets up to a mile long. Also in 2019, a Greenpeace investigation found that twenty-five supertrawlers, including the four biggest in the world, fished in thirty-nine of the UK's MPAs, quite legally.[123] One avowed objective of several of the MPAs was to protect porpoises, but over 1,000 died in 2019 alone, caught as bycatch. Of the twenty-five supertrawlers, fifteen were Russian, nine Dutch and one Polish. In 2020, during the COVID lockdown that prevented local fishers going out to fish, the supertrawlers more than doubled their time catching and carrying off fish from MPAs around Britain.[124]

In response to Greenpeace, the National Federation of Fishermen's Organisations made a remarkable statement:

> Greenpeace regard supertrawlers as an easy target, but
> their arguments about fishing in MPAs are a red herring.
> The majority of MPAs exist to protect seabed habitats
> and these trawlers fish mid-water and so do not affect
> the seabed. Most of our fish stocks range well beyond the
> boundaries of MPAs. So, controls on how much fish can be
> caught are far more relevant to the sustainability of stocks
> than limiting access to catches within MPAs.[125]

This surely ignores the nature of healthy ecosystems, where everything is connected to everything else. A marine system does not consist of only one part of it. The statement sounded like a defence of industrial fishery interests. To add to that impression, surely influenced by the same lobby, the government blocked an amendment to its 2020 Fisheries Act that would have imposed a ban on supertrawlers in MPAs.

Globally, evidence suggests that marine reserves, if strictly managed, can lead to an encouraging revival of fish and other marine life, and to larger and more diverse fish.[126] But industrial fisheries have resisted their establishment. And governments linked to industrial capitalism have tended to support the big firms and their lobbyists. In the UK, the Labour government before 2010 drew up a list of 127 proposed inshore and offshore marine conservation zones (MCZs), after years of consultation and much expense. In 2013, the Conservative-led coalition government cut that back to twenty-seven and not one was designated as 'strictly protected', with a no-take fishing rule. The government argued that having more MCZs would have an excessive economic cost for fisheries, to which Callum Roberts responded, 'It's bollocks. These MCZs will not put fishermen out of jobs; they will protect them in the long-run.'[127]

The Conservative government later approved sixty-four extra MCZs, bringing the total in English waters to ninety-one by 2019. But they are not well protected and, as in other countries, it is mainly left to outside bureaucracies to do the protection. Counting both inshore and offshore MPAs around the whole of the UK, by 2020 there were 357. But trawling and dredging could only be halted in inshore waters up to twelve nautical miles from the coast, while few MPAs had 'no-take' zones. The respected Marine Conservation Society reported that, although UK MPAs covered an area over nine times the size of Wales in 2020, less than 1% was considered by its scientists to be well-managed. Calling them all 'paper parks' may be an exaggeration. But overall the protection seems very limited. This is a classic case where local commoners should have the authority to preserve the resources and regenerate threatened nature.

Britain is not alone. One detailed study covering 727 EU-designated MPAs concluded that industrial trawling for fish was greater *inside* MPAs in European waters than in unprotected areas, largely because fishing was easier and more 'efficient' in MPAs.[128] No less than 59% of all the MPAs were trawled commercially. In December 2020, the European Court of Auditors issued a report saying that MPAs in the Mediterranean were failing and showed no meaningful signs of progress.[129] The relevant countries were using just 6% of the fund set aside for protection. The Court concluded that of the 3,000 MPAs in European waters, most still allowed commercial fishing.

MPAs are also contentious because their boundaries are often hard to define and because the gatekeeper role is hard to apply. Leading long-distance fishing nations, notably Norway, Russia, Japan, Iceland and South Korea, want them regulated by RFMOs, which have no mandate for marine ecosystem conservation. As the Chilean Ambassador to Norway told a group looking at the issue, 'Many fishing nations are not true believers in marine protected areas.'[130]

The reality is clear. Industrial fisheries seek short-term profit maximization, and financial interests are oriented almost exclusively to the short term. Unless control of legislation and conservation policy is taken away from those interests, nobody should expect real improvement. It is essential to put in charge those whose real long-term interest is in reproducing the blue commons, and to strengthen the gatekeeper role by governance reform and financial assistance.

One promising study concluded that a 5% expansion of highly protected MPAs would improve future fish catches by up to 20%.[131] This is encouraging, but caution is in order. Existing highly protected MPAs tend to be in remote and little trafficked areas such as Antarctica, where it is relatively easy to identify rule-breakers and enforce that degree of protection. Extension to other areas would need to be accompanied by stricter monitoring and punishment of those abusing the rules. An MPA established in a well-managed fishing area tends to reduce the total catch, but in already overexploited, poorly managed fisheries the total catch may actually increase. In other words, the impact on fish catches depends on the system in which the MPA operates.

The picture on MPAs is not uniform. Some have been developed in partnership with local fishing communities; assessments have concluded that MPAs can help when they are, and damage fishing communities when they are not. This reinforces the case for giving the interests of blue commoners – whether fishers or those involved in other activities – high priority in the establishment of MPAs and variants. Too often, they have been excluded from consultations or presented with a *fait accompli* when asked to participate in the process. Industrial fisheries should be given minimal priority, and preferably be excluded from their establishment and from access to them afterwards.

The 'Great Deceleration'?

As stated at the outset, this is an unfinished story, a narrative of evolving crisis stretching over seven decades. The essential dishonesty of the rentier capitalism model is the subject of the next chapter, which shows how industrial fishing is inherently a crimogenic form of capitalism. Meanwhile, the combination of capacity expansion aided by subsidies, constant technological innovation and mercantilist national strategies has meant that there is scarcely anywhere in the world's oceans for fish populations to find refuge.

Unless there is a transformation, the situation can only become worse. Think of the power of seabed mapping; global positioning systems; fish-finding electronics; lighter, stronger nets; massive trawl gear; huge factory ships fed by giant fishing vessels, and so on. Where there are protection mechanisms at all, they are weak, underfunded and mostly focused on selected high-value fish populations, ignoring the need to preserve biodiversity.

We come back to a standard claim of neoliberal economics, that a 'free market' economy fosters the efficient allocation of resources or factors of production, which promotes growth of GDP and thus material wealth. The drive for 'efficiency' and 'productivity' is virtually compulsory; producers who are less efficient and productive will be driven out. In industrial fisheries, this claim is a form of madness. The enormous nets dragged along the seabed in bottom trawling are certainly 'efficient', sweeping up everything in their path. But they destroy marine ecosystems and turn vast areas into barren zones. What is more, by churning the seabed, trawling releases sediment that is increasing ocean acidification and disturbing the world's largest carbon sink. Trawling is thus responsible for pumping out one gigaton of carbon every year, significantly more than is released by aviation in a normal year.[132] It is disappointing but predictable that the main reaction by politicians has been to suggest that such trawling should be restricted to certain areas rather than banned altogether or heavily taxed.

One trend in global fisheries is clear. Conglomeration is growing. Globally, the seafood industry is increasingly governed by a potential cartel of transnational corporations, not by governments or regional bodies. In 2012, just thirteen seafood companies, comprising 0.5% of the 2,250 registered fishing and aquaculture companies worldwide, accounted for 11–16% of the global marine catch, 18% of the global value of seafood production and 19–40% of the most valued species. They have been dubbed 'keystone actors' that alone can affect what happens to marine ecosystems.[133] They operate with hundreds of subsidiaries, have greater resilience to recessionary shocks, and can use them to buy up vulnerable smaller firms. Companies related to Japan's Mitsubishi conglomerate, for example, now own 40% of all tuna caught around the world through investments in fleets, fishing equipment, processing plants and branded tuna products.[134]

Since 2012, connections between those thirteen corporations have increased. Their rent-seeking abilities must have increased accordingly. Similar trends have been taking place within individual countries, as we will see in the case of the UK. The trend to conglomeration is a feature of rentier capitalism and financialization, associated with increased mark-ups of prices over costs of production and hence with increased profitability.[135]

The competition for fish is also exacerbating political and military tensions, with the devastation wreaked by Chinese fisheries in particular increasingly in the spotlight. But the granting of so little of the ocean to the world's most populous country in the UNCLOS Great Enclosure of 1982 was unjust. The carving up of much of the world's continental shelf for national ownership was bad enough, but giving the United States, France and the UK ten times as much as China smacked of neocolonialism. International action to curb the plunder of the seas must take that into account.

What about the high seas beyond the Exclusive Economic Zones? This is often depicted as the new great frontier. But the fish species out there are, metaphorically, awaiting political decisions. The ongoing UNCLOS-based negotiations on biodiversity protection in the deep sea do not include fishing. So, the fish have little hope there. Although fishing in areas beyond national jurisdiction has been limited, with just a few big fishing nations involved, it has nevertheless been causing severe environmental damage.[136]

The pervasive tension between blue commoners, the industrial juggernauts and their complicit governments is discussed later. But the evidence presented in this chapter should be sufficient to show that the squeeze on small-scale and artisanal communities not only impoverishes those communities but presages disaster for the world's fish populations and fisheries of the future.

Commercial Fishing: Crime Under Other Names

> It is impossible for any skipper with a boat over 80 feet to stay viable now without breaking at least one of the three main rules – misreporting, using smaller mesh or making illegal landings. Impossible on the quotas we have now. We are being forced to be criminals.
>
> — Tim Oliver, *Fishing News*, 26 April 1991[1]

The sea has always been a zone of banditry, piracy, smuggling, daring rogues and rough justice. In recent years, as fish populations have come under more intense pressure, there has been rising concern about the perceived growth of so-called IUU (illegal, unreported and unregulated) fishing. However, some of the most egregious activities in the sea are formally legal, and result from manipulation of laws and lobbying by powerful commercial interests. A fixation on IUU fishing easily leads to neglect of more damaging actions and the misleading idea that if only IUU fishing could be controlled, all would be well.

Many illegal practices in the seas reflect a combination of factors, including globalization and conflicts of interest. The fate of the European eel, once so plentiful, encapsulates many of the issues. Long a staple food item across Europe, such as jellied eels in the East End of London, and famed for their mysterious practice of swimming thousands of miles to breed only in the Sargasso Sea, they are now critically endangered. Young 'glass eels' are still being caught in large numbers, particularly in Sweden. And they are being illegally smuggled out of the European Union despite a ban on international trade since 2010. In 2019 this illegal trade was described as 'the most serious wildlife crime issue the EU currently faces'.[2] The eels go mostly to China and other parts of East Asia, where they are fattened up and fetch high prices, and where overfishing has long depleted the local eel population.

Is this straightforward criminality? Or do the respective states also have responsibility for what is happening, by lack of effective action? Complicity is a form of criminality; it is certainly a failure of stewardship. In general, there are issues of morality and legality. Some practices may be legal but amoral, some may be legal yet endanger the blue commons, deliberately or unintentionally. Worst are the actions that are amoral, illegal and ecologically and socially destructive, which are all too widespread in the world's fisheries.

State-corporate crime

It is a convenient myth that there are or could be free markets, in fish or anything else. Neoliberal economists claim that markets can and should be deregulated, because in their view private actors will self-regulate efficiently. In reality, corporations everywhere interact with politicians and civil servants to construct and reshape institutions and processes to suit their interests. Markets and economic practices operate to benefit the powerful, often giving legitimacy to what might otherwise be regarded as illegitimate, if not criminal.

The result has been the unprecedented rentier capitalism of the twenty-first century, in which states and their governments have acted ruthlessly in the interest of their corporations and financial institutions. The following well describes the process by which rentier capitalism was strengthened in the United States in the 1990s:

> Executives conducted a decade-long march through the institutions, waving banners of a free market and singing psalms in praise of investors, when, in fact, they were waging aggressive lobbying campaigns (with their investors' money) to change the rules in ways that would buffer them from scrutiny.[3]

This is a particularly strong tendency in the blue economy. Fisheries the world over – and not just in developing countries – tend to generate collusive networks that favour 'market-bending' methods.

Advocates of deregulation often argue that what have been called 'reputational intermediaries' such as auditors and accountants will ensure that corporate executives abide by rules of integrity and probity, because if they did not the intermediaries would lose their reputation and their fee income. This claim was made most famously by Alan Greenspan, a fan of the extreme right-wing thinker Ayn Rand. Greenspan became the most powerful banker in the world as chairman of the US Federal Reserve between 1987 and 2006.[4] In 2002, after three decades of insisting otherwise, he finally admitted he was wrong.

A feature of any crimogenic industry is that much business is done in private non-market deals, between firms or between firms and state institutions, politicians, political parties and state bureaucrats.[5] This is a fundamental reality of rentier capitalism. And it is an inherent feature of industrial fisheries, in part because so much of what is done is out of sight, easily concealed, or is so profitable that amoral or illegal activities are worth the (usually nugatory) risk of detection and punishment. Legality and illegality are often combined.

For obvious reasons, in many countries there is a lack of data about such deals, so we must rely on what is often well-informed rumour. However, every now and then, an odious arrangement comes into the open. Thus, in late 2019, 30,000 documents leaked to Wikileaks, dubbed the Fishrot Files, revealed that the largest fishery company in Iceland, Samherji, had bribed Namibia's fishery and justice ministers to acquire a large lucrative quota, mainly for horse mackerel, a nutritious local staple, in the country's fish-rich waters.[6] Allegedly, the bribes came to over £6 million, substantial for the recipients but small change for the Icelandic company, given the revenue it expected to obtain.

Between 2011 and 2019, Samherji channelled £54 million of the revenue, via a maze of offshore firms, to a shell company in the tax haven of the Marshall Islands. The whistleblower who leaked the documents said the company 'habitually does whatever it takes to get its hands on the national resources of other nations'. It was no doubt a coincidence that Iceland's fishery minister had previously been managing director of the company. Another revelation was that one-fifth of Namibia's MPs held shares in fishery companies. So, the

Icelandic arrangement is unlikely to be unique except, per-haps, in being exposed.

The corruption inherent in the global fishing industry endangers small-scale artisanal fisheries, eroding the blue commons on which the reproduction of marine ecosystems depends. The message of this chapter is that a free-market approach based on private property rights is not only in-compatible with the 'blue growth' model – the win-win-win promise of sustainable growth, ecosystem conservation and benefits for local communities – but threatens to do the op-posite, almost guaranteeing the near-destruction of the blue commons.

The underside of fishing access agreements

To start with the globalized jigsaw of cross-national fishing access agreements, Chapter 4 dealt with their formal side, focusing on EU agreements. But they are very rarely what they seem. Many are secret. Of those like the EU's that are not, almost all contained confidentiality clauses until polit-ical pressure in Europe led the EU to drop them.

From the outset the morality of these agreements has been dubious; they have been powerful rent-seeking devices. The agreements could best be described as 'neo-colonial' and 'neo-mercantilist'. To recall, they stemmed from the concept of maximum sustainable yield (MSY), the idea that there is a scientific measure of how much fish can be taken from an area without risk of depletion. Claiming that many coun-tries were not fishing anywhere near that maximum, fish-ing powers pushed for the UNCLOS rule requiring countries to allow foreign fisheries to take up the 'surplus'. This rule was aimed at developing countries for the benefit of long-distance fisheries from rich countries.

The waters of the EEZs of the twenty-four West African countries, blessed with plentiful fish, were primary victims. Economically impoverished, desperate for foreign currency and with politicians eager to escape poverty themselves, these countries were easily corruptible targets for European, Russian and latterly Chinese governments, whose long-distance fleets offered money or aid in return for monopolistic fishing access agreements.

Most host countries could not estimate their MSY and did not have industrial fishing vessels that could have caught whatever it might have been. They were pressured to accept that foreign vessels could take 'surplus' fish, and foreign governments and fishing fleets could claim, disingenuously, that there were no data to judge sustainable catch limits. They, or the international financial agencies supposed to be helping developing countries, could have provided the technical expertise to make estimates. They did not do so.

Access agreements have done lasting damage to the blue commons and their communities. Overfishing by long-distance fisheries, aided by processing and storage ships offshore, and frequent trespassing into near-shore waters supposedly reserved for the exclusive use of domestic small-scale fishers, have slashed catches of local fishers and forced them to go further out to fish. This has reduced their profitability and viability, while often putting themselves in mortal peril. And, since the fish caught by industrial boats goes primarily for export, foreign fisheries not only destroy the livelihoods of local fishers but undermine their ability to provide local communities with fish to eat.[7]

Apologists might claim that development aid linked to such agreements by the EU, China, Russia and, before 1991, the Soviet Union, compensated countries for foreign access to fish stocks. However, such aid could scarcely compensate for the enormous value of fish catches by foreign fisheries, especially since whatever financial and technical assistance has been given is often earmarked for management services or infrastructure facilities, largely if not exclusively for the benefit of foreign fisheries. By ignoring the adverse effects on the blue commons, such agreements distort the appearance of economic development.

A case in point is Japan's controversial 2018 tuna access agreement with Mauritius, in return for Japanese investment in fish processing, port development and maritime security, including a radar system.[8] Even before the deal, Japan's Mitsubishi, estimated to control 40% of the global tuna market, had built up a large tuna processing company in Mauritius employing 10,000 workers and generating $400 million in sales each year. But until 2018 Japan did not have significant fishing rights in Mauritian waters. Within months of the agreement being signed, however, there was a huge increase in Japanese fishing operations out of Mauritius, not only in the Mauritian EEZ but across the Indian Ocean and beyond.

Japanese boats have added to the pressure on already overexploited tuna populations from European vessels covered by long-standing fishing access agreements between the EU and Mauritius. Local fishers say they cannot compete with the foreign fleets, which use advanced industrial fishing techniques including fish aggregating devices. Catches by mostly small Mauritian fishing boats have shrunk, not just of tuna but of other valued fish for the domestic market that the foreign boats treat as bycatch. Meanwhile, the government aims to double its 'blue' GDP to 20% in the medium term, with an emphasis on industrial fishing that threatens to further deplete fish populations and damage marine ecosystems.[9] And in a further blow to artisanal fishing communities, a massive oil spill in 2020 from a Japanese bulk carrier devastated protected marine areas and fishing grounds, the effects of which were still being felt in late 2021.

Linked to a persistent and notorious lack of transparency is what might be called a quasi-privatization of deals nominally between governments or between local governments and foreign fisheries. When UNCLOS came into full effect in the 1990s, it was celebrated as offering developing countries control over their marine resources. But politicians and bureaucrats were easily enticed into turning access agreements into private exchanges, without public deliberation, knowledge or consent.

Private deals have characterized the commercial extraction of most natural resources but are particularly venal in fisheries. So much is unseen and must be taken on trust. So much, in fisheries in all countries, involves opportunism of the worst kind. Few governments have acted as loyal stewards of the blue commons, guarding their long-term reproductive interests. Corporate capital has been all too willing to collude with them. But it must always be emphasized that it takes at least two sides to collude in corruption.

Another aspect of fishing access agreements is the pitiful

amount paid in resource use fees – fees or royalties paid by foreign countries and corporations for the right to extract natural resources. In the case of minerals and energy, it is reckoned that foreign companies pay developing-country governments royalties of between 20% and 40%. In the case of timber, resource use fees have been about 8.5% of gross profits, which most development and environmental experts regard as amorally low. The situation in fishing is worse.

Fishing access agreements have been among the most lop-sided economic agreements in modern history. In the 1960s, there were thirty-six known agreements, in the 1980s there were 242 and by the early 2000s there were over 300.[10] That was not counting so-called 'domestic' offshore fleets consisting of reflagged European and Chinese vessels. Excluding reflagging, one assessment of EU and Chinese agreements with West African countries concluded that on average EU agreements enabled African countries to obtain just 26% of the value of recorded catches, while with Chinese agreements the added value of aid supposedly provided in return came to about 40% of the value.[11] However, when account was taken of unreported (legal and illegal) catches, the respective figures were just 8% and 4%. This is plunder and super-exploitation on a disgraceful scale.

Many African countries, and tropical small island states elsewhere, depend on resource use fees for their development spending. For example, during the 1990s, following a protracted civil war, the Mozambique government gained 50% of all its revenue from fisheries, mainly from prawn trawling for export. In other countries, such as Guinea-Bissau and Mauritania, over 25% of government revenue comes from foreign fisheries, much from licence fees. Several Pacific island states depend on fisheries for over half of government income, with Kiribati recording 65% in some years. These figures could be mischaracterized as lucrative transfers obtained by poor states for doing little other than administering permits. Yet the dependency on foreign fishing fees merely highlights the extent of their impoverishment. They cannot rely on much else.

Fishing access agreements are clearly mechanisms of what is called 'unequal exchange'. The foreign industrial fisheries have not paid anything like the full costs of what they have gained. Under the agreements, resource use fees have been based on the size and attributes of vessels granted entitlement to fish, or on a percentage of the value of landed catch. Neither approach factors in the host states' management costs, or compensates them for the damage caused by fishing, such as pollution and habitat destruction, or the loss of income by local fishers and the disruption to local communities. Non-payment of those 'externalities' constitutes rental income obtained by foreign capital and by citizens of richer countries through cheaper fish prices than they would otherwise have to pay.

The amorality does not stop there. Where fees are based on reported catches, host governments must rely on the information that foreign distant-water fleets provide. While all resource sectors suffer from illicit extraction beyond prescribed limits, fisheries are uniquely vulnerable to deceit, since the fishing takes place out of sight, and the total catch is not landed in the country to be weighed, counted or processed.

In response to systematic under-reporting, some countries have increased the number of onboard observers as monitors. However, although they may improve the accuracy of reported catches, there are doubts about their ability to blow the whistle for transgressions. Their salaries are often paid by the vessel owners, and they can be required to sign confidentiality agreements. While they are well-placed to share information on realities at sea, there has been little research to see what effect they are having.

In addition, licence or resource use fees are often determined by the value of target species specified in the access agreements. Yet substantial bycatch, for which there may be only a nominal fee, or none at all, is often retained and sold. In many fisheries, bycatch is a lucrative component of catches, such as snapper and other demersal (bottom-dwelling) fish caught by trawlers licensed to fish for small pelagic species. EU evaluations of Moroccan fisheries during the mid-2000s showed that foreign trawlers targeting small pelagics caught more demersal species than the entire fleet of local fishers, although they were not licensed to catch these species. Bycatch may even generate higher profits than the target species. For example, the value of shark fins can easily exceed the market value of tuna and billfish in longline tuna fishing. On a conservative estimate, global bycatch may account for 10% of all fish caught,[12] so the absence of fees on bycatch amounts to a serious form of exploitation.

Then there is the truth about fishing vessels. Estimated catches, and thus fees, are often based on information supplied by foreign fishing countries on the physical attributes of their vessels. Misreporting is rife. Greenpeace found that official records substantially underestimated the size of Chinese vessels in West African waters, allowing them to qualify for lower licence fees. This has been going on for three decades. Coastal states have lost massive amounts in fees, and fish populations have suffered from concealed overfishing.

With these caveats in mind, how much are foreign fishing fleets paying? The International Centre for Trade and Sustainable Development, which made comparisons with mining and timber, has suggested that resource fees of at least 30% of the value of the catch would be justified.[13] In reality, resource fees in fisheries are a small fraction of that.

Some in the fishing industry claim that fishing is not very profitable, pointing to high operating costs, such as fuel and labour, shrinking fish stocks and the structure of global seafood trade that means much of the profits go to processors and retailers. They argue that higher licence fees would put fishing companies under pressure, unless consumers paid higher prices. Certainly, the fishing industry suffers from fluctuating profits, which vary between types of fisheries and parts of the world. And certainly, fish processors and retailers hold considerable power. But the evidence available suggests that foreign fishing boats, which are heavily subsidized, could afford to pay much more. It would be up to them to bargain for more from those further up the seafood chain.

One assessment of fees was commissioned by the World Bank, undertaken by a team of experts with long experience in fisheries management in West Africa and with unique access to otherwise confidential government data.[14] They estimated that payments to coastal states in the bottom-trawl sector were about 2% of corporate profits. The one exception was Guinea-Bissau, where the figure was close to 8%. But this included the EU's payment for access to the fish population. The 2% figure approximated what the companies were paying in licence or resource use fees.

Moreover, the study only considered profits from the market value of landed fish, and not the additional profits from processing and selling fish products. The authors recognized limitations in the data and the possibility that company profits were larger due to under-reporting of catches, including retained bycatch. So, almost certainly, resource use fees paid to the West African governments for these fisheries amounted to under 2% of net profits.

This suggests that at least part of the fisheries industry may be the world's most inequitable natural resource sector in terms of benefit-sharing. Further research is needed in other fisheries. But it does appear that developing states have been pressured into selling access to fish too cheaply. This is corroborated by the experience of the Pacific islands. For years they followed other countries in negotiating access fees with powerful distant-water fishing nations. Without good data or collective bargaining, the price for access was easily driven down to what has been paid in Africa. Then, in 2009 a group of Pacific states collaborated in developing an auction-based system to sell fishing days to purse-seine fishing companies. Payments by distant-water fishing fleets rose from $60 million in 2010 to over $500 million by 2015, adding credibility to the view that fishing companies had been highly exploitative.

However, auctions come with risks. Companies with the lowest operating costs and most unethical practices may outbid competitors. Self-reported information for 2012 supplied to the Federated States of Micronesia showed that, for landing about 6,000 tonnes of skipjack tuna, a Japanese boat gained net income of $1.3 million, while a Chinese boat gained $5.8 million. The discrepancy partly reflected different levels of government subsidy, but also much lower operational costs for the Chinese vessel, including $2 million less spending on crew salaries.[15]

African countries have been urged to copy the Pacific model. However, the only African auction experiment was a disaster. In 2020, in the wake of the damaging Icelandic corruption scandal, Namibia attempted to auction fishing quotas with the objective of redistributing them for developmental ends. The auction was publicly presented as a way of generating funds to fight the economic impact of the COVID-19 pandemic. According to initial press reports, the quotas were auctioned for $40 million, over twice what the government usually charged. The Minister of Finance declared that this had finally revealed the true value of the resource to private firms.

Yet it soon emerged that hardly any of the winning bids were genuine. Only 1.3% of the money was paid. While the story was still unclear at the time of writing, the fishing industry may have hijacked the auction to prevent a rise in quota fees, or (as is more likely) the quotas were purchased by financial speculators hoping to resell them to fishing companies after having cornered the market, but who then could not raise the capital in time to secure the quota.

Thus, foreign fishing access agreements have been highly inequitable, serving the short-term profit-making interests of foreign industrial fishing fleets, and have been systematic vehicles for amoral dealings. And they have contributed significantly to the plunder of fish populations and marine ecosystems, at the expense of local fishing communities and the ocean environment.

Asymmetrical joint ventures

The potentially good news that fishing access agreements may have passed their zenith is spoiled by the fact that so-called 'joint ventures' have become the main vehicle for foreign access to the remaining fish populations in the EEZs of countries around the world. They have similar drawbacks, and some are even worse.

Much foreign fishing in developing countries happens outside formal bilateral agreements. Public information is scarce. Many coastal states do not publish lists of vessels that are licensed to fish in their waters. Estimates of unlicensed fishing by foreign companies are dubious since we do not know how many commercial vessels are licensed. Joint ventures and chartering arrangements are murky; often local partners are not identified.

The European Commission used to publish statistics on joint ventures involving European companies when it was subsidizing them; now that has stopped. In the early 2000s, the EU reported that it had helped establish 152 joint ventures in developing countries, involving over 240 vessels. By 2006, after EU subsidies ended, there were apparently 220 joint ventures with Spanish companies alone, involving over 550 vessels. Since then, public information on joint ventures involving European companies has largely dried up.

Secretive joint ventures abound, as in Senegal. In 2006, it

became the first country to refuse an extension of an EU fisheries agreement, on the grounds that it provided poor returns and had led to overfishing. The EU claimed that negotiations soured when the government demanded increased payments and refused to commit to using the funds for fishery development.[16] Whatever the reasons, having rejected the extension, Senegal prioritized joint ventures instead. In 2011, over 130 were operating in its waters, involving Korean, Russian, Spanish, Italian and Chinese companies. Many were joint ventures in name only, with declared local shareholdings as low as €150.[17] Such ridiculous amounts enable the company to pay a local to hold a nominal 51% shareholding to qualify as a joint-venture company. The Senegalese authorities are aware of the abuse but have done nothing to prevent it.

A similar situation has been revealed in Ghana. Despite a law banning joint ventures, seen as hindering local fisheries, the Environmental Justice Foundation observed seventy-six industrial fishing trawlers operating off Ghana in 2018; almost all were front companies for Chinese firms.[18] Elsewhere, there have been numerous reports of secretive joint ventures with local politicians as local partners, as in prawn fisheries in Mozambique and fishing more generally in Angola, Madagascar and Namibia.

The World Bank has urged fishing authorities to publish vessel registries, even making this a soft condition for loans. But it admits it has failed to convince governments to do so. In 2018, the governments of Mauritania and the Seychelles helped launch a global Fisheries Transparency Initiative, which commits signatory countries to publish contracts of fishing agreements and licences, among other things. However, as of end-2021, only three other countries – Madagascar, Cape Verde and Senegal – had formally joined the initiative and only Mauritania and the Seychelles had submitted the called-for reports.

The spectrum of legality and illegality

No aspect of global fishing attracts more attention than what is called 'illegal, unreported and unregulated' (IUU) fishing. However, the implied dichotomy with 'legal' fishing is misleading; fisheries are inherently on the borderline of illegality. Many practices should be classified as criminal or at least amoral, which is why it is appropriate to regard fishing as a crimogenic industry.

International fisheries consist of three categories. First, there are those that are registered in their nation and that abide by national and international regulations, or at least are presumed to do so. Second, there are privateers that fly flags of convenience, registered in countries such as Panama, Liberia and Mongolia. Since UNCLOS only requires ships to be subject to the regulations of their country of registration, flags of convenience help ships to avoid tax and escape safety regulations and regulations designed to preserve fish stocks.

The third category consists of boats that ignore all jurisdictional dictates of international agreements. The overused term 'pirates' is not in fact appropriate in relation to illegal fishing, since a pirate was and is someone who takes by force from other boats or from land. Nevertheless, a common claim is that globally 'fish piracy continues to be part of almost every fishery and in every size of vessel.'[19] Yet the ratio of illegal to legal fishing covers a spectrum. Very few industrial trawlers fish 100% legally, never destroying habitats, jettisoning bycatch, discarding nets or other fishing gear, or catching excess fish.

Roughly half the countries with fishing ports have signed up to Port State Authority rules obliging them to act against foreign fishing vessels found to be breaking international regulations. But boats can offload at 'ports of convenience' to avoid inspections, or process and sell their fish at sea to other fisheries before returning to their home port. The industrial-scale processing of catch on board large transhipment vessels facilitates 'fish laundering', enabling legal and illegal fish to be mixed and/or mislabelled. Long-distance fisheries can catch fish in various national waters and mislabel those taken excessively from one country as having been caught in another. One effect is to inflate estimates of remaining populations of quota-constrained high-value fish. Or fisheries can process their catch at sea and label fillets as something else to disguise their origin.

An investigation covering thirty countries found that over a third of seafood samples from restaurants, fishmongers and supermarkets were mislabelled, usually selling a lower-priced fish for a higher-priced fish on the label or selling farmed fish as wild-caught.[20] The highest rates of mislabelling were in Canada and the UK. If you see the word 'snapper' on a fishmonger's slab, be suspicious. But while cheating is pervasive, industrial fishing conglomerates can conceal this practice by controlling the whole value chain through to retail outlets. Governments have helped. The US government decided in the 1970s that some fish species needed to be renamed to improve their 'edibility profile'.

Where is the boundary between legal and illegal activity in the sea? Consider Somalia, which has the longest shoreline (3,333 kilometres) and richest marine resources in mainland Africa.[21] The collapse of the Siad Barre government in 1991 and the ensuing civil war led to the disbanding of Somalia's navy and coastguard. Unhindered, European and Asian trawlers entered the country's Exclusive Economic Zone and plundered the sea of tuna, shrimp, spiny lobster, snapper and other species, intruding in inshore waters supposedly reserved for domestic artisan fishers. According to the High Seas Task Force, in 2005 there were over 800 foreign vessels fishing illegally in Somali waters. Other foreign boats, some allegedly linked to the Italian mafia, dumped toxic waste, poisoning not only marine life but also the inhabitants of coastal communities.

When some Somalis subsequently took to their boats to drive off trawlers they were accused of 'piracy'. Others, in desperation, took to kidnapping for ransom. Later, this developed into a lucrative business for warlords and terrorist groups, prompting the major powers to send naval vessels to protect their ships. But they had done nothing to protect Somalia from the earlier marauding industrial fishery armada, even though that was illegal and largely explained the initial resort to 'piracy'. Somali fishing communities continue to struggle under pressure from better-equipped foreign vessels, operating without permits or with permits granted on dubious authority, though an FAO-led project to create an integrated local fishing community may show a way to improve the lot of these artisanal fisheries.[22]

While we must be careful about attributing responsibility

for illegality, illegal forms of fishing are undoubtedly part of the unfolding story of the blue commons under duress, unfairly affecting legal activities.[23] Although a messy concept, illegal fishing is clearly extensive and almost certainly growing.

To give some idea of the scale, it has been estimated that between 20% and 32% of the weight of wild-caught seafood in the USA is either illegal or unreported, in violation of the 1990 Lacey Act that prohibits the import or export of any animal or plant product taken by illegal means.[24] This is for a country with a relatively well-enforced regulatory system. In Japan, one investigation found that between 24% and 36% of the 2.15 million tonnes of wild seafood imports in 2015 were of illegal and unreported origin, valued between $1.6 billion and $2.4 billion, out of total imports of $13 billion.[25] In the Antarctic fishing area about a quarter of all fish caught are reckoned to be illegally taken.[26]

Another way of conveying the scale of IUU fishing is that every time a customer buys fish or eats fish in a restaurant there is a one in five chance it has been caught illegally.[27] Various estimates suggest that IUU fishing may amount to between $19 billion and $45 billion annually. But no one really knows; the main statistics on IUU fishing are largely made up. Even the FAO has admitted this. There are hardly any reliable data.

Putting illegal, unreported and unregulated fishing together in an overarching concept made this inevitable; what it includes has been muddled from the outset. 'Illegal' fishing has in principle a coherent definition; it is fishing that breaks the law. But some define illegal fishing as foreign fishing in the EEZ waters of another country without permission, whereas domestic fishery violations of fishing regulations are not treated as 'illegal'.[28]

Others use the term more broadly to cover three types of activity: opportunistic overfishing by usually law-abiding fisheries, which under-report catches; overfishing by artisanal fisheries unaware of fishing regulations; and premeditated overfishing by industrial fisheries.[29] The third form is most worrying, since those involved evidently do not care for the long-term sustainability of fish stocks. And it is a low-capital, fairly low-risk and high-return business.

The graphic on page 224, taken from a useful report by the US National Intelligence Council, summarizes the common forms of IUU fishing.[30] That occurring in the mid-grey area is the responsibility of the nation state to which the EEZ belongs, while IUU fishing in the light-grey area is nominally the responsibility of the relevant regional fisheries management organization.

However, mixing 'unreported' with 'illegal' fishing makes little sense: it is either illegal if the fishing vessel is mandated to report specific data and does not do so, or it is not illegal if there are no clear obligations to report, which is often the case. Much of the unreported catch is linked to the inevitable tendency of industrial fisheries, with their elaborate fishing gear, to catch a high ratio of bycatch to targeted catch. Often, it is not illegal to catch species for which a vessel does not have a licence or quota. Often, bycatch is not reported because vessels are not required to do so. But it is rampant. As with all fishing statistics, estimates of unreported catch must be treated with caution. However, one study suggested that unreported catch averages 53% of reported catch, mostly due to discarded bycatch.[31] In other words, unreported catch is more than a third of the total catch.

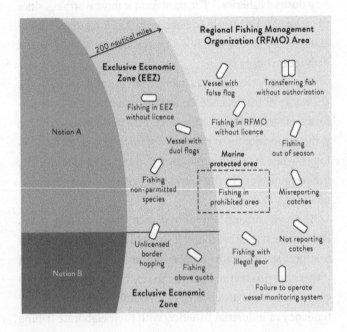

Unregulated fishing may also occur on the high seas, outside any Exclusive Economic Zone (EEZ) or Regional Fishing Management Organization (RFMO) area.

National Intelligence Council, *Global Implications of Illegal, Unreported and Unregulated Fishing* (Washington, DC: Office of the Director of National Intelligence, September 2016).

Meanwhile, according to another study, unreported catches that are sold could be worth $9-17 billion a year in traded value, costing economies anything from $26 billion to $50 billion by diverting revenue from the 'legitimate' trade system.[32]

Further confusion arises in defining what is 'unregulated'. The usual definition covers vessels flagged to states that do not cooperate with regional fisheries management organizations (RFMOs), as well as vessels operating in fisheries that are not well managed according to international norms. Although some studies on IUU fishing try to measure all three aspects, most focus on illegal or unreported fishing. Things become even more confusing when you realize that much of the world's commercial fishing is both unregulated and unreported, not because this is what fishers want, but because of a failure of fishery management.

The conventional narrative uses IUU as an adjective for certain fishing vessels, also called 'pirate fishing vessels', and there are numerous 'IUU fishing vessel' lists. This creates an artificial divide – goodies and baddies.[33] In reality, there are few industrial fishing companies that could honestly claim to be saintly, and almost all could meet the definition for inclusion on these lists. Listing is political, often decided by RFMOs, which typically represent the main fishing nations and industrial fisheries.

The conventional narrative also suggests that IUU fishing is down to a minority (although a sizeable number) of deviant fishing companies. It assumes that if we can catch the baddies then the industrial fishing sector will be managed by good sustainable companies. Catching the baddies is to be done with the assistance of the goodies. This perspective is based on a law-enforcement model that assumes that corporate crime is caused by a few bad apples and needs a strong law-enforcement approach with the assistance of industry groups. In fisheries, law enforcement is political, and in the rush to 'fight IUU fishing', state and corporate interests have tended to bend laws and the enforcement of them to their advantage. Tough law-enforcement approaches are frequently the cause of human rights abuses and unfair victimization. The big countries most often get away with it.

For one thing, illegal fishing is treated as a civil offence, not a criminal one that would involve a real threat of incarceration for skippers and owners. Instead, punishments tend to be fines or confiscations that companies can easily afford or evade. However, a carding system introduced by the EU in 2010, based on soccer's yellow and red cards for rule infringements, is having some success in getting countries to tackle illegal fishing more vigorously. As of early 2021, twenty-seven countries had been yellow-carded, while six had received red cards since 2010.

Red-carded countries – Cambodia, the Comoros, and St Vincent and the Grenadines in 2021 – are banned from supplying EU markets. Countries with yellow cards – in 2021 Cameroon, Ecuador, Liberia, Panama, Sierra Leone, St Kitts and Nevis, Trinidad and Tobago, and Vietnam – are put on notice that they must do more to comply with international rules to combat IUU fishing or face red-card listing. Most yellow-carded countries have had their 'pre-identification' revoked within two to three years, after being judged to have sufficiently addressed concerns.

There have been calls for the USA and Japan to issue cards jointly with the EU, which would make this system more powerful and effective.

The trouble with the EU scheme is that it is being used against smaller and weaker countries, while China has escaped censure.[34] Ranked the worst of 152 countries for its record on IUU fishing, China is the second-biggest exporter of fish products to Europe after Norway, accounting for 7% of total value.[35] Is Europe intimidated? It seems the EU issues 'red cards' to small coastal states, but would not consider doing so to China, or to coastal states with which it has lucrative fishing agreements.

It is easy to explain the growth of illegal fishing. Because fish populations have been shrinking and the demand for fish has been escalating, prices have risen sharply. Tuna, for example, used to be a low-cost fish; now it is a luxury, the better varieties selling for extraordinary prices. In January 2021, the owner of a Japanese sushi restaurant chain paid a record $3.1 million at auction for a 278-kg tuna caught off the northern Japan coast. Accordingly, the economic return to illegal fishing has gone up. Against that, the risk of being caught is not high, and the penalties if caught have been modest or negligible relative to the income to be gained.

Illegal fishing hits licensed fisheries because those fishing illegally typically operate at lower cost. For example, industrial vessels that fish illegally tend to hire workers in virtually slave-like conditions, many lured into debt bondage. They are also associated with other crime, such as bribery of port inspectors, money laundering and fraud. Among the challenges for regulators is that vessels are only weakly constrained by RFMO boundaries. Some illegal vessels regularly change colour, name and flag state, making it hard for RFMOs to keep identification records or to apprehend them. And there has been a failure to design and enforce a system of registration of beneficial owners, who often hide behind shell corporations. Attempts to use documentation schemes to identify them have been hampered by forged documents, misreporting and shifts of boats to an RFMO area where they are not listed. It is all an elaborate game.

One revealing example of the feeble response to illegal fishing, known as the *Volga* Case, came before the International Tribunal for the Law of the Sea (ITLOS) in 2002. The Australian authorities had arrested and compounded a Russian-flagged vessel fishing illegally in the Antarctic region and said they would only release the vessel if the beneficial owner was disclosed. The Russian government objected, and the Tribunal ruled that it was not reasonable to require information about a beneficial owner. In setting the boat free, the ITLOS ruling supported state collusion in IUU fishing. The Russians clearly had something to hide, and ITLOS allowed them to do so.

Problems in tackling IUU fishing also arise because of the difficulty of coordinating the layers of authorities, within and across nations.[36] And detecting illegal activity in the vast expanse of oceans is a challenge, since fishing per se is legal and fish are an easily transformable commodity, making identification of their source and type, if filleted, hard if not impossible.

In 2001, FAO members agreed on a voluntary code known as the International Plan of Action to Prevent, Deter and

Eliminate IUU Fishing. It is not enforceable or legally binding. This was followed in 2009 by the binding Agreement on Port State Measures to Prevent, Deter and Eliminate Illegal, Unreported and Unregulated Fishing, which finally came into force in 2016. This agreement asserts extra-territorial jurisdiction over foreign vessels by controlling use of 'ports of convenience' to offload illegally caught fish, denying access to ports, prohibiting landing and transhipments, and making more inspections of suspect vessels. It is a step in the right direction. However, many countries are not signatories and do not have port regulations. By early 2021, sixty-nine countries and the European Union had ratified the Agreement, but that left seventy coastal nations not signed up, including China, which operates fourteen of the fifteen busiest fishing ports.[37]

Another effort to combat illegal fishing is the International Monitoring Control and Surveillance (IMCS) Network for Fisheries-Related Activities, which aims to improve information collection and sharing among its seventy member countries and institutions. However, its activities have been dogged by its lack of legitimacy within the FAO. Like the other measures taken so far, it is partial and voluntary. In short, the regulatory governance of IUU fishing is clearly ineffectual.

Many of those concerned about IUU fishing put their faith in better monitoring and tracking of fishery vessels, of which there are 4.6 million around the world. Some have called for the compulsory onboard use of electronic monitoring equipment as a mandatory condition for access to EEZs.[38] Others hope that an automatic identification system (AIS) could track the 40,000 or so large-scale vessels over 100 tons. According to Global Fishing Watch, a platform leading this initiative (partially funded by Leonardo DiCaprio),

> We are revolutionising the ability to monitor the global commercial fishing fleet, offering near real-time tracking of fishing activity via a public map, for free, to track fishing boats and download data about their past and present activities.

Unfortunately, boats can switch off the AIS in questionable locations. In one notorious case, about 1,000 Chinese industrial fishing vessels entering North Korean waters turned off their automatic identification systems while catching large quantities of squid.[39] AIS signals can be manipulated to disguise temporarily identity and location. And trackers cannot tell if vessels are fishing illegally when most governments do not publish information on licences. The emphasis on tracking and monitoring also assumes that IUU fishing is the principal cause of unsustainable and inequitable fishing whereas, as we shall see, much 'legal' fishing is highly damaging and cannot simply be 'policed away'.

State-corporate collusion

The international focus on IUU fishing threatens to divert attention from the biggest challenge of all: systemic state-corporate collusion and tolerated unethical practices. The most obvious of these relate to bribery, extortion and embezzlement, often seen as 'the cost of doing business' and frequently benefiting both sides. The industry is rife with opportunities for corruption at all levels, from skippers and port officials to corporate leaders and government ministers.[40]

For instance, few African countries publish or audit information on payments for licences or fines, so these can go missing with little risk of detection.[41] In Senegal, out-of-court settlements to speed up cases are open to abuse. On the other side, fishing firms that pay bribes gain from being allowed to circumvent the rules, a mutually beneficial outcome. In a corrupt environment, vessel owners can rationalize paying bribes because a weak state means 'everyone does it'. And an environment characterized by bribery and embezzlement is conducive to other crime.

Corruption is only part of the crimogenic state-corporate setup. Regulatory capture often explains weak management rules and state failure to control illegal or criminal activities. In Chile, for instance, where illegal overfishing and conflicts between corporates and small-scale fishers have been endemic, weak rules on access and overfishing are the result of intense lobbying by powerful fishing firms with ties to political elites.[42] This has enabled a cartel of firms to protect themselves from potential competitors and exceed quota limits with impunity; the regulatory agency has simply refused to impose sanctions.

It is not always powerful firms who gain from special dispensations; occasionally, fisheries management is captured by small-scale fishing interests and environmental groups.[43] In India, for example, government authorities normally side with powerful business interests in conflicts between trawlers and small-scale fishing communities. But in the run-up to elections, they suddenly side with small-scale fishing communities, as important sources of votes.[44] The support does not last long. In Senegal too, these political dynamics have been clear in commitments by politicians to revoke licences for foreign trawlers just before elections. Yet overtures to politicians are mostly ineffectual. The power of votes from small-scale fishers in African countries as a counter to corporate interests is undermined by weak democracies and because fisheries remain peripheral in deciding most elections.

Regulatory capture by corporate capital reflects the subordination of the state, even if it is often personalized. The role of political elites in extractive and other industries is ubiquitous in Africa, but not only there. Political and economic power are intertwined. In fisheries, national policy encourages (via tax incentives) or mandates (via fisheries law) joint ventures between foreign and local businesses, as in Senegal, Namibia, Mauritania, Mozambique and Angola.

Foreign partners can contribute capital and expertise, and support integration of domestic firms in the commercial sector, historically dominated by foreign companies. But the ideal local partners are those offering political influence. Lack of competitive tendering for joint ventures, or for fishing quotas needed to set them up, increases the advantage of access to insider knowledge by those in government. Thus, in South Africa and Namibia, indigenization of commercial enterprises historically dominated by colonists is part of a narrative of postcolonial transition, yet it does little to undermine business interests or help marginalized groups.[45] It has transferred control from one elite to another.

There are many variants of the theme. In the 1990s in Mozambique, where the prawn trawling sector was dominated by Japanese and Spanish companies, the policy of insisting that companies form joint ventures to access quotas was a way of enriching members of the government and the security forces.[46] Former President Armando Guebuza, nicknamed 'Mr Guebusiness', who built a business empire in Mozambique and southern Africa, has substantial interests in fisheries first acquired when he was Minister for Transport and Ports.[47] The involvement of Guebuza and senior military officials in ownership of joint-venture shrimp fishing companies was allegedly one reason why shrimp quotas were set too high and why allocation of fishing rights was concentrated among a few large firms.[48]

Guebuza is just one well-documented case of close links between politicians and the fishing industry that reflect conflicts of interest and help to explain institutional failures that facilitate harmful corporate behaviour. Political elites may intervene in the work of fishing authorities or may quietly undermine them by starving them of resources or moral support. Meanwhile, those responsible for regulating fishing vessels may be inhibited by knowing that their actions may hurt powerful interests and thus lead to career-destroying retribution.

Reflecting the hypocrisy in the treatment of commercial fishing activities, governments of distant-water fishing fleets rarely prosecute or punish their own firms for illegality in foreign waters or help host countries in their investigations. In some cases, boats have evaded prosecution or escaped with reduced fines due to pressure exerted by the home government. In Senegal, for example, the Russian government has used various tactics, including bullying of officials, threats of litigation and financial inducements, to advance the interests of its firms and avoid regulation or prosecution.

For their part, governments of host countries hold back from harsh punishment of foreign firms to maintain smooth diplomatic relations or foreign investment in other sectors, such as mining or the military.

There is ample evidence of how rich countries act unethically to further their fishing companies' interests abroad. The most common avenue is through bribes or gifts in negotiating bilateral access agreements, including 'goods-and-services' contracts that conceal gifts, as was documented in relation to tuna fishing agreements in the Pacific region.[49] Foreign negotiators also influence outcomes by providing first-class air tickets for officials and their spouses to attend meetings, accompanied by generous per diems, lavish hotel accommodation and entertainment, and even overseas tuition fees for the children of ministers.[50]

Most fishing nations, including Japan, South Korea and Taiwan, also make development aid conditional on fisheries access.[51] Russia's latest fisheries agreements with Senegal and other West African countries have used development aid to persuade host governments to grant access that contradicts fisheries regulations and threatens the sustainability of other parts of the fisheries sector. In Ghana, where Chinese companies are active in fisheries and other extractive industries, the Chinese state paid for four patrol vessels to fight illegal fishing and oil-related piracy. The vessels were supplied by China Poly Group Corporation, one of China's largest weapon manufacturers, which is the parent company of Poly HonDon Pelagic Fishery.[52]

In Namibia, funds from the Spanish Cooperation Office (the main provider of Spanish overseas aid) were used to lobby the Namibian government to promote Spanish fishing interests.[53] In recent years Spain has given over €50 million for development projects in Namibia, which has dissuaded the Namibian government from signing access agreements with the EU. These would open Namibian waters to 'foreign' competition, that is, other EU member states engaged in distant-water fisheries, such as France. Here and elsewhere, a combination of domestic conflicts of interest, regulatory capture and foreign influence has shaped unethical and criminal corporate behaviour. This aspect of state-corporate crime is systemic.

Illicit behaviour of foreign fishing firms is supported by collusion and abuse of power between firms, host governments or political elites, and foreign governments. States and corporations are 'functionally interdependent'; the deviant actions of one usually occurs with assistance, either by omission or facilitation, from the other. The institutional setting that encourages or fails to stop deviance is created by the interests of firms, investors and states. Corporations do not contest imperfect institutions; they are integral to their creation.[54]

This is illustrated by the negotiations on tuna fishing access agreements between Pacific island states and distant-water fishing nations including Japan, South Korea and the EU. The resultant overfishing and skewed benefit-sharing were the outcome of intense political lobbying, coercion and innovative ways in which fishing companies responded to new regulations. The story testifies not just to uneven power relations between distant-water fishing nations and developing host nations but also to the ability of fishing fleets to strengthen their position in changing conditions, including lobbying home and host governments, and adjusting their production methods to circumvent regulations and shape management systems.[55]

The multiple strategies used by fishing companies in the face of regulatory change suggest that illegal fishing can be understood as profit-maximizing survival. 'Deviant' behaviour is an outgrowth of competitive and financially insecure fisheries, characterized by overcapacity, dwindling resources, increasing fuel and other costs, and volatile financial markets. Illegality is a tactic. In some cases, multinationals deploy older vessels to fish illegally (the cost of losing them being modest), while modern vessels are deployed elsewhere, perhaps even using eco-labels to improve market access.[56] Some vessels may catch legally for part of the year, illegally in others. Inside corporations, criminality may be evident to different degrees within subsidiary companies or individual boats.

Other forms of corporate crime, seen in private military groups and the banking sector, indicate how larger companies organize criminality. They may outsource more criminal ventures to others less vulnerable to detection or reputational damage, or launder the proceeds through supply chains in ways that support the financial stability of otherwise law-abiding enterprises. These sorts of dynamics are found in some fisheries sectors, including global tuna fisheries.[57] The 'pirates' may be the most visible part of crimogenic business, but focusing on them distracts from bigger threats.

The next two sections consider the most egregious cases of dubious morality and legality perpetrated by the Russian and Chinese states. But all the powerful fishing nations are complicit. For instance, Indian Ocean yellowfin tuna has been described as the worst managed yellowfin stock in the world.[58] The responsible regional fisheries management organization is the Indian Ocean Tuna Commission (IOTC), a collection of regional coastal states and distant-water fishing nations. In 2014, its scientific committee recommended a 20% cut in the annual catch of yellowfin tuna if there was to be a 50% chance of recovery. The IOTC compromised on an 'interim' 15% and then allowed fisheries to cut by less still. Predictably, in the following year total catches of yellowfin tuna went up, not down. Even by 2017, the EU's long-distance fisheries operating in the Indian Ocean had only cut catches by 5%. There was no sanction for breaching the rule.

In April 2019, the South African government complained to the European Commission that the Spanish long-distance fleet's tuna catch in the Indian Ocean had been under-reported and that their catch had been 12% higher in 2017 than the average of the preceding five years. A subsequent investigation by the Commission found that in 2018 the Spanish fleet had exceeded their legal quota by 30%, or nearly 9,000 tonnes.[59] Yet the only punishment imposed on the Spanish fisheries by the Commission was to reduce their total allowable catch in 2019 by the amount of the 2018 excess. By not imposing a proper penalty, the Commission effectively allowed illegal fishing to continue. The penalty should have been sufficiently stiff to deter both the offenders and others who might be tempted. Instead, the outcome illustrated the EU's hypocrisy in condemning illegal fishing.

Russia: scrambling for resources

When the Soviet Union collapsed in 1991, so did its fisheries and the mix of fishing access and joint-venture agreements it had negotiated with a number of developing countries between the 1950s and 1980s. Russian fish catches fell by 50%, and many of the 2,500 Russian vessels fell into chronic disrepair.[60]

In the 1990s, as 'shock therapy' was imposed on the Russian Federation, the regulatory state withered. The reform strategy pushed by the USA and its allies, through the World Bank and other international agencies, was to privatize the economy while shrinking the state. Salaries of politicians and civil servants crashed to levels well below subsistence. The free-for-all that followed enriched a kleptocracy that developed into a thuggish oligarchy, epitomized by the rise to political power of Vladimir Putin. The revival of Russia as a global fishing force took place within that mould, as billionaires moved easily into shipping and global fisheries. Shadowy figures emerged as owners of giant supertrawlers that flouted morality and laws.

Meanwhile, the post-Soviet government set out to revive fishing access agreements, particularly in Africa, and subsidized the construction of a new generation of supertrawlers and a predatory fishing fleet. The resurgence of Russian fishing in West Africa has been part of the country's 'scramble for Africa's resources' as a major player in its extractive industries.[61] In 2009, Moscow announced a $2.5 billion investment in its fishing industry, which helped to fund new fisheries agreements in West Africa.

A feature of Russia's fishing agreements is their secrecy, or lack of transparency. Senegal's experience, which happens to be unusually well documented, is likely to be characteristic.[62] Facing the Atlantic Ocean, Senegal has long been West Africa's largest producer of marine fish. Recorded exports rose from 500,000 tonnes in 1950 to a peak in the early 2000s of 5.5 million tonnes.[63] By the mid-2000s, the fisheries sector employed some 60,000 fishers, over 90% of them working in the small-scale sector, with an additional 540,000 people engaged in related services and trade. About 17% of the labour force depended on marine fisheries for their livelihood.[64]

For several decades, most foreign fishing firms operated under bilateral access agreements, with the EU signing its first in 1979, later joined by agreements with China and the Soviet Union. However, in 2005 Senegal decided to reject all bilateral agreements and instead, through tax incentives, encourage foreign firms to establish joint-venture partnerships with Senegalese firms.

Artisan fishers have mostly targeted small pelagic species, such as sardines and mackerel, which enter Senegalese waters in large numbers between December and May. But these shoals also attracted industrial trawlers owned by companies from Europe, Russia and Asia, many over 100 metres long and capable of catching up to 250 tonnes of fish a day. Such is the scale of the nets that fish are not landed on board by hauling them in but are pumped up in vacuum pipes. Moreover, big trawlers net huge bycatch, including other commercially or locally important species. Thus, the impact of supertrawlers goes beyond excess catches of small fish, threatening a country's entire fishing industry.

By the late 1990s it was clear that small pelagics were being overfished, and authorizations for industrial vessels targeting them were phased out. However, Senegal still allowed industrial fishing for high-value demersal species (bottom-dwelling fish) and migratory tuna and billfish, for export. And the suspension of foreign small-pelagic fishing did not end the decline of its all-important fishing sector. It has suffered prolonged chronic overcapacity, partly stimulated by government investment in local fisheries development, including generous fuel and boat-building subsidies. This has led to migration by Senegalese fishers to other West African countries, while the Senegalese government has negotiated bilateral access agreements with Mauritania, Gambia, Guinea-Bissau and Cape Verde to enable its fishers to fish legally in their waters.

The 2000s saw illegal fishing become pervasive, with industrial boats operating in restricted areas, and both industrial and artisanal boats using banned fishing gear (such as ultra-fine nets) and misreporting catches. One 2010 study estimated that illegal fishing in Senegalese waters equalled 35% of the official reported catch.[65]

Overcapacity and illegal fishing forced local fishers to spend more time at sea though catching less; the fish caught were smaller, and some once abundant species became hard to find. Fisheries laid off employees and downsized, and the number of pirogues (fishing canoes) fell by half. Prices, particularly for the small pelagic species that dominate local markets, rose sharply. And lower catches and rising prices threatened the food security of millions of Senegalese, for whom fish was the main source of animal protein.

Against this background, in 2010, it was discovered that

the Minister of Maritime Affairs had authorized foreign supertrawlers, mostly Russian or Russian-owned, to target small pelagic species, despite the dire state of local fisheries.[66] The circumstances surrounding these authorizations, the first in more than ten years, were not made public; local fishing organizations claimed the authorizations were illegal, and there were suggestions that political pressure and/or bribes had been involved behind the scenes. Before the authorizations were granted, the Senegalese National Institute for Fisheries Research had recommended a 50% *reduction* of fishing of small pelagic stocks to stem overfishing. Yet the foreign vessels' fishing capacity was several times that of the whole Senegalese fleet.

Later, it was argued that the authorizations fell under a protocol signed between Russia and Senegal. However, the protocol, subsequently leaked to local NGOs, did not include access to fish for Russian boats. It was an agreement to provide development assistance to Senegal, including research and support for combating illegal fishing. In turn, the agreement was outcome of a military cooperation pact signed in 2007. At the time, the Russian foreign minister, Sergey Lavrov, said 'our wish is to sign a fishing accord with Senegal' and suggested it could be structured on EU fishing access agreements linking access to financial aid for fisheries development. The two foreign ministers issued a joint statement, stating that 'the private sector must be the engine of their co-operation' and that 'fishing is a priority sector which will be very profitable for the two countries'.[67]

This was not the only such arrangement. In 2011, Russia signed a similar confidential protocol with the Guinea-Bissau government, apparently worth €15 million.[68] It too was ostensibly directed to capacity-building and combating illegal fishing, but it allowed Russian trawlers access to Guinea-Bissau's waters. It was also in contradiction with national laws; Guinea-Bissau law restricts trawler size to 2,000 gross registered tonnage (GRT), but the Russian fleet operating in West Africa consists of boats two or three times as large. As with Senegal, this was not the first fishing agreement between Guinea-Bissau and Russia. In the 1980s, the Soviet Union paid the government for fishing access, known to be a swap deal involving the supply of Soviet military equipment.

In Senegal, information about how many trawlers were given licences emerged only gradually in the public domain after persistent pressure from representatives of local fishers. Over a two-year period, the number of authorizations for supertrawlers reached forty-four, although only twenty-nine did any fishing before their licences were revoked in 2012. Fifteen of the trawlers were flying the Russian flag, with the others flagged to Belize (ten), Peru (five), Lithuania (three), Latvia (two), and one each from the Comoros, Georgia, Vanuatu and the Faroe Islands. A majority of the owners were Russian. And most of the boats had been in the Soviet Union's fishing fleet, taken over by Russian and former Soviet oligarchs after being privatized and fragmented in the 1990s.

Licence fees in Senegal are normally based on 30% of the landed price of the catch, and the international market value of small pelagic fish at the time was about 400 CFA a kilo. Yet the foreign trawlers were asked to pay only 17 CFA a kilo, just over 4% of the market value. The fisheries ministry reported that the government was set to receive five billion

CFA (€7.6 million) from licensing. That was a pittance, given that the trawlers could catch 300,000 tonnes during just one season, with a market value of €183 million.[69]

What is more, only a fraction of the licence money due reached the finance ministry, amid suspicion that the rest went towards President Abdoulaye Wade's 2012 unsuccessful re-election campaign. Wade's legacy was marred by claims that ministers had amassed fortunes. They included his son, who was later arrested and faced a highly publicized trial for unexplained wealth of $240 million.

Anger over the ecological and economic impact of the foreign boats led to strikes and a protest march in Dakar in March 2011. In April 2012, the new president, Macky Sall, announced that all licences for foreign trawlers had been revoked. A new fisheries minister promised an investigation. Sall himself gained international praise, receiving the prestigious Peter Benchley Award for ocean conservation in New York in April 2013. Yet hours later, he caused controversy by saying the licences were only suspended and that his government would allow the Russian vessels back.[70] His fisheries minister added that the licences had been suspended simply to allow a biological rest period and an assessment of fish stocks.

Senegal and Russia subsequently concluded a joint research operation to establish new data on fish stocks, and Russia announced it was offering free university scholarships for Senegalese fisheries officials, as well as vehicles, office equipment and other resources to help negotiate long-term access agreements in Senegal, which it was also offering to Mauritania, Morocco, Guinea-Bissau and Namibia.[71]

However, in early 2013, relations soured again, when

Senegal impounded a Russian trawler, *Oleg Naydenov*, for fishing illegally, and detained its crew of sixty Russians and twenty-three citizens of Guinea-Bissau. The trawler, whose Senegal licence had been revoked in 2012, was then part of a fleet granted licences by Guinea-Bissau under a bilateral agreement with Russia. Russia claimed the boat had been operating in the waters shared by Guinea-Bissau and Senegal when arrested and accused Senegal of 'piracy'. The *Oleg Naydenov* was eventually allowed to leave port after an out-of-court settlement, reportedly following a payment of $1 million by the owners, though the amount was not confirmed or accounted for.

In 2014, local organizations discovered that a new charter arrangement was being established for Russian vessels, this time through Africamer, Senegal's largest fish-processing company until it went into liquidation in 2011. At its peak, the company owned thirteen freezer-trawlers, processed 20,000 tonnes of fish annually, and employed 2,500 people. Yet while still in liquidation Africamer applied for ten new licences, ostensibly to give the company a supply of fish for processing and so restore its viability.[72] That this was clearly a Russian enterprise was made clear when Africamer was formally acquired in 2015 by a Russian-owned company, Flash Afrique Sea Products. As of December 2019, however, Africamer was still dormant.

The 2010 decision to grant fishing licences to Russian and other boats also affected relations with the European Commission and with Spain, the biggest beneficiary of EU access arrangements with developing countries. After Senegal's decision in 2005 not to renew a fisheries agreement with the

EU, there was a further attempt at renegotiation, and in 2007 the EU provided €6 million to the Senegal government to help fund fisheries development. So, news of the Russian agreement came as an unwelcome surprise.

In January 2010, the EU had introduced its 'red and yellow card' system to stop illegally caught fish entering the European market. The Commission said that if there was evidence of malpractice in Senegal's licensing decision, it would consider 'carding' the country for allowing illegal fishing. However, no card was ever issued, and the EU successfully reopened negotiations for a new fisheries partnership agreement covering tuna and black hake, initially signed in 2014 and renewed in 2019.

China: scouring the seas

The adverse impact of Russian fisheries is dwarfed by what China's mighty long-distance fishing fleet is doing to global fish populations and the blue commons more generally. Fisheries are one component of the 'going out' strategy. Vast subsidies have helped them expand globally and take pressure off the degraded China Sea.[73] Excess capacity has created a competitive environment where overfishing and rule-breaking are inevitable.

Much of China's expansion into the world's marine fisheries has been technically legal but morally dubious, involving not just 'unequal exchange' with developing countries and their fishing communities, but also unsustainable and damaging blue economy development. This applies particularly to its web of fishing access agreements, which exemplify the three illegitimate features of such agreements identified earlier: not paying for 'externalities', being quasi-private deals and underpaying resource use fees.

While the number of Chinese agreements in operation is unknown, they are numerous and spreading. In line with the concept of 'odious debt' – debt incurred against a country's true interest – the agreements could be characterized as 'odious leverage', foisted on developing countries as part of an integrated package that includes debt relief or infrastructural investment and loans linked to quite different economic spheres.

China has done little to help locals develop the capacity to catch, process and export the fish themselves. It has been a conspicuous feature of these agreements that, in return for access to the fish, it has financed non-fishery related investments in the country concerned, usually with its own firms and workers, such as constructing football stadia or other buildings, or in the case of Mauritania supplying military jets. According to one comparative review, Chinese agreements have never included financial contributions to support monitoring and surveillance or scientific research on fish stocks.[74]

An example of an odious deal is a confidential fisheries protocol signed in 2011 between the Mauritanian government and the giant Chinese state corporation, Poly HonDon Pelagic Fishery. Although there had been persistent rumours circulating among local NGOs about the agreement, it took a member of parliament to leak a copy to a journalist for the details to be confirmed. The journalist was arrested, prompting a successful international petition for his release. But the experience highlighted the immense difficulties facing local civil society in opposing such deals.

The protocol promised investment in local fisheries but gave remarkably generous fishing access to Chinese boats for no fewer than twenty-five years, as well as a tax holiday for the company.[75] The scale of authorized fishing increased overcapacity in several fishing areas, and the twenty-five-year period was much longer than EU agreements, which typically last five years. Poly HonDon was granted the right to set up a processing factory and bring in fifty fishing vessels, with an annual quota of 80,000 to 100,000 tonnes of fish (unspecified). Some of these boats are designed to target small pelagic fish, but some are semi-industrial trawlers that target coastal demersal species. The vessels use highly productive gear, including long lines with thousands of hooks, long trawling nets and complex traps for species such as octopus and lobster, long a mainstay of local small-scale fisheries.

By leaving it vague what types of fish could be taken or in what quantities, the agreement allowed the company to exploit the fishing potential as it saw fit. In return, the company pledged to invest $100 million in Mauritania's fishing sector, including building the fish-processing factory and support for local, small-scale fisheries. So, it was dressed up as an agreement that blended commercial interests with charitable contributions to help develop local fisheries.

Years later, the completed processing factory, exclusively used by Poly HonDon and claimed as the hub of China's largest overseas fishery base, is protected by a high wall and armed security guards. It does not look like a community empowerment investment and is resented by the local fishing community.[76] In 2020 a Mauritanian parliamentary enquiry commission accused Poly HonDon of breaking the terms of the agreement and pillaging the country's marine resources, listing 146 occasions of fishing in proscribed areas between 2017 and 2019.[77] Yet the government has insisted on maintaining the accord.

It is a feature of China's fisheries agreements that they are often just one component of a web of investment contracts and business deals. So it is perhaps no coincidence that other members of the Poly Group, Poly HonDon's parent company, have won contracts in Mauritania to build ports, roads and other infrastructure. And Poly HonDon, which is thought to have about 130 distant-water fishing vessels in all, has reportedly been negotiating with other African states for similar agreements, including a proposal for an 'industrial fisheries hub' on the island of Zanzibar, Tanzania.

One of China's largest state-owned corporations, the Poly Group has been described as 'the most important company you have never heard of'.[78] It is thought to be owned by the People's Liberation Army, and the chairman is a delegate of the National People's Congress, China's parliament.[79] The company is reported to be engaged in an extraordinary range of commercial enterprises, including armaments, mining, pharmaceuticals, real estate development and the art market. Amnesty International has implicated the Group in illicit arms trading to developing countries.[80] The USA imposed sanctions on it for its arms trade with Iran, North Korea and Syria, which are subject to international arms embargoes.[81] Still, the Poly Group has also become the supplier of choice for marine patrol vessels in Africa. For example, it has provided the navies of Ghana and Cameroon with boats to help combat piracy and illegal fishing,[82] and in 2016 it signed a deal to build three armed vessels for the South African government.[83]

Chinese agreements materialize without publicity or public consultation. By contrast, several announced agreements have never materialized. A press release from the China-Africa Forum held in Beijing in 2018 announced a ten-year fisheries agreement between a Chinese company, Taihe Century Investment Developments, and the Madagascar government. This was to allow a staggering 330 vessels access to Madagascar's waters in return for financial investment in fisheries of $2.7 billion. The press release described the deal as part of Madagascar's commitment to sustainable blue growth and was accompanied by a photo of the Chinese company's CEO signing the agreement in the presence of the president of Madagascar.[84]

Hardly anyone in Madagascar knew about it, including the ministers of environment and fisheries, both of whom denounced it. The deal sounded unbelievable; 330 vessels seemed far too many, while the investment was larger than anything ever seen in the fisheries sector. For over a year, civil society organizations in Madagascar and abroad opposed the deal, which included a letter to the president with over 20,000 signatories. The main criticism was that Chinese vessels would inevitably target fish in coastal zones, since Madagascar already had agreements with Chinese companies for offshore tuna and sharks that were being decimated by overfishing. Inshore fishing remained crucial for local small-scale fisheries.

Then it became apparent that the deal had collapsed after the president lost his re-election bid. It turned out the deal had been announced for political reasons.[85] However, in 2020 the new government signed two new fisheries agreements with Chinese companies, allowing thirty industrial vessels long-term access to Madagascar's waters.[86]

China's lending for port development as part of its Belt and Road Initiative is another way of gaining and improving access for Chinese fishing vessels. Thus, China is lending Sierra Leone $55 million to build an industrial fishing harbour and a processing plant ostensibly intended to boost the West African country's fish exports.[87] However, this will create valuable facilities for Chinese boats, which comprise three-quarters of Sierra Leone's deep-water fishing fleet. Local fishers, who provide 70% of fish for the domestic market, accuse the Chinese boats of exceeding catch limits and depleting the sardines, barracuda and grouper on which the locals depend. And there has been no environmental assessment of the risks to marine and other ecosystems, although the plan threatens 100 hectares of pristine beach and protected rainforest bordering a bay that is visited by whales and dolphins and is a key fish-breeding area.

China's murky deals are not only with African governments. In November 2020, the fisheries minister of Papua New Guinea (PNG) and China's trade minister announced an agreement in principle to build a fisheries industrial complex on the island of Daru, including a processing factory and a landing jetty for large vessels. The project was to be handled by Fujian Zhonghong Fishery Company with a budget of $200 million.

This is a contentious proposal, since impoverished Daru, with about 12,000 people, shares coastal waters with Australia.

Under the 1985 Torres Strait Treaty, indigenous communities are granted joint access to this region with Australian fishers. The arrangement seems to work, largely because Daru fishers are few and use traditional fishing methods. But Australian fishers believe the agreement is a back-door deal to allow Chinese vessels to assume Daru residency, and so enter the area legally flying the PNG flag. China has already used this tactic to increase 'legal' fishing, as in Ghana, where 90% of Ghanaian-flagged vessels were found to have Chinese involvement in 2018.[88]

Access to the valuable lobster fishery is considered a primary motive, although the scale of investment suggests the company will build a facility that will suck in fish from a wider region. Others worry that fishing is not the main motive, and that Daru island will become a Chinese military base.[89] There has been no local consultation, with the mayor of Daru apparently unaware of the deal until he saw the government's press release.[90]

In addition to the web of fishing access agreements weaved by the Chinese state and its complex corporations, Chinese vessels have increasingly been involved in blatant and rapacious illegal fishing. China's illegal fishing for squid in North Korean waters is indicative of the depth of the crisis. Over 700 Chinese vessels were reportedly fishing there in 2019, in breach of UN sanctions policy. Squid populations have dived by 70%, driving small North Korean boats to fish further out in dangerous waters. Between 2015 and 2020 over 500 North Korean 'ghost boats' washed ashore in Japan containing the corpses of their crew. Such has been the death toll that some fishing communities are now called 'widows' villages'.[91]

In mid-2020, Ecuador raised the alarm when a flotilla of 340 Chinese vessels was found to be fishing just outside the EEZ surrounding the iconic Galapagos Islands, whose unique biodiversity inspired Darwin's theory of evolution. The fleet was mainly fishing for squid – essential to the diet of Galapagos fur seals and endangered scalloped hammerhead sharks – but also for tuna and billfish important for Ecuadorian fishers. Amid international outrage, the Chinese embassy declared that China had a 'zero tolerance' policy towards illegal fishing.[92] But Ecuador reported that nearly half the vessels had at some point switched off their satellite communications to prevent monitoring, and some had even changed their names.

'Going dark' by switching off transponders so their locations cannot be identified is a widely documented practice by Chinese vessels. Of the 300 or so boats fishing for squid in the South-West Atlantic Ocean near Argentina in February 2019, more than 250 had intermittently turned off their vessel tracking system, almost all of them flagged to China.[93] Like many other countries, Ecuador has a difficult balancing act in seeking to prevent unsustainable fishing off its coast while avoiding a confrontation with China, its largest financier and a major market for its shrimp exports.

And in another instance of rule-breaking, in December 2020 a Chinese vessel, along with six smaller boats working for it, was caught illegally harvesting sea cucumber – a delicacy known as bêche-de-mer in its dried form – off the tiny Micronesian archipelago of Palau in the Pacific. The quantity of sea cucumber had a market value of about $180,000, a lot for a small island economy. Palau, a pioneer in marine conservation, has banned all foreign commercial fishing.

In 2020 China tightened the rules against illegal fishing by its distant-water fleet, including harsher penalties for captains and companies.[94] For the first time, Chinese regulations emphasize sustainability, ban IUU fishing by name, and pave the way for China to fulfil its 2017 commitment to join the Port State Measures Agreement. They also require hourly transponder reporting and monitoring of high-seas transhipment, and introduce seasonal closures of squid fishing. Conservation groups welcomed the new rules, though it remains to be seen how strictly they will be enforced. In addition, some of the worst offenders, though Chinese-owned, are flagged to other states and operated through shell companies, away from China's direct jurisdiction. Most importantly, measures against IUU fishing, even if enforced more vigorously, do nothing to alter the state-corporate collusion and associated illegality that is the primary threat to fish populations and the blue commons.

In addition, China's voracious demand for fish and other marine life has encouraged illegal harvesting and overfishing by fishers of other nations and attracted criminal gangs. To give just a few examples, soaring prices for sea cucumbers – which are viewed as an aphrodisiac as well as a delicacy – have led to deadly violence in Mexico, involvement with the *yakuza* criminal organizations in Japan, smuggling between the Tanzanian mainland and Zanzibar, and poaching in the Lakshadweep archipelago off the south-west coast of India.[95] Illegal fishing with gillnets for Mexico's endangered totoaba fish, whose swim bladders fetch eye-watering prices in China as a supposed aphrodisiac, threatens a rare porpoise known as the vaquita marina with extinction.[96] And seizures of illegally harvested giant clam shells in the Philippines have been linked to demand from China's traditional ivory carving centres, now that trade in elephant ivory has been banned.[97] All these sea creatures play a vital role in marine ecosystems that support the livelihoods and wellbeing of coastal communities.

Flag hopping

Reflagging is part of many of the dirty deals that are driving fish populations and local commons towards extinction. Like other ships, fishing vessels can have one or more 'owners' and a choice of country where ownership is registered. A vessel owner can choose the flag state that will exercise jurisdiction over the vessel and can change this at will, a practice known as 'flag hopping'. As one commentator put it, 'There is probably no more compelling example of the cosmopolitan nature of today's fishing business than the possibility of ships using one flag to pick up government subsidies, another to get higher quota, yet another to employ banned fishing gear, and a further one to market the catch.'[98]

As noted in Chapter 1, flags of convenience – open registries that do not require domicile in the flagging country – are routinely used by ship owners to avoid taxes and regulations of their home state, including safety and environmental standards. They can also protect vessel owners from legal action or scrutiny by obscuring their identity. And the well-documented poor treatment of crews on flag of convenience vessels – including abandonment of crew members in foreign ports, forced labour and safety issues – underlines the links with illegal fishing and unfair competition, lowering labour costs and thus increasing profitability.[99]

In fisheries, a similar practice involves reflagging to countries that are not parties to regional fisheries management organizations that set rules on fishing methods and catch levels. These vessels can then opt out of management rules they would otherwise be bound by. A related phenomenon, noted in relation to China, is the reflagging of vessels to fish in the waters of countries where foreign boats are banned or restricted. In many developing countries, particularly in Africa and the Pacific, the national industrial fishing fleet is largely foreign owned and operated. Industrial fisheries formed and owned by locals are rare.

One investigation found that over 500 Chinese fishing vessels were flagged to African countries, while hundreds more were flagged to other countries, including flags of convenience.[100] Most of the Chinese vessels flagged to Africa are bottom trawlers that have the most destructive effects on seabeds and are most prone to operate with exploitative labour and safety standards. This adds to their competitive advantage over domestic small-scale fishers.

However, though the numbers are large, the share of Chinese distant-water vessels flagged to other countries is small – just over 5% of its 17,000 vessels, compared with 20% of fishing fleets on average globally. One reason is that there is little incentive to do so because of lax regulation by China, which is effectively its own flag of convenience![101]

The use of flags of convenience is highlighted by the outlandish case of the largest fish factory vessel in the world, 228 metres long or the length of two football pitches, capable of processing 547,000 tonnes of fish a year. Launched in 1980 in Japan as a Norwegian oil tanker, it was converted to a fish-processing vessel in China. It has so far been renamed seven times and has moved around the world under the flags of Peru, Belize, Moldova and, as of 2020, Russia, under the name *Vladivostok 2000*.

For a while the boat, then called *Lafayette*, was owned by China Fishery Group, a fishing giant that went spectacularly bankrupt in 2016 amid allegations of massive fraud (see next section). Its latest owner is DVS-R, a Singapore-based company controlled by the Russian fishing oligarch Dmitrii Dremliuga. In 2014, it was put on a list of IUU boats by the South Pacific Regional Fisheries Management Organisation (SPRFMO), and in 2015 was fined $800,000 for dumping waste in the sea and for illegal fishing. It never paid the fine. It was arrested again in Peru in 2018 but released a few months later after it promised to pay a reduced fine for its previous offence.

This persistent rogue activity demonstrates the weakness of international rules and institutions in controlling blatantly destructive and illegal activities. At least three member states of SPRFMO – China, Panama and the Cook Islands – have allowed this huge boat to dock in their ports, contrary to explicit rules of the Organisation. Out at sea, it continues to operate with impunity.

Much more could be done to combat flags of convenience and flag hopping. International rules should be tighter and enforced. The FAO operates a database of the world's fishing vessels, the Global Record of Fishing Vessels, Refrigerated Transport Vessels and Supply Vessels, that aims to include vessel, company and owner information and assign a unique vessel identifier (UVI) that remains the same throughout the vessel's life. UVIs, which are issued by the International Maritime Organization, are already compulsory for cargo and passenger ships above a certain size. However, nearly thirty years after such a global database was first mooted, it is still a work in progress, participation by states is voluntary, and just 23,000 vessels had been assigned UVIs as of early 2021.

National rules on reflagging have also been weak, as there is no legal obligation on countries to bar their nationals or companies from using flags of convenience or those of states that ignore international rules on IUU fishing. It is also worth pointing out that the practice was started by Western governments, and most registries are still operated by multinationals from OECD countries. The United States, which prohibits its citizens from involvement in IUU fishing anywhere in the world, is an outlier, though Japan, Australia and New Zealand also restrict their nationals from working on boats from certain flag states. However, the European Union has permitted its fishing vessels to reflag to non-EU countries as part of its effort to reduce overcapacity, only to find vessels hopping back to EU flag states when it suits them, to gain subsidies or fish in waters covered by EU access agreements.

Some of these returning boats were flagged to states the EU had identified as not doing enough to combat IUU fishing, and could be regarded as complicit.[102] In 2018, the EU tightened the rules for granting member-state flag authorizations to prevent abusive flag hopping, and clamped down on deals between EU nationals and third countries that allowed EU boats to continue to fish, outside the terms of EU fishing agreements, by reflagging to the relevant state. As of

2021, it was too early to say how effective these stricter measures will prove.

Financialization of amoral fishing

Finance, like flags of convenience, is accentuating the crimogenic character of the commercial fishing industry, making money from its profitable but amoral activities. To take one example, in 2010, the US-based international investment firm Carlyle Group invested $190 million in China Fishery Group. It reported to its shareholders that this would help the Chinese company expand in West Africa, which it described as having enormous money-making potential as a source of fish and a consumer market. In reality, the investment enabled more supertrawlers to enter a region already well known to be suffering chronic overfishing.

China Fishery Group was a subsidiary of Pacific Andes, a huge seafood conglomerate, which in 2016 filed for bankruptcy amid allegations of fraud of over $5 billion.[103] Aided by Carlyle's investment, China Fishery had invested in *Lafayette*, the world's largest fish-processing vessel, which operated mainly between West Africa and South America. Despite optimistic projections, the *Lafayette* apparently ran at a huge loss.[104] But it helped China Fishery in its plunder of developing-country fish stocks.

Another example, Mozambique's $2 billion 'tuna bond' scandal, has been described by a former World Bank anti-corruption expert as 'the most egregious corruption offence of the decade'.[105] In 2013 and 2014 Mozambique borrowed $1.4 billion from Credit Suisse and Russian bank VTB, tied to maritime security projects, alongside a $850 million bond arranged by the two banks to finance a tuna fishing fleet. The boats were purchased at a hugely inflated price that masked embezzlement and kickbacks.

As of 2021, the scandal was the subject of several ongoing court cases and criminal investigations in the USA, the UK, Switzerland and Mozambique. Corruption and money laundering charges had been brought against bank officials, employees of a Gulf shipbuilding company, the former Mozambican finance minister, Manuel Chang, and more than a score of others, including the son of former President Armando Guebuza. US Department of Justice prosecutors alleged that those charged had 'created maritime projects that conducted little to no legitimate business activity to funnel at least $200 million in bribes and kickbacks to themselves, Mozambican government officials and others'.[106]

The bank loans were questionable from the start and surely qualify as 'odious debt' that should not have to be repaid. They were taken out in secret by Mozambican state-owned companies, without the legally required approval of the Mozambique parliament, and backed with hidden government guarantees. The discovery of the loans by the IMF in 2016, when it was due to make an emergency loan to the impoverished country, prompted donor countries and the World Bank to cut off aid. After its debt rating was downgraded, Mozambique plunged into economic crisis and debt default. Its total debt at that point amounted to 85% of GDP.

The $850 million 'tuna bond' itself was not secret, since it was designed to attract investors, but the circumstances aroused early suspicions. Guaranteed by the Mozambican government and paying 8.5% interest over six years, it was the sole backing for the launch of a tuna fishing company, EMATUM. About a third of the money was to buy thirty vessels; the remainder was for fish-processing factories and training.[107]

Ownership was split between government and military agencies, although it was a private corporation. There was no competitive tendering for the shipbuilding contract, or public documentation on how the money would be spent. The country was exposed to financial risk, yet no due diligence was shown. Although foreign donors threatened to end budgetary support unless there was more transparency, they did not follow through with their threat, possibly because they wanted to maintain good relations with a country then experiencing a mining boom.

The lack of transparency, the inflated value of the bond (much more than needed), and the speed at which the deal was completed were all points of concern, especially as the confidential investor prospectus was only three pages. *The Economist* noted that investors were aware that EMATUM was a risky venture, but 'know there are huge gas reserves off the shores of Mozambique that will eventually bring in lots of foreign exchange, even if tuna does not'.[108] They were also prepared to fund a company that would add to overfishing, notably of sharks and billfish that would be caught alongside tuna. Once again, we see fish populations being treated as collateral damage in the pursuit of growth and profits.

Fishing agents

Fishing access agreements, flags of convenience and global finance are the external factors shaping an inherently criminal industry. It takes mechanisms inside countries with rich fishing waters to complete the process. Just as the trading of flags is a mechanism for rent-seeking, so other forms of intermediation generate rental income for their practitioners. In many countries, intermediaries known as fishing agents play a crucial role in the amoral commercialization of marine life, linking foreigners unfamiliar with the local language and culture with opportunistic bureaucrats and politicians.

The fishing agent is a powerful personality in fisheries, particularly in much of Africa. Very little has been written about fishing agents in Africa, and virtually nothing about their activities in other areas of the world. But their role is widely regarded as problematic. In a different framework, they could have been gatekeepers helping to defend the commons. Instead, they have been instrumental in destroying the blue commons. They represent 'regulatory capture', as brokers for the rentiers and rent-seekers, and are themselves a source of corruption and unethical business practices.

Agents play a critical role in facilitating the operations of industrial fishing in Africa. All vessels use at least one agent, if not more. And in most African countries, the use of a nationally based agent by a foreign-flagged fishing vessel is obligatory in law.[109] In EU fisheries agreements with African countries, the use of a local agent for vessel owners is also mandatory. This has opened the way for endemic corruption, fuelled by informal payments by foreign industrial fisheries to local agents.

The history of fishing agents in West Africa began in the early 1980s, when the extension of territorial waters by UNCLOS coincided with intensification of industrial fishing and growth in the number of foreign vessels. Previously, industrial fishing had been dominated by state-owned companies from the Soviet Union and by European vessels operating under bilateral or quasi-private access agreements negotiated between governments.

The 1980s also saw implementation of 'structural adjustment' policies imposed by the international financial institutions that cut state bureaucracies and weakened regulatory oversight. In some coastal countries, prolonged civil conflict further enfeebled state capacities. Soon, hundreds of large vessels, many from Asia, were invading the waters of countries with barely functioning administrations, ineffective legislation and inadequate resources for securing compliance with what laws there were.

Staff in local fishery authorities, who had previously relied on funds from bilateral agreements, endured prolonged periods of no pay. The situation was ripe for the entry of new commercial actors, who saw an opportunity to make money by acting as go-betweens for fisheries and governments. Today, agents provide a wide range of services: organizing licence acquisition, arranging vessel inspections, recruiting crews, providing food and water supplies for vessels, arranging refuelling, passing information between vessels and the authorities, and even removing rubbish from vessels when they are in port. Some agents have become companies providing all these services to several large vessels on a regular basis. More commonly, vessel operators use different agents for different services. Some agents focus on the lucrative business of obtaining licences, subcontracting other services to specialists.

Even under bilateral access agreements, individual

fisheries will pay a local agent to obtain licences and may expect the agent to keep a licence on their behalf. European vessels have reportedly been paying €1,500 a year to agents for this service, beyond what they pay for the licence itself. Indeed, there have been reports that some owners have been charged over €10,000 a year. In short, a successful agent makes considerable revenue.

Although most agents are locals, some foreign agents have also set up in business. Even diplomats have dabbled in remunerative sidelines. For some years, the Spanish consul in Guinea-Bissau was the business contact for Spanish vessels, facilitating the purchase of licences and offering informal diplomatic services.

In some countries, such as the Seychelles, agents are registered and certified. In others their legal status is unclear, and they operate in an informal manner. For example, Dutch vessels operating in Mauritanian waters have reportedly been using one local agent for years without any formal contract. This seems widespread.

Is this institutionalized corruption? Agents do appear to provide a useful service or set of services that benefit the fisheries and the local authorities. As one fishery representative from Europe pointed out, 'To work without an agent in countries like Angola or Guinea would be impossible.'[110] For local authorities, it is useful to have a local contact in communication with foreign companies that are rarely in their ports. For many vessels, all dealings with the authorities are handled by their agent, including the reporting of their catches and days of fishing.

Nevertheless, there are serious conflicts of interest and

potential for corruption. Many successful agents were formerly employees of fishery departments or senior politicians
or military personnel. Some are even still in these positions.
In 2015, the Seychellois executive secretary of the Indian
Ocean Tuna Commission, which is based in the Seychelles,
was forced to resign when it was found that he had established
a fishing agent company offering services to tuna fisheries out
of the Seychelles. He had transferred ownership of the company to his wife in an attempt to cover up his double role as
both regulator and agent. However, during an investigation by
Interpol of an incident in which up to five alleged Somali pirates were shot in cold blood, his company was found to have
licensed the Taiwanese fishing vessel involved.[111]

Many countries have long-standing arrangements under
which fees paid to agents are shared with members of the
local authorities as illegal, institutionalized kickbacks. This
has been a source of considerable income, supplementing
depressed wages. In 2019, the director of fisheries in one
country was on a monthly salary of $500; others had even
lower salaries.

Embezzlement of fishing licence fees has also been
widespread. In countries such as São Tomé and Príncipe,
Guinea-Bissau, Tanzania and Mozambique, some vessels
have reportedly paid licence fees and fines directly into the
personal accounts of senior officials. More often, however,
agents act as intermediaries, taking their cut in the process.
This is unlikely to be happening without the knowledge of
the fishing vessels involved. EU tuna fishing vessels have
been paying millions of euros to agents in some countries,
knowing full well they were financing kickbacks to officials.

This would put them in breach of their home countries' laws on paying bribes in a foreign country but there is no sign that anyone in the chain of activities has attempted to regulate or penalize what has been happening.

Some EU vessel owners, and some countries such as Mauritania, have tried to prevent corruption by insisting that licence fee payments are made only into the central bank. This may have limited the flow of money going to corrupt officials, but it also seems to have led agents to come up with more innovative ways of obtaining illicit cash, increasing the cost of their other services to compensate.

In Liberia, the law requires vessels to pay for annual inspections, which normally take half a day. But the inspections must be organized through agents, who reportedly invoice inspection fees for four days and charge a daily rate for each inspector of €300, on top of costs for flights, hotel accommodation and food. As a result, vessels can pay agents €5,000 for one inspection. In one instance, Spanish and French operators discovered that they were paying the same agent and the same inspectors for the same days! And where vessel inspections are a means of corruption, the inspections themselves are unlikely to be honest or proper.

Another lucrative activity for agents and government officials involves out-of-court settlements for fisheries offences. Even exorbitant payments may be preferable to long court cases, plus possible IUU listing by international organizations and risk of confiscation of the vessel. In 2009 the authorities in Guinea-Bissau arrested a Panamanian oil tanker and two Spanish fishing vessels for refuelling at sea without authorization. The owners of the tanker, *Virginia G*, claimed that the refuelling was done outside Guinea-Bissau's territorial waters and the court case dragged on for several years.

The crew of the tanker were detained for fourteen months, although the Spanish boats and their crews were released the day after the arrest. The case eventually went to the International Tribunal for the Law of the Sea. In evidence to the Tribunal, the tanker owners said its captain had been told by the skippers of the two fishing vessels that they had paid the local agent, that is, the Spanish consul, €100,000 for their release, which was then allegedly transferred to the private bank account of a senior security official.[112]

More generally, the most successful agents work closely with government officials, and often the latter recommend specific agents to the vessel owners. Relationships are not always amicable. The head of Mauritania's fisheries inspection service between 2005 and 2010, Cheikh Ould Baya, was widely known to be pocketing nearly 50% of the sums paid in penalties, which may have amounted to as much as €10 million a year. This enabled him to become one of the wealthiest businessmen in the country, with investments in fishmeal processing among others, and an influential adviser to the fisheries minister, including in negotiations with the EU on access to Mauritanian waters in 2015.[113] In 2018, he became president of the National Assembly.

Baya later claimed the penalty share was legal and was for the entire team of inspectors, though former inspectors denied receiving anything. And when the agent liaising with the EU fleet wrote a newspaper article detailing the scale of the scam, two vessels using that agent were arrested on a bogus charge. Owners of the fishing fleet were 'recommended' to use another agent, who, they were told, would also ensure that their trawlers could circumvent laws on fishing restrictions close to shore. Presumably mindful of EU rules, the fisheries rejected this illegal offer and refused to change their agent.[114]

In Mauritania and elsewhere, agents also play a shadowy role in the recruitment of domestic crews for foreign vessels. Vessels needing to pick up local crews use agents, which provides more opportunities for kickbacks, such as recruiting untrained or poorly trained people prepared to pay them to be hired, as well as through imposing abusive labour contracts. The tuna industry now vets all contracts provided by agents for local crews, but this is not usual for demersal trawlers.

EU fisheries say agents often offer them attractive licences, which, as in Mauritania, may help them avoid regulations such as prohibitions on fishing in restricted zones where only artisanal and semi-industrial fishing is allowed. In Gabon, an agent claimed to offer licences allowing industrial boats to use at-sea supply vessels, prohibited under the EU-Gabon access agreement. Other vessels fishing through private agreements in Gabon apparently had licences supplied by the agent. Sometimes these deals are scams, such as one that offered French tuna companies licences for purse-seine vessels in the Maldives, where they are banned. But there is clearly an incentive for agents to supply industrial fisheries with permits to undertake damaging fishing.

In 2017, the president of Liberia proposed to abolish the law prohibiting industrial fishing in the six-mile zone from the coast, at the instigation of an agent working for Asian fisheries, who happened to be a relative of a senior government official. The reform would have facilitated the sale of licences, the prospect of which had induced the Asian companies to promise investment in onshore processing facilities. Fortunately, public outrage and protests from other fishing countries halted the move.

Agent-official corruption partially explains why governments have been reluctant to rein in industrial fishing. According to one expert working on large-scale donor-funded projects in West Africa, 'If you want to understand why the fishing industry is so poorly regulated, and what drives seemingly bad decisions, including selling too many licences, then you have to understand the role of fishing agents and the flow of money.'[115] It is not known how much foreign fisheries pay above the fees stipulated in fishing agreements to agents and government officials. But anecdotal evidence suggests it is a lot, which explains their resistance to reforms. As the expert put it, 'We have tried to organize meetings with the fishing industry, but the minister refuses to allow us to meet the industry without the agents being invited.'

The role of agents has been largely ignored in proposals to curb overfishing in Africa, which is depicted as an unequal fight between under-resourced countries and illegal fishing vessels 'plundering the oceans', backed by powerful foreign corporations. This leads to an overemphasis on law enforcement rather than systemic reform, when the larger threat to fish populations, marine ecosystems and the blue commons comes from 'legal' fishing legitimized by licences and private agreements. Law enforcement can be corrupted by vested interests and can serve as another vehicle for illicit flows of cash to agents and government officials.

Of course, not all agents are dishonest, nor is the problem unique to Africa. But there should be more transparency and public registries of agents. Corruption could be curtailed if information about licensed vessels, terms of licences, details of payments and the fees charged by agents for supposedly public services were all made public. And governments should draw up rules to avoid conflicts of interest and 're-volving doors' by stopping officials and their families from becoming agents. This would help, as would a rise in the currently very low wages of fishery officials so as to reduce the temptation to demand or accept bribes.

Of course, in an ethical industry there would be no need for many of the services agents claim to provide. Often, their services are just filling in for the deficiencies, or abdication of responsibility, of national fishing authorities. Why should vessel owners pay agents to process and collect fishing li-cences, when the licensing authority could do this online? When negotiating EU access agreements, for example, instead of mandating the use of agents, negotiators should insist that services including licensing are carried out by competent national authorities.

The same could be said for other functions of agents. Is it necessary for agents to arrange government inspections, handle communications with vessel owners and collect data from fishing vessels? All of these are government services. If the argument for use of agents is to avoid working with opaque and bureaucratic governments, the answer lies in improving government services, not in creating money-making opportunities for well-connected but unaccountable intermediaries. International efforts should aim to phase out agents and informal channels of corruption by building up the state, not weakening it as neoliberal institutions and donors have done since the 1980s.

World Bank flops

Shadowy and destructive intermediation reflects the weakness of the state and global governance of the marine economy. Part of the responsibility for this lies with the World Bank's 'structural adjustment' programmes enforced on developing countries and reinforced by the austerity strategy pursued around the world after the financial crash of 2008.

Over the past few decades, the World Bank has tried to promote economic growth in developing countries by creating and expanding commercial fishing industries. Latterly, the Bank and international development agencies have emphasized 'blue growth', supposedly linking industrial efficiency and modernization with environmental sustainability and poverty reduction. But it should have been obvious from the start that the neoliberal incentive-based approach would fail to achieve blue growth, given the inherently crimogenic character of commercial fisheries.

Ghana provides one of the most frustrating examples. In 2012, the World Bank provided a $54 million loan to improve fisheries management, although only $38 million was disbursed by the project's end in 2018. There were optimistic predictions that, if fully implemented, fish stocks would expand, revenue from commercial fisheries would rise, and the net benefit over thirty years would be $140 million. Much of the loan was for improving fisheries governance, reducing industrial fishing effort, increasing transparency and improving compliance by other fisheries.

At the start, the government agreed to a five-year fisheries plan, drafted by Bank consultants, which included a moratorium on industrial fishing licences, followed by a reduction in the number of licences of at least 50% and a tripling of licence fees. However, according to the Bank's evaluation, the project proved 'moderately unsatisfactory'. Fish biomass fell: the government allowed increased fishing intensity and increased the number of licences issued to foreign trawlers. Several million dollars were spent on developing a web-based information portal, including a vessel registry, with the names of companies and their owners. But the government decided not to publish the information. The project evaluation was candid in concluding that conflicts of interest and industry power had blocked reform, the overriding objective being to maximize short-term gains, while offences and collection of fines were neglected.[116]

What had happened, as in other countries, was 'regulatory capture' by foreign industrial companies and their agents, which were able to dictate fisheries policy. One outcome was a licence fee that was by far the lowest in West Africa. Whereas Guinea was charging demersal trawlers $315 per gross registered tonnage of each vessel, Ghana charged only $35, later raised to $200.

Much is troubling about this case. The Bank absolved itself of blame, although it admitted that its three-year pre-project preparation 'did not include an in-depth analysis of the political economy risks to project outcomes . . . especially toward reductions in the industrial fishing effort'. Similar anomalies have characterized other Bank projects for fisheries reform, including in Kenya, Tanzania, Mozambique and Madagascar.

In the vision of blue growth, the problem of unsustainable fisheries is reduced to one of 'resource constraints' and a 'funding gap', requiring large amounts of aid and private financial investment. This is a misleading diagnosis; the problem is a political one, which large development loans, as still envisaged, may well make worse.

The impasse

The global commercial fishing industry is inherently corrupted. It is out of control, with little prospect of effective remedial reform. A global industry of consultants and conservation NGOs depict fighting IUU fishing as a moral crusade, yet while this is all well and good, it does not attack the rottenness at the industry's core. Much could be done to combat criminality, including illegal fishing, if there were the international will to do so, such as measures to combat flag hopping and collusion between governments. The standard refrain is to call for more surveillance, better catch and trade documentation, higher penalties and more international coordination.[117] These are worthy policies, but they do not get to the heart of the structural problem, which is the corporate model.

Encouragingly, a lobby is building in favour of banning all fishing on the high seas, where regulation and monitoring are largely absent. Some of the most illicit activities are simply displaced into areas where weaker governance exists,[118] and a ban would be easier to police, at least in principle.

Yet no reforms directed simply at IUU fishing could

overcome the opportunistic pursuit of short-term profits. A 'free market' based on private property rights, neo-mercantilist fishing access agreements and the spreading intrusion of financial capital threatens to destroy the world's fish populations and the communities that rely on them. Only a commons-based artisanal structure that supported the preservation and reproduction of local marine life could overcome the crimogenic realities that couple high levels of dishonesty and greed with damage to the environment and society.

Relying on a legalistic definition of crime is inadequate, partly because corporate-state interests ensure that many damaging practices are not criminalized. Corporate-state collusion is more than a two-sided form of 'corruption'. Much of what is wrong with industrial fisheries is technically legal although morally deplorable. Corporate lobbying, regulatory capture by vested interests, and a culture of corruption enable commercial interests to gain rental income legally, in marine seafood as in other industries.[119] There have been improvements, with stronger regulations in some parts of the world. But it is misleading, as global statistics on IUU fishing suggest, to think of 'illegal = bad', 'legal = OK'. Without a fresh approach, the legal and illegal plunder of the blue commons will not be stopped.

The European Union's Common Fisheries Policy . . . and Brexit

> I think at this stage of the game, they could promise and will promise anybody anything. They'd have you believe that fish were going to fall from the sky.
>
> — Jeremy Percy, director, New Under Ten Fishermen's Association[1]

On 15 June 2016, a grand flotilla of fishing boats made its way up the River Thames to the Houses of Parliament in Westminster to protest that the European Union's Common Fisheries Policy (CFP) was destroying the livelihoods of Britain's small-scale fisheries. It was a stunt that may have tipped the impending Brexit referendum on Britain's membership of the EU in favour of Leave, which won with 52% of the vote. On board the flagship boat was Nigel Farage, leading campaigner for Leave, alongside the campaign's controversial multimillionaire financier, Arron Banks.

One of the boats taking part, the *Christina S*, was a big industrial trawler that had been involved in a notorious illegal fishing scam and was now owned by a multimillionaire family owning extensive fishing quotas in UK waters. It was a strange choice for a flotilla supposed to highlight the alleged damage to Britain's small-scale fishers inflicted by the CFP. It had been plundering the fish while small-scale fishers were duped into pinning all the blame on the European Union. The stunt was an exercise in hypocrisy that nevertheless exploited the emotive power of the plight of local fishing communities to win votes for the Brexit side.

The recent history of the fishing industry in Britain is a prime illustration of how promoting private property rights through quotas and subsidies, combined with feeble conservation mechanisms, easily gives way to state-corporate collusion and tolerated illegality, to the detriment of the blue commons and the sustainable balance between marine ecosystems and human activity. However, the story needs to be understood in the context of the evolution of the CFP and how the UK chose to use its mechanisms to benefit big fishing corporations, including foreign-owned conglomerates, rather than the small-scale fishers of popular imagination.

Despite policies intended to promote sustainable use of marine resources, European boats continue to overfish in the EU's own waters and those of other countries, aided by large and harmful subsidies. When it comes to fisheries, the EU's vision of blue growth is a chimera. The EU's Blue Growth Strategy, which imagines sustainable growth alongside ecosystem preservation and benefits for local communities, does not even include marine fisheries, recognizing that they do not offer sustainable growth opportunities. Yet EU fisheries policy continues to be dominated by a mindset that emphasizes economic growth, making neglect of ecological and social objectives almost inevitable.[2]

The CFP as muddled subsidiarity?

Europe has played a pivotal part in the evolution of the global fishing industry, and has contributed to its several crises. The Great Acceleration of the 1950s was centred on the area that was to become the European Union, and it was the evidence of overfishing that set the context for its defining policies. But it took a collapse in the herring population in the North Atlantic in 1975 to prompt the then European Economic Community (EEC) to develop a Common Fisheries Policy.

Although Brexit removed about a sixth of what had been EU waters, and about the same proportion of its fishing capacity in terms of tonnage, the EU, led by Spain, remains an important centre of fisheries and of commercial fish populations. It is the world's biggest trader in fish, counting both imports and exports,[3] and also has the most highly regulated fisheries sector and market, which makes it a heavyweight in international negotiations on fisheries trade and conservation.

Without the 6,000 or so UK-registered boats, the EU fishing fleet still exceeds 75,000, including a sizeable long-distance armada of some 250 vessels dominated by Spanish, Portuguese and French boats. About three-quarters of the EU catch has come from the prolific North-East Atlantic, which includes UK waters, and roughly a fifth is caught outside EU waters, under fishing access agreements or on the high seas in areas managed by regional fisheries management organizations (RFMOs). British boats, which fish almost exclusively in British, EU and other northern European waters, accounted for about a fifth of the 4.5 million to 5.5 million tonnes live weight of EU recorded catches between 2010 and 2019.

The CFP starts from a presumption that fishing areas comprise a 'common pool resource' that requires rules for sharing limited fish stocks. In 1983, drawing on principles set for the EEC in 1970, the CFP introduced a quota-based management system, still used today, that aims to ensure 'long-term environmental, economic and social sustainability', while giving all EU fishing fleets equal access to EU fishing grounds.

In December each year, after negotiations between fisheries ministers of member states, the EU Council of Ministers establishes the total allowable catch (TAC) for each of the 124 major species in EU waters. Intended to be the overarching conservation tool, the TAC is then divided into fixed quotas for each member state, based on a pragmatic concept known as 'relative stability'. Member states are allocated a share of the TAC determined by their historic track record, which, when the CFP was set up, was based on catches in the five-year period between 1973 and 1978.

In deciding on the total allowable catch, ministers are supposed to be guided by recommendations on sustainable fishing by the independent International Council for the Exploration of the Sea (ICES), a venerable body set up in 1902, comprising marine scientists from countries bordering the North Atlantic. But, to please their fishery communities, ministers negotiate to obtain national quotas that collectively exceed the recommended TAC. Between 2001 and 2015, the total allowable catches agreed by ministers were

20% larger on average than the TACs recommended by ICES and, despite a target to end the practice by 2020, TACs in 2021 were set to exceed scientific advice for about a third of EU fish stocks.[4]

Once the TACs are agreed, member states can distribute their allocated individual quota free of charge to their fishing companies as they see fit. Although quotas cannot be traded freely between member states, they have sometimes been exchanged. But essentially the EU gives common pool resources to states, which can then give private companies rights to access and profit from those resources. As we shall see, in the UK the allocation has favoured big corporations, which is also the case for other fishing nations, such as Denmark and Spain. In effect, the industrialization and conglomeration of European fisheries in recent decades has been driven by national governments, not the EU per se.

A primary reason for this is the power given to devolved fishery management bodies known as producer organizations, of which there were about 180 across the EU in 2019. The producer organizations system, a key plank of the Common Fisheries Policy, is governed by the 'CMO Regulation' of 2013, where CMO stands for the Common Organisation of the Markets of Fishery and Aquaculture Products. Its rules require producer organizations to be open, transparent and democratic, have many fisheries as members, give due weight to the needs and aspirations of small-scale fishers, and support sustainable fishing.

However, although the producer organizations are institutionalized at EU level, how producer organizations are designed is left to each member state. In practice, they have mainly operated for the benefit of large-scale indus-trial fisheries and maximization of 'growth', rather than for small-scale fisheries and resource conservation. In most cases, governments hand quotas to the producer organiza-tions, which can choose how and to whom they are allocat-ed. There is no transparency, as illustrated by Denmark, by volume the EU's second-biggest producer of fish after Spain. In 2017, its national audit office investigated how 'too much quota has ended up in too few hands' and bewailed the fact that 'neither the ministry nor the public has an accurate pic-ture of the concentration of quota ownership'.[5]

In Ireland, fisheries management is in the hands of four producer organizations that represent under 10% of the Irish fishing fleet but land 90% of the fish by volume and 70% by value. They comprise a majority on the country's Quota Management Advisory Committee, which determines the free distribution of national fish quotas. Thus large-scale fishing companies are enabled by the Irish government to abuse a dominant market position for rent extraction.[6]

The system in Germany has also been structured in favour of large-scale corporations, such as Parlevliet & Van der Plas Group, Europe's biggest fishing company, which is head-quartered in the Netherlands. It is a prominent member of Seefrostvertrieb, one of thirteen producer organizations in Germany, whose stated aims make no reference to the CMO guidelines on sustainable fishing or small-scale fisheries.[7]

As for the Netherlands, just one producer organization represents the entire Dutch pelagic freezer-trawler fleet. In every respect, it contravenes the CMO Regulation. By defin-ition, it has a dominant position and has only four member companies, including the Parlevliet & Van der Plas Group. In addition, one of the remaining three is fully owned by another, giving that company, Cornelis Vrolijk, 50% of the votes.[8] Cornelis Vrolijk also has indirect membership of Germany's producer organization system and remains a powerful player in Britain's post-Brexit fisheries management, as its main trawler is registered as British.

In this way, producer organizations operate as rent-seeking institutions for industrial fisheries, acting against the interest of the blue commons and accentuating depletion of common pool resources. Along with excessive TACs, they are part of the reason why the CFP has failed in its objective to restore all exploited EU fish stocks to healthy levels. The European Commission claims that overfishing in the North-East Atlantic has fallen to 40% of assessed stocks as of 2020, compared with 66% a decade earlier. However, it remains rife in the Mediterranean, the world's most overfished sea, where fish populations have plunged.

Although there is an EU-level inspection service designed to ensure that member states enforce the rules on quotas, hygiene, fish size, documentation and so on, non-compliance has been widespread, due to weak enforcement and risibly small penalties. In 2008, illegal fishing in some European countries was estimated to account for one-third to one-half of all catches.[9] Compliance may have improved since, but the cases that do end up in court suggest that illegal fishing by EU boats remains substantial.

European fisheries policies, at EU and national levels, have also failed to safeguard the blue commons around the coasts of Europe that have nurtured fishing traditions over countless generations.[10] Policymakers have failed to address the growing inequalities in fisheries, which subsidies and quota systems have intensified. As a result, decommoning has been accelerated by privatization and simple neglect.

Over the years of the CFP, there have been calls for more respect for the principle of subsidiarity, that is, for leaving governance as much as possible to national or local levels of decision-making. This would have more appeal if it would strengthen the voice and agency of small-scale fishers. But neither growth-oriented national governments nor the domination of fisheries by industrial corporations makes that likely.

So, it is misleading to claim, as the Leave campaigners did, that the CFP imposes a straitjacket on national sovereignty. On the contrary, the CFP has left too much to national governments and corporate fisheries. As a natural common pool resource, marine life depends for its health and long-term sustainability on international governance. Regional agreements like the CFP need to be strengthened, not jettisoned, as Britain has done in leaving the European Union.

Brexit lies

The countries that make up the United Kingdom have always been fishing nations. Fishing is part of the national personality. More people participate in recreational fishing of all kinds than in any other sport. For generations, fishers from the many fishing communities roamed the Atlantic and a few went out long distances to the resource-rich waters around Iceland, Greenland and the Faroe Islands. The first fishing supertrawlers were built in Scotland in the 1950s, but the UK never developed a global long-distance fleet, as Spain and others did.

There is also a long tradition of foreign boats fishing close to British shores. Under the 1964 London Fisheries Convention, reconfirmed when the UK joined the EEC in 1973, fishing fleets of other member states were free to fish outside a twelve-mile coastal band, while some countries continued to have historic rights inside that zone.

Until the 1970s, the British position was that, beyond its narrowly defined coastal waters, the seas should be open to free access for everyone. This was what motivated fishers and politicians in the three cod wars with Iceland mentioned in Chapter 1. Yet views changed dramatically in the years leading up to Britain's decision to leave the EU. Critics talked of 'returning sovereignty' to large swathes of the sea around Britain, ignoring the fact that in 1973 Exclusive Economic Zones had not been established so there was no sovereignty to return to.

The reality is that for over a century Britain's fishing industry, or at least its small-scale fishers, like those elsewhere in Europe, have struggled in the face of declining fish populations and growing competition from other fishing nations. Although the fishing industry now accounts for about 0.1% of British GDP, less than Harrods, the upmarket department store, the perceived crisis became a core emotional issue in the 2016 Brexit referendum and in the subsequent trade negotiations between Britain and the EU that dragged on through 2020.

In the Brexit campaign, and in the two subsequent general elections, the Leave advocates and the Conservative Party built on a sentimental slogan of the Fishing for Leave campaign: 'British fish for British people'. Over 90% of those in the fishing industry are said to have voted for Brexit, and the Conservatives made substantial electoral gains in fishing communities both in 2017 and, more spectacularly, in 2019 under the leadership of Prime Minister Boris Johnson.

Undoubtedly, by 2016 fisheries were suffering, particularly small-scale artisanal fisheries. But the EU's CFP was not the primary villain. This did not stop the leaders of the Brexit campaign misleading the public. Symbolically, Johnson waved a smoked kipper during a speech attacking the EU, claiming that EU rules dictated extra packaging. There was no such rule; packaging standards were set entirely by British authorities.

Catches vary widely from year to year, but in 2019, a relatively poor year, UK-flagged boats caught 502,000 tonnes of fish in British waters.[11] This compares with the 675,000 tonnes caught by EU fishing fleets in UK waters – about 60% of the total – while UK boats caught just 88,000 tonnes in the waters of other EU states.[12] This would appear to back up one of the Brexiteers' claims, that boats from other EU countries were taking 'British fish'. But catches by weight tell only part of the story.

In value terms, the percentages are reversed: British boats caught fish with a value of 60% of all fish caught in UK waters, while other EU boats caught 40%. The reason is that UK vessels targeted higher-value fish, notably shellfish, as well as mackerel and herring, while EU boats took more low-value fish such as sand eels and whiting. In addition, pre-Brexit, UK-based fisheries exported about 80% of the fish caught in UK waters, mostly to the EU, while 70% of the fish consumed in Britain was imported. This largely reflected consumer preferences. For instance, over 90% of UK-caught herring was exported, mainly to Norway and the Netherlands.[13]

For many years the biggest sector in the UK fishing industry has been shellfish, not cod or other white fish preferred by British consumers. Pre-Brexit, cod made up only 5% of the UK catch, and haddock 7%. About 83% of cod consumed in Britain each year was imported, as was 58% of the haddock. Under the CFP, shellfish catches were quota-free or allocated mainly to the UK, and the single market meant they could be traded freely within the bloc. Over 80% of shellfish caught off the UK, mostly by small-scale fishers, went to continental Europe, mainly to Spain and France. Over 40% of active fishing boats were devoted to shellfish, accounting for over half of all full-time equivalent jobs in the industry.[14] The future of the shellfish sector post-Brexit is more important for small-scale fishers than the future for cod and haddock, on which the media and Brexiteers concentrated.

Brexit has thus left small-scale fishers and local producers – the core of what should be the blue commons in the UK – more vulnerable rather than less. The fact is that the woes of small-scale fishers cannot be put at the door of the European Union but are almost entirely due to British government policy pressured by the corporate fishing industry. The story epitomizes an underlying theme of this book – depletion of common resources due to privatization and excessive commodification, destruction of commons communities, and government support, implicit and explicit, for capitalistic industrial fisheries, favouring rentier capitalism.

Cod woes

In 1983, Britain did badly out of the CFP's allocation of cod quotas, which were based on historic fishing levels in the 1970s when many of its biggest boats were trawling the waters around Iceland. The UK was given only a tenth of the quota for cod caught in the English Channel, with EU boats, mostly French, taking the rest. Nevertheless, the long-term decline in catches of cod – long regarded as Britain's national fish – cannot be blamed on the CFP. The decline in cod populations began in the late nineteenth century, falling by 94% between 1892 and 2010, with most of the decline coming long before the UK joined what became the EU in 1973.[15] And it was after losing access to waters around Iceland at the end of the acrimonious cod wars that fisheries in places like Grimsby, Hull, Fleetwood and Aberdeen went into steep decline, although this was conveniently misattributed to the CFP.

Between 1970 and the early 2000s, fishing took 40–60% of North Sea cod resources each year, which was unsustainable. Stocks only began to recover after 2007, when the European Commission launched a Cod Recovery Plan. This included improved controls on catches, a requirement for larger holes in nets, more controls on the number of days cod trawlers could spend at sea, some decommissioning of boats, and more controls on where they could fish, notably by banning fishing in nursery areas.

In 2017, in the euphoria of an apparent resurrection of cod populations, the European Commission was urged by fishing ministers to drop the Plan, abandoning days-at-sea controls and raising limits on allowable catches. The Marine Stewardship Council (MSC) awarded the cod zone its certificate of sustainability. Mike Park, chair of the Scottish Fisheries Sustainable Accreditation Group, said at the time: 'This is a massive development for the catching sector and is a testament to the power of collective action. The years of commitment to rebuilding North Sea cod has [sic] shown that fishermen are responsible and can be trusted to deliver stable and sustainable stocks. The consumer can now eat home-caught cod with a clear conscience.'[16]

Yet revised estimates by ICES showed that cod stocks had not recovered to sustainable levels by 2017, as it had previously thought, and the MSC certificate should not have been awarded, especially since it had accompanied a relaxation of fishing regulations.[17] In July 2019, ICES reported that North Sea cod stocks had fallen to critical levels, and recommended a 63% cut in the annual catch, coming on top of its recommended cut of 47% in 2018. The MSC hastily suspended its certificate of sustainability. Cod thus joined haddock, another staple which had been removed from the MSC's list of sustainable seafood in 2017.[18]

The future of North Sea cod and haddock remains bleak, whoever controls the waters. Spawning is at an all-time low, not just because of overfishing but also because of warming sea temperatures, as cod spawn requires water close to freezing to develop into fish. And overfishing may have been underestimated due to the widespread discarding of dead juvenile fish to keep within quotas.

Brexiteers also claimed that foreign boats were breaking the rules on quotas and fishing practices with impunity. However, enforcing the rules has always been the responsibility of individual countries. In Britain, the main regulatory body is the Marine Management Organisation (MMO). Between 2010 and 2015, as part of its austerity drive, the UK government slashed the MMO's budget by over £10 million. The predictable result was a sharp drop in inspections and investigations of fishery violations, and a similar drop in warnings and prosecutions, encouraging a pervasive culture of quota malpractice. This was entirely due to national policy and practice, not EU policy. It illustrates the accelerated encroachment of the blue commons through neglect.

The shift from EU-wide to national control of British waters is unlikely to lead to a strengthening of the regulatory system. In October 2020, the British government successfully opposed amendments to the fisheries bill, now law, that would have required it to act against overfishing on the recommendation of an independent scientific committee and would have barred supertrawlers from fishing in the country's marine protected areas. And in late 2021 it granted licences to more than 1,000 UK and EU boats that would allow bottom trawling and dredging in all but a few of Britain's MPAs.[19]

The UK's quota system

Britain's quota system long predates the EU's introduction of quotas in 1983. It was first introduced by the Sea Fish (Conservation) Act of 1967. Industrial fishing has dominated UK fisheries for many years and, for these companies, quotas make sound business sense. Well over two-thirds of fish landed are caught by just 4% of boats, those over 24 metres long. They have been responsible for the extensive labour displacement that has occurred in recent decades; today the number employed in all commercial fishing is a quarter of what it was before the Second World War.

Brexiteers alleged during the referendum campaign that the CFP allocated the quotas.[20] This was another lie. Once the total allowable catch is set, the allocation of quotas is decided at national level, and EU countries have very dissimilar systems.[21] The UK from the outset operated a system based on allocation of quotas free of charge, which has been described as permitting a public asset to be 'squatted' by private interests, in a legally dubious form of privatization.[22]

Neither the 1967 Act nor any subsequent legislation created property rights in the quota system. In law, the UK government cannot transfer a commons asset that is not its property – the state does not 'own' the fish in the sea or the 'rights' to take them. And it cannot rightly transfer a public asset to private hands without valuing the asset and selling it at a price that reflects the valuation and that preserves the asset value in the public domain. No government or regulatory agency has attempted to value the quotas, let alone set an appropriate price for the transfer. That is why the analogy with squatters' rights is relevant. Quota holders 'occupy a property' without it being valued in market terms. What is more, as with squatters on land, after a certain time occupation can become 'possession', a quasi-property right. In effect, in an act of enclosure, the state has taken an asset from the commons to transfer the acquired rights to private interests.

The system has two tiers. A portion of quota is put into a 'pool' for collective use, mainly for small-scale inshore fisheries, and the rest is managed by producer organizations. In early 2021 there were twenty-three in the UK, the first of which was formed by a group of fishers in the Shetland Islands in 1982. Quotas for small-scale fisheries that are not in producer organizations are managed directly by the fishing authorities, which allocate quotas from the pool. But vessels that join a producer organization can take their share of quota out of the pool to be managed by the producer

organization. Joining a producer organization is generally
not to the advantage of small-scale fishers, since they stand
to gain only limited rights to quota within the producer organization and lose their entitlement to a share of the pool.
Of the 4,299 boats under ten metres, only fifty-three were
producer organization members in 2018.[23] But gradually, as
more of the larger trawlers joined producer organizations,
the pool has been stripped of almost all its quota, while the
producer organizations have been captured by a few large-
scale quota holders which effectively control British fishing.

In 2017, for example, 94% of the UK's total allowable
catches were allocated to 902 vessels that were producer
organization members, representing 15% of the UK fishing
fleet. The remaining 85% – 4,649 vessels – were supposed to
share 6% of all TAC tonnage, only part of which was actually allocated to them by the government. Although the quota
system was derived from the CFP, this denial of access to
most small-scale fishers was entirely a British affair.

The procedure for allocating quota was originally based
on the 'catch history' or track record of a vessel on a rolling three-year period. But this encouraged a 'race to fish'
as boats tried to maximize landings to maintain or enlarge
their quota in subsequent years. It also encouraged 'over-
reporting', that is, reporting larger catches than were actually
landed. So in 1999 rolling track records were replaced by fixed
quota allocations (FQAs) based on the three years 1994–96.
This curbed the race to fish but structurally disadvantaged
small-scale fisheries. In the 1990s they were not required to
keep written records of their catches, so they could not provide a catch history under the FQA system. This meant they

could not join a producer organization and were dependent on the pool.

Meanwhile, from the mid-1980s, worried by depletion of fish populations, the government restricted the issue of new fishing licences. The only way for entrants to obtain a licence was to buy one from fisheries prepared to sell theirs, which usually meant also buying the vessel and its track record. But in the mid-1990s, the government allowed members of producer organizations, known as 'sector' fisheries, to transfer licences, with their track records, between vessels covered by the PO. This meant vessels could increase their quota allowance by acquiring licences from other vessels.

Then, in 1996, the government relaxed rules on the swapping of quota between producer organizations, so that a straight exchange was no longer required. This made it much easier for a vessel in one producer organization to lease or sell quota to a vessel in another producer organization, further hurting small-scale fishers who were not producer organization members.[24] Later, the rules were relaxed further to allow trade with non-sector vessels. And the move to fixed quota allocations made quotas even easier to swap, sell or lease out. Fish quotas became fully commodified.

The government allowed the producer organizations to determine their own method of quota allocation between members. As trade in quotas became easier, more POs switched from managing quota among their members to individual transferable quotas (ITQs), enabling their members independently to purchase individual quota to expand their initial allocation. A key development came in 2007 when, in the context of decommissioning old vessels, the government allowed owners to keep their quota without it being attached to a particular vessel. The government made the telling statement in support of that decision that the quota 'was not ours to take back'.[25]

The implication that quotas were to be treated as private property rights, despite the lack of legal title, strengthened the financialization of British fisheries, since banks were able to accept quota holdings as collateral for loans to expand. They became a new tool for conglomeration and 'accumulation by dispossession'. Financial interests saw a lucrative opportunity in purchasing quota and leasing it out, joining the ranks of 'slipper skippers' – owners of boats with quota who do not (or no longer) fish but make money from those who do.

Under EU rules, notably the CMO Regulation, producer organizations were supposed to be a devolved mechanism for democratic governance and management, set up by groups of producers to manage the allocation of quotas between members and other joint activities. They were required to take 'the specific situation of small-scale producers' and 'transparent and objective' environmental criteria into account, respect competition rules, not abuse a dominant position in a given market, and reveal their membership and sources of funding.

Over many years, the British government and the MMO have been indifferent to those principles. Only in 2013 was information made public on quota holdings and, even then, producer organizations could withhold information about the ultimate controlling parties of the quota holdings they manage. After detective work based on 'following the money', a research team concluded that 'the vast majority of

English POs have either one or two members holding 50% or more of their FQA holdings, giving them controlling stakes in those organisations.'[26]

Another investigation found that one British producer organization, the North Atlantic Fish Producer Organisation, set up in 2010, had just two company members, one listed as 'dormant', and both wholly owned by Cornelis Vrolijk Holding, the Dutch holding company that dominates the main PO in the Netherlands.[27] The UK authorities do not seem to have queried whether a single 'ultimate controlling party' could establish a PO, which under the CFP rules was supposed to be an entity 'set up on the own initiative of a group of producers' (plural). The CMO Regulation also stated that 'Member states shall carry out checks at regular intervals to verify that producer organisations and inter-branch organisations comply with the conditions for recognition' and 'a finding of non-compliance may result in the withdrawal of recognition'. This appears to have been ignored.

Between 2016 and 2019, Cornelis Vrolijk owned the *Cornelis Vrolijk*, a 114-metre giant which was the largest vessel in the British fishing fleet. This one boat had been given 23% of England's fishing quota, four times as much as all small-scale inshore fishing boats put together. It landed much of the fish it caught in the Dutch port of Ijmuiden, where the company is based. Being UK-registered, the *Cornelis Vrolijk* could have continued its lucrative fishing in the post-Brexit era. Instead, the parent company transferred it to sail out of Namibia under the Namibian flag. Lest any reader think this means more 'British fish for British fishers', the company's UK subsidiary now has an even bigger Dutch-owned vessel in its place, the *Frank Bonefaas*, of which more is said later.

CHAPTER 6

Quotas, 'codfathers' and the betrayal of artisans

As noted earlier, quota systems contribute to the conglomeration of fisheries, which facilitates rent-seeking. Giving evidence to a House of Commons committee in 1999, Iain MacSween, chief executive of the Scottish Fishermen's Organisation (SFO), predicted that moving away from treating fish as commonly owned, or owned by nobody, and instituting ITQs as private property rights would lead to the destruction of fishing communities.

In Iceland, he said, privatizing fishing rights had led to 'those who own the property rights . . . sitting in Florida and leasing them out to other people to go and catch', adding: 'Norway, for example, which is the largest fishing community in Europe, would have the heebie-jeebies if you even suggested ITQs, because they want to maintain viable coastal communities in remote areas where there are no permanent economic opportunities.'[28]

MacSween concluded, 'It seems to me, without being overly dramatic about it, that the confirmation of property rights in the fishing industry will do for coastal communities what highland clearances did for the agricultural sector.' He was referring to the eviction of thousands of crofters, small-scale tenant farmers in the Scottish Highlands, by the likes of the Duke of Sutherland in the eighteenth and early nineteenth centuries. They were driven off common land into the slums of Glasgow or abroad, enabling the duke to enclose over a million acres for his own use and profit.

At the time of MacSween's testimony, the market value

of track records had already 'increased to such a degree that most individual fishermen find it impossible to compete with those that have the financial clout of large companies behind them', according to the Anglo-North Irish Fish Producers Organisation.[29]

The predictable outcome of conglomeration provides fertile space for monopolistic rentier capitalism, where informal cartels can dominate what happens. Over two-thirds of UK fishing quotas are in the hands of just twenty-five companies. Only 6% have gone to small-scale fishers, with boats of under ten metres, even though they make up 79% of the fishing fleet. Well over a quarter (29%) have been handed to just five families, all of whom were on the *Sunday Times* Rich List in 2016: Lunar Fishing Company, owned by Alexander Buchan and family; Interfish, owned by Jan Colam and family; Klondyke Fishing Company, owned by Robert Tait and family; Andrew Marr International, owned by Andrew Marr and family; and JW Holdings, owned by Sir Ian Wood and family.[30] These families also had a commercial interest in a further 8% of the quota. In England alone, just three companies hold 61% of all the fishing rights.[31]

In 2011–12, directors and partners of thirteen of the twenty-five privileged companies were convicted in a huge overfishing case in Scotland, known as the 'black fish' scam. The companies had clandestinely landed 170,000 tonnes of undeclared herring and mackerel, worth about £63 million. Yet the convictions did not stop those companies from continuing to receive their large quotas. It is a case to cite against those who claim that quota systems – private property rights – encourage long-term conservation and sustainable fisheries.

Ironically, one of the boats involved in the 'black fish' scam, the *Christina S*, took part in that flotilla of fishing boats that sailed up the Thames to the Houses of Parliament in June 2016. The 72-metre trawler was acquired after the scam by Andrew Marr International. However, former owner Ernest Simpson and his son Allan, who were convicted in 2012, still had a stake in the trawler in 2016.

Another scandal concerned two large vessels, registered in the UK but owned by the Vidals, a Spanish fishing family already fined several times for illegal activities. In 2012, the family was fined £1.6 million for falsifying logbooks, failing to register the transfer of fish between vessels, false readings for weighing fish at sea, and fiddling fish quotas. The judge condemned them for 'flagrant, repeated and long term abuse' of the fishing quota system, which involved hake, 'a species of fish on the verge of collapse'.[32] Yet the family was allowed to continue to hold 11,600 fixed quota allocations (FQAs) and the right to fish for ling and hake, two of the species it had been fined for overfishing.[33] This was a UK decision, not the EU's. Other cases ignored by the UK authorities include the *Bergur*, a fishing trawler that, despite being in a rust-yard in Galicia since 2012, still had 5,868 FQAs on the MMO's register in 2016.

The persistent failure to pursue, prosecute and ban illegal overfishing has hurt small-scale British fishers. Yet the failure is entirely due to the British government, not the EU as claimed by the Leave campaign. Even with the MMO budget cuts, penalties for those caught could have been increased. And under Article 17 of the CFP the authorities had the right and duty to take compliance history into account in allocating quota. They simply did not do so. That might have offended large-scale industry interests. This made the MMO and government complicit.

The government's White Paper on post-Brexit fishery policies, published in mid-2019, stated that there would be no change in the quota distribution and made no mention of redistributing quotas to small-scale fisheries. This was confirmed in the Fisheries Act of 2020, reflecting the power structure in the fishing industry and the ideology of private property rights.

Nearly twenty years after MacSween's perceptive testimony, in a complete reversal of perspective, the Scottish Fishermen's Organisation agreed with the chief executive of the National Federation of Fishing Organisations that the distribution of UK fishing rights should 'remain the same' after Brexit. This, he claimed, would recognize 'the investments made by fishermen and fishing businesses over the past 20 years, and as such [help] to maintain business stability within a period of great political uncertainty'.[34] The fishers' organizations have become defenders of entrenched property rights and the conglomeration of fisheries. And, by generating expectations that pre-existing quota allocations would be preserved after Brexit, the government deprived itself of the ability to manage fisheries in the public interest.[35]

Meanwhile, the rentier character of UK fisheries is exemplified by an example from Northern Ireland. In 2015, the largest fishery company there sold its 76-metre boat, the *Voyager*, which held 55% of Northern Ireland's fishing quota. While waiting for a replacement that was only delivered in September 2017, the company earned £7 million simply by leasing out its quota, reporting an operating profit of £2.5 million from doing so. By 2020, the new 86-metre *Voyager* still had not landed any fish in Northern Ireland, and was most unlikely to do so, because it is too big for the province's Kilkeel Harbour. Instead, it operates out of Killybegs, the Republic of Ireland's biggest fishing port.

The quota system has also produced some absurd outcomes that the regulatory bodies have been unwilling or unable to prevent. In the south-west of England, in a small marina in Exmouth, a five-metre fibreglass dinghy named *Nina May* owns nearly one-fifth of all the quota fishing rights in the whole of the region, amounting to 1,500 tonnes of fish a year, or four tonnes a day.[36] The owner gifted with that property has done rather well. He happens to own twelve much larger fishing vessels and merely transfers quota units to the dinghy, so that those boats can write off their catches against the dinghy's allocation. This means the twelve boats can fish without risk of being penalized for exceeding quotas.

The manipulation arises because there are no regulations restricting the number of FQA units that can be held on one licence. The owner said: 'We fish about 90% of the quota we have and lease the rest. We use the MMO's set rates or the landing price to guide us. But market prices move. It's all about supply and demand. Quota is a currency you can swap.'[37]

For years fishers worried about exceeding their quotas have discarded less valuable fish, throwing them dead into the sea. Seemingly to help remedy this, a sort of 'spot market' in quotas has been allowed to emerge, whereby small-scale fisheries, if they find they have exceeded their quota, can buy (rent) additional quota. Since this must be done quickly, because the extra fish have to be sold while fresh, the sellers of quota can usually demand high prices.

A feature of all tradable quota systems is 'quota hopping', whereby foreign boats register locally so they can buy quota to fish in domestic waters. While big companies have been buying up quotas held by smaller firms, foreign firms have bought up 'British' quotas by registering their boats in the UK. In this, they were helped by EU-sponsored decommissioning rounds in the 1990s, aimed at reducing overfishing by reducing fleet capacity, when fisheries were given cash incentives to give up licences and remove their boats from the fleet. This created an open market in licences and quotas, which were snapped up by Dutch and Spanish fisheries prepared to pay over the odds. The creation of tradable private property rights combined with unfettered foreign capital investment has meant that nearly half of all English and Welsh fishing quota is today owned by foreign companies.[38]

Almost a quarter of the English quota is possessed by the *Frank Bonefaas*, the 120-metre flagship fishing trawler owned by Cornelis Vrolijk through its British subsidiary, the North Atlantic Fishing Company. In 2015, the owner and skipper of the *Frank Bonefaas* were fined £102,000, including costs, by a British court for illegally catching 632,000 kilos of mackerel.[39] But they were then allowed to sell the fish, which fetched £437,000, and to keep their enormous quota. That made the illegal activity rather profitable.

The Brexit deal

On 24 December 2020, after acrimonious negotiations in which UK demands for 'control of its waters' became a sticking point, the UK and EU reached a deal on tariff-free trade for goods, including fish. The accord provided for a 25% cut in quota for EU boats over five years, front-loaded to 2021, with annual negotiations from 2026 on how the catch will be shared. The UK will then have the rights to about two-thirds of estimated fish stocks in British waters. It can exclude EU boats completely from 2026, but the EU could respond by imposing tariffs or denying UK boats access to EU waters. Britain failed to secure an exclusive twelve-mile limit for UK fisheries, which was left at the previous six miles, and failed to enlarge its quota share for Channel cod.

When the UK left the EU's customs union, fish trade became subject to additional checks at national borders, for which both the government and the industry were unprepared. And Britain no longer has the enforcement back-up of an EU-level inspection service. Without devoting more resources to monitoring, it risks more rule-breaking and loss of fish stocks. The Royal Navy and Scotland's Marine Sea Fisheries Inspectorate have only twelve protection vessels to monitor fishing practices in a sea area three times the size of the UK. And, after a decade of austerity-induced cuts, the civil service no longer has the staff or institutional knowledge to operate an enlarged regulatory or governance system.

In characteristically jingoistic manner, as the deadline for a negotiated agreement approached, the government announced that from January 2021 four armed Royal Navy patrol ships would be deployed to keep unauthorized vessels out of the UK's EEZ waters. A former Rear-Admiral, who had been chair of the MMO, said provocatively, 'I would seek to make an example and take a boat or two into Harwich or Hastings. Once you had impounded them, the others would not be so keen to transgress without insurance.'[40] Fortunately, the immediate prospect of another 'cod war' was averted by the final agreement which, at least until 2026, allows EU boats to fish in UK waters, though at a reduced level.

In the House of Commons debate on the earlier withdrawal agreement, on 22 October 2019, Boris Johnson asserted that 'we will take back 100% control of the spectacular marine wealth of this country.' But, aside from the fact that fish are not 'wealth' or naturally 'national', this ignored trading realities. British fishers have been dependent on trade with the EU, in both directions, but for small-scale fisheries shellfish exports to the rest of the EU were a principal source of revenue, worth £430 million a year or over a quarter of all UK fish exports by value.[41]

As of 2021, the signs for protecting this revenue were not encouraging. The European Commission refused to exempt the UK from shellfish regulations it applies to all third countries. The extra paperwork and need for quayside veterinary inspections resulted in higher costs and delays, crucial for live crustaceans. Shellfish exports plummeted. Consignments rotted awaiting shipping. A month into the new arrangements, one leading lobster producer announced it was closing down and other shellfish companies said they were threatened with bankruptcy.

And the UK was struggling to maintain access for British boats to the waters of other countries, such as Norway which supplies much of the cod and haddock for the nation's beloved fish and chips. As a member of the European Economic Area (EEA) Norway grants access to EU boats as part of its arrangements with the EU, but Britain now has to negotiate separately as a 'third country'. Jane Sandell, UK Fisheries chief executive, said after failure to reach a deal with Norway for 2021 that fishing crews and the Humberside region wanted to know why the government 'was unable even to maintain the rights we have had to fish in Norwegian waters for decades, never mind the boast of a "Brexit bonus", which has turned to disaster'.[42]

The British government was forced to create a special compensation fund for fishers whose exports had been hit. Fishers interviewed in Brixham, a Channel fishing harbour in the west of England, said that pre-Brexit fish consignments had required three documents; after Brexit, they required forty. The delays caused by extra paperwork meant the fish were less fresh, prices fell, and many buyers looked elsewhere. Fishers were earning lower incomes and going out to sea in harsh conditions ('pushing weather') to compensate. One local fish merchant, who had voted for Brexit, was reported as saying: 'Boris Johnson came here and said we were going to get all our fish back and have free trade. That's turned out to be nonsense.'[43]

Meanwhile, the government was allowing a fleet of so-called 'fly-shooting' fishing boats unfettered access to the Channel. 'Fly-shooting' boats – sometimes called Danish or Scottish seiners – drag huge lead-weighted nets along the seabed, encircling entire shoals of fish and scooping up anything else they encounter. Each fly-shooter can cover a million square metres of seabed on each fishing trip, leaving vast areas dead zones and dwarfing what local artisanal boats can catch.

Some of the seventy-five fly-shooters involved were UK-registered, the rest being Belgian, Dutch and French. But the failure to stop what they were doing was Britain's responsibility. The Department for Environment, Food and Rural Affairs (DEFRA), the licensing authority, had not made any assessment of the damage from the fly-shooting technique. After months of protest from local fishers, DEFRA's spokesperson said: 'We are considering the potential effects of fly-shooting fishing gear used by vessels in UK waters, and have been discussing this with different sectors of the industry. Any future decisions on the use of this, or any other gear, will be based on the best available evidence.' The metaphor of closing the barn door after the horse has bolted comes to mind.

Other detrimental aspects of Brexit may take longer to manifest themselves. For example, though the government has claimed it supports 'discard-free fisheries', reduced trading opportunities may encourage more discarding. As long as there was an accessible market for species not valued by British consumers but valued in the EU, the tendency to discard good edible fish was held in check. Now that access to EU markets has become more difficult, there is less incentive to keep fish that may be hard to sell domestically.

The trend towards monopolization in the British fishing industry can also be expected to affect attitudes and business strategy. Large-scale owners, who dominate the English and Scottish fishing industries, will be unconcerned by a reduced number of fisherfolk or vessels. They may even respond to shrinking fish populations by squeezing out more marginal players, gaining more of the total catch and raising prices due to reduced competition.

This is what the Brexit saga in fisheries has really been about. Large-scale industrial fisheries have plundered the blue commons through their control of quota. Yet they have managed to pin the blame on the European Union, diverting the wrath of small-scale fishers towards the EU and 'foreign' boats.

Meanwhile, nominally British fisheries have long been dominated by foreign capital, alongside a few rich families, 'codfathers' and their ilk. Unless the power of the rentier alliance dominating British fisheries can be broken, decommoning and the depletion of fish populations will persist.

What is next?

What has happened to British fisheries encapsulates the failings of rentier capitalism in the blue economy. The plunder of the commons has left communities that were built on generations of artisan fisherfolk both insecure and marginalized, while corporate industrial fisheries have gained from the possession of most of the quotas, aided by subsidies effectively paid for by commoners of the land. Although the UK government acknowledged in a legal case that fish are a public resource, it has been negligent in its duty of stewardship and gatekeeping, first by gifting property rights to an elite and then by demonstrably failing to monitor and regulate blatant disregard for rules of resource reproduction.

Just because a trawler caught a lot of fish some years ago is no moral or legal justification for giving its owner privileged access to a lot of valuable fish now and in the years ahead. There is no moral or legal justification for allowing companies to keep gifted quota when they have been caught flagrantly breaking the rules to the long-term detriment of fish populations and fishing communities. And there is no justification for giving much of the transferable quota for valuable fish to producer organizations that can choose to whom they give the rights, without accountability to the public.

The artificial and arbitrary creation of private property

rights in UK fisheries through the quota system also limits the scope of government policy, because the claimed sanctity of private property rights means the state implicitly promises not to interfere with them. As one review of the legal position points out, 'The threat of litigation, even on relatively thin legal grounds, makes it hard for public administrators to make transformative decisions.'[44] With enclosure and privatization, the commons is potentially lost; the state loses control. It is unclear whether these informal property rights over a resource amount to a 'legal lock-in' and thus preclude adaptive public management, but since the resources should belong to the commons, there should be no presumption that these claimed rights amount to legal title.

This chapter has told the core part of an evolving crisis. Still, there are heart-warming stories of fisherfolk and valiant attempts to preserve and revive marine habitats around British shores. Although the UK has a very mixed record on establishing and implementing marine protected areas, without doubt there are many well-meaning people keen to improve the management of the waters around the UK. As elsewhere, it is not too late. But time is running out.

CHAPTER 7

Aquaculture: Saviour or Threat?

> Aquaculture – not the internet – represents the most
> promising investment opportunity of the 21st century.
> — Peter Drucker

Fish farming has existed for many thousands of years. In Australia, Aboriginal peoples were practising a form of aquaculture as far back as 40,000 years ago, using fish traps to capture and hold fish. Chinese farmers raised carp in their paddy fields 2,500 years ago, and around the same time primitive aquaculture may have started in ancient Egypt, with the farming of tilapia.

Traditionally, fish farming took place in rivers and lakes that were part of the commons. In England, the 'right of piscary', the right of commoners to catch and keep fish, was enshrined in the Charter of the Forest of 1217. But in recent years fish farming has expanded dramatically all over the world, encouraged in part by the crisis of overfishing and degraded marine ecosystems, in part by globalization and its impact on world trade, and in part by advances in technology and the pursuit of corporate profits.

The growth of industrial fish farming has produced an unprecedented value chain, whereby fish bred in one country or region are taken to another to be processed, and exported to yet another to be sold and consumed. In 'tuna ranching', wild juvenile fish are caught and reared in cages or pens in the sea, and sent later into the global trading system.

In 1950, aquaculture accounted for less than 3% of global production of fish by weight. Twenty years later it still only accounted for about 4%. But between 1970 and today, particularly since the late 1980s, production has expanded exponentially. In the 1950s, global production was less than a million tonnes; in 2018 it was eighty-two million tonnes, and worth some \$250 million.[1] By 2000, aquaculture accounted for over a quarter of all production and in 2018 just under half. A monumental transformation has taken place.

With capture fishery production broadly static since the late 1980s, aquaculture overtook wild fish for human consumption in 2016, and the World Bank has predicted that it will supply two-thirds of human consumption of fish by 2030. It is by far the world's fastest growing food-producing sector, easily outpacing human population growth and the increase in food production on land. If the Great Acceleration in the 1950s marked the first Industrial Revolution in the blue economy, the surge of aquaculture could be said to mark the second.

Although more than 500 aquatic species are farmed around the world, including some rare and threatened species, commercial production centres on about twenty-five species – mainly salmon, carp, clams, pangasius, shrimp and tilapia. Salmon and shrimp are two of the top five species consumed by Europeans; virtually all the salmon and half of the shrimp consumed now come from aquaculture.

Farming of freshwater fish has historically been the main focus of aquaculture, and still accounts for nearly two-thirds of aquaculture fish production by weight. Freshwater aquaculture is dominated by plant-eating (herbivorous) finfish, led by several varieties of carp. Alongside marine bivalve molluscs such as clams, oysters, mussels and scallops, herbivorous fish make up the 30% of farmed food fish – freshwater and saltwater – that do not require artificial feeding. However, this proportion has fallen from 44% in 2000.

That is because the main growth areas have been in high-value marine species, most notably shrimp – dubbed by some as 'pink gold' – and salmon and marine finfish. Farmed shrimp (or prawns, as Europeans call them) have become the most popular seafood eaten in the United States.[2] They and most other farmed marine fish eat processed feed such as fishmeal made from wild fish species, putting additional pressure on wild fish populations, especially small pelagics, vital to marine ecosystems and the livelihoods of many artisanal fisheries.

The main producer is China, which since 1991 has produced more farmed fish than the rest of the world put together. Along with India, Vietnam, Bangladesh and thirty-five other nations, China produced more farmed fish than wild-capture fish in 2018. In another twenty-two countries the proportion of farmed fish was over a third. But aquaculture has taken off almost everywhere. In the EU, which is also a big importer of farmed fish, aquaculture employed about 75,000 people in 2017 and produced 1.4 million tonnes of fish and shellfish, on a par with Norway. The top EU producers were Spain, the UK, France, Italy and Greece, with mussels comprising about a quarter of production by weight, and Atlantic salmon and rainbow trout (the main species raised in the UK) together accounting for a third by value.[3]

Aquaculture also includes creatures such as sea cucumbers and frogs, and there has been rapid growth in the cultivation of marine plants, especially seaweed such as kelp. Seaweed is used as food or as a food additive, but also in other sectors, such as pharmaceuticals and cosmetics. There is also a growing use of algae as feedstock for biofuel.

Three aspects of aquaculture illustrate the themes of this book. It has increased the commercialization and commodification of the fishing industry. It has had a damaging impact on blue commons communities and marine reproduction systems. And it has increased the scope for rent-seeking from the blue economy. In the background is a conventional belief, expressed by the FAO among others, that further exploitation of land for agriculture is limited so, to produce more protein for a growing population, the world needs to increase reliance on marine sources. Since wild fish are under stress, fish farming must be expanded.

Aquaculture pros and cons

Aquaculture is often presented as an alternative to marine wild catches, a way of relieving pressure on marine fish stocks. Some have referred to a 'blue transition' as 'the passage from fish biomass reduction to recovery in exploited aquatic resources, enabled by aquaculture'.[4] One study has claimed that aquaculture could replace the capture of all wild fish using less than 0.015% of the global ocean area.[5] However, the growth of aquaculture has not coincided with a decline in wild-capture fishing or a recovery in wild fish populations. Moreover, only certain species are amenable to farming, or are commercially worthwhile, so that many marine fish that are diet staples around the world cannot or will not be replaced by farmed varieties.[6] Commercial aquaculture is likely to continue to focus on international trade, mostly in high-value species such as salmon, sea bass and shrimp for affluent consumers in richer countries.

Another reason for doubting that aquaculture is removing the pressure on marine fish stocks is that many fish raised in fish farms are taken as juveniles from the sea for use as stock. This practice, which includes shrimp, milkfish, eels, yellowtail and southern bluefin tuna, depletes marine fish stocks and involves other kills as bycatch. Many farmed fish also rely for food largely on wild fish. Some rather alarming estimates of the Fish In–Fish Out (FIFO) ratio a few years ago calculated that one kilo of shrimp required four kilos of wild fish to produce, one kilo of Atlantic salmon required five kilos of wild fish, and one kilo of farmed tuna required twenty kilos of wild fish.[7]

FIFO ratios have declined somewhat since then as producers have tried substituting fishmeal with plant-based protein such as soya.[8] But they still suggest that aquaculture is not a sustainable replacement for overstressed wild marine fish. In the Mediterranean, the ranching of species such as bluefin tuna that are high up the food chain (fish with so-called high 'trophic value') has resulted in a net loss of fish since the weight of farmed tuna is far outweighed by the destruction of wild fish populations.[9]

Aquaculture is also seen as a key component of blue

growth strategies and a big employment generator. The EU, for example, claims it has a 'high potential for sustainable jobs and growth'. Globally, in 2018, over twenty million people were employed in aquaculture, up from 12.6 million in 2000, accounting for over a third of all employment in fisheries. In developing countries, aquaculture is touted as a way of providing food security and, through exports of high-value fish, as a source of foreign exchange. However, while aquaculture has increased the supply of fish for consumption by low-income consumers in some places,[10] in others it has displaced coastal wild-catch fisheries and hit nutritionally vulnerable people, who neither obtain the farmed fish nor benefit from the industry's profits.[11]

These issues are being played out in Africa, where aquaculture is less well developed than elsewhere but is spreading rapidly. For instance, a Norwegian firm has been setting up fish farms in nine African countries.[12] And US-based World Neighbors, a non-profit development organization, has sponsored projects combining fish production with vegetable growing around Lake Victoria in Kenya, with plans to extend into Uganda and Tanzania.[13]

An EU-funded five-year project known as True Fish, with FAO's technical assistance, also aims to boost African aquaculture to overcome the decline in wild fish catches.[14] The initiative is linked to campaigns by local fishery organizations, led by the Tilapia and Aquaculture Developers Association of Nigeria (TADAN), for their governments to ban the import of cheap farmed tilapia from China. TADAN claims that they are cheap because taxes are not paid on them, adding:

These fishes being brought from China are rejected fishes that cannot enter the European or American market because of the issue of growth hormones and the very bad water conditions where these fishes are raised in volumes can hamper the health of people.[15]

Resisting this is not easy. After Chinese fish imports into Kenya more than trebled in monetary value between 2015 and 2017, the president ordered a ban, only to reverse it after China threatened to withhold funds for completion of the strategic Standard Gauge Railway between Nairobi and the port of Mombasa.

Governance or security concerns may also deter investment in aquaculture to feed local populations. The coast of Kenya south of Mombasa, for example, has high potential.[16] But Kenya has suffered terrorist attacks and political violence. In a pessimistic assessment of prospects in sub-Saharan Africa to 2030, the World Bank said growth of capture fisheries and aquaculture would fall well behind rapid population growth, leading to declining per capita consumption of fish with 'far-reaching consequences for the intake of protein and micronutrients important for human growth and development'.[17]

Proponents of aquaculture argue further that it is a more environmentally friendly form of food production than farming on land. The EU Seafood and Aquaculture Initiative even claims aquaculture could 'decarbonise' the fishery sector. However, some estimates suggest that industrial fish farming has a carbon footprint double that of wild fishing, as bad as poultry and pig rearing.[18] And aquaculture has been directly responsible for environmental damage through massive changes in land use, including the destruction of mangrove forests, pollution of neighbouring waters with effluent, and the spread of disease among fish.

These concerns remain, despite new technologies and incentive schemes such as eco-labelling that are beginning to improve practices.[19] Disease, which can wipe out entire fish stocks, can be combated by low-tech methods such as the establishment of integrated fish farms (known as 'integrated multi-trophic aquaculture') that use shellfish to absorb fish excreta.[20] Integrated farming can mix fish production with animal husbandry or vegetable growing. Other developments that aim to avoid environmental damage are indoor farming of marine fish using so-called 'recirculation aquaculture systems' (RAS) and polyculture, involving combinations of fish, molluscs and seaweed or other vegetation.[21]

According to some enthusiastic commercial fish farmers, the future of aquaculture is indoors. The head of Blue Ridge Aquaculture, based in Virginia, USA, compared what he was doing with breeding battery chickens, telling *National Geographic*, 'My model is the poultry industry. The difference is, our fish are perfectly happy.'[22] When asked how he knew they were happy, he said they would die otherwise.

RAS still only account for about 1% of all aquaculture production. However, indoor fish farms are being planned on a vast scale. Norway's Nordic Aquafarms has received authorization to construct a $500 million salmon farm in Maine, USA, designed to 'optimise fish densities and tank volume'. Its tanks will have three times the volume of an Olympic swimming pool and the firm expects to produce 33,000 tonnes of fish a year, about 8% of US consumption.[23] The company notes that the famous Monterey Bay Aquarium's Seafood Watch now ranks RAS-farmed fish as one of the most sustainable choices available. Meanwhile, Israeli aquaculture firm AquaMaof has been building indoor facilities in Canada, Germany, Japan, Norway, Poland, Russia and Slovakia. Its plant in Newfoundland, Canada, is the world's largest indoor salmon facility.[24]

Risks and threats

Before discussing the risks and threats for humans and the environment, we should recognize that, in the pursuit of profits, industrial aquaculture has treated fish abominably. The leading farmed high-value fish is the Atlantic salmon, which was the first carnivore fish to be farmed for human consumption.[25] Although breeding methods may be refined, the current system should disgust anyone with a care for living creatures.

Female salmon are given hormone baths and injections to increase their roe. When 'ripe' they are cut open to extract eggs. Milt from killed males is sprayed on the eggs, and the fry are hatched in plastic trays in incubators. Once weaned, they are exposed to light for 24 hours a day to accelerate growth. After a year, they are transferred into huge, overcrowded net-pens in sea bays, and fed fishmeal, which can transmit dangerous chemical toxins to other marine life.

The problems of contamination and price rises have prompted the industry to reduce fishmeal in favour of more plant-based protein. But this, combined with the crowding in pens, produces flabby, unappetizing grey flesh. So the salmon are fed a petroleum-derived synthetic, allowing fish

315

farmers to choose from a range of colours, from mild pink to bright red. Farmed fish take in the faeces of others and easily pass on pathogens; they are also vulnerable to infections, including viruses. Moreover, they can pass on diseases to wild stocks, while algae blooms generated by the concentration of undigested food and faeces kill off shellfish. And densely packed salmon are eaten alive, slowly, by sea lice, which include parasites that eat the skin on a salmon's head until it dies of exposure.

There have also been many instances of wipe-outs of farms. The known disasters have been huge. A sudden algae outcrop in Chile killed over 30,000 tonnes of salmon in just one area. On the other side of the world, in Northern Ireland, a swarm of jellyfish known as mauve stingers annihilated an entire reputable organic salmon farm. Other wipe-outs have been caused by storms or disease.

In another worrying development, the US Food and Drug Administration (FDA) ruled in 2015 that Atlantic salmon genetically engineered to speed their growth were fit for human consumption and did not have to be labelled as genetically modified in restaurants and take-aways. In 2019 this genetically engineered salmon, developed by Aquabounty, a US biotech company, became the first genetically modified animal to be approved for sale in the USA. Aquabounty has taken a gene that regulates growth hormones in Pacific Chinook salmon and a 'promoter', a sort of genetic on-off switch, from another species, ocean pout, and introduced them into Atlantic salmon. The salmon, dubbed by some a 'Frankenfish', grows to market size in half the time taken by unmodified farmed fish.

However, transplanting alien genes entails unknown and

unpredictable risks, for salmon, for humans and for ecosystems, including the spread of new pathogens and changes in the genetic makeup of wild salmon through interbreeding. Environmental activists have called for a boycott of genetically engineered salmon, and big US supermarket chains such as Walmart, Costco and Whole Foods say they will not sell it. Surely prudence should prevail over profits. Yet salmon is just one of thirty-five species of fish currently being considered for genetic modification.

Genetically modified fish aside, the FAO argues that aquaculture methods have improved.[26] Sea lice, for example, can now be largely controlled by stocking so-called cleaner fish, which feed on the parasite. However, solutions bring with them their own problems. Adding lice-eating fish such as wrasse into salmon pens may deplete those fish populations. Treating the salmon with chemicals endangers other species in the surrounding water, including lobster. And use of antibiotics by fish farms to treat and prevent disease is contributing to the global increase in drug-resistant strains of bacteria, a major threat to human health.[27] To avoid this, some companies are growing pathogen-free larvae in sterile, carefully managed hatcheries, but these are mainly confined to rich-world fish farms.

Countries are also using regulations to tackle bad practices. In Norway, the world's largest source of farmed salmon, licences for fish farming are now only given to companies with plans to address waste, sea lice and escaped fish. However, controls are less stringent in Asia, the biggest source of farmed fish. The USA imports 90% of its seafood, mostly from Asia, and only about 2% is inspected by the FDA. In those

limited inspections, it has discovered numerous banned substances, including carcinogens.[28]

Even with controls, a report in 2021 covering the four main
countries of salmon farming – Canada, Chile, Norway and
Scotland – painted a depressing picture. The mortality rate
on Scottish farms, for example, quadrupled from 3% in 2002
to about 13.5% in 2019, with at least a fifth of the deaths due
to sea lice infestations and perhaps much more, since many
other deaths had unknown causes.[29] In addition to high mortality rates, the report identified heavy social and environmental costs that the aquaculture companies do not pay for. It
estimated that about 40% of the total cost of salmon farming
is borne by society, in pollution, loss of other fish populations
and impact on the surrounding environment.

Mowi, a Norwegian company that produces a fifth of the
world's farmed Atlantic salmon, accounted for an estimated
fifty million premature fish deaths between 2010 and 2019.
It responded to the report by saying: 'We are pleased that the
report finds that, when considering the full range of benefits
and impacts, the business of salmon farming demonstrates
overall positive benefit. We agree that there are opportunities for continued improvements for our business.'[30] This
seems rather an understatement.

Elsewhere, aquaculture has polluted freshwater sources
with nutrient wastes and harmful chemicals, and caused depletion and salinization of potable water, salinization of agricultural land, escapes of non-native species and the spread
of disease to native species.[31] The introduction of 'foreign'
species for farming may inadvertently wipe out native species or devastate the local ecosystem. In a notorious example

from Africa, the introduction of carnivorous Nile perch into Lake Victoria in the 1950s has led to the extinction or near-extinction of several hundred native species. Other examples of damaging introductions include non-native tilapia and crayfish.[32]

Climate change is also exacerbating the risks associated with aquaculture, which is vulnerable to increasingly frequent extreme weather events, such as floods, storms, hurricanes and drought. Some countries are particularly exposed: they include Norway and Chile for marine aquaculture, and Vietnam, Thailand, Ecuador and Egypt for 'brackish water' aquaculture in water adjoining the sea.[33] Tidal surges and flooding can change salinity in aquaculture ponds, leading to losses of fish, stunted growth and mass escapes.

In the US state of Washington in 2017, strong currents destroyed a net-pen owned by a Canadian company, Cooke Aquaculture, and released 250,000 farmed non-native Atlantic salmon into the Pacific Ocean. The threat to already depleted wild Pacific salmon and other species so alarmed the state authorities that they passed a law banning net-pen salmon farming. The company was forced to pay $2.75 million for that and other violations after legal action by environmental groups. But in 2020 it was granted a permit to raise a partially sterile form of steelhead trout, which environmentalists say is capable of interbreeding and exchanging pathogens and parasites with endangered wild Puget Sound steelhead.[34]

In another example, when Storm Ellen hit the Scottish Isle of Arran in August 2020, strong winds and tides damaged mooring ropes attaching ten salmon pens to the seabed. The huge North Carradale sea farm was one of twenty-five salmon farms off Scotland operated by Norway's Mowi. Those ten pens held 550,000 salmon, of which 49,000 escaped, 31,000 died and 125,000 were harvested, prematurely.

Stiffer regulations, certification of cage equipment, modification of pond systems and management reforms are needed to reduce escapes and the risk to native fish populations. New strategies to adapt to climate change, such as moving floating fish cages further offshore, would also be beneficial.[35] Yet without access to funds and technical advice, these investments will be out of reach of small-scale fish farmers.

It is often claimed that, since small-scale producers account for most aquaculture production, they will benefit from its expansion. Yet they are being squeezed by commercial aquaculture, unable to afford the technologies needed to check disease and pollution and lacking the financial resources to recover from shocks from disease or weather. And, in a vicious cycle, these risks will continue to deter financial institutions from providing insurance or low-interest loans to small-scale fisheries.[36]

Globalization, which has driven much of the growth of aquaculture, has also had adverse consequences. Chile is a prime example. It is one of the world's ten largest producers of farmed fish, with over 3,000 aquaculture farms (called 'concessions') along its long coastline. About 45% raise salmon, with most of the remainder dedicated to mussels and edible algae. An early testbed for neoliberal economic strategy, Chile was encouraged to produce high-value farmed fish largely for export. The concessions were subsidized for that end.

Domestic food consumption of fish in Chile has dropped far below that of most fishing nations. Most wild fish is turned into fishmeal for fish farms, while high-value farmed fish, such as salmon, the mainstay of Chile's aquaculture, is exported to richer countries. Farmed fish is rarely found in the shops or local markets.[37] Even when it is, it is too expensive for most Chileans. Thus, Chile is no longer producing cheap seafood for domestic consumption. In this country with abundant fish, the commodification that has come with industrialized aquaculture has deprived the country's citizens of fish. The commons have been sacrificed to the god of economic growth.

Ecuador is another example of the threat posed to the blue commons by aquaculture. It is the world's fifth largest producer of farmed shrimp; the industry employs some 250,000 people. But clearance of mangrove forests to construct fish farms has reduced the forested area from over 360,000 hectares to just over 100,000, even though mangrove forests can sustain the livelihoods and provide food for eight times as many people as the shrimp industry, according to c-CONDEM, the local member of the World Forum of Fisher Peoples.

Local business owners acquired wetlands with loans from the Bank of the Pacific, and evicted entire communities as the land was enclosed and then privatized. After the first of the new landholders went bankrupt in 1997, a 'Collective' of over seventy families with ancestral ties tried to reclaim the land. But in 2010 the Bank sold it to another business. This was contested by the Collective, which won a court ruling in its favour. But the government did not restore their right to the land or its resources.[38] It was a sad case of 'accumulation by dispossession', a defeat for the commons.

The fishmeal question

As noted earlier, most farmed fish require artificial feeding and commercial aquaculture has required a huge expansion in the capture of fish to make fishmeal. Although fish trimmings make up a rising share, fishmeal and fish oil are largely derived from small pelagic marine fish known as wild forage fish, which are oily fish such as anchovies, sardines, sprats, mackerel, herring and sardinella.

About a quarter of all fish captured in the sea is destined for purposes other than direct human consumption, mostly for reduction to fishmeal and fish oil.[39] About two-thirds of all fishmeal is used for aquaculture, with most of the remainder going for pig and poultry feed. About 75% of fish oil is used for aquaculture, although it is also in demand for its omega-3 content as an ingredient of cosmetics and skincare products.

Mauritania, Senegal and the Gambia, which have among the world's best conditions for pelagics, have seen a boom in fishmeal and fish oil processing, entirely controlled by foreign investors with production almost exclusively intended for overseas markets.[40] Production increased more than tenfold between 2010 and 2019, from 13,000 tonnes to over 170,000 tonnes.[41] The EU is a major investor and consumer market.[42] Russia has re-emerged as a big player, and companies from Turkey and the USA are also involved. But China has been the leading foreign investor. In the Gambia, all three fishmeal factories are owned by Chinese firms, while about a quarter of fishmeal factories in Mauritania are Chinese. Many of the smaller fishmeal factories are run as joint ventures with local partners, or are presented as such, since the true beneficial owners are hard to identify.

In 2011, the Chinese company Poly HonDon received authorization from the Mauritanian government to build a fish-processing plant to handle up to 100,000 tonnes of fish annually. Although the agreement did not specify the types of fish, it allowed the company to process and export substantial quantities of fishmeal and fish oil. In 2017, the government authorized another Chinese firm, Sunrise Oceanic Resources Exploitation Company, to build a fishmeal factory over three times the size of Poly HonDon's and allowed it to bring its own fishing fleet. Who would have thought commodified fishmeal production would be a neo-colonial activity of the twenty-first century?

For many years, the fishing industry in West Africa was dominated by industrial vessels from Europe and Russia. Most of the small pelagic fish they caught was sold frozen or tinned for human consumption, mainly in African markets. However, to promote the fishmeal sector and check the impoverishment of small-scale fishing communities, governments lowered the quotas of small pelagics that foreign vessels could take. In 2012, Mauritania banned them from inshore areas, where the highest concentrations of round sardinella are found. In that period, most of the fish for fishmeal factories was supplied by local artisanal fisheries.

Later, as China's involvement grew, along with the number of fishmeal factories, locals were increasingly squeezed out. Several Chinese factories brought their own fishing boats. They were not alone. Since 2015, huge Turkish purse-seine vessels have been operating in Mauritanian waters to supply three Turkish-owned factories. Their boats were then contracted to supply Chinese factories as well, and a secretive fisheries agreement between Mauritania and Turkey extended their involvement.[43] Over forty Turkish vessels now fish in Mauritanian waters.

Foreign fishmeal activities are weakly regulated and official data on production are woefully incomplete. The factories are rarely monitored. Dubious government deals have exempted some Chinese factories in Mauritania from rules on customs control, so their catches are excluded from statistics on fish exports.[44] Some factories have responded to processing limits by misreporting sardinella as other species for which limits are not set.

The FAO, which has tried to quantify fish landed in Mauritania for fishmeal processing, suggests that landings rose from about 50,000 tonnes in 2010 to 550,000 tonnes in 2018. Before 2010, Mauritania had just one fishmeal factory processing waste fish and offcuts. By 2019, it had thirty-nine factories, most using whole fish. And more factories were in the pipeline.[45] These are operating alongside six factories in Senegal and three in the Gambia.

Governments in the region have blocked efforts to monitor the fisheries, according to the FAO's working group on North-West Africa's small pelagics.[46] However, independent evidence indicates that fish stocks are dwindling alarmingly due to overfishing, driven by the fishmeal and fish oil industry. Pelagics are also moving northwards and southwards away from West Africa as ocean temperatures rise. In 2018, an acoustic survey by a Norwegian vessel indicated that fish populations were the lowest on record.[47] The FAO has called for an urgent 50% reduction in fishing effort for sardinella.[48] Yet government authorities and companies involved continue to insist that the fishing is sustainable.

In the Gambia, declining fish populations have led to conflicts with Senegalese fishers who have been contracted by factories to supply fish from Gambian waters. There have been protests from women who have long earned their livelihood as fish processors. Some fishers have been lured into debt bondage to factories, which have lent them money on condition that they supply their fish to the factories. The factories have also caused serious pollution by pumping waste and chemicals into the sea, even dumping loads of surplus fish on beaches.[49]

While the Chinese and Russian governments have negotiated shady and conspicuously generous deals with host governments, some European firms claim to be championing sustainability. In Mauritania, the French firm Olvea, one of several cosmetics firms that own fishmeal factories in the country, is supporting a Fisheries Improvement Project (FIP) alongside other companies investing in Mauritania's fishmeal and fish oil industry, including Norwegian firms supplying fishmeal to European salmon farms.[50] This FIP is one of several industry-backed FIPs around the world, described as 'a pragmatic, stepwise approach to enhancing the sustainability of a fishery, encouraging harvesting to continue, while continual improvements are achieved'.[51] However, the primary purpose of FIPs is to gain eco-labels, in this case for West African fishmeal and fish oil products, to burnish the companies' brand image as much as to champion sustainability.

The pursuit of eco-labelling through FIPs is part of a global campaign involving well-funded lobbying by rich-country fisheries. Meanwhile, local artisanal fishery organizations have no voice in the FIP framework. When the industry's trade organization – the International Fishmeal and Fish Oil Organisation (IFFO) – contracted a British firm to study the impact of the industry in West Africa, it dismissed protests by local artisan fishers, as well as expert opinions by EU scientists, as handling the subject too 'emotively'.[52] This is 'bluewashing' pure and simple.

Demand for fishmeal and fish oil has led to supply shortages and rising prices, which has stimulated the search for substitutes and production of fishmeal using fish waste. However, even with a reduced reliance on fishmeal per farmed fish, the projected expansion of industrial aquaculture is likely to result in higher demand for fishmeal overall. And small pelagics are expected to remain the main source of fishmeal and fish oil, increasing pressure on stocks. This also reduces the food supply of larger predator fish, causing stunted growth, lower fertility and further erosion of those fish populations. Quota systems that focus on high-value commercial fish have neglected the depletion of wild forage fish. An ecosystem management approach would be more appropriate, yet small pelagics are rarely managed in this way.[53] Since 1950, stocks of small, short-lived forage fish have had as many collapses as better known high-value fish populations,[54] with severe knock-on effects on the larger fish, seabirds and marine mammals that feed on them.

Small pelagics have long been the main source of income for local fishers and fish traders in West Africa, and are part of the staple diet for millions of people in coastal communities and beyond. Communities traditionally dependent on these fish have been made more vulnerable. In Senegal, foreign industrial fishery vessels first devastated the stocks of thiof (white groupers), a long-standing staple of the Senegalese diet, and then devastated stocks of sardinella, which had replaced thiof as the staple. Most sardinella is taken by foreign vessels for fishmeal. As one researcher said: 'Sardinella is at the bottom of the food chain. If sardinella stocks are depleted, there won't be much else to fish. Losing those species would drive the entire ecosystem to collapse.'[55]

This has already had terrible human ramifications. In recent years sardinella has accounted for three-quarters of all the fish consumption in Senegal and has been the main source of protein. Diminishing supply led to a trebling of domestic sardinella prices between 2009 and 2019, threatening the food security of much of the population. And the impoverishment of traditional fishing communities has caused mass migration to Europe. Many thousands of Senegalese have been driven to undertake the perilous voyage across the Mediterranean, captured in Wolof slang as 'Barca or Barsaax', meaning 'Barcelona or die'.[56] And many have died or are missing in the attempt.

The hypocrisy involved in this tragic situation is disgraceful. The EU provides hefty subsidies that enable its vessels to take fish off West Africa that are the mainstay of local fishing communities, and then gives more than a billion dollars' worth of aid to countries in the region to curb illegal migration. The fisheries researcher described the attitude of would-be migrants to Europe rather well:

It is a sign of frustration saying that why does our fish not need a visa and we do? You're taking our fish away from our waters; you're taking our livelihood away from our waters. I am entitled to go to Europe because you took everything away from me.

The plight of pelagics is so grave that the only sustainable course would be to close the fishmeal factories and ban industrial fishing for small pelagics altogether. 'Bluewashing' by fishmeal investors is simply concealing overfishing. Short of a ban, foreign governments should stop subsidizing their long-distance industrial fishing vessels, which would otherwise be uneconomic, and bar imports that contribute to destruction of the commons and local commoning communities. Local people must have priority in access to and use of local fish for direct human consumption.

Mangroves and other wetlands

Mangrove forests are a magical part of the earth's ecosystem. These unique trees, which grow in salt water between the land and near-shore marine environments in tropical and subtropical regions, support diverse communities of plants, birds, fish, crustaceans and mammals. The forests act as nurseries for shrimp, crab and offshore fish; one study has suggested that almost 80% of global fish catches are directly or indirectly dependent on mangroves.[57]

Mangroves' dense root systems and leaves filter salt and other materials, protecting coastal lands from salinization. They also act as a barrier to sea surges, mitigating the impact of tropical storms. In the other direction, they trap sediments flowing down rivers and off the land, helping to stabilize the coastline and prevent erosion. By filtering out sediments, the forests protect coral reefs and seagrass meadows from being smothered. Globally, they are a source of carbon sequestration, storing three to four times as much carbon as tropical upland forests, and supply essential organic carbon to the world's oceans.

Although mangroves comprise only 0.5% of the world's forest area, millions of people depend on them for food and income, and for the protection they provide to coastal land areas. But the growth of aquaculture, especially shrimp farming, is destroying the forests and the communities that depend on them. Globally, as much as a third of mangrove cover has been lost since 1980, half of which represents clearing for aquaculture; agricultural and urban development account for the rest. As a result, 16% of mangrove tree species and perhaps 40% of mangrove animal species are at high risk of extinction.[58]

The global growth in shrimp farming, which alone may have caused nearly 40% of mangrove loss, was encouraged by the World Bank, which provided loans to establish farms and urged governments and intergovernmental agencies to support them. They bear responsibility for the impoverishment of communities and associated environmental degradation. Clearance of mangroves has continued, unchecked by protective regulations. In addition, the farms pollute groundwater and estuaries, while salt from the ponds seeps into groundwater and onto agricultural land, making it unfit for crops, most notably in Bangladesh. Even more inexcusably, shrimp aquaculture rarely benefits local poor communities; they cannot afford the shrimp, and most is intended for export.[59]

Indonesia has the largest mangrove cover, accounting for over 20% of the world's mangroves. But it has lost half its mangrove areas since the 1950s, due mainly to aquaculture and timber logging and despite government efforts to curb deforestation. The Centre for International Forestry Research (CIFOR) has concluded that mangroves deteriorate more in areas where community rights are not respected or recognized, and where the important economic and social roles played by women are ignored. Without respecting community rights, mangrove rehabilitation efforts also fail.[60]

Tanzania provides an instructive example. The Rufiji river delta, home to the largest continuous mangrove forest in East Africa, supports the country's most important fishery, including wild shrimp. In the 1990s the government gave the go-ahead for what would have been the world's largest shrimp farm, involving the destruction of much of the mangrove forest, before the project was abandoned in the face of local opposition and an international outcry. Yet subsequent state protection has had only limited success in checking the clearance of mangroves for rice paddies and firewood. Locals have also allowed outsiders to harvest timber and charcoal illegally to sell in the capital, Dar es Salaam. A CIFOR researcher summed up the situation: 'The threats are increasing and the government alone cannot deal with all these threats. People will always come up with creative ways on how they can access and use the mangroves, regardless of how much protection the government imposes.'[61]

Recognizing that local communities need good reasons to defend the mangroves from outsiders and manage them sustainably, CIFOR with others tested three models of community engagement. Supporting the claim in this book that only a commons approach will suffice, the model that was based on providing individual property rights was the least successful. The Tanzanian Forest Service (TFS) gave farmers renewable one-year licences to farm rice in exchange for regenerating mangrove trees on their plots. Once the trees grew to a certain height, the farmers had to move and repeat the process. But this gave them an incentive to prevent mangrove recovery.

A second approach relied on group rehabilitation of mangroves. Local people were paid for each day they replanted trees or weeded around them. But this gave no sense of community ownership. In a third approach, known as the Joint Forest Management scheme, the TFS negotiated cost and benefit-sharing arrangements with communities and transferred some decision-making powers to them. It turned out to be the most promising of the three schemes and can be seen as a move towards recreating a commoning community.

Although not wholly successful in checking mangrove loss, the Tanzanian case contrasts with other countries where corporate aquaculture has predominated. FAO experts claim that most companies now have policies to curtail mangrove destruction for shrimp farming.[62] But still, fish farm ponds are often exploited for several years and then abandoned, while mangrove ecosystem rehabilitation is costly and hard to achieve.

Draining mangrove swamps for aquaculture is even more damaging to the climate than cutting down rainforest to provide pasture for cattle. CIFOR found that clearing mangroves was by far the main contributor to shrimp farming's carbon footprint, and that a kilo of farmed shrimp was responsible for almost four times the greenhouse gas emissions as a kilo of beef. Turning mangrove areas into zones for aquaculture for export has such damaging ecological and social effects that in a sensible world it would be stopped.

Meanwhile, the growing investor interest in 'blue carbon' projects – carbon stored and sequestered in mangrove forests, seagrass meadows and tidal salt marshes – to reach decarbonization targets has stimulated a fledgling carbon-offset market in which conservation groups sell carbon credits to fund their work in protecting mangroves, seagrass meadows and salt marsh ecosystems. Investors include shipping companies, renewable energy firms and finance companies, and blue carbon mangrove projects are in development or under way in Colombia, Kenya, Senegal, Madagascar, Vietnam and the Sundarbans in India.[63] The biggest so far is in Pakistan's degraded Indus delta on the Arabian Sea where the Sindh regional government is working with Indus Delta Capital, a development company, to protect or restore over 350,000 hectares of mangrove forest. This project aimed to sell a million credits in 2021, increasing to 30 million over the next ten years. However, whatever their proponents like to claim, financing mangrove restoration with blue carbon-offset credits risks acting as a licence to pollute by those buying the credits, the offsets may not be equivalent, and those groups gaining the funds control how the money is used, including taking a cut for themselves. The involvement of local communities can be treated as an optional extra.

Financialization of aquaculture

> We believe that the industry can help to meet the nutritional
> needs of a growing global population, while also generating
> environmental social benefits, and providing attractive
> investment opportunities with compelling financial returns.
> — The Nature Conservancy and Encourage Capital[64]

The expansion of industrial aquaculture since the 1970s in
Asia, Latin America and Africa has been driven largely by foreign finance. Initially that came mainly through grants and
loans from bilateral development agencies, notably those of
Japan, the USA, Norway and the UK, and then increasingly
from loans from the World Bank, the IMF and regional development banks. Billions of dollars have gone into large-scale
commercial shrimp farming for export to rich countries.

The World Bank has contended that the expansion reflected market forces, a supply response to rising global demand.
In reality, it was fuelled by loans from financial agencies and
IMF pressure through its 'structural adjustment' lending for
a shift to export-oriented fish production.[65] Substantial sums
of money went to support the growth of foreign control of
farmed shrimp, with funds used to aid corporations from the
USA, Japan and Europe. Japan's Mitsubishi, BP Nutrition's
Aquastar, and Ralston Purina of the USA have all benefited
from loans for fish farming and aid for construction of necessary infrastructure.[66] Financial aid has propelled the evolution of a 'world shrimp commodity system', part of the
so-called 'blue revolution'.

Expansion of fish farming on a massive scale was financed

before any assessment of possible ecological and social damage. Only after two decades of pumping money and technical assistance into shrimp farms did the World Bank set up, with WWF, FAO and the Network of Aquaculture Centres in Asia and the Pacific, a Consortium Program on Shrimp Farming and the Environment to conduct case studies of management strategies for sustainability.

In the early 1990s, the giant US construction corporation Bechtel International joined forces with the nutrition division of BP, the UK-based oil giant, in constructing a $100 million prawn farm in Thailand. They transformed subsistence rice paddies into 1,700 prawn ponds, each the size of a football pitch, with supporting canals, electrical generating facilities, feed mills, hatcheries and processing plants. Finance was raised by Bechtel Financing, the corporation's investment arm.

The rice farmers were induced to sign contracts agreeing to buy products and services from Bechtel and BP, the former providing infrastructure and technical services, the latter selling the black tiger prawns on the market. BP's Nutrition Division was soon selling vast numbers of prawns to Japan and the USA. In a media puff, the vice-president of Bechtel Financing proudly said that not only had it taken 'substantial equity' in the project but had forged the laws of Thailand. He said, 'We took a proactive position and essentially got together with the Thai government and wrote many of the laws dealing with aquaculture and shrimp farming.'[67] The former rice farmers did well financially, but the communities and local economy were obliterated.

Mergers and acquisitions in the sector have created an

oligopolistic industry – that is, a global commodity system controlled by a few giant players. The tendency for big corporations to eliminate competition by buying up their rivals is classic rentier capitalism. In this form of capitalism, firms acquire each other as commodities rather than compete with them in the market for goods and services.

To take a few examples, in 2014 Mitsubishi of Japan, best known as a car manufacturer, acquired the large Norwegian salmon farming corporation Cermaq for $1.4 billion. In 2015, SHV Holdings, a Dutch family-backed investment firm, paid €3 billion for Dutch animal feed specialist Nutreco. Later that year, Cargill, a US agricultural and trading behemoth, bought Norwegian salmon-feed firm EWOS Holding from two private-equity companies for $1.47 billion. And in 2015, the UK's Benchmark Holdings bought Belgium's INVE Aquaculture from two big banks for about £227 million ($322 million), giving it a 20% share of the world's market for shrimp and fish hatcheries and nurseries.[68]

Meanwhile, Norway's Mowi (formerly Marine Harvest), the world's biggest producer of farmed Atlantic salmon, has continued to take over other firms. When it bought a Norwegian fish farming company in 2019, one analyst commented, 'They can be willing to pay a high price, because they want to get rid of a competitor.'[69] Mowi's largest shareholder is a company controlled by oil and shipping magnate John Fredriksen, a multibillionaire, who was Norway's richest man until he took Cypriot citizenship in 2006. He also owns the world's largest oil tanker fleet and, among other businesses, offshore driller Seadrill.

We are seeing a systemic process of horizontal and vertical

conglomeration, aided by global finance, in which multi-nationals consolidate control over parts of the chain from production to sale of fish products (vertical integration) and/or monopolize specific parts of the chain (horizontal integration), notably in fish production. The capital-intensive nature of commercial aquaculture means it is dominated by a few vertically integrated corporations, notably Mowi, Japan's Nippon Suisan Kaisha and Spain's Nueva Pescanova, as well as retailers such as Walmart and Carrefour.

Conglomeration is encouraged by bank investment, led by DNB, Norway's largest bank, which invested over $1 billion in 2019 alone, Denmark's Nordea Bank and Rabobank, based in the Netherlands. Commercial aquaculture has also become an enticing sphere for private equity, which is prominent in other industries exhibiting a trend to conglomeration. Funds with interests in aquaculture include California-based Paine Schwartz Partners, Dutch private equity fund Aqua-Spark, and Bonafide, based in Switzerland and Hong Kong.[70] In 2019, the US investment fund Amerra Capital became the majority shareholder in AquaShip, a company that then owned and operated a global fleet of twenty-eight service boats.

Nueva Pescanova, based in Galicia, Spain, is a major producer of farmed shrimp and one of the world's largest producers of farmed turbot. The company has a controversial history. In its previous incarnation, as Pescanova, once the world's biggest fishery company, it went bankrupt in 2013 after piling up huge debts. In October 2020 its former president, Manuel Fernández de Sousa-Faro, son of the founder, was sentenced to eight years in jail for fraud and falsifying documents that led to the bankruptcy. The company was rescued by a consortium of financial institutions including vulture funds. As part of the subsequent restructuring, one of its salmon farming businesses in Chile, Nova Austral, was sold to EWOS and is now owned by private equity companies Altor and Bain Capital. In March 2020 ABANCA Corporación Bancaria, a Galician bank, took a majority shareholding in Nueva Pescanova itself.

Other financial firms with interests in aquaculture include Alimentos Ventures, a venture capital firm based in Germany, whose CEO is also co-founder of HATCH, described as the world's first accelerator programme focused on sustainable aquaculture start-ups. Among the most intriguing is Coastal Enterprises, based in Maine, which operates as a non-profit organization and can thus take on more risk because it can lend money from US federal or state funds, which is a form of state subsidy.

Private equity is also penetrating indoor 'recirculation aquaculture systems' (RAS) in a big way. For instance, the Israeli firm AquaMaof has partnered with 8F Investment Partners, a Singapore-based private equity firm consisting of former Deutsche Bank executives, in an Atlantic salmon facility in Poland. AquaMaof claims its facilities can deliver a high rate of return over four to seven years.

Private equity funds operate on a short-term profit-maximizing business model, expecting to make their profit and then sell up and shift to other investments with a time horizon of about seven years. Profit, not conservation, is the priority. And promoters of financial investment in aquaculture claim it can yield an internal rate of return of up to 22% annually. These are very high rates of profit, indicative of the rents being earned in the sector.

Thus, in 2018, US-based investment company Encourage Capital structured its Pescador Holdings for private equity returns of 15–25%. And the founder and managing partner at Aqua-Spark told an investor conference that his firm expected a return of 22%, stating that, 'The view that aquaculture is not profitable is as false as it gets.'[71] He added that 'disrupters like Google are looking at aquaculture, though they haven't invested yet.'

A year later, the consultancy Spheric Research described aquaculture as 'the hottest investment play on the globe' and said there was 'an unprecedented level of interest in disrupting aquaculture from an array of impact investors, venture capitalists, philanthropists and governments'.[72] It added that the needed and expected capital inflow would transform the sector: 'Disruption could put thousands of smallholder shrimp farmers across southeast Asia and China out of business.'

Clearly, financialization represents a global threat to small-scale independent fishery communities, and a structural threat to marine commoning in general. But now it is expanding into aquaculture, its predatory model can be expected to accelerate its destructive tendencies. Not for nothing has private equity been described as 'termite capitalism'.

And so: saviour or threat?

Aquaculture has the potential to be the best food system available to mankind.

— Mike Velings, founder, Aqua-Spark, global investment fund[73]

Is the growth of aquaculture a saviour for beleaguered wild fish populations or a threat to the blue commons and to commoning in fishing? Aquaculture clearly has the potential to serve humanity's food security needs. But so far it has had serious environmental costs and unquestionable adverse effects on blue commons communities. It is a modern form of enclosure, which facilitates privatization and commodification. When practised in the coastal sea, aquaculture typically converts what was a common pool resource into a private property resource, which only the owners of the fish farm can access. In this way alone, aquaculture is a major way by which the blue commons are lost.

Historically, aquaculture was a commoning activity and in places it still is, providing food and livelihoods for local communities. But industrial aquaculture largely ignores the commons. Those who gain are effectively rentiers, with access to financial capital and global markets. They also profit from publicly funded research and development of technological tools and infrastructure, as well as subsidies that mitigate risk. This is relevant to the proposals detailed in the final chapter.

Commodifying the Sea: The Mining Juggernaut

To imagine the seas as a commons opens up a vast and daunting vista that is conceptually hard to grasp. It requires us to go beyond thinking of the vast expanses of deep water as a basin of resources for humanity to discover and use. It is neither state property nor private property, though it can artificially and arbitrarily be made so.

The seas and all that are in or on or underneath them belong to nobody and yet belong to everybody. Many people would contend that the seas and what is in them are an integrated whole that should be left undisturbed. Here, however, it is accepted that humanity will continue to exploit what is in, on or under the sea. The challenge is to find ways of doing so that respect the reproduction needs of all of nature and that ensure that all of us, as commoners, share equitably in the process.

For millennia, human activities in the oceans were confined to navigation and fishing. But the twentieth century changed the way humanity looked at the sea. Technological breakthroughs enabled us to catch fish in the deep, and to drill for oil, gas and minerals. Like the land, the seas are now being used for multiple purposes, including the building of human habitats on new islands. But the trend was started by the shift to the sea for energy.

The first offshore oil well was drilled in 1937 off the US state of Louisiana. By 1980, offshore oil and gas provided 20% of world consumption; by 2014, it provided 30%, with more coming from depths of over three kilometres.[1] Over two-thirds of the oil and gas discoveries in the twenty-first century have been under the seabed, and energy companies are moving steadily into areas of greater depth. Since 1970, the oil and gas industry has drilled thousands of deep-ocean wells, and in 2020 the French-owned oil giant Total announced plans to drill off the coast of Angola at a record depth of 3.6 kilometres. The mining of minerals has followed the same path into deeper water, including the extraction of sand and gravel for the insatiable global construction industry.

The probability of accidents increases with depth, so the move to deeper waters raises the risk of serious oil pollution incidents.[2] The damage to ecosystems and livelihoods of the 2010 Deepwater Horizon disaster in the Gulf of Mexico, to date the largest oil spill in marine history, is still being felt today. The explosion of BP's Deepwater Horizon oil rig, which killed eleven workers, led to 750 million litres of oil being poured into the ocean over three months, fouling more than 2,000 kilometres of coast, devastating marine life and destroying jobs in fisheries and tourism.

Ecosystems will take decades to recover. A decade after the spill, fish were still contaminated with hydrocarbons.[3] And tens of thousands of people, including fishers, who helped with the clean-up became sick from the toxic haze, including known carcinogens, caused by the mixing of oil and the chemicals used to disperse it. For some, the illness is chronic. Others have died. And, on a smaller scale, accidents and oil leaks are common. One well off Louisiana has been leaking since 2004.

Inshore drilling is also controversial. In Britain, the Corallian Energy company was given a licence for exploratory drilling off the Dorset coast in the winter of 2018–19, which resulted in identification of enough oil deposits to justify commercial production.[4] This iconic coastline includes designated Areas of Outstanding Natural Beauty and England's only natural UNESCO World Heritage Site, the Jurassic Coast. Local groups mounted strong opposition, including court challenges, that pointed out the risks of oil spills, including to Dorset's renowned beaches, and the threat to sensitive protected species such as bottlenose dolphins, rare seahorses, rays and breeding populations of seabirds. Plans for commercial drilling now appear to have been abandoned.

Whatever the outcome, it is a further example of the global trend to the commodification of everything in and under the sea. And the invasion of the blue commons does not stop at mining and drilling. Reclamation of land from the sea has accelerated. Land reclamation has long been extensive in the Netherlands (now partially reversed), Japan, the USA and Mexico. However, it is now being led by China, which for decades has been extending its coastline by hundreds of square kilometres every year. Between 1985 and 2010, 755,000 square hectares of wetlands were drained along China's coastline, with severe ecological effects on marine ecosystems.[5] Since 1949, over two-thirds of China's mangrove habitats and over 80% of all its coral reefs have been lost.

Increasing water shortages on land have boosted desalination projects that remove salt from seawater to produce drinking water. Desalination globally has tripled since
the start of the twenty-first century, with some 16,000
industrial-scale desalination facilities in 177 countries churning out ninety-five million cubic litres a day.[6] However, for
every litre of potable water, most desalination systems produce 1.5 litres of toxic brine, contaminated with chlorine and
copper. This is usually dumped in the ocean, where it depletes oxygen and poisons marine life.

Opportunities for blue growth appear to be everywhere.[7]
Millions of kilometres of fibre optic cables and submarine
pipelines have been laid on or under the seabed, disrupting ecosystems there. The more than 1.3 million kilometres
of undersea fibre optic cables are responsible for 99% of all
international telecommunications.[8] Protruding from the sea
are many thousands of wind turbines, gathered in gigantic
wind farms; recent studies show that more wind power can
be generated further offshore, making deep-water environments the next frontier for renewable energy. Ocean biodiversity has enticed corporations to prospect for marine
genetic resources, for medicines and other uses. Ocean space
is also being considered for carbon sequestration, storing
carbon dioxide in deep-sea sediments to mitigate climate
change, in a risky form of 'ocean dumping'.

Then there is deep-sea mining for the ocean's mineral
riches. In its Blue Growth Strategy document of 2012, where
deep-sea mining is one of the sectors earmarked for development, the European Union admitted that there were 'considerable environmental concerns and uncertainties' related

to deep-sea mining and that 'effects on the ecosystems are difficult or even near impossible to predict'.[9] Yet if potential damage cannot be predicted, the precautionary principle should be respected and, according to the public trust doctrine, no reduction in the commons should be tolerated.

Alongside seabed mining, marine biotechnology and ocean energy are the two other deep-sea sectors identified by the EU as targets for blue growth, generating sustainable economic growth alongside environmental conservation and community benefits. The reality is very different. The deep sea is increasingly a 'wild west frontier' of commercialization and privatization. The basic principles of the commons – the precautionary principle, the public trust doctrine principle and the intergenerational equity principle – are ignored, rejected or abused.

UNCLOS and beyond

The known resources of the sea-bed and of the ocean floor are far greater than the resources known to exist on dry land. The sea-bed and the ocean floor are also of vital and increasing strategic importance. Present and clearly foreseeable technology also permits their effective exploitation for military or economic purposes. Some countries may therefore be tempted to use their technical competence to achieve near-unbreakable world dominance through predominant control over the sea-bed and the ocean floor. This, even more than the search for wealth, will impel countries with the requisite technical competence competitively to extend their jurisdiction over selected areas of the ocean floor.

— Arvid Pardo, 1967[10]

Arvid Pardo, the Maltese diplomat remembered as the 'father of the Law of the Sea Conference', showed remarkable prescience in his electrifying 1967 speech to the UN General Assembly, in which he urged countries to regard all the sea beyond immediate territorial waters as the 'common heritage of mankind'. He was to be sorely disappointed.

The first UN Conference on the Law of the Sea in 1958 had basically codified the Truman Proclamation of 1949 by recognizing coastal states' ownership of resources on or under their continental shelves. This prepared the legal ground for offshore oil and gas extraction. The UN Convention on the Law of the Sea (UNCLOS), signed in 1982, eventually provided a legal framework for the exploitation of mineral resources beyond territorial waters. But though UNCLOS incorporated the notion of the seabed and its resources as the 'common heritage of mankind', it was far from treating them, or the seas more broadly, as a commons, to be managed in the interests of all.

UNCLOS was conceived in 1973 at the zenith of faith in regulations for protection and redistribution. By the time it was finalized after nine years of wrangling, neoliberal faith in deregulation was in the ascendancy. Ronald Reagan opposed UNCLOS in his presidential election campaign and then refused to submit it to Congress for ratification. Bill Clinton tried half-heartedly and unsuccessfully to push for ratification. Later US presidents, for reasons of conviction or political expediency, have kept the USA out of its orbit.

The aims of UNCLOS, which became fully operational in 1994, were: to codify traditional rules of navigation; to regulate territorial boundaries at sea, notably sovereignty over

200 nautical miles (370 kilometres) of sea from a country's coast; to establish an International Seabed Authority which would also determine mandatory royalties on deep-sea resources; and to require transfer of revenue to landlocked and developing countries. While admirable in scope and ambition, it was a messy set of compromises. In the end, the Convention was accepted because coastal states obtained 200-mile EEZs, the superpowers obtained freedom of navigation in every sea beyond the 12-mile territorial limit that became a universal rule, and developing countries thought they had obtained a seabed mining regime that protected prospective mining rents.

However, UNCLOS ignored the interests of blue commoners. It is an intergovernmental instrument, committed to the commercialization of the sea and marine resources. While early meetings of the Law of the Sea Conference recognized that local fishing communities deserved special attention, the emerging law of the sea did not take that forward in rules on fishing, still less on other ocean resources.

Meanwhile, by staying out of UNCLOS, the USA has weakened its effectiveness. It has been resolutely mercantilist, even imperialistic. It has preferred to rely on its naval strength to enforce its commercial interests in its designated waters and has baulked at the idea of sharing benefits with other countries. As a report for the Heritage Foundation, a right-wing libertarian institute, put it: 'US accession would penalize US companies by subjecting them to the whims of an unelected and unaccountable bureaucracy and would force them to pay excessive fees to the International Seabed Authority for redistribution to developing countries.'[11]

This encapsulates the denial of the principles of the blue commons and shows contempt for the legitimacy of the United Nations and multilateralism. The 200-nautical-mile privilege is an arbitrary rule. The bounty and benefits of the oceans belong to humanity. Implicitly, the UNCLOS rules recognize this in transferring royalties on seabed resources to the International Seabed Authority, a collective body. But that is where it stops.

By refusing to adhere to global rules agreed by governments, the USA gained commercially in the short term. But it has weakened the ability of the international community to develop new rules for the preservation of the global blue commons and the protection and enhancement of communities of blue commoners. For instance, the Heritage Foundation refers to China's failure to respect a UNCLOS ruling on its claims in the South China Sea as evidence of 'international organizations' lack of ability and authority to prevent such aggressive acts'. Yet this authority might have been strengthened had the USA supported the UNCLOS framework from the outset rather than stayed out.

When UNCLOS was being forged, the main concern was that the two superpowers, the USA and the USSR, would colonize the deep seas and come into conflict over the struggle for their resources. Now, the main geopolitical struggle concerns a struggle for supremacy between the USA and a resurgent China. Under President Donald Trump, the USA was in wholesale retreat from multilateralism, epitomized by his repudiation of the Paris Agreement on Climate Change and his withdrawal of US funding for the World Health Organization in April 2020. Both these decisions have been reversed by President Joe Biden. But that was not all.

Also in April 2020, Trump issued an Executive Order authorizing mining the moon for minerals and expanding commercial exploration of outer space. This extended a law passed by the US Congress in 2015 that allows US companies to use resources from the moon and asteroids. The US moves were contrary to the international agreement signed in 1979 known as the Moon Treaty, which makes the moon and its resources the 'common heritage of mankind'. The USA had not signed the treaty but had tacitly accepted it. Henceforth, it no longer did so. As a non-member, Washington could do the same with respect to UNCLOS, overriding the rules of any multilateral deep-sea mining agreement.

UNCLOS itself has permitted the extended enclosure of the seabed under the open sea, ushering in a hidden geopolitical transformation. Article 76 allows countries to claim an extended continental shelf to explore and exploit resources of the seabed beyond the 200 nautical miles of the EEZ. The first claim was made by Russia in 2001 for a large part of the Arctic. By 2020, eighty-three countries had made submissions to the UN Commission on the Limits of the Continental Shelf, encompassing over 37 million square kilometres of sea floor.

To add perspective, that ocean grab is eighty times as much as the land grab that has taken place since the beginning of the twenty-first century. As a result, some small island states have become very large ocean states! For instance, Kiribati, with 726 square kilometres of atolls and reef islands, has an EEZ of 3.5 million square kilometres – over 4,800 times as much sea as land. And some countries have benefited from having one or more small islands to secure vast areas of additional seabed. Alongside UNCLOS itself, this latest phase represents the biggest plunder of the commons in history. It is justly described as the Blue Acceleration.[12]

The international governance of the blue economy, and thus the blue commons, is piecemeal, fragmented and inadequate, with separate rules for different sectors rather than a holistic approach. This is especially so in the governance of the ocean beyond national jurisdiction, which is divided into the 'high seas' – the waters beyond the EEZs – and 'the Area' – the seabed, ocean floor and subsoil beyond national jurisdiction. The high seas have been largely subject to free and open access, whereas the Area is held to be the 'common heritage of mankind', subject to an explicit requirement to share economic and other benefits from marine science and mineral resources. To complicate matters, they have different boundaries: the high seas cover 64% of the ocean area, while the Area covers 54% of the seabed.

UNCLOS is an umbrella framework. But commercial fisheries are managed by regional fisheries management organizations, shipping is managed by the International Maritime Organization, mining in the Area seabed is in principle regulated by the International Seabed Authority, and a separate committee is responsible for the boundaries of EEZs. There are also gaps in the system, notably for management of marine genetic resources. The Global Ocean Commission, a business-oriented lobbying group, has described the fragmented regulatory system as a 'co-ordinated catastrophe'. It is hard to see the coordination; the catastrophe is real.

The International Seabed Authority

The International Seabed Authority (ISA), established by UNCLOS, was set up in 1994 with headquarters in a pair of modest buildings in the harbour area of Kingston, Jamaica. It is mandated to organize, regulate and control all mineral-related activities in the seabed outside the limits of national jurisdiction, so is nominally responsible for regulating all mining activity in just over half the world's ocean area. Its annual budget has been about $9 million, a derisory amount indicative of the low priority given to the issues it is supposed to cover.

Equitable governance of the International Seabed Authority was curtailed at the outset, when rich countries refused to accept a 'one country, one vote' rule, since that would have given more strength to developing countries. Majority rule was abandoned in favour of consensus. Alongside inadequate funding, this has contributed to the ISA's feebleness. And the ISA does not cover seabed mining within the 200-nautical-mile zones – the coastal blue commons – where governments have exclusive jurisdiction. Thus, no international body exists to oversee the *global* conservation and use of geologically scarce mineral resources, wherever they are found in the oceans.[13]

The ISA has still not established a long-delayed marine Mining Code for regulating deep-sea mining activities. Without such rules, companies and governments have been able to explore the seabed for minerals and metals but could not start commercial mining. However, in 2021 the Pacific nation of Nauru, fed up with the slow pace of negotiations, triggered an obscure 'two-year' rule buried in UNCLOS, which means that if the ISA does not succeed in finalizing a Mining Code within two years countries will be able to start mining regardless after July 2023. The prospects for agreement on a Code are by no means certain, since that will require consensus of the ISA's 168 members (167 countries plus the EU). And if there is no agreement, 2023 could see the start of an unregulated mining free-for-all.

The ISA aims to *promote* 'the orderly, safe and rational management of the resources of the Area for the benefit of mankind as a whole'. It does not question whether deep-sea mining should take place at all.[14] It is charged with mitigating the damage from seabed mining, but not with stopping or even limiting it.[15] And, despite paying lip service to the need for effective protection of the marine environment, the ISA has no mechanism to stop activities that pose environmental risks, nor adequate means of assessing what they might be.

By 2021, the ISA had issued thirty licences to twenty-one governments and mining conglomerates to search for potential mine sites in roughly 1.5 million square kilometres of the Pacific, Atlantic and Indian Oceans. China holds five of these licences, more than any other nation, to explore an area roughly the size of the UK. Given the scale of these search areas, the ISA is hardly equipped to monitor what mining companies are actually doing. One licence stretches across 7,240 kilometres (4,500 miles) of the Pacific, about a fifth of the circumference of the planet.

UNCLOS commits the international community to preserve 'the common heritage of mankind'. According to international law, this imposes on the ISA a trusteeship obligation, including that 'the interests of future generations have to be respected in making use of the international commons'.[16] The ISA is therefore bound to respect the intergenerational equity principle, which it has not done. It has also lagged in developing and implementing the precautionary principle. It did so partially in 2012 when it adopted the deep seabed's first environmental management plan for the important Clarion-Clipperton Fracture Zone in the Pacific, the site of most exploratory activity. But the ISA lacks the authority to be effective. Nor can it be truly representative of 'mankind' because it is an interstate body, whose staff are appointed by governments. The world's commoners do not have a voice.

Exploration contracts for deep-sea mining, mainly for cobalt and nickel, are dominated by a few European and American multinationals, which have even taken the place of government officials at ISA meetings.[17] The ISA has not rejected any of the thirty licence applications, for each of which it is paid $500,000 (£374,000), equivalent to about 7% of the ISA's regular budget.[18] The process is opaque. The 'revolving door' between Britain's civil service and corporations has seen Cabinet officials go to work for Lockheed Martin, whose UK Seabed Resources subsidiary, in partnership with the British government, has two contracts to explore in the Pacific.[19]

Thus, the ISA is evidently more concerned with eventual extraction of valued minerals from the seabed than with protecting the environment. Environmental impact assessments are conducted, if at all, only by the contracting company and are not independently verified.[20] The ISA is certainly not a body structured to preserve or enhance the blue commons, or commoners' interests in the world's seas.

Deep-sea mining: the lure of minerals

> The rush to mine this pristine and unexplored environment
> risks creating terrible impacts that cannot be reversed.
> We need to be guided by science when faced with
> decisions of such great environmental consequence.
> — Sir David Attenborough

Mining in the deep sea is seen as an almost inexhaustible source of materials wanted for industrial growth. Multinationals and financial capital are queuing up to go ahead at full speed, excited by the prospect of 'mind-boggling quantities of untapped resources' lying 200 metres or more below sea level.[21] Unfortunately, the harm to the environment could be equally mind-boggling.[22]

One example concerns commercial drilling for oceanic methane hydrates, an energy source claimed to be sufficient to supply the world for thousands of years at current levels of global energy demand.[23] But drilling to release and collect the methane gas in the hydrates could be potentially catastrophic, for the environment and for people. Methane is a potent greenhouse gas, so releases will add to global warming. And methane hydrate releases water at the same time as gas. Releasing large amounts of water and gas together risks destabilizing the seabed, causing underwater landslips and even destructive tsunamis. The hydrates also support unique marine species, from bacteria to tubeworms and crabs, that live off the methane as their source of energy.

Methane hydrates are present off the coasts of many countries worldwide, unlike oil, which is concentrated around a few countries. And all countries now have exclusive control over resources in their EEZ, where most hydrates are located. Despite the known risks, some countries, like Japan, will be tempted to drill to reduce their dependence on energy imports. But hydrate governance in the Area, where the ISA has jurisdiction, has also been given worryingly scant attention. It is vital to embody the precautionary principle in rules for governing this potential 'resource' before any take-off of a new industry.

Although the ISA says on its website, 'No mining operations have started anywhere in the world', some of the so-called 'exploration activities' look very much like mining. The result has been dubbed 'the new gold rush'.[24] The deep seabed contains nickel, copper, cobalt, lithium, gold, silver, manganese, platinum, zinc, gemstones and rare-earth elements such as yttrium. Many of these are wanted so that capitalist industry can manufacture and sell more smartphones, iPads, laptops, Kindles, batteries, LED bulbs, flat-screen TVs, fuel cells, wind turbines and so on, including, of course, parts for advanced military technology.[25] There is also an anxiety to secure supplies of minerals and rare earths that are not dependent on China, which has a near-monopoly in mining for rare earths and processes 72% of the world's cobalt and 61% of its lithium.[26]

Deep-sea mineral resources are found in sulphide deposits around hydrothermal vent sites and polymetallic crusts at seamounts. But most exploratory activity is aimed at recovering 'polymetallic nodules', potato-sized lumps containing combinations of minerals, that are scattered across soft deep-sea bottoms. The area identified as the most productive is the Clarion-Clipperton Zone between Hawaii and

Mexico in the Pacific where, 4,000 metres down, lie an estimated 21 billion tonnes of nodules containing more cobalt, manganese and nickel than all known deposits on land.

Proponents of deep-sea mining claim it is more environmentally sustainable than terrestrial mining, leaving a smaller 'footprint', that seabed mining will have a shorter extractive lifespan, and that it will have 'no human impact'.[27] They also argue that to combat global warming, humanity must shift rapidly from burning fossil fuels to other forms of power. Switching to 'clean' electricity for heating and transport means increased reliance on storage batteries. If, as some predict, there will be a billion electric cars on the world's roads within a couple of decades, there will simply not be enough copper, nickel, cobalt and other elements needed for storage batteries and vehicle electronics to be found on land, while they exist in large quantities under the sea.[28]

If everybody in the world were to achieve the same lifestyle and accumulate as much stuff as those in industrialized countries, global metal stocks would have to be an estimated three to nine times larger than currently available.[29] But much more could be done to recuperate and recycle the metals already mined. Less than 5% of lithium-ion batteries, used in mobile phones and laptops as well as electric vehicles, is recycled.[30] And shortages would provide more impetus for desirable changes in human lifestyles to minimize use of resources. So it is not the case, as the mining industry and some governments claim, that deep-sea mining is 'inevitable'.

The making of a 'natural resource' is a complex process, going beyond exploration or discovery, production costs and the conventional economic discourse of externalities and social costs. It encompasses the impact on the 'landscape', 'seascape' and 'minescape', and on ecosystems. And deep-sea mining presents both known and unknown dangers.

About 85% of the global seabed remains unmapped. Scientists have only been able to explore the three zones closest to the surface – the 'sunlight zone', where plants thrive, the 'twilight zone', and the 'midnight zone'. They have been unable to explore the two lowest depths of the ocean – 'the abyss', the frozen flatland that has been visited, and the 'hadal zone', named after Hades, the Greek god of the underworld, which lies more than 6,000 metres below the ocean surface.

Polymetallic nodules can be scooped up by scouring the seabed with giant machines. But this disturbs sediment that will directly destroy habitat where the mining takes place and indirectly degrade the sea and areas of the seabed far from where the mining is done. 'Loss of biodiversity will be unavoidable.'[31] Over fifty years after a 1969 test in the Pacific, which ploughed only a small area, the site has still not recovered; characteristic animals such as sponges, soft corals and sea anemones have yet to return in any number.[32] And while the ISA uses an estimate of sixty-two miles for drifts of sediment plumes, others say sediment plumes may travel hundreds of miles, including into the hadal zone, where they could smother life on the seabed yet to be discovered and do untold environmental damage.[33]

Moreover, while commercial interests claim that deep-sea mining will help reduce greenhouse gas emissions, scientists fear it will damage the ability of the sea to act as a carbon sink.[34] Deep-sea mining could disrupt the ocean's 'biological pump' that is crucial to its capacity to store carbon: cold, denser water sinks, taking with it dissolved carbon that can stay at the bottom of the ocean for hundreds of years, before upwelling currents bring the cold water to the warmer surface where some of the CO_2 is released. Deep-sea mining threatens to destroy the millions of microbes attached to polymetallic nodules that play a key role in carbon storage.[35]

These microbes could also be the basis of new drugs and antibiotics to treat human ailments. According to genetic scientist Craig Venter, the companies doing mining exploration 'should be doing rigorous microbial surveys before they do anything else'.[36] The ISA recommends, but does not require, companies to include data on microbes in environmental impact assessments (EIAs) for exploration licences, and the planned Mining Code does not include the comprehensive regulations on safeguarding microbial ecosystems that scientists consider necessary.[37]

The potential destruction of seabed ecosystems is also irreparable. Lifting nodules off the sea floor removes a habitat that took millions of years to grow; recreating much of what is destroyed would take centuries if not thousands of years.[38] Marine mining, where it has been done, has been shown to destroy marine biodiversity,[39] but the scientific knowledge needed to assess the full impact on the marine ecosystem is perhaps decades away.

A few intrepid explorers have established that there is considerable life in the lowest depths, although most of it and the extent of it are unknown. Timothy Shank, a pioneer deep-sea explorer, has said of the hadal zone, 'I think we'll be looking at hundreds or thousands of species we haven't seen before, and some of them are going to be huge.'[40] Deep-sea mining will almost certainly do damage and lead to what Edward Wilson has called 'anonymous extinctions'.[41]

Closer to the surface, deep-sea mining may clash with fisheries.[42] For example, deep-water phosphate deposits off Namibia, New Zealand and Mexico are targeted for fertilizer, but the deposits also provide nutrients for the marine life on which fisheries depend. Taking them will hit fish populations and fishing communities. Nor should the impact of noise from underwater mining equipment be forgotten; it travels vast distances, harming the migration patterns and reproduction of marine mammals and other sea life, including fish.

Despite these fears, the ISA seems to presume that mining will start in the near future. Its Secretary-General says blithely: 'I don't believe people should worry that much. There's certainly an impact in the area that's mined, because you are creating an environmental disturbance, but we can find ways to manage that.'[43] As one critic put it, 'the ISA has been entrenched in the mindset of a developer rather than a custodian of the common heritage of humankind.'[44]

Meanwhile, extensive and essentially unregulated exploration is taking place within EEZs. Japan and South Korea are working on projects to exploit offshore deposits. Elsewhere, the De Beers Group is using a fleet of specialized ships to drag machinery across the seabed off West Africa in search of diamonds. In 2018 they extracted 1.4 million carats of diamonds from the coastal waters of Namibia.[45] De Beers has even commissioned a new ship that will scrape the sea bottom twice as quickly.

Papua New Guinea was the first country to award a deep-sea mining lease, which went to the Canadian corporation

Nautilus Minerals in 2011 to mine offshore for copper, gold, silver and zinc.[46] The government took a 15% stake in the project, but stayed out of its governance, leaving the company to deal with social aspects. This was privatization, with the government playing neither a stewardship nor gatekeeper role.

As seabed mining usually takes place far from shore, identifying the community of direct interest can be difficult. Nautilus Minerals came up with the concept of 'coastal area of benefit', which did not please communities outside the arbitrarily decided designated area. The company's agreement with the government specified that the area was to receive 20% of the royalties collected by the government. This percentage was another arbitrary decision. Eventually, vehement opposition by local communities helped lead to the bankruptcy of Nautilus Minerals in 2019. As a result of its 15% stake in the project, the government was left with debts equal to a third of the country's health budget.

There is a deeper story around this venture. A community member on the Duke of York Islands told anthropologist John Childs: 'How do we show this company that when they mine this seabed, they mine our culture?' Deep-sea mining disrupts the fabric of life and a sacred link with the land and sea. As one woman put it, 'the resources are part of who we are'.[47]

Devious practices are not confined to developing countries. In 2011, the UK government granted deep-sea exploration licences to UK Seabed Resources, a subsidiary of the US arms company Lockheed Martin. The government refused to reveal the details of the licences, but they were released by the company, after pressure from environmental groups, in March 2021. The licences run for fifteen years, five more than legally permitted, and cover twice the exploration area in the Pacific in which UK Seabed Resources is permitted to operate. There is also no requirement for an environmental impact assessment. As the executive director of Blue Marine Foundation rightly said, 'If governments cannot be trusted to get the exploration phase right, what hope is there of them managing potentially environmentally catastrophic deep-sea mining responsibly?'[48]

BP: destroying deep-sea corals

Disregard for environmental destruction and harm to local communities is also a feature of a state-corporate agreement on drilling for oil and gas off the coasts of Mauritania and Senegal, which threatens the world's largest known deep-sea coral reef.[49]

In late 2018, British Petroleum (BP), in partnership with US-based Kosmos Energy, gained approval from the Mauritania and Senegal governments to start operations in the Greater Tortue Ahmeyim (GTA) deep-sea development, covering 33,000 square kilometres. Seabed drilling at a depth of about 3,000 metres is expected to produce fifteen trillion cubic feet of gas over the next twenty years or so, for export and domestic use. BP described the investment as hugely important for the region, and claimed the partners were 'committed to operating in a transparent, ethical and sustainable way'.[50]

BP's acquisition of mining rights for the GTA has been at the heart of a corruption scandal in Senegal involving millions of dollars paid by the company to the previous rights holders, which included the president's brother.[51] While this scandal was probably the biggest political risk facing BP, less publicized was an open letter to BP by ten of the world's leading marine scientists expressing outrage at its weak environmental and social impact assessment.[52] The letter claimed the assessment had ignored their research and had rationalized installation of a pipeline through the reef.

The assessment had not been subject to peer review, nor had it been published or shared widely. The scientists saw it only when the Dutch government assured the Senegalese government that it would pay for a review of the social and environmental assessments undertaken by oil and gas companies in its waters. The Senegalese government then shared the report. But this was too late; only a month after the scientists raised their concerns, BP received the green light for drilling operations.

The importance of deep-water coral ecosystems is internationally recognized. In 2004, the UN Environment Programme, the governments of the UK, Norway and Ireland, and WWF, produced a landmark report on cold-water coral reefs, the lead author of which was also in the group writing to BP in 2018.[53] The report describes these reefs as exceptionally complex, long-lived and diverse, noting that they are vital for the breeding of marine wildlife, including commercially important fish species. They are also seen as exciting areas for pharmaceutical research and as bio-archives for the study of climate change. However, they are extremely fragile.

The most obvious damage has been caused by bottom trawling and dredging for fish. But the report highlighted how destructive offshore oil and gas exploitation can be. In his introduction, the Norwegian environment minister, Børge Brende, said: 'These reefs are underwater oases, biological treasures and important habitats for fish. It is amazing that such major new discoveries can still be made. The reefs are slow growing and extremely fragile, and must, as a matter of urgency, be protected from further damage.'

Shortly before that report was published, the Norwegian government set an example by banning bottom trawling and oil and gas exploration on cold-water reefs in its waters.[54] In 2004, the UK also gained approval from the European Commission to ban trawling and other disruptive activities on the Darwin Mounds' cold-water coral reefs in the North-East Atlantic.

Among the scientists who wrote to BP were several who had been working on the marine ecosystems of Mauritania for many years. The unique deep-water corals were first discovered by an Australian oil and gas exploration company, Woodside Energy, in the early 2000s. Woodside later published a report with Australian scientists that recognized the damage oil and gas exploration could do to the reef ecosystem, which is thought to be over 200,000 years old.[55] As a result of research based on this discovery, the Mauritanian deep sea is one of the best studied areas in the world. The scientists who complained to BP argued that the project should apply similar environmental standards in Mauritania as in places such as Norway. Others have proposed that the area be designated a deep-water marine protected area. This would be disastrous for BP, as it has publicly committed not to drill in or near MPAs.

BP and Kosmos contracted the US consulting firm CSA Ocean Sciences and the Canadian consultants Golder Associates to undertake an environmental assessment. But these firms did not have the expertise to undertake the analysis required and did not consult any of the marine biologists and scientists working in the region. As a result, their report contained remarkable errors, suggesting that it was a 'cut and paste' job from reports for other parts of the world.

For instance, the fish species and marine mammals listed as identified in the area off Mauritania are not all found there. The list of the largest marine animals omitted the Omura's whale, a species recently discovered in the area, which has generated international coverage.[56] Many of the coral and other benthic (sea-bottom) species cited by BP have never been found in the region but are endemic to the Gulf of Mexico. Such sloppy analysis is common in reports paid for by mining companies. BP's disaster risk assessment for its Deepwater Horizon drilling in the Gulf of Mexico identified sea lions, seals, sea otters and walruses – creatures from the Arctic not found there.[57]

Yet the most controversial mistake made by those consultants was to downplay the importance of the deep-water coral reef that the pipeline will cut through. The reef spans about 600 km (potentially further, although less is known about what exists in Senegal's waters), making it the largest known deep-water coral reef anywhere on the planet. The consultants described the reef as mostly dead and said BP had chosen a path that did not impact 'relics of carbonate mounds'. They claimed to have reached this conclusion from extensive underwater mapping using a remotely operated vehicle. In reaction, the independent scientists wrote in their open letter to BP:

The photos taken with a Remotely Operated Vehicle clearly show living Lophelia pertusa, which you fail to recognise. Lophelia is categorised by the European Commission's Habitats Directive (92/43/EEC) as a reef-forming coral species creating critical habitat for fishery resources – the main pillar for long-term development of the West African societies.

Although the coral reef is indeed degraded – parts of it are inactive and its future is in doubt from warming oceans caused by climate change – it remains one of the most biodiverse spots off the Mauritania coastline, critical for the survival of endemic biodiversity. BP's pipeline will trespass on one of the most sensitive parts of the reef identified by scientists, and the only area containing black coral, among the oldest living organisms in the world. Furthermore, deep-water coral reefs are productive carbon sinks, while this reef is a unique bio-archive recording how the climate has evolved over the past 200,000 years.

In 2012, the UN Development Programme (UNDP), in partnership with several other bodies, funded a five-year study to help Mauritania's government mainstream biodiversity in its oil and gas sector, and understand the environmental and social implications of oil and gas drilling. The project document highlighted Mauritania's extremely low capacity to monitor environmental impacts, and the lack of needed regulations and procedures. One recommendation was for Mauritania to monitor its marine environment as part of a strategic environmental assessment for oil and gas drilling. These assessments are normal in developed countries and provide a plan for managing underwater and coastal developments before exploration or drilling licences are granted.

Unlike environmental impact assessments, strategic environmental assessments are not financed by oil companies but are based on publicly financed research. A strategic environmental assessment was never done for Mauritania, but the UNDP-led study provided information and data archives for use by the government and the oil companies and underlined the importance of the biodiversity reliant on the coral reef. Nevertheless, the study was ignored by the government, BP, Kosmos and CSA Consulting. This could hardly have been an oversight, especially as the health and safety manager of Kosmos was previously a consultant for the UNDP's project.

The lack of an independent environmental assessment is all the more shocking given the inherent conflicts of interest involved in oil and gas projects. Besides the problem of kickbacks or bribes paid to government and political elites – as seems to have been the case in Senegal – oil and gas projects are often joint ventures, with a profit-sharing arrangement for the host government. In both Senegal and Mauritania, the state-owned oil and gas companies have a 10% stake in the GTA project, although details of benefit-sharing arrangements between BP, Kosmos and the governments of both countries have not been made public. Both sides thus have a commercial incentive not to have stringent environmental regulations in place.

The World Bank has not helped. Despite making a pledge in 2017 to withdraw financing for oil and gas projects on environmental grounds, it provided a grant of US$29 million to Senegal and one of US$20 million to Mauritania.[58]

The ostensible purpose was to strengthen the governments' negotiating power in dealing with oil and gas companies and to help develop communication strategies to ensure support by investors and national stakeholders.

The consultants that carried out the environmental impact assessment claimed to have undertaken extensive consultations with local people. However, these were largely a public relations stunt designed to ensure that BP, Kosmos and the two governments achieved what they wanted. The report acknowledged that small-scale fishers were worried about the environmental impact and that they were unlikely to be compensated for disruptions to their livelihoods. Local communities were aware of what had happened elsewhere, as in Nigeria where oil and gas companies have destroyed coastal ecosystems.

These concerns duly noted, the consultants then argued that 'experienced' members of fishing communities recognized the benefits of oil and gas, adding in an extraordinary claim that, 'although stakeholders have concerns about potential negative impacts of the project, the consultation process has highlighted a general trend that gas discovery in Mauritania and Senegal is a gift from God.'

Since the approval of the contracts for BP and Kosmos in 2018, Mauritania's small-scale fishing organizations have publicly raised their concerns about the process and likely impact. This has not gone well. A spokesperson for small-scale fisheries was threatened by the environment ministry and told to stop publicizing their grievances.

Another issue is the silence of some international environmental NGOs. Birdlife International, for example, has a bird-preservation project in Mauritania specifically aimed at reducing harm from the offshore oil and gas sector. The coastline is a stopping point for millions of waterbirds on their annual migration along a route known as the East Atlantic Flyway. Yet, though informed of the threat to seabirds from offshore oil and gas developments, Birdlife International has not criticized what BP is doing, perhaps because it receives funds from BP.

This raises a wider concern. BP's spending on 'corporate social responsibility' targets environmental organizations and causes. As the company stated in a brochure:

> In Senegal, as part of our commitment to environmental conservation in the region, we have helped train 50 members of the local community in biodiversity monitoring and management. We also provided equipment for wildlife parks in both Mauritania and Senegal.

This smacks of 'bluewashing' and underscores the need for environmental impact assessments to be conducted by publicly funded, independent scientists, who are less dependent on industry money than NGOs and less easily bought off.

Not that this is always the case, however. In March 2018, BP financed two seminars – one in Mauritania, one in Senegal – run by the Oxford Centre for the Analysis of Resource-Rich Economies (OxCarre), entitled 'Oil & Gas Governance – Learning from the Past'. The seminar in Dakar was led by Sir Paul Collier, an Oxford academic and former World Bank chief economist. Yet familiar governance problems associated with oil and gas were not raised. Perhaps that had something to do with the fact that, although OxCarre is part of the Department

COMMODIFYING THE SEA: THE MINING JUGGERNAUT

of Economics at Oxford University, it was established with a generous grant from BP.[59]

The immediate challenge is to oblige BP, Kosmos and the governments of Mauritania and Senegal to acknowledge the flaws in their environmental impact assessment, and to arrange a serious international and independent assessment of the ecological and social impact of this project, before drilling and installation go much further. BP is already putting out contracts worth hundreds of millions of dollars to US and Norwegian engineering firms to install equipment in the seabed. It would be deeply irresponsible for the companies to press ahead on the basis of the existing assessment, yet that is clearly what they plan.

Intellectual property: colonizing marine genetic resources

The medicinal properties of some marine species have been known for millennia. The first recorded medicinal use dates from almost 3000 BC in China. And in 400 BC, Hippocrates, the 'father of medicine', recognized the antibiotic properties of sponges in recommending they be applied to soldiers' wounds.[60]

Who owns the resources in the sea? The answer should be 'everybody'. Instead, corporations are being given ownership through the so-called 'intellectual property rights' regime. Under the World Trade Organization's Agreement on Trade-Related Aspects of Intellectual Property Rights (TRIPS), inventions are granted patent protection for twenty years, giving the patent holder a monopoly income and preventing others from producing or using the invention without permission.

In the case of pharmaceuticals, special rules can extend this monopoly protection further.

Since 1995, when TRIPS came into force, the number of patent applications filed has tripled to some three million a year. Yet, rather than stimulating innovation, the system is being used to bolster corporate power.[61] Giant corporations are stifling competition by buying other companies for their intellectual property or hoarding patents to prevent their use by rivals.

Using these tactics, corporations have been moving into the blue economy with the intention of establishing intellectual property rights over as much as they can, and the biggest growth area has been in 'marine genetic resources' (MGRs). Under the Convention on Biological Diversity (CBD), which came into effect in 2003, MGRs are defined as 'genetic material of actual or potential value'. While it is generally agreed that 'discoveries' of products of nature cannot be patented, and so cannot be converted into private property, patents can be taken out on novel applications of organisms and specifically their genes.

The establishment of property rights in MGRs has led to a burst of activity by genetic prospectors, who are scouring the world's oceans and seas. As of 2018, more than 13,000 patents had been taken out for the genetic sequences of over 860 marine organisms. These are concentrated in very few hands.[62]

The world's largest chemicals company, BASF of Germany, owns 47% of all the patents. Another 220 companies own 37% of the patents between them. Meanwhile, the commercial arm of the Weizmann Institute of Science in Israel holds 56% of all patents held by the world's research institutes.

Slicing the numbers another way, entities headquartered in just three countries own about three-quarters of all patents linked to MGRs – Germany (49%), the USA (13%) and Japan (12%). Ownership of these patents guarantees monopoly income flows from the blue economy for many years and gives rich corporations in rich countries a research and development advantage over the rest of the world.

The true biodiversity of the oceans is unknown, making the potential for discovery virtually limitless. This applies most of all in the microscopic sphere, which holds out extraordinary potential for medical and other breakthroughs of real value for humanity. There are on average one million bacteria and ten million viruses in each millilitre of seawater, and the universe of viruses is thought to kill 20% of the living material in the ocean every day.[63]

Deep in the oceans, extremes of pressure and temperature produce 'extremophiles' with unique qualities. They include slugs, sponges, strange fish, worms, seaweed, algae and bacteria. Genetic material from the seas is one hundred times more likely to have anti-cancer properties than that from the land.[64] Commercial interest in these largely untapped marine genetic resources is understandable, especially as some have already led to breakthroughs in the treatment of leukaemia, other cancers, HIV and chronic pain. Some 34,000 marine natural products have already been identified for possible use in medicine, food and cosmetics.

The Nagoya Protocol on Access to Genetic Resources and the Fair and Equitable Sharing of Benefits Arising from their Utilization, adopted in 2010 as an addition to the CBD, covers exploitation and benefit-sharing in areas under national jurisdiction, on land and in the sea. It was designed to combat 'biopiracy', the taking of genetic resources for commercial gain without payment to the country of origin or to indigenous communities, which are often the source of information about organisms of interest. For example, sponge extract from the sea off East Africa, with a wide range of medicinal uses, was patented without any benefit-sharing with the local people.

The Nagoya Protocol makes it mandatory for companies prospecting for genetic resources to negotiate benefit-sharing agreements with the country concerned. No doubt it is hard to ensure that is done fairly.[65] But at least the principle has been established in international law. Still, the Protocol took effect only in 2014, covers only 'areas of national jurisdiction', and does not include the USA, the only UN member not to have ratified the CBD.

If a discovery is made within a country's EEZ, under the Protocol it has a right to share in the benefits of exploitation. Outside EEZs, in nearly two-thirds of the ocean area, the situation is unclear.[66] There are no regulations or benefit-sharing mechanisms for MGR discoveries in areas beyond national jurisdiction. Negotiations under UNCLOS auspices on a new international convention that would fill that void failed to conclude as planned in 2020, with negotiators split on whether the high seas 'open access' model or the Area's 'common heritage of mankind' model should apply, and to what.

It was not until 2018, after years of discussion and pressure from developing countries, that UNCLOS began the process of designing an international treaty to protect biodiversity in areas beyond national jurisdiction. This is often called the Global Ocean Treaty or the High Seas Treaty, though (or because) the official name for the negotiating body is the Intergovernmental Conference on the Conservation and Sustainable Use of Marine Biodiversity of Areas Beyond National Jurisdiction.

The respected International Union for Conservation of Nature (IUCN) has urged negotiators to agree ten 'enabling conditions' to future-proof the treaty, most crucially to 'recognise that the Global Ocean is a "commons" whose health is a common interest of all humanity'.[67] One is inclined to add 'and all that share the planet with humanity'. UNCLOS had been clear in stating that resources in the Area, the deep seabed, are the 'common heritage of mankind', which meant the sharing of benefits from their exploitation. But back in 1982 marine genetic resources were not considered significant, so the International Seabed Authority was charged only with setting rules for equitable sharing of benefits from minerals exploitation.

Furthermore, MGRs are not confined to the deep seabed but are also found in the waters above. So negotiators need to decide whether MGRs should fall under the regime of the freedom of the high seas, which allows users to keep whatever they find, or under the regime of the common heritage of mankind, which requires equitable sharing. There have even been suggestions that choice of regime should depend on where the MGRs are found, a recipe for confusion and conflict.

The IUCN also emphasized that the new treaty should 'establish clear requirements for implementing the precautionary principle'. This is fundamental because little is known about the conservation status of many species from which MGRs are drawn. While bioprospecting in its discovery phase may require collection of only a little bio-mass, for later clinical trials much more may be needed, and unless the genetic material can be synthesized (or produced through aquaculture) commercial application might entail large-scale harvesting of species, which would threaten their sustainability.

This is already the case for horseshoe crabs, whose copper-rich blood is used in tests to detect contamination in shots and infusions. The crabs are bled and although most are returned to the ocean after bleeding, many die and those returned are weakened. Overexploitation off the Atlantic coast of North America has severely reduced the crab populations, with serious impacts on seabirds that feed on their eggs as a critical food stop in their northward migration. The red knot, whose 9,500-mile migration from the tip of South America to the Arctic is among the longest of any bird in the world, is for this reason classified by the USA as 'threatened'.[68] A synthetic test for contamination exists, but until 2018 it was under patent and drug companies were reluctant to rely on a single supplier. And although there are now several suppliers, synthetic tests have yet to be authorized as equivalent to horseshoe crab blood, which is still the industry standard for safety tests.[69]

Even some microbes – notably those in extreme environments – could face extinction from unregulated harvesting.[70] And many MGRs have been discovered in already vulnerable and threatened ecosystems such as coral reefs and the polar regions – threatened by global warming – and sea mounts, which are being damaged by deep-sea fishing and, potentially even more so, by deep-sea mining.

The crux of the challenge is whether the commercial potential of marine genetic resources belongs only to the discoverer – most likely to be powerful multinational corporations, backed by governments – or whether the benefits should be shared among all nations. Application to all MGRs of the 'heritage of mankind' principle, under the auspices of an international regulatory body, would profoundly change the legal status of the high seas. At present, all countries have the right to navigate, conduct scientific research and fish in the high seas. They are regarded as 'open access resources' and are not protected as a commons. There are no stewards and no gatekeepers. The UN negotiations can thus be interpreted as a global attempt to turn the high seas into a commons. But the omens are not propitious.

Wind power in the sea: an example of royal plunder

It is not just taking from the sea that matters. It is also use of seaspace, which is part of the commons. And seaspace is being used increasingly for the generation of wind power as demand for renewable energy rises.

Much of humanity has had a historical fascination with wind power. By the ninth century wind power was being used in Persia (now Iran) to grind flour and pump water, and windmills spread across Asia and the Middle East. In Europe, they were in use by the twelfth century, most famously in Holland. And the first wind turbine for producing electricity was built in Scotland in 1887 by Professor James Blyth, an electrical engineer, who used it to power the lighting of his holiday cottage.[71]

However, it took a further century, and the push to reduce greenhouse gas emissions from burning fossil fuels, for wind energy to be recognized as a major source of renewable energy to replace coal, oil and gas. From negligible generation of wind energy in 2000 and just 180GW of installed capacity in 2010, capacity rose to 565GW in 2018 and is expected to near 1,000GW by 2024. Though most wind energy will continue to come from onshore installations, the most rapid growth is predicted for wind farms offshore, fixed to the seabed or on tethered floating structures in deeper water.[72]

It has become a comforting presumption that expansion of wind energy, along with solar energy, can boost economic growth while benefiting the environment. This is an oversimplification, if not a delusion. For one thing, the construction of wind turbine generators requires large amounts of metals and rare-earth elements, adding to pressures for deep-sea mining and its environmental hazards.[73] Meanwhile, tonnes of balsa wood, a stiff light wood also used in model aeroplanes, go into the core of the huge 100-metre-long blades. Demand for balsa has fuelled illegal logging, deforestation and exploitation of indigenous communities in Ecuador, which provides three-quarters of the world's balsa supply.[74] And PET, a synthetic foam increasingly substituted for balsa, is made using naphtha, an oil derivative.

Apart from the materials used in construction, offshore wind turbines themselves pose environmental risks to marine and shoreline habitats, the full extent of which is still not known. More research is needed, while the commons and commoners' interests should be protected. The UK example points to critical issues that must be resolved.

In early 2021, the Crown Estate, the commercial business that manages Crown property, announced the results of an auction for leases of areas of the seabed around Britain to develop offshore wind farms. This was the fourth round of seabed sell-offs for wind farms by the Crown Estate since the first in 2001, and will raise £9 billion over ten years for the monarch and the British Treasury. Yet they have no moral right to the proceeds from this annexation of the blue commons, which rightly belong to us all.

Ever since the Charter of the Forest was sealed alongside Magna Carta in November 1217, reversing the monarchy's unmerited enclosure of common land and waterways, the commons have been regarded as public wealth. In 1297, King Edward I issued a decree to that effect, which the monarchy has been expected to respect ever since. For centuries, a commons was accepted as such if it had been treated as a commons for 'time out of mind of man', that is, for as long as anybody living could remember. In 1623, the Limitation Act set the time limit at twenty years, still the rule today. The seabed clearly meets this criterion, unchallenged as a commons for hundreds of years.

Recall three features of any commons. First, all who constitute the commoners have equal rights in the commons. Second, formal owners, including government and the monarchy, must operate as stewards, as trustees, acting to protect and preserve the commons for the benefit of all commoners, according to the public trust doctrine. Third, the stewards, as trustees, must respect the principle of intergenerational equity, that is, the advantages of the commons must flow as much to future generations as to current generations.

In other words, that which is public should be passed on to future generations in as good a state as, or better than, when we inherited it. Edmund Burke, the Conservatives' favourite thinker, put it best when he remarked that 'we are temporary possessors and life renters' of our inheritance.

It offends all three principles for the Crown Estate to award large parts of Britain's seabed to multinational corporations that enables them to exploit common resources for private profit, in addition to the cut that the Crown Estate and the Treasury are taking for themselves. Much of the private profit will be syphoned abroad.

Overseas-based companies already owned over 90% of Britain's wind generating capacity, and of the four auction winners in 2021, three have foreign ownership: German energy firm RWE Renewables, German utility EnBW (with Britain's BP) and French oil giant Total (with Green Investment Group, a subsidiary of Australian financial firm Macquarie). UK-based Offshore Wind has won the smallest of the areas up for auction. The fourth leasing round thus consolidated foreign domination of Britain's offshore wind energy sector.

Until the mid-twentieth century, there was no claim to ancestral ownership of the seabed by the Crown, to which all the land of the United Kingdom notionally belongs. The seabed grab by the monarchy, prompted by the discovery of North Sea or Scottish oil, began only in 1962, when the Queen told the First Commissioner of the Crown Estate that she had seen something about 'taking over rights on land under the sea'. In 1959, the Estate's legal adviser had proposed enshrining in law the extension of Crown lands to the continental shelf. However, other Estate officials argued that seeking Crown ownership by legislation would not be expedient 'since this would focus attention on the fact that there was no existing legislation declaring Crown ownership of the bed of the sea below lower-water mark'.[75]

In 1951, the Foreign Secretary, Herbert Morrison, stated that the continental shelf around the UK was *res nullius* (nobody's thing), that is, not owned by anybody but available for occupation. Nevertheless, in 1964, in response to demands by drilling companies for legal clarity, the Conservatives passed the Continental Shelf Act, which extended Crown lands to the continental shelf, so granting the monarchy ownership of everything on or under the seabed, including oil, gas and minerals. That was inexcusable enough. Yet that enclosure did not alter the commons status of the seabed. Rather, the Crown, and the government as its agent, became its stewards. They have not respected their obligations.

The British government has responsibility for managing oil and gas exploitation, whether on land or offshore. The Thatcher government granted drilling licences for North Sea oil at give-away prices, treating the revenue as a windfall and squandering it on tax cuts for the wealthy. Adding insult to injury, the oil multinationals were given large, publicly funded subsidies for drilling and transporting the oil and gas. And after making tidy profits they are now being given more public money to help them pay for dismantling their oil rigs.

By contrast, Norway retained ownership of its share of North Sea oil and put the proceeds into a national capital fund, which has become the biggest such fund in the world. It respects the principle of intergenerational equity by retaining the capital value of the national asset, the oil, to build the fund, only paying out the annual net returns.

Similarly, the US state of Alaska set up the Alaska Permanent Fund to accumulate oil royalties, which have been used to pay out dividends to all Alaskan residents equally since 1982. The scheme is insufficiently independent of the state government, which has led to its use as a political football in recent years. But the Fund and dividends are very popular.

Britain's North Sea oil debacle stands to be repeated in a different form with offshore wind and wave energy, adding an extra twist. While all the revenue of North Sea oil went to the Exchequer, even though the Crown nominally 'owned' the seabed and the resources under it, in 2004 Tony Blair's New Labour government passed the Energy Act, which gave the monarchy the right to a share of the revenue from offshore wind and wave electricity production.

Then in 2012, George Osborne, as Chancellor of the Exchequer, ended the 'civil list', which provided the Crown with an annual fixed sum for royal expenses. Instead, it was to receive 15% of the Crown Estate's net returns, all of which had previously gone to the Treasury. The monarch's share was raised to 25% in 2017 to meet the costs of refurbishing Buckingham Palace, with a review due in 2022.

In the fiscal year 2021–22, the monarchy received over £86 million from the Crown Estate.[76] Its share of the income from auctioning the seabed will be on top of that. And in the fourth round of leasing the Crown Estate acted even more like a Sea Lord by requiring the winning bidders to pay an annual 'option fee', years before any income is generated by the wind farms. Previously, the Crown Estate's income from wind generation was confined to a 2% share of the revenue from the sale of electricity once wind farms began production, which already amounted to £41 million in 2018–19.[77] Now it is taking big down payments as well.

Planned offshore wind-farm projects will expand the number and size of wind turbines dramatically. On average, each project will have 300 wind turbines stretching into the distance. Worse than a spoiled view is the harmful impact on the seabed, marine habitats, marine creatures and bird life. These effects are not being properly assessed or addressed.

Whereas developers must do evaluations of environmental threats before obtaining approval for mining on land, in the case of the seabed, that is left to the Crown Estate, which has an interest in maximizing its revenue. Under the EU's Environmental Impact Assessment (EIA) Directive, in operation since 1985, before any decision is made on locating infrastructural developments, there should be demonstrable consideration of alternative sites to see if the one selected is optimal. This was not done for the first three rounds of sale, when Britain was an EU member, and the Crown Estate does not seem to regard it as something it should do.

In fact, as the Estate itself admits, there are no data with which to make objective assessments. One lame excuse in Britain is that the government's renewable energy targets mean there is no time for thorough evaluations. Another device is to differentiate between strategic and local or regional effects. If there are no data at local or regional levels, data from somewhere else can apparently be used.

To see why this is a nonsense, take a stylized example. Suppose there were 1,000 birds of a rare species scattered equally over ten sites. A 50% mortality rate in one local area would be catastrophic. But using the strategic methodology, deaths would be only 5% of the whole population at national level. If the project were approved because of that low figure, what would happen if ten projects were approved? If that area had been just typical, half the birds would be killed, perhaps leaving the remaining number below the survival threshold level. This absurd procedure has contributed to a 'race to the water' by companies that have won bids for projects, which in turn has led to hasty plan preparations.[78]

Then there is the offset practice. At the end of 2020, the Danish energy company Ørsted received approval for a project off the North Yorkshire coast that will affect the Flamborough and Filey Coast Special Protection Area, home to England's biggest colony of seabirds, including endangered kittiwakes. The government accepted that the project would threaten the kittiwakes, which slalom through wind turbines to access feeding grounds rather than circumvent them as other birds do.

Nevertheless, the project was given consent after the company said it would install artificial nesting structures onshore to offset deaths with births, a ludicrous and callous proposition. The Royal Society for the Protection of Birds said it would take at least ten years to see if this works, by which time the wind turbines would be up and running.[79] It is a sad instance of ignoring the precautionary principle.

Another critical deficiency is that the government's Planning Inspectorate treats each application on its own, without considering the cumulative effect of multiple offshore wind farms on wildlife and ecosystems. Furthermore, the body with responsibility for advising on wind-farm applications and enforcing licences is the Marine Management Organisation, which has had its budget and staff slashed in the austerity drive since 2010 and has been woefully ineffectual in preventing other skulduggery such as illegal overfishing.

In December 2020, the UK government set up a partnership with the Crown Estate to consider environmental issues around renewable energy production in the sea. That was an admission that they did not know the risks or dangers. Yet for twenty years, they had allowed industrial-scale projects to go ahead and were continuing to pursue more expansive plans. In a characteristically bombastic pronouncement, Prime Minister Boris Johnson said the UK, after China the largest offshore wind-power producer, could become 'the Saudi Arabia of wind'. The National Federation of Fishermen's Organisations, which said the expansion of wind farms was a major new threat to fishing, claimed that the government was 'in thrall to the conservation lobby'. Their ire was misplaced; it is in thrall to corporate capital.

Apart from the threat to seabirds, there is a long list of environmental concerns, many still poorly understood. Wind-farm construction obviously involves huge disruption, but once operating, the wind turbines continue to cause noise and vibration in the sea, which harms sea mammals such as harbour porpoises and disturbs fish migration patterns and breeding.

The cabling infrastructure damages coastal mudflats and salt marshes, not only disrupting habitats but interfering with their role in carbon sequestration. Disturbing them releases carbon dioxide into the atmosphere, the very opposite of what renewable energy is supposed to achieve. Similarly, the turbines and cabling can damage undersea coral reefs as well as seagrass meadows and kelp fields that are important carbon stores besides providing breeding grounds, food and shelter for numerous marine species. Other issues include the impact on sensitive marine creatures of electromagnetic fields generated by the electric current passing through undersea cables. European eels, for instance, use an electromagnetic 'sixth sense' to navigate during their long migration to the Sargasso Sea, while sharks, rays, skates and sawfish can detect the tiny electric signals given off by all living organisms to find and capture their prey.

There are possible environmental benefits: wind turbine foundations act as artificial reefs, attracting shellfish and the animals that feed on them, including fish and marine mammals. And there is a sheltering effect: exclusion of boats from wind-farm areas can create de facto marine reserves by barring fishing, including destructive bottom trawling. That said, we should be cautious in talking of 'balance' when assessing environmental impacts. How many additional mussels make up for a dead kittiwake?

Immediately after the Crown Estate auctioned the fourth round of leases, covering England and Wales, the Scottish authorities changed tactics, impressed by the rental income prospects. Instead of capping the amount developers could offer at £10,000 per square kilometre, Crown Estate Scotland supported by the Scottish government set the cap at £100,000, with the expectation of gaining windfall revenue of £860 million.[80] Firms could bid for areas totalling 8,600 square kilometres, enough to power every Scottish household.

COMMODIFYING THE SEA: THE MINING JUGGERNAUT

Unlike the situation in England and Wales, Crown Estate Scotland, through ScotWind Leasing set up in 2020, manages 'the Queen's property' but pays over all the revenue to the Scottish Consolidated Fund, which finances the Scottish government. Though very enticing in revenue terms, here again was a reckless expansion of privatized energy without assurance that environmental safeguards would be imposed or respected.

While Britain is in the vanguard of offshore wind power generation, alongside China and Germany, the USA is now set for take-off with approval by the Biden administration in early 2021 of an 84-turbine site twelve nautical miles off the Massachusetts coast. This will be the first large-scale offshore wind farm in the United States and is intended to be the first of many in the decade to 2030. One estimate suggests the world's offshore wind capacity may reach 254GW by 2030, more than seven times the level in 2020.[81] Yet, as in Britain, there are significant environmental concerns that have yet to be assessed in the pell-mell rush to claim the seaspace, the blue commons, for private interests and profit.

Can the juggernaut be stopped?

Under no circumstances . . . must we ever allow the prospects of rich harvests and mineral wealth to create a new form of colonial competition among the maritime nations. We must be careful to avoid a race to grab and to hold the lands under the high seas. We must ensure that the deep seas and the ocean bottoms are, and remain, the legacy of all human beings.
— US President Lyndon Johnson, 1966[82]

Contrary to Lyndon Johnson's plea, exploitation of the deep sea – whether for minerals, genetic resources or wind energy – has become a mix of enclosure, commodification, privatization and neo-colonialism, the features of unchecked rentier capitalism. We must instead treat nature in and under the sea as held in common, which, if exploited, should benefit all commoners, and benefit all humanity if we are talking about the global commons – the high seas and the Area.

We should nevertheless be wary of declaring that the high seas, like the Area, are the 'common heritage of mankind' (or 'humankind'). Such language *encourages* unsustainable exploitation. It promotes the idea that all states have a right to an equitable share of the economic benefits of deep-sea mining, and could legitimize the right of all states to access marine genetic resources in areas beyond national jurisdiction.[83] It is a perspective in which every country has an interest in maximizing the pot available for sharing.

The seas and the seabed should be managed as true commons, with stewards and gatekeepers legally bound to respect the three basic principles of a commons: the public trust doctrine, the precautionary principle and the intergenerational equity principle. And new mechanisms are needed to share the benefits, financial and otherwise, flowing from the discovery and exploitation of ocean resources.

Treating the seas and seabed as commons also implies strong protections for biodiversity and habitats. We are now far more aware than UNCLOS negotiators were in 1982 both of how interconnected and sensitive ocean ecosystems are, and of the depth of our ignorance about the impact of human activities on those ecosystems. We should not start from the arrogant premise that the oceans are there to supply 'resources' to humans. We are beginning to learn just how much we owe the oceans in ensuring a planet fit for humans to live on. Given the imperfect state of our current knowledge, following the precautionary principle will often mean we should leave well alone. In 2021 hundreds of scientists and policy experts signed a Deep-Sea Mining Science Statement calling for a global moratorium until the full impacts of deep-sea mining are understood, and support for a moratorium is growing as the warnings grow louder.[84]

Yet this is a message that business and finance do not wish to hear. In so far as problems are acknowledged, they are usually focused on conflict between human activities – between seabed mining and fisheries, for example, rather than between profit and nature and ecosystems. Finance is accelerating the industrialization of the oceans, while the World Bank is playing its customary leveraging role. By 2018, it valued its 'blue economy' portfolio at more than $4 billion.[85] Venture capital has poured into companies with licences to explore the Area seabed, in the expectation of juicy returns once mining is allowed.

The deep sea should not be seen as a zone of capitalist extraction but as a space where we need to foster a new sense of ecological justice. This is an aspect of the blue degrowth perspective explored in the final chapters.

Resistance and Rebellion

> Every human group or class that wants to defend their
> interests and rights in society, needs to organize.
>
> — Gabriela Cruz, President, National Federation of
>   Fisheries Cooperatives, Ecuador

Blue commoners come in various guises – as artisan fishers,
as small-scale fishers, as coastal and estuarine dwellers and
even as 'peasants', surviving by combining marine activities
with small-scale farming or craft work. Over the past century,
particularly in the neoliberal phase, most such communities
around the world have experienced an erosion of their commons, their ability to common and their ability to reproduce a
lifestyle oriented to ecosystem sustainability. This has hit not
only the marine life on which they depend, but also their land,
water and supporting communal institutions and activities.

But they have not gone gently into the night. They have
resisted the encroachment, enclosure, commodification and
neo-colonization of their commons, and their own crimi-
nalization too. They have particularly resented and resisted
the entrance of new interests competing for marine space.[1]
Their resistance has taken various forms, with mixed success. Overall, it has been an uphill struggle, one lesson of

which is that for sustained success the state must play a positive role.

However, the very existence and also the extent of resistance exposes as false the continuing presumption that a 'partnership model' can provide an equitable way of exploiting marine resources while ensuring local communities benefit from blue growth. In reality, state-corporate corruption and manipulative rent-seeking are destroying the commons and marginalizing commoners.

The most dramatic struggles have come in response to the imperialistic logic of capitalism. Capitalistic industrialization needs constantly to advance to new 'commodity frontiers', extract new resources and create new commodities, producing waste and undermining the commons as it does so. Resistance to the resultant 'accumulation by dispossession' and the consequent destruction of a way of life defines the human condition.[2]

Today, resistance arises from the structural 'unequal exchange' that characterizes the frontier character of the blue commons.[3] Industrial fisheries, other marine corporations and their financial backers at the core of the blue growth strategy extract resources and commodify nature. They export these resources and commodities from what were commoning communities to rich consumer markets, at prices that do not reflect the depletion of resources and other costs, including pollution and the damage to livelihoods. In a sense, resistance often reflects an attempt to impose the full cost on the plunderers.

The resistance is sometimes sullen and silent, sometimes vocal and angry, sometimes collective, sometimes anomic.

Sometimes it is retributive, rather than consciously aimed at overthrowing or reversing the loss of the commons. Much depends on where the forces of loss come from, and on the balance of strength and the institutions of the state.

Where commoners are numerous and the threat to the commons comes from outside the community without legitimation by the state, active resistance is relatively likely. But where the commoners are already weakened and fragmented, or where they know or believe that the institutions of the state are aligned with corporate capital or other corroders of the commons, they will be more likely to indulge in passive, sullen, anomic resistance. However, the absence of overt resistance need not mean the absence of resistance altogether, or tolerance of the erosion of the commons.

To understand resistance, it is helpful to distinguish between the formal possession of rights (or entitlements), the ability to claim and use them, and the power to do so. In the first, custom is usually the main source of legitimacy. Commoners, by definition, have enshrined rights, usually moulded by 'social memory', as noted in Chapter 3. They also often have 'claim rights', that is, claims that stem from past patterns of commoning, and popular feelings that such rights should exist. These may include rights of access, rights of withdrawal and rights of reproduction of resources, as well as rights of governance, distribution and social protection of members and the community.

In all these respects, the commoners in the community may or may not have the *ability* to give their rights reality. They may have lost the capacity or institutional mechanisms to put them into effect. The lost ability may reflect internal conflicts or, more likely, suppression by outside intervention. And the ability to realize rights should be distinguished from the *power* to exercise or obtain the rights. Some analysts have treated the two terms as similar.[4] But in many commons, the commoners retain the technical ability, but lose the power to exercise it. And the loss of power usually comes from outside forces.

So, in general, resistance is directed against loss of recognized rights, loss of ability to exercise them and loss of power to do so, or, as some commentators put it, loss of 'bundles' of rights, abilities and powers. While they are all connected, most attention has been given to the struggle against loss of power and the struggle to regain power. Perhaps more should be given to the other two aspects, since loss of power has often stemmed from the erosion or corruption of institutions set up to defend the commons and commoning.

We must also distinguish between the resistance by blue commoners against erosion of their commons as an 'environment' and resistance by small-scale fishing communities against loss of their ability to take a commons approach to fishing. Erosion of the commons as an 'environment' includes coastal grabbing or ocean grabbing by commercial interests unrelated to the main activities of those communities, sometimes involving transfer of property rights to outside interests.[5] It also includes invasive aquaculture in coastal communities, where expropriation of mangroves for shrimp farming has reduced food security and marginalized the community inhabitants, a practice that has led to many conflicts worldwide.[6] The latter may arise within communities simply because different groups no longer feel bound together by common interests.

Shrimp farming is an example of loss through outside intervention. This is often an itinerant activity, with fishing communities shifting ponds at regular intervals, similar to crop rotation schemes in farming. Most intensively farmed ponds are productive for only five to ten years, because of disease outbreaks and build-up of an organic ooze, rich in uneaten food and prawn faeces. But the rotation system has been disrupted by commercial shrimp farmers, who dispossess community access to mangroves and then, once they have fully exploited the former mangrove zone, move on, spatially advancing the 'commodity frontier' and leaving behind impoverished communities.[7] It is hard to resist this sort of dispossession.

Resistance by small-scale fishers unable to institute a fishery commons was poignantly illustrated in Luchino Visconti's 1948 film, *La Terra Trema*, a 'docufiction' hailed as a masterpiece of Italian neo-realist cinema. Filmed in a small fishing community in Sicily, using local people as actors, it told the story of the fishers' failed attempt to break the stranglehold of the powerful middlemen who monopolized sale of the catch and drove down the price they paid for it. *The Spectator* magazine said it was 'surely one of the greatest films ever made'. But it was a tale of defeat.

Globalization has brought the intrusion of powerful corporate and financial forces into once self-contained communities with little capacity to fight back. Resistance is made still harder where corporate-state collusion has deliberately created confusion and ambiguity about what rights commoners

possess, and blocked channels of legitimate action to retain
or recover their rights. In Brazil, India and Thailand, for instance, jurisdictional ambiguity – leaving rights and duties
unclear, contradictory or incomplete – has compromised
rights of access to and use of mangrove swamps.[8] Resistance is obviously hard when the legal system becomes an
instrument of dispossession. It has ever been thus; from the
Middle Ages onward, much of the commons in Britain was
lost through legal action. But these losses grew more pervasive in the neoliberal era, which greatly strengthened private
property rights around the world.

One important aspect of resistance concerns the varying
roles of women. The modes of resistance and the source of
conflict will depend in part on women's role in the production process, and the resistance itself can alter their status
and consciousness. When women are prominent in part of
the production process, as they are in processing and marketing fish in much of Africa, for instance, then they are likely
to play a key role in collective action. There have been few
successful cases of resistance where women have not been
an integral part of the action.

Many successful commons have used rituals and festivals
to express the joy and longevity of commoning and reinforce
community solidarity. This can be a defence against possible
erosion or a form of resistance to existing threats. A feature
of the early English commons was the annual practice of 'per-
ambulations' at Rogationtide in May (Ascension Week in the
Christian calendar), when whole communities mobilized to
walk around the boundaries of their commons, with 'cakes
and ale' along the way. Numerous 'holy-days', harvest festivals

and rites of passage continue around the world today. Some celebrate and defend the success of past skirmishes; the National Octopus Festival in Mauritania recognizes how local artisanal fisheries wrested back full control of octopus fishing from EU long-distance fleets.

This aspect of commoning acts as a 'soft power' defence, intimidating outsiders threatening to disrupt traditional procedures and rights. Another 'soft power' defence is the international attention generated by the celebration of World Fisheries Day each November and the declaration by the United Nations of 2022 as the International Year of Artisanal Fisheries and Aquaculture. But however well-intentioned, these initiatives cannot fulfil the function of an embedded defence stemming from local traditions and ceremonies. This is not to suggest there is no place for them. It is to return to the point that in a globalized blue economy system, just as there are multiple layers of government (global, regional, multilateral, national and local), so countervailing defence mechanisms have to be identified, defended and constantly reinvigorated.

Silent protest: the power of sabotage

Historically, the powerless have almost always resisted their decommoning. One way of rebelling against state-led enclosure and commodification has been described as 'the art of not being governed'.[9] They just do not comply. For example, even though it might have been in their future interest, local small-scale fishers in Pondicherry, India, refused to take part in a government-initiated safety drill linked to the establishment of a new chemical factory in their area. They rejected remedial action because it would imply they accepted the legitimacy of the factory, which they wished to be closed.[10]

Beyond non-cooperation, the most passive form of protest against perceived injustice is sabotage. This form has been little discussed, because it is concealed and possibly because the authorities want to minimize awareness of what it could do. Throughout history, it has been used by individuals and groups denied legal routes to challenge injustice or lacking the collective strength and solidarity to do so. Sabotage can draw attention to the harms being done and, by imposing costs and uncertainty, it can sometimes induce concessions.[11] But the likelier reaction is more draconian suppression, as history attests. For every successful Robin Hood, there are many lost souls.

Some sabotage can be deliberately self-destructive, as if the community is saying that if they cannot have the resources, nobody can. On Misali Island off the west coast of Zanzibar, the Muslim fishing community dynamited the inshore coral reefs in a desperate attempt to maintain their catches after overfishing by foreign industrial trawlers depleted fish populations. However, the reefs were spawning grounds for the very fish they wanted to catch. Belatedly, the fisherfolk were persuaded that dynamiting the reefs was against Muslim teaching. But considerable ecological and economic damage had been done.

The key to understanding sabotage – and why it should be differentiated from collective action as discussed later – is that it is surreptitious, deliberately concealed, knowingly breaking rules perceived to be illegitimate and imposed on those being dispossessed. Sabotage may be motivated by a desire for structural change, but the action does not itself put changes into effect.

In the case of fisheries, there are usually internal tensions within commoners' communities. There is always scope for resentment, that someone is 'too big for their boots' and should be 'brought to heel'. A fisherman who breaks the informal rules to take opportunistic advantage over his fellows is likely to find his nets cut.

In the green commons, a classic form of silent resistance has been poaching from forests, farms or other land previously taken by enclosure and privatization. This form of retributive justice, which lowers actual and potential profits, is harder in the blue commons. It could include fishing without a licence or deliberately exceeding quotas, as a response to perceived injustice in the award of licences or the allocation of quotas. In the longer term, deliberate overfishing might be self-defeating. But if the commoners feel their community economy is doomed anyhow, because industrial fisheries are plundering their resource base, they might feel justified in taking as much fish as possible as quickly as possible.

A response to mangrove destruction by commercial shrimp farmers and corporations has been the night-time destruction of shrimp ponds, and the subsequent replanting of Rhizophora (mangrove tree) seedlings. This form of retributive justice has been exacted by dispossessed commoners in countries such as Bangladesh, Ecuador, Honduras, India, Indonesia, Malaysia, the Philippines, Sri Lanka and Thailand.[12] Such action has often resulted in violent retaliation against protesters, without achieving great success in recovering mangrove forests. But it has more than symbolic value, to the extent that it may deter further expansion by commercial interests.

In some cases, it may evolve into more effective resistance to the tragedy of enclosure, such as the transition from silent to active resistance to shrimp farming in Ecuador. Mobilization that linked local commoners with civil society organizations led to what one observer characterized as a liberation of women and nature.[13] Information gathering and dissemination are also important ways for movements to identify longer-term trends and risks from commodification of everything in and around the sea, and to prepare the ground for active resistance at a later date.

Some acts of sabotage by blue commoners are openly defiant. An imaginative example comes from the picturesque Tuscan fishing village of Talamone, where Paolo Fanciulli, a small-scale lifetime fisher, has taken direct action to stop illegal trawling near the coast, which has devastated fish populations.[14] The trawling nets are weighted with chains that drag along the sea bottom, uprooting the seagrass – crucial to the Mediterranean ecosystem – in which sea bream, lobsters and red gurnards lay their eggs. Though trawling within three nautical miles of the coast is banned by law, the fishing is so profitable that illegal trawling continues, often at night or with transponders turned off to evade the coastguard.

Fanciulli started by organizing other local fishers and activists from Greenpeace to block a commercial port. Then he graduated to destroying trawling nets with barbed wire. By this time, he had become a local celebrity, albeit one threatened by the local mafia. But in 2006, the Tuscan regional government tried a new deterrent by dropping concrete blocks on to the seabed to snag the nets.

After Fanciulli argued that more blocks were needed, he obtained permission from the Regional Environmental Protection Agency to drop eighty blocks at his own expense. Then, taking inspiration from underwater shipwrecks, he asked a quarry in Carrara, just up the coast, if they would donate two marble blocks to make sculptures. So supportive was the quarry that it donated one hundred blocks. News circulated about his ambition, and via online crowdfunding and contributions from tourists, he persuaded several famous artists to carve sculptures. Then he took the sculptures out and lowered them into the sea.

The result is an underwater 'museum'. The seagrass has started to recover, and marine life of all kinds appears to be returning. Commoning has worked. This small act of resistance shows how the sense of connection that is nurtured in a commons, between the humans, the environment and the resources, fosters sustainability. A long-term perspective comes from attachment to the commons, whereas corporate capitalism focuses on short-term profit.

Activists have also used the concrete-block tactic to prevent bottom trawling in places around the British coast. This surely has potential as a disruptive and conservation tactic. But it stops short of being a tactic to revive the commons. That requires other actions.

Direct action for heritage rights

Indigenous communities are a special type of commoner community whose rights have gained increased recognition in recent years. In Australia, Canada and New Zealand, for instance, there has been an intense struggle by indigenous groups to preserve and revive their ancient fishing rights in traditional blue commons that were usurped by colonial settlers.

An example concerns First Nations' claims to the right to harvest the land and waters of their ancestors in Nova Scotia.[15] After years of agitation, in 2000, Canada's Supreme Court ruled that the indigenous descendants had a right to fish their lands, in pursuit of a 'moderate livelihood'. But the court's decision came with a caveat, stating that the federal government had the authority to regulate fisheries in the public interest and for conservation purposes. And 'moderate livelihood' was never defined. It was a prime example of how commoners' rights can be frustrated by 'jurisdictional ambiguity'.

In 2020, the Sipekne'katik First Nation in Nova Scotia issued the first licences to its fishers to catch lobster. Furious local commercial fishers attacked the First Nation fishers with flares and hauled up their traps, accusing them of overfishing and of fishing in the close season. Sipekne'katik leaders noted that the federal authorities had granted 979 commercial inshore lobster licences in the area, whereas it had issued just seven to its fishers. So, they could not be the primary cause of overfishing. The standoff exemplified a form of commoners' resistance that usually requires legislative resolution. The commercial fishers argued that traditionally the First Nations had not fished for lobster, so they could not be given back rights they never had. But that does not alter the fact that they had an ancient right to fish for what they wished in those waters.

In late 2020, another First Nation achieved what seemed a remarkable coup by joining with a commercial food company to purchase the huge Nova Scotia-based Clearwater Seafoods in a deal worth C$1 billion. One of their chiefs proudly announced, 'For 13,000 years, the Mi'kmaq have sustainably fished the waters of Atlantic Canada, and today, on this truly transformational day, we are owners of a global leader in the fishery.'[16] The communities would henceforth own Clearwater's coveted offshore fishing licences, allowing them to harvest lobster, scallop, crab and clams in a vast tract of ocean.

Will this lead to a revival of traditional fishing communities and sharing systems, or will it merely herald a change of corporate ownership? Local commercial fishers were sceptical, suggesting that Clearwater would use First Nation treaty rights to gain access to lobster licences that it could not have obtained otherwise. The scene was set for further confrontations.

Collective action

A potentially promising form of resistance is collective agitation, such as mass protests and symbolic strikes. This can be directed against stewards or gatekeepers perceived as corrupt or not doing their jobs, or against outside bodies, such as corporations or the state more generally. However, agitation may not impose sufficient costs on those taking away common rights, or on the authorities that are the effective stewards. And the costs borne by the commoners taking the action may not be sustainable for the time needed to gain concessions.

Certain preconditions are usually necessary for sustained effective resistance. There must be a widely shared sense of 'perceived injustice', often built around a sense that traditional rights or reciprocities have been abrogated. In Tamil Nadu and Gujarat, for example, local self-governing fishing communities, which had traditionally regulated coastal fishing through village councils, found themselves in competition and conflict with large-scale trawler fisheries, heavily promoted by the Indian government from the 1950s onwards.[17] It was an unequal struggle they were bound to lose. Trawling depleted the fish populations, small-scale fishers lost their livelihoods and their communities disintegrated.

In general, righteous indignation and frustration are insufficient on their own to galvanize collective action. There is also a need for 'perceived efficacy', that is, that the action has a good prospect of restoring abrogated rights. Those participating in collective action may in fact realize that there is a low probability of 'winning'. But they should at least believe that, if their demands were met, their livelihoods and rights would be restored or enhanced. For collective action in such circumstances, there is usually a need for strong and charismatic leadership.[18]

One well-documented example of the failure of collective action concerns small-scale fisheries in the north of Sri Lanka, where the population is overwhelmingly Tamil. Banned from fishing their traditional inshore waters for twenty years during the civil war between the government and Tamil separatists, their rights to fish were restored after the war ended with the crushing of the insurgency in 2009. But in the meantime, about 2,000 industrial fishing trawlers from the Indian state of Tamil Nadu had moved into the Sri Lankan waters.[19]

The injustice felt by the Sri Lankan small-scale fishers reflected four factors. The foreign trawlers had usurped their access and withdrawal rights, taking most of the fish they had previously caught, including grouper, snapper, bream and skate, and leaving the locals with low-value alternatives such as sardines. The trawlers came during the night, often destroying the local fishers' nets. Bottom trawling was turning the seabed into a lifeless desert. And, ironically, while the Indian trawlers did not need fishing permits, the locals were required to pay for fishing passes.

This was an example of permitted colonization of the blue commons, in which the weakness of local commoners dictated what sort of action they took. Initially, there was sporadic collective agitation, including demonstrations, strikes, petitions, press conferences and even the hijacking of Indian trawlers. The Sri Lankan government soon clamped down, suspicious of anything involving collective action by Tamil fishing communities, which had supported the separatist Liberation Tigers of Tamil Eelam during the civil war. Appeal to the government, the 'steward', to take action resulted in several navy ships being sent to the area, but only symbolically. Diplomatic pressure from the Indian government meant any arrested Tamil Nadu trawler was soon released. The Sri Lankan state was disadvantaging its own small-scale fisheries, for largely geopolitical reasons.

The local fishing communities have since been sullen but silent. Many youths left for jobs in the city or the Gulf. And military surveillance of the Tamil population created an atmosphere of fear and distrust. As a local priest told a researcher, 'It's a saying here that we only open our mouths for food.' Collective action no longer had 'perceived efficacy'. Fishers became disillusioned by their lack of agency and believed they were powerless to bring about change. Not only were they unable to have a meaningful dialogue with the navy, politicians and government officials, but their cooperative societies, the fishers' primary collective organizations, were undermined by parallel fisher representative organizations set up by the government and based on political patronage. Obtaining government subsidies was conditional on joining these bodies.

The Tamil fishing communities had a bundle of increasingly unrealizable rights. They still possessed *capacities* – the technical ability to exercise their rights, in possessing adequate fishing equipment and skills, but the power to access the resources had been taken away. Quite simply, the voice of local fishers could not match the effective lobbying power of foreign industrial fisheries and their government. The Sri Lankan state found it expedient to let the communities wither.

Although the commoners in this case might have hoped for successful restoration of their rights, not all forms of collective action are motivated by an expectation of achieving the stated goals. There are also protests emanating from dying commons, the classic example being the destruction of textile machinery by artisan weavers, the Luddites, in the early nineteenth century. This is usually misinterpreted as an anarchic and futile protest against the replacement of workers by machinery, so that 'Luddite' has come to mean someone opposed to technological progress. In fact, the Luddites were protesting against the destruction of their way of living and working, without remedial reciprocity. This may be a sentiment motivating many protests in the blue commons as well, though it has received little attention in the literature on collective action.

Probably the main conflict within fisheries is between systemic winners and losers, usually a reflection of growing class differentiation. This tends to occur within all occupations unless there are institutional constraints to prevent it. In the case of fisheries, an elite, often consisting of externally owned or funded industrial fisheries, may capture the governance of local fishing, in effect reducing small-scale artisanal fishers to the status of a precariat. No longer having the ability or power to exercise customary rights or contest changes to the rules, they are reduced to wage labourers, paid on a piece-rate basis, such as share of catch, or by time at sea.

This is not just a developing-country issue. For example, most small-scale fishers have vanished from Sweden's Baltic Sea coast, and the remainder have struggled to keep going, due largely to neoliberal policies adopted at national and EU levels.[20] These policies have aimed to maintain fish stocks while maximizing profits and efficiency, benefiting large mobile fisheries that gain competitive advantage through economies of scale and substantial subsidies.[21] There and elsewhere, social and ecological objectives, despite being written into the EU's Common Fisheries Policy, have been subordinated to economic growth imperatives. The commoners have little chance of resisting the commercial steamroller.

However, there are occasional successes. In the coastal municipality of Simrishamn on the Baltic coast, historically nicknamed 'herring town', resistance has taken the form of a communal fishery strategy designed by and for local interests.[22] The aim is to implement at local level a true blue growth strategy in which sustainable exploitation of fish goes hand-in-hand with benefits for the fishers and their community. Among other things, fishers have begun direct sales of fish to consumers, enabling them to gain from higher prices by excluding intermediaries, and are campaigning to win a regional cod quota which would not be subject to Sweden's individual transferable quota (ITQ) system. The strategy has been shaped by a feminist-inspired alliance named the Community Economy Collective, whose objective has been 'to bring marginalized, hidden and alternative economic activities to light in order to make them more real and more credible as objects of policy and activism'.[23]

Nigerian fishers organized a mass campaign in 2008 to take Shell to court for polluting their fishing grounds. In 2015, Shell agreed to pay $83.4 million in compensation, with $35 million going to the fisher families and the rest set aside for health clinics and schools. The fishers gained over $3,000 each, but this merely made up for what they had lost over the previous seven years. Meanwhile, the oil spills had dislocated the fishing community. It was a pyrrhic victory.

Successes elsewhere include a 2009 campaign led by fisher organizations in Venezuela that persuaded President Hugo Chávez to ban trawler fishing completely. In Chile, small-scale fishers have created an alliance with student bodies to lobby government to protect their communities. And in the UK in 2013, a small-scale fishers' organization, the New Under Ten Fishermen's Association (NUTFA), won a High Court ruling that quotas were not the industry's private property, so that the government had authority to take unused quota from large-scale boats to give to small-scale boats.[24] This was potentially important, since successive UK governments had allowed extreme concentration of quota ownership.

Another form of collective action might be called 'shaming the state'. For a long time the Mauritanian government, for whatever reason, refused to acknowledge systematic illegal fishing by foreign trawlers that were plundering local fish populations and damaging the livelihoods of local artisanal fisheries. After years of protest, the locals took out to sea some naval officers who, after coming under attack from illegal fishers, were forced to accept the inconvenient truth that dozens of foreign trawlers were breaking the law. The challenge, of course, will be to enforce the law, for which Mauritania is notoriously ill-equipped.

If there is one general conclusion from recent experiences, it is that to mount effective collective action the group struggling to retain or recover common rights must be able to politicize its identity and articulate its struggle so as to resonate with a sufficient class interest outside its own community. Unfortunately, this has often been lacking.

Collective bodies

There is an obvious difference between action that is confrontational and action through collective bodies that is organized and integrated in some way into the state. These bodies, varying in scale and formality, can be divided into five categories.[25] The first, evidence for which dates back to medieval times, comprises 'customary organizations', formed around a shared local or occupational identity, whose actions are consensual and initiated by the community based on customary rules. Customary organizations could be seen as blue commons variants of occupational guilds.

A second category is cooperatives. Cooperatives began to be formed in the early 1900s and became widespread in the 'development decades' of the 1950s, 1960s and 1970s. Closely related to the essence of the commons, cooperatives may yet experience a new surge, as they are seen as more oriented to ecological protection and sharing activities than capitalistic endeavours. However, they require the state to provide institutional protection. And a perennial challenge has been the 'succession problem': ensuring that a cooperative set up by pioneers is maintained when the initial founders pass on the mantle of management.

A third category consists of associations and unions, mainly adversarial towards the state, which proliferated during the 1980s. Another comprises 'supported' organizations, mostly set up since about 2000. These tend to be cross-class and multi-interest bodies, linked to the state, non-governmental organizations and, often, international bodies. Finally, there are hybrid and networked arrangements, which have spread since the financial crisis in 2007–8. In this fifth category, collective action is partly organized online.

It is not too fanciful to see fishery-based collective bodies evolving in similar ways to labour-based industrial relations, where the vocabulary has morphed from industrial action to the vague and non-threatening social dialogue, from confrontation to accommodation and supplication. The danger is that they are co-opted by the state and made less threatening to powerful interests.

Customary organizations, closest to the historical commons, probably stemmed from rising resource constraints and were set up to defend and preserve the commons as a sharing sustainable community. Customary norms were mostly unwritten laws, with implicit sanctions and retributive justice for those who did not respect them.

The main mechanism was moral suasion, supported by rituals, ceremonies and 'holy-days', many of which might appear to the modern commercial eye as recreational and non-work, but which usually had a material work orientation. In such a system, the autonomy of individuals, households and extended families was circumscribed, at least ostensibly in the interest of preserving the commons and, implicitly, respecting the precautionary and intergenerational equity principles. Customary organizations can be effective in maintaining internal disciplines. But they are weak in defending against commodification and colonization.

An example of an unequal struggle against unequal exchange is taking place in Ghana, where Chinese trawlers have usurped the fishing of sardinella, long the staple fish of artisanal fisheries. The trawlers have been catching about 100,000 tonnes of the fish each year, worth some $50 million, selling much of that to local traders at sea in a process known as *saiko*. The Chinese trawlers have thereby severed the fishing and marketing arms of the fishing communities. Meanwhile, the government has done nothing, tacitly supporting the trawlers that pay it about $135 per tonne of fish and have registered as Ghanaian by linking up with Ghanaian frontmen.

In response, the locals have formed the Ghana Canoe Fishermen Council to lobby for action. The odds are against it. The state, as in so many countries, has been captured by commercial 'partners'.

For their part, unions have been relatively strong in bargaining for redistribution of shares of revenue within fisheries, but weak in protecting the commons character of the community or in protecting the 'right of withdrawal' of resources. They too have been powerless against destruction of the resource base of local commons. They do not have the ability to impose costs on those trampling on the rights of commoners.

Moreover, unions have often been co-opted. In the Sri Lankan case described earlier, collective agitation in defence of the small-scale local fishers was initially led by a local Fisheries Union. However, this was subsequently taken over by a local politician loyal to the government, resulting in merely symbolic protests and loss of faith by the fishers themselves.

The fourth and fifth forms of collective body perhaps offer the best hope of defending and reviving the blue commons. But they depend crucially on support from a progressive state against the rent-seeking power of corporations and foreign nations. It is necessary but not sufficient for bodies to exist at local level, given that we live in a multi-level world.[26] And collective action will often depend on outsiders having some sort of affinity and empathy with the local commons, to share the moral outrage that lies at the heart of such action.

One example of a hybrid organization is the Foundation of Ecological Defence (FUNDECOL). This early grass-roots organization was set up in the coastal region of Muisne in Ecuador in 1989 to defend the mangroves against expansion of illegal shrimp farms, and to restore them and the traditional local mangrove-dependent communities.

After some years, FUNDECOL started receiving support from radical academics, mainly women. This was no doubt partly because the organization was mainly led by women, which in turn reflected the traditional division of labour in the mangrove coastal communities. Women and children were responsible for crabbing and other activities in the mangroves, while men were responsible for sea fishing. Indeed, at the outset, women formed 'user groups' against often violent opposition from the men in the community. The movement itself acted to liberate local women from previously rigid patriarchal relations.[27]

Later, FUNDECOL began to link up with supportive organizations in Quito, the capital, and was soon aided by Greenpeace, whose activists visited Muisne aboard the famous ship *Rainbow Warrior* and participated in a big conference and collective destruction of an illegal shrimp pond. At about the same time, a national network was created, the Coordinating Committee for the Defence of Mangroves, giving the movement a stronger political platform. Two years later an international arm was formed, the Redmanglar International, which has been mainly active in Latin America.

Thus, a multi-level organizational structure has been built up. Which way is it leading? FUNDECOL has moved from being a protest-and-restore organization to being more transformative. It has helped subsistence communities to become small-scale commodity producers, brought together to supply a local 'ecological market'. This could be one of the classic routes to capitalist relations or could evolve into a form of

411

'socialism from below'. The outcome will depend in part on the posture taken by the state, and the globalizing pressures from international institutions. If Ecuador is pushed back into depending wholly on export-oriented production of primary products, FUNDECOL may be marginalized.

There have been developments that suggest resistance to capitalistic commodification. In 2003, the government accepted the creation of a 5,000-hectare mangrove reserve to be managed by FUNDECOL. Unlike other reserves devoted to conservation, this was an 'extractive reserve' in which coastal communities could fish and collect animals and plants from the mangroves. Thus, FUNDECOL started by agitating for human rights, which then became an environmental campaign. While never explicitly feminist, it has liberated women. Over time it has evolved into a potentially transformative organization. The question is: Can it revive and support the commons and commoning, or will it merely facilitate commodification and petty accumulation?

Another somewhat encouraging example of a collective body is the Kenyan system of Beach Management Units, introduced by the government in 2006. The fisher mentioned in the Preface belonged to one of these. The idea is fine. They are multi-stakeholder bodies, with an executive and their own by-laws. They exercise some control over local fishers but have limited control over commercial fishing by foreigners. What they have shown is that a fightback is possible.

The judicial route

So, what about the law? In 1217, Magna Carta and the Charter of the Forest together established what is in effect the principle of the 'civil commons', that the weak should have equal recourse to justice with the strong. This principle has never been respected by the powerful, and in the era of neo-liberalism commoners have systematically been denied access to justice.

However, one landmark legal case of resistance concerns a community of low-income fisherfolk in the Indian state of Gujarat. In a deal orchestrated by the then Chief Minister of Gujarat, Narendra Modi, the International Finance Corporation (IFC), the corporate lending arm of the World Bank, helped to finance the construction by India's Tata Group of a huge coal-fired electricity generating plant near the shore of the Gulf of Kutch. The Mundra Ultra Mega Power Project was advertised as eventually supplying 2% of India's electricity needs.

The construction work had devastating effects on the livelihoods of fishers and their communities, hitting fish stocks, polluting drinking water and poisoning the air. Running the Tata plant requires four billion gallons of cooling water each day. This is taken from the Gulf of Kutch, and the heated water is then discharged back into the sea through a four-mile-long outflow channel. This is leading to mass die-offs of fish in the Gulf. In addition, in constructing the plant, the whole area was dredged, which turned coastal settlements into peninsula communities, surrounded on both sides by water channels. Many villagers are now cut off from the road leading to the area's few shops.[28]

In 2008, desperate local fishers, led by their Association for the Struggle for Fisherworkers' Rights (MASS), contacted a Delhi-based NGO, the Centre for Financial Accountability.

A petition was sent to the president of the World Bank in Washington DC, calling on the Bank to recognize the IFC's violation of its environmental policy and to 'develop remedial action that has a clear timeline'.

No remedial action happened then or in succeeding years, even though the IFC's Compliance Advisor Ombudsman issued a scathing report confirming that the IFC had failed to ensure that the project complied with environmental and social conditions attached to the loan. The report was ignored by IFC management; the insolence of office prevailed.

But the World Bank, the IFC and Tata had not counted on the fisherfolk, and in particular on the stubbornness of a 58-year-old fisherman named Budha Ismail Jam. Aided by the Delhi NGO and EarthRights International in the United States, in 2015 the fishers filed a class action suit for damages with the District Court of the District of Columbia, where the IFC is based. In 2016, the court ruled against Jam, the lead plaintiff, on the grounds that the IFC, as an international organization, had 'absolute immunity' against legal action. A year later, the Appeals Court upheld the decision. It seemed all was lost.

However, in 2018, aided by another NGO, the Stanford Supreme Court Litigation Clinic, the suit was lodged with the US Supreme Court. The fishers cannot have had much optimism, since of the 7,000 or so requests to be heard each year, only about 100 are selected for hearing. Surprisingly, it was chosen.

At this point, it is essential to understand the full context of the Supreme Court case, *Jam v. International Finance Corporation*. Before confirmation of the $450 million loan to Tata, the IFC had been obliged under its standard procedure to conduct a review to determine the project's likely social and environmental impact. In 2006, the World Bank, the IFC's parent body, stated its conclusion that the project was 'expected to have significant adverse social and/or environmental impacts that are diverse, irreversible, or unprecedented.' Despite these early warnings, the Tata Mundra project went forward in 2008.

The IFC states that its mission is to 'carry out investment and advisory activities with the intent to do no harm to people and the environment'. By that criterion, said the lawyers on Jam's behalf, 'The Tata Mundra plant is thus a mission failure.' However, that was not enough to win Budha Jam the lawsuit and damages. The case ran up against the legal obstacle that the World Bank and other international organizations were granted immunity against prosecution for misdeeds under the US International Organizations Immunities Act (IOIA) of 1945, which gave them the same 'absolute immunity' as foreign governments. This became the heart of the matter. Indeed, the US Supreme Court only consented to hear the part of the suit relating to the immunity issue, not that part which could have determined whether Budha Jam and his community should receive damages, or how much.

Although the 1945 Act had made the World Bank above the law, the Supreme Court ruled that the Foreign Sovereign Immunities Act of 1976 excluded commercial activities of foreign governments from immunity and, since international financial institutions were to be treated like foreign governments under the 1945 Act, they were liable to prosecution. By a majority of 7-1, the Court ruled in favour of Budha Jam.[29] It was truly a landmark case. As one law professor remarked afterwards, 'It was one of several moments when the voice of ordinary citizens got to reverberate in the international law system.'

However, the Supreme Court left the matter of damages to lower courts while noting that the exception to immunity specified by the 1976 Act related to 'commercial activity carried on in the United States'. The Court said it was not clear whether development banks' activities would qualify as commercial activity and that, to come within the jurisdiction of US courts, the activity would need to have a sufficient nexus to the United States.

In July 2021, a federal appeals court in Washington DC upheld a lower court ruling that the World Bank Group could not be sued for damages caused by its lending, despite the Supreme Court decision, because the plaintiff had not proved that the action was 'based on' conduct 'carried on' or 'performed in' the USA.[30] The ruling said the 'gravamen' or 'core' of the complaint was not the IFC's approval of the loan, which took place in the USA, but its failure to ensure that the plant was designed, constructed and operated with due care so as not to harm the plaintiff's property, health and way of life – conduct that was based in India. The plaintiffs, represented by EarthRights International, said they would appeal further and go back to the Supreme Court if necessary.

The Supreme Court ruling may in practice have only a limited impact. Most international organizations, including the International Monetary Fund, have a separate source of immunity in statutes or ratified treaties in addition to the IOIA, and will not be affected. According to EarthRights, eighty-five international organizations are designated under the IOIA but only seven do not have immunity from another source.[31] Four of these are part of the World Bank Group.

Nevertheless, the Jam judgment marks an important breach in the claimed immunity (and impunity) of international financial institutions, at least in the USA, and could open the way for more challenges by victims of their lending activities. And it should make international financial organizations rethink their dispute procedures to avoid action in national courts.

Courts outside the USA have taken a different approach to the issue of immunity, judging challenges based on the existence (or lack) of reasonable alternative means of redress.[32] This approach has the advantage of allowing challenges to non-commercial activities of international organizations, such as issues arising from the UN's peacekeeping operations. There has been increasing willingness to argue that the bar to jurisdiction violates claimants' rights to access a court and to a remedy, though most cases have been unsuccessful.[33]

The protracted judicial process unleashed by the impoverished but determined fisherfolk of Gujarat demonstrates the scant attention given by international finance, and the World Bank in particular, to protecting the livelihoods of commoners or the commons environment. The case also shows how loaded the international legal system is in favour of financial interests, leaving commoners with legal mountains to climb, with costs and prospective costs that most could not contemplate. Budha Jam and his fellow fishers found a group of fantastic advocates. But how many communities could be so fortunate?

There is another aspect of the Gujarat case, which is that all the land adjoining the seashore had been virtually gifted to two billionaires by the Modi Gujarat government, much of it for as little as one US cent a metre, after being taken by the government from the villagers. Such a case could be construed as land grabbing or a mix of that and ocean grabbing. In 2016, the International Criminal Court indicated that it was considering moving into the area of environmental crime involving land grabbing and the violent displacement of residents in order to exploit nature.[34] There have also been calls for 'ecocide' to be made a crime subject to international jurisdiction.

International rules are also making it possible for commoners to take legal action and seek redress for environmental and social harm caused by governments and business. The Aarhus Convention, ratified by forty-six countries and the European Union, affirms the right of the public to have access to justice in environmental matters, and requires ratifying states to put the necessary mechanisms in place. The UN Guiding Principles on Business and Human Rights have spurred European legislation making respect for human rights and the environment mandatory for business. And the Hague Rules on Business and Human Rights Arbitration adopted in December 2019, though voluntary, may provide a further route to obtaining justice for commoners. Although in many countries access to justice remains difficult and costly, if not impossible, the trend to hold corporations and governments to account in judicial processes should be regarded as a modest source of encouragement.

Resistance by alliances

One promising site of resistance at the international level involves partnerships between national and local organizations in various countries, and between fishers' organizations and NGOs. Although often small-scale in coverage, some initiatives by international NGOs are showing how the blue commons can be revived.

For instance, in Honduras the Coral Reef Alliance, a non-profit body based in California with the mission of saving the world's coral reefs, has been working with reef-dependent fishing communities to combat overfishing and other threats to the reefs. The Alliance is helping with boat purchases for reef patrols, providing salaried jobs for monitors, and helping to diversify income-earning opportunities to draw locals away from exploiting vulnerable ecosystems.

The Alliance director commented, 'We are building resilience in the human community and that translates to resilience in the coral reef community as well.'[35] There are two crucial points here. First, if action is coordinated and serious, vital reefs of the world can be preserved and revived, even in the face of global warming. Second, the best way of doing this is to combine local energy and vernacular knowledge with resources and scientific knowledge from outsiders, especially if they are not involved in commercial ventures.

Another example of an alliance between civil society and government illustrates how fragile they can be. In 2012, just before the Earth Summit in Rio de Janeiro, the World Bank launched the Global Partnership for Oceans, a collaboration between the Bank, which acted as the secretariat, and over

150 other partners from governments, intergovernmental organizations, many of the world's largest environmental NGOs and a long list of multinational businesses, including the world's biggest seafood and oil and gas companies.

The Norwegian government was initially the Global Partnership's main funder but withdrew its support in 2015 after small-scale fishing organizations claimed the Partnership was insensitive to their needs and had produced recommendations that threatened coastal fishing communities, including privatization of fishing rights. As a result, the Partnership was quietly disbanded. One of the complaining NGOs was the International Collective in Support of Fishworkers (ICSF), long a beneficiary of Norwegian aid. Then in 2018, under another political party, Norway ended funding for the ICSF, claiming it was unable to demonstrate its effectiveness. In reality, the Norwegian government had become far more favourable to neoliberal policies for the oceans.

It is still to be hoped that supportive governments can foster civil society resistance to loss of the commons. But so far, few arrangements have had any sustained success. The experience of the Faroe Islands (population 49,000) is instructive, where even a sovereign government failed in an attempt to restore a fishing commons.[36] In December 2017 the Faroese Parliament passed a law declaring that all living resources in Faroese waters belonged to the islands' people and restricting the transfer and accumulation of fishing licences by large corporations. This was an attempt to break up the oligopoly of four companies holding most of the licences, led by Dutch-owned Parlevliet & Van der Plas (P&P) and Iceland's Samherji. The new law was in force for just a year before being repealed by a new government, after the Dutch prime minister, Mark Rutte, threatened the Faroe Islands' free trade deal with the European Union. The threat worked. P&P and Samherji, which has close ties with P&P, remain the uncontested dominant players in the Faroese fishing industry.

Reviving blue commoning

A central claim of this book is that, if fish populations and marine life are to be rescued, it is vital that capitalistic industrial fishing is drastically curbed while communities of blue commoners are revived as local stewards and gatekeepers. Blue commoners surely have the most interest in preserving the reciprocities of humanity and nature. And commoners are much more likely to exert moral suasion on fellow commoners to respect conservation and quota rules than large-scale corporate multinationals backed by global finance.

The essence of commoning is the idea of shared activity, shared participation in a common endeavour. Regrettably, the notion of 'participation' has been captured to some extent; international efforts to help local communities gain or regain control over their livelihoods and local resources have been over-professionalized in a 'top-down' sort of way. No doubt, much of this is well-intentioned. But techniques dressed as scientific knowledge must be subordinated to vernacular wisdom, or at least be balanced by it.

This does not mean that science should be ignored or overruled. But science can easily be captured or deployed selectively by those preoccupied with 'progress' and 'improvement', 'efficiency' and 'productivity', all narrowly defined to suit industrial fisheries. Vernacular wisdom is more geared to respect for essential inefficiencies, and for traditions that have literally stood the test of time.

One reaction to pressures on the environment has been to create partnerships between donors, multilateral agencies and NGOs, on the one hand, and local commoners on the other. The main objective has been to enable locals to monitor and regulate abuses of the commons. But these schemes risk creating a version of the emerging global class structure,[37] with the foreign agencies sending in 'proficians', as consultants, employing a small 'salariat' of bureaucrats to handle the more technical tasks, and requiring local commoners to do the more menial monitoring and regulating tasks, as an 'eco-precariat'.[38]

Inducing local commoners to participate can also inadvertently penalize their commons community. For instance, if they are charged with monitoring and reporting 'illegal' fishing, which tends to be lumped in with unregulated and unreported fishing, this may penalize small-scale artisanal fisheries, which have a high propensity not to report what they catch.[39] So they could criminalize their fellow commoners. Meanwhile, they may be unable to combat determined rule-breakers, either because they are out of reach or out of sight, or because to do so would invite severe retribution. The real requirement is to create partnerships led by the commoners.

The appeal of guidelines

Revival of the blue commons and blue commoning requires coordinated international action. This is made harder by the ideology guiding most multilateral organizations and the financial power behind industrial fisheries and industrial-scale exploitation of ocean resources. There are numerous organizations comprising blue commoners around the world, but they have struggled to develop a coherent countervailing strategy.

Internationally, there has been a lot of rhetorical commitment to support small-scale fisheries. In May 2012, after years of work by a coalition of small-scale fishers and other environmental organizations from around the world, the FAO's Committee on World Food Security endorsed the Voluntary Guidelines on the Responsible Governance of Tenure of Land, Fisheries and Forests in the Context of National Food Security, a mouthful fortunately soon shortened to the Tenure Guidelines.

In June 2014, the FAO's Committee on Fisheries adopted the Voluntary Guidelines for Securing Sustainable Small-Scale Fisheries in the Context of Food Security and Poverty Alleviation, another mouthful that became known as the Fisheries Guidelines. The mood was euphoric, as the Small-Scale Fishers' Declaration at the time made clear:

> This is the first instrument that deals specifically with the small-scale fisheries sector all through the value chain . . . This is a historic moment for small-scale fishers. The Guidelines are comprehensive and deal, in one instrument, with all significant aspects of small-scale fishing communities within a human rights perspective. The Guidelines will also assist fishing communities to engage in meaningful dialogue/negotiations with the state and other sectors towards securing access to their living and livelihood space and in protecting this space from various threats.

Both sets of Guidelines were forged through an ambitious process of participation, facilitated by the FAO, involving governments, companies, multilateral organizations and numerous civil society organizations and social movements that work to protect indigenous groups and rural communities. This effort to involve grass-roots organizations in an empowering way, to define and write an international agreement affecting their lives, was unprecedented, certainly in the fisheries sector.

Of course, the text of the Guidelines was a compromise. The wording is vague in places, giving scope for interpretation. Nevertheless, their contents have been described as a 'historic victory'. Contrary to the neoliberal imperative of economic growth, they give precedence to food security and poverty reduction, stating that the value of natural resources cannot be reduced to private profit and resource rents for governments. Instead, they urge states to implement tenure reform and other measures to support small-scale food producers that would be more productive and beneficial for local food security than large export-oriented commercial systems.[40]

Moreover, the Guidelines emphasize that conservation of biodiversity and sustainable use of resources are more likely where local communities have control over the management of the resources on which their lives depend. And they stress the value of collective systems of resource stewardship, recognizing that fisheries, land and forests around the world have existed and still exist as commons, which play a unique role in supporting community wellbeing. This contrasts with mainstream policy advice on resource governance that treats commons as unproductive and unsustainable, and in need of privatization to make them more 'efficient'.

Although they are not binding, the Guidelines provide tools for political struggle by challenging the dominant economic model that has caused the transfer of natural resources and commons to corporate interests. According to the People's Manual on the Guidelines, they are intended to help dismantle 'extractive models of development', which sacrifice the commons in the interest of economic growth. These models, it says,

> favour patriarchal structures that systematically discriminate against women and privilege the accumulation of wealth and power, in particular by the transnational corporate sector. These models are highly dependent on public funding, thus increasing the external debt burden of countries where such investments are made.
>
> These dynamics have had negative impacts on the economic, social and political lives of peoples across the world, and have particularly affected the territories, the living conditions and well-being of indigenous peoples and communities living in rural and coastal regions. In those regions, tensions and conflicts have arisen between local communities and transnational corporations, elites and governments because of differing visions of the ecological, social, cultural, and economic values and uses of land and the commons. Land and water play vital social, cultural and spiritual functions for peasant, pastoralist and fishing communities.[41]

This is well stated, but implementing the Guidelines will be a monumental challenge, since it requires genuine political will by governments and powerful interests that gain from the status quo. Simple recognition of customary tenure is hard enough. The Rights and Resources Initiative estimated in 2015 that 65% of the world's land was owned through customary tenure arrangements, but only 18% was formally recognized as such.[42]

Even within this 18%, institutions protecting customary land rights are often weak. Large-scale transfer of resources, including from coastal lands and coastal marine areas, continues to occur without the consent of local communities. The corporations behind these land grabs tend to target areas with weak governance, often with high rates of food insecurity and poverty. And efforts to defend people's rights to their resources are undermined by oppression and violence in many countries. The 2018 CIVICUS Monitor report, which tracks the ability of civil society to speak out on actions by their governments, including in natural resource decisions, found that 60% of countries had an oppressive or closed approach to civil society voice.[43]

More governments are passing laws to limit media freedom and civil society activism, while the number of peaceful protests confronted by violence has increased. The Committee to Protect Journalists estimates that reporters who expose land grabs and the environmental impacts of transnational corporations are – after war reporters – the most at risk of intimidation and physical harm.[44] The scale of these human rights violations prompted the UN Human Rights Council in 2018 to draft a United Nations Declaration on the Rights of Peasants and Other People Working in Rural Areas, which restates the core messages of the Guidelines. As before, however, fine words need translation into effective action. That is yet to come and seems a long way off.

A luta continua

Like other commoners, blue commoners usually have rights without the power to exercise or defend them, whereas industrial fisheries and corporations have power, often exercised without rights. This brief review of forms of resistance suggests that what is needed is stronger and more ethical, rights-based 'steward' organizations, with independent management and governance systems at local, national and international levels. But equally important, stronger 'gatekeepers' are also required, bodies that do not simply monitor community resource management but also act as agents for 'contestatory collective action' to defend and enhance common rights.

Perhaps the ultimate form of resistance is against the hegemonic paradigm that maximizing economic growth is the key to development. While the World Bank and others say they support the Guidelines, they continue to promote policies that create the problems the Guidelines seek to address. Commoners must struggle for 'revalorization' to give value to sharing and reproductive activities that go beyond matters of technical efficiency and profits. The integrated Swedish example cited earlier, linking feminist and ecological objectives, needs to be scaled up, as does the Ecuadorian action to recover mangroves from commercial shrimp farms. Good local initiatives need to be identified, saluted and emulated.

Mobilization of resistance from 'below', from within commoning communities, can have liberating effects that go beyond contestation with commodifying forces. Where women play a prominent role, resistance has the capacity to erode patriarchal hierarchies and traditional discriminatory practices. By the nature of their customary tasks and activities, women may attach a high value to their local environment and its ecology, relating not only to conservation but also to reproduction and regeneration.

Resistance can reduce costs imposed by the unequal exchange between rich and poor countries and between corporations and commoners, which underpins the plunder of the blue commons. It can at times even reverse the process or halt it temporarily. But this will usually be at great cost to those resisting. To keep going, commoners need assured material resources and for their voices to be protected and respected by the state.

In recent years, there have been a series of initiatives to identify and restore the rights of indigenous peoples who occupied land before the arrival of European or other settlers, embodied in the UN's 2007 Declaration on the Rights of Indigenous Peoples. However, surely an agenda for what are really citizenship rights – and what Hannah Arendt referred to as 'the right to have rights' – should apply just as much to established commoners in their commons. If indigenous peoples have rights to safeguard or recover their access to resources, so should commoners in general. Article 31 of the UN Declaration asserts, 'Indigenous peoples have the right to maintain, control, protect and develop their knowledge, sciences and intellectual property over such.' If this applies to indigenous people who can demonstrate an ancient connection with the land, should it not also apply to commons or former commons communities that can also be traced way back?

The main conclusion from this brief foray into resistance is that unless the state acts as a proper steward seeking to preserve or revive the commons, and unless commoners have assured material resources and income security, transformative success is unlikely. Resistance, even revolt, is vital. But there must be a vision to motivate it and to guide its energies.

From Blue Growth to Degrowth

> You are undone if you once forget that the fruits of the
> earth belong to us all, and the earth itself to nobody.
> — Jean-Jacques Rousseau

Nature exists in its own right. Whatever lives or exists in the sea and on the seashores, estuaries and wetlands is no one's property. And to claim that it is the common heritage of humankind does not mean we 'own' it or that it is just there to provide resources for humans to exploit. We should think of ourselves rather as collective custodians, with responsibility for maintaining the blue environment. If we take anything from the blue parts of the planet, we have a duty both to nature and to humanity today and in the future, to ensure that those zones and their ecosystems are left in a state at least as good as we find them.

Moreover, if certain interests, corporations, governments or individuals take from the blue environment for their own profit, creating a blue economy with blue resources, they have a duty to compensate the commoners who are thereby deprived of those resources. How can ordinary people, all of us, be compensated, preferably in ways that help revive the commons and commoning? Common justice requires compensation for past loss of commons and the resources inherent in the commons, penalties for those responsible for current losses, and the capacity to preserve and enhance common-wealth in the future. Of course, that is a lofty objective that is hard to translate into feasible policies. But we should at least try.

Neither business as usual, in the form of rentier capitalism, nor blue growth, the win-win-win illusion that growth of the blue economy is compatible with environmental sustainability and social inclusion, will succeed in arresting the damage to marine ecosystems and the commons. Both models are charging in the wrong direction by pursuing economic growth. The only way to reverse the destructive tendencies shown in this book is to foster a global blue commons, in which local communities take charge of regenerating the blue economy and giving it resilience, while reviving the ethos of the commons and commoning as shared participation. This must be supported by states committed to curbing corporate power and the political abuse of power.

The COVID-19 pandemic could be a transformative moment for humanity and for the global economy. Unless there is a transformation in the sense made famous by Karl Polanyi, one that 're-embeds' the economy in society, a dark period lies ahead. The domination of the economy by financial capital and rent-seeking corporations creates such widespread inequalities and insecurity that there is a threat to civilization, social accord and ecological survival. This threat can only be averted if the state remakes the economy to serve society through new mechanisms of regulation, distribution and social protection. This requires a new progressive vision and politics, or that dark period will rush towards us. Today, that vision must be centred on a revival of the commons, equitable sharing and localized governance free from domination by financial capital or elites.

Any commons needs rules and people with the authority to implement and enforce them. Governance of the blue commons requires three groups with clear roles. By virtue of our humanity, we are all 'custodians', and as such we all have a moral duty to respect, preserve and reproduce the blue commons, considered as an environment, or more specifically a 'seascape'. But we as commoners do not govern the commons. That is the responsibility of the stewards – governments, local authorities and international bodies – which have constitutional obligations to maintain, reproduce and strengthen the commons.

To ensure that the stewards diligently carry out their responsibilities, monitoring bodies or gatekeepers are needed with enough power to hold the stewards to account. International bodies and governments have done remarkably little to promote or support gatekeepers in the blue commons, sometimes deliberately. And ideally, both stewards and gatekeepers should be answerable to the commoners as a community. The emerging popular idea of 'citizens' assemblies', or citizens' juries, may be one way forward, drawing on the idea of popular assemblies as operated in ancient Athens. In their modern form, they are groups representing the wider population, charged with deliberating and deciding on specific policies or actions. In Britain they have been asked to make recommendations on funding adult social care and how the UK can reach its net zero carbon emissions target by 2050, as well as local issues such as improving air quality in urban centres.

At present, the blue economy is poorly governed. Stewards ignore their responsibilities or succumb to pressure from corporate and financial capital. Gatekeepers, where they exist, tend to be feeble and toothless. And attempts to cooperate internationally are typically weakened in the course of intergovernmental negotiations, in order to obtain a consensus. Any agreement reached in an international arena must then be ratified by national legislatures and incorporated into national law. An enforcement agency must be identified and be well led, with adequate powers and resources. All this is so much harder for the blue economy where resources straddle national boundaries.

Some apparently laudable agreements can even be counterproductive, giving the false impression that something is being done. An example is the dysfunctional politicized wrangling in the 1973 Convention on International Trade in Endangered Species of Wild Fauna and Flora (CITES) over the classification of fish species by degree of endangerment. CITES classifies species in three categories: species so endangered as to be banned from international trade; species likely to become endangered unless trade is restricted; and species that are not endangered globally but at risk in some places. Various countries have lobbied hard to keep fish that are important to them off the list altogether. For instance, Japan, with its large tuna fishing fleet and appetite for tuna sushi, led a successful campaign in 2010 to stop the listing of the hard-pressed bluefin tuna.

The crimogenic character of fisheries is also partly due to

weak international governance. Regulation is mainly left to regional bodies that are easily subject to corporate-state capture and corruption down the line. The ability of large-scale industrial fisheries to ravage targeted areas and then move on to others means that only more localized governance, involving commoners with a vested interest in reproducing the resource base of their environment, can achieve real sustainability.

One hopeful development is that many people around the world have become aspirational commoners, realizing not only that marine ecosystems are in serious danger but that they themselves should engage directly in combating the threats, as well as pressuring governments and corporations to do so. In Britain, for example, according to the Director of Living Seas of the Wildlife Trusts, 'The extent of the nature and climate emergency is becoming increasingly clear, and more people than ever are volunteering to be citizen scientists and conducting important surveys or taking action to tackle the profound problems of marine litter and plastic pollution.'[1] Many other countries, rich and poor, report similar stories of growing public engagement. We can only hope this will extend to everything happening in the blue part of the planet. The following measures would help.

The imperative of blue degrowth

> Capitalism can no more be 'persuaded' to limit growth than a human being can be 'persuaded' to stop breathing.
> — Murray Bookchin

The fetish of economic growth must be rejected. The belief that GDP growth should be the primary measure of societal improvement is dogma. Yet in 2018 William Nordhaus of Yale University, a proponent of the primacy of growth, received the Nobel Prize in Economics, the highest accolade his profession can award. This was ostensibly for his work on climate change, where his main contribution has been to argue that policymakers should give economic growth priority over mitigating climate change.[2]

His argument, in a nutshell, is that global warming of over 3 °C would be acceptable as the cost of rapid economic growth because future generations would be richer and therefore better able to deal with the consequences. He has opposed a high carbon tax, which would help to reduce global warming, because it would slow economic growth. On receiving news of his Nobel Prize, he told his students, 'Don't let anyone distract you from the work at hand, which is economic growth.'[3]

Because sectors most vulnerable to climate change, including fishing, account for only a small percentage of global GDP, the cost of the loss of fish populations could be regarded as minimal. This type of reasoning must be rejected. A commons-based perspective geared to values of reproduction, and an income distribution system that compensates commoners adversely affected by the impacts of economic growth, are preferable for human welfare and preferable for the blue planet.

Let us reflect on what needs to be done to roll back the tide of neoliberalism that has led to rentier capitalism in the seas and seashores. Of course, the power of finance and corporate conglomerates means that this is easier said than done. It requires reversing the industrialization of the blue economy, since modern globalized capitalism is driven by financial capital and its dictates.

For that reason, despite its stated aims, the blue growth model is simply incompatible with sustainability and inclusiveness, and no rhetorical commitment to corporate social responsibility and good intentions will change that. Short-term profit maximization through growth is the nature of the beast, and the beast is devouring the habitats and environments of marine ecosystems around the world.

Patrick Bresnihan has coined the oxymoron 'neoliberal commons' to describe how community co-management fisheries can be created in, and coexist with, the rentier capitalist system.[4] And in a few places the blue growth model, in all its variants, has been adapted to support the commons. But this has involved reshaping and co-opting the commons – and the ethos of commoning – for its own ends and in its own imagery. Thus Walmart Canada is selling 'indigenous-made' hot-smoked Atlantic salmon with the claim that it is farmed and packaged by the Kitasoo/Xai'xais First Nation in Klemtu, British Columbia. But the salmon is raised and processed through a joint venture with Mowi, the world's largest producer of Atlantic salmon, which can thereby burnish its image as well as earn profits from its First Nation partnership.[5]

Combating blue growth requires subordinating the extension of private property rights to 'common rights'. This means halting and delegitimizing the long-standing strategy of international institutions such as the World Bank and the IMF to extend private property rights at the expense of public and common property rights, and ending their privatization programmes for production systems and infrastructure.

There is a place for private property. But private property rights must not be presumed to be superior to, and predominate over, common property rights. As Article 17 of the Universal Declaration of Human Rights states:

(1) 'Everyone has the right to own property alone as well as in association with others.

(2) No one shall be arbitrarily deprived of his property.'

An economy and society without respect for – and protection of – common property will veer inexorably towards predatory rentier capitalism. For instance, millions of hectares of land, including land adjoining the coastline, have been grabbed by private commercial interests, often backed by foreign capital based in rich countries.[6] The international financial agencies have not done anything serious to protect communities, while they have devoted considerable resources to assist privatization and commodification of such land.

This points to the need for robust legislation, regulations and collective action to protect the commons, and sustained action against the powerful financial and corporate lobbies that have perverted global politics and institutions in the past four decades. That too, of course, is easier said than done. But those who wish to protect and restore marine ecosystems must risk being condemned as extremists in opposing plutocratic corporate and financial involvement in policymaking at all levels. There is no moral, legal or economic justification for privatizing the seabed, even if doing so would boost GDP growth.

Staff of international organizations and those who work for them on contracts should be required to adhere strictly to 'civil-service' principles, answerable only to the commoners of the world, not to any sectoral or other special interest. International organizations charged with upholding human and natural rights should also stay clear of 'soft money' donated for special interest projects. However well-intentioned corporate or individual donors might be, it is profoundly undemocratic, and open to corruption as well as lobbying power, for governance institutions to depend on their largesse. Enforcing core civil-service principles is especially important in matters relating to the blue economy. Given that so much of what transpires is crimogenic, moral codes are vital.

In practice, the blue growth model externalizes the depletion of resources and the wider ecological and social damage entailed by pursuit of rapid economic growth. Offers or requirements to pay for 'externalities' are likely to be 'bluewash', that is, exercises in public relations designed to make the activities look better, while leaving the damage done. Nobody can bring back a destroyed reef that was shaped over millions of years; nobody can resurrect an ancient mangrove forest or a fish species driven to extinction. The only way to stop the damage is to internalize respect for nature in the economic model.

That need for respect applies also to blue commoners and blue communities. The growth imperative has treated damage to their livelihoods and community systems as an unvalued externality, almost as collateral damage. Devoting time and resources to valuing nature and 'natural capital', without valuing what neoliberals might call 'commons capital', further highlights the absurdity of trying to put a price on our green and blue worlds.

Besides having implications for patterns of production, respect for nature also has implications for us as consumers and as citizens. We should admit that we overeat as well as overfish, and that we are likely to overconsume resources from the seabed as well as overexploit them. To preserve the blue as much as the green world, we must change the way we live.

For instance, globally, and especially in rich countries, we must eat less fish. There have been efforts to reduce consumption of some species, through eco-labelling, which in principle we should applaud. But we need to go further than that. How much further will be an increasingly contentious public debate in the years ahead. But merely recognizing the need for such a debate is a civilizational issue of mounting importance.

The enormous growth of global tourism, at least before COVID-19 intervened, has caused a disturbing extra threat to high-value fish. For example, in the Balearic Islands off Spain, there has been a marked shift from cheap local fish consumed by local people to expensive species consumed by tourists, paradoxically leading to an increase in fish consumption but a sharp reduction in local fishing jobs.[7] The message should be clear. For the sake of local commons, local commoners and the environment, eat local fish!

The world needs to stop trying to maximize GDP growth. GDP growth without resource depletion is a fantasy; absolute decoupling of growth from resource use is not going to happen.[8] And even if it were possible to achieve relative decoupling – GDP growth using fewer resources per unit – it would be unsustainable because some resources would soon be exhausted. Politicians and economists must stop making growth of GDP their prime objective. That is even more vital in this era of rentier capitalism, since more and more of the gains from economic growth are going to the plutocracy, elite and parts of the salariat.

Defenders of prioritizing economic growth have claimed that, while the benefits might go disproportionately to the rich, much will trickle down to the rest of the population through spending and investment channels. But with rentiers at the top taking an increasing share, ever higher rates of growth are needed for any substantial trickle-down to take place. The trickle-down thesis is a recipe for accelerated resource deple-tion and ecological crisis, leaving billions of people mired in economic insecurity while a rentier elite profits from plunder-ing the commons.

There are two ways to think of alternatives to blue growth – 'blue degrowth' and 'blue economic growth'. The second derives from the perspective of ecologist Herman Daly, who has argued that 'uneconomic growth' occurs when increases in production come at the expense of depleted re-sources and wellbeing that are 'worth more than the items made'.[9] However, the distinction between 'uneconomic' and 'economic' growth risks confusing the argument, so the term 'blue degrowth' is used here, even though 'degrowth' conjures up an unhelpful (and misleading) image of cuts in living standards. Perhaps the right term for what is needed is 'anti-growthism', that is, a strategy of simply not making GDP growth an objective.

However alternatives to growth are framed, the chal-lenge is how to raise the living standards of the majority of people who are still chronically impoverished. The standard response is 'redistribution', a term associated in people's minds with higher income taxes to pay for it. Taxing incomes after they have been 'earned' causes resentment and resistance, and certainly would do so on the scale needed to raise the living standards of the majority.

While more progressive taxation is desirable, the proposals put forward later in this book come closer to 'predistribution', that is, altering the flow of pre-tax incomes and imposing costs on those who take advantage of the commons to gain income and wealth. Given conventional forms of redistribution, many people would support more GDP growth, which in their view would generate more taxable income for redistribution. By contrast, in the proposed degrowth strategy, more GDP growth would generate less income for those driving it, because they would have to pay for depleting resources and causing public 'bads' by plundering the commons.

Consider a few common resources. When minerals are mined and sold, the standard approach is to add the marketed value of the minerals to measures of GDP growth; it is a one-off 'windfall' gain. But no adjustment to GDP is made to take account of the depletion of the asset value of the minerals. A negative adjustment should be made. The same could be said of fish. If the amount of fish taken depletes a fish population, affecting its ability to regenerate, that should be deducted from any measure of economic growth.

In addition, companies mining the seabed, if mining is permitted at all, should pay a 'rental' levy that reflects the depletion of the resource and damage to the environment.

This would go to the state to benefit the commoners. One of the most complex issues in the negotiations on the Mining Code relates to the amount the International Seabed Authority will charge in fees and royalties for minerals exploitation, and how that will be distributed. While there seems to be acceptance in principle that companies should pay both for depletion of a non-renewable resource and the environmental costs involved in minerals extraction, the ISA's desire to encourage seabed exploitation suggests it will set charges too low.

In the case of fish, the 'rental' levy should be determined by what is needed to deter catching beyond the natural reproduction rate. Clearly, the levy would be well above the user fees that have been implemented in standard fishery access agreements and joint ventures. Since local commoners would gain from reproducing rather than depleting the fish population, because that would give them future compensation, they would have a vested interest in monitoring fishing effort and catch levels, to help ensure that those taking more than allowed would be penalized. How this could be achieved is the subject of the final chapter.

The imperative of definancialization

The primary driver of global rentier capitalism since the 1980s has been financialization. Financial capital has penetrated every aspect of life, systemically commodifying both the human and the natural world. It encourages short-term profit maximization, and even requires it, contrary to the needs of conservation, let alone a commons perspective. And it fosters 'excessive speculation', where speculators rather than producers and consumers set market prices, causing large and unpredictable swings in prices, as well as 'contagion effects' when other markets become speculative targets. All these hit low-income communities particularly hard. The spreading tentacles of financial capital must be severed if the blue planet is to recover.

The major banks must be persuaded not to invest in corporations that practise overfishing or other predatory marine activity. Following the recommendations of the Marine Stewardship Council (MSC) – the international body that certifies sustainable fish – is not necessarily a reliable guide. Critics claim it sets the sustainability bar too low. An umbrella group of marine activists, On the Hook, has already forced the MSC to ban 'compartmentalization', that is, fisheries presenting one, not all, of their activities for assessment.[10] Banks are also over-sanguine about aquaculture. A spokesperson for the Dutch bank ING defended its investment in aquaculture by saying, 'Farmed fish brings a solution to reduce overfishing, although more research is required to do this in a truly sustainable way.'[11] Yet as we have seen, aquaculture in its present form is far from being a 'solution' to overfishing, and its headlong expansion may be on track to make things worse.

Bankrolling Extinction, a report published in 2020, estimated that the world's fifty biggest banks, led by Bank of America, Citigroup and JP Morgan, had provided more than $2.6 trillion (£1.9 trillion) in 2019 alone in loans and credit to sectors having a high negative impact on biodiversity.[12] The report made three demands that we should all support. Banks must disclose and reduce their impact on nature, and stop financing fossil fuels, deforestation, overfishing and ecosystem destruction. Governments must stop protecting banks' role in biodiversity destruction and hold banks liable for damage caused by their unethical lending. And people everywhere must have a say in how their money is invested and 'the right to stop banks from causing serious harm to people and planet'.

Some prominent financiers, led by Larry Fink, founder and CEO of BlackRock, the world's largest asset manager, have expressed confidence that financial institutions can induce better environmental practices by corporations. This pretension was rudely shattered by someone in as good a position as anyone to know. Tariq Fancy, an investment banker appointed as BlackRock's chief investment officer for sustainable investing, left the job after about a year, convinced it could not happen.

In an interview in March 2021, he said, 'It's not because they are evil, it's because the system is built to extract profits.'[13] Pointing out the obvious fact that investors and executives have a fiduciary duty to maximize returns to shareholders and clients, Fancy made the equally obvious point that effective action will require government intervention, including carbon taxes. One fear must be that the illusory hope of 'stakeholderism' could impede such action by persuading governments that firms will regulate themselves.[14]

Fancy predicted that, while more investors and firms would market themselves as 'green', they would not do much in reality. Investing that took into account environmental, social and governance (ESG) factors was 'little more than marketing hype, PR spin and disingenuous promises'. Sure enough, current finance-led initiatives purporting to guide investment towards more environmentally friendly companies are characterized by rampant 'greenwashing'. An investigation by *The Economist* revealed that funds claiming to take ESG factors into account were investing in fossil-fuel producers, including coal mining.[15]

A study looking at 183 firms that signed a Business Roundtable statement on corporate purpose found they had failed to 'walk the talk'.[16] They had higher environmental and labour compliance violations, and spent more on lobbying. Another investigation by *The Economist* compared companies pressured to reduce their carbon footprint by Climate Action 100+, whose members hold over $50 trillion of assets, with a portfolio of about 100 large emitters not engaged by the investor group. The impact of CA100+, compared with what firms were doing anyway, looked modest. '$50trn-worth of investor pressing does not seem to result in much change,' it concluded.[17] And the Bank for International Settlements found that firms issuing 'green' bonds tended to produce the least carbon anyway, so that green-bond issuance did not lead to decarbonization.[18]

There is no agreed methodology for giving companies ESG scores. An IMF study that looked at listed companies accounting for close to 30% of global emissions since 2002 found little or no correlation between ESG scores and emissions growth, for example.[19] And there is plenty of scope for gaming the ratings in order to qualify for 'ethical' investment. An egregious example concerns major oil producers which are divesting billions of dollars of less profitable oil assets under increasing pressure to take more action on climate change. These assets are being snapped up by independent operators backed by private equity, and by energy traders and state oil companies, which face less public scrutiny and are not accountable to shareholders. They have an interest in maximizing short-term profit by producing as much oil as they can, as fast as they can. So, paradoxically, the oil majors' divestments not only do nothing to reduce emissions, in the short term they may increase them.[20]

This is already happening in the North Sea oilfields, where companies such as BP and Shell have been shedding assets. More than a third of North Sea licence blocks now have a private or state-backed controlling interest, including Siccar Point, backed by private equity groups Blackstone and Bluewater; Ineos, the private chemicals firm owned by billionaire Sir Jim Ratcliffe; and state-owned companies from China, Russia and the Gulf.[21] And despite a warning from the International Energy Agency that all development of new fossil fuel resources must cease after 2021 to keep global heating to within 1.5 °C,[22] the UK (alongside the USA and others) has given the go-ahead for further offshore oil and gas exploration. While the government says new developments will have to pass a 'climate checkpoint', the fact that the majority of members of the UK's North Sea regulator, the Oil and Gas Authority, have close links with, and/or shareholdings in, the very industry they are supposed to be regulating does not inspire confidence.[23]

Stopping financiers turning everything into a frenzied casino of commodity speculation must now be a priority. Taming and reversing financialization in the blue economy will ultimately depend on the re-emergence of an egalitarian political culture, based on a revival of the commons and commoning.

Global governance of the blue economy

In December 2020, the High Level Ocean Panel, comprising the leaders of fourteen countries, launched what was described as the biggest ocean sustainability initiative ever. Speaking on behalf of the panel, Erna Solberg, Prime Minister of Norway, said, 'For too long, we have perceived a false choice between ocean protection and production. No longer. We understand the opportunities of action and the risks of inaction, and we know the solutions.'[24]

The report contained a worthy list of conventional policies – rolling back 'harmful' fishery subsidies, setting a target to protect 30% of the world's oceans by 2030, monitoring fishing, eliminating the discarding of 'ghost' fishing gear, preventing plastic pollution, setting targets for reduced emissions and investing in offshore wind. The omissions were glaring. There was no recognition that the economic structure underpinning blue growth might be the most harmful factor of all.

Nevertheless, the initiative was a welcome rebooting of multilateralism. It came in the wake of a prolonged failure, due in part to the global disengagement of the USA. When UNCLOS was agreed in 1982, the United States refused to ratify it, refused to be a member of the newly established International Seabed Authority, and refused to help fund either. That was a sign of imperial power. The USA was to be the special one, which did not have to abide by international rules and conventions. Similarly, it has always refused to ratify most of the Conventions on labour standards negotiated in the International Labour Organization.

The US decision not to ratify UNCLOS meant it could ignore international regulation of fisheries. Washington refused to accept coastal state sovereignty over migratory tuna stocks as well as limitations on the marauding activities of its fishing boats. Whenever its vessels were arrested by coastal states, the US government simply reimbursed their expenses, calling the seizures 'illegal'. And the monetary value of penalties was subtracted from any foreign aid committed to the coastal state, which was also barred from receiving defence assistance. The USA only began to respect EEZ boundaries when little Kiribati (population: 117,000) threatened to allow Soviet fishing fleets into its waters in the 1980s.[25]

The USA is no longer the world's imperial hegemon. But having refused to abide by common rules and to help design and implement them, it surely has no moral right to try to dictate what the organizations it has not joined should or should not do. In August 2020, China's candidate to be a judge on the International Tribunal for the Law of the Sea (ITLOS) was elected as one of its twenty-one judges. This was after the USA, from the outside, had urged UNCLOS member governments to vote against him.

The USA should join the global community and respect democratic governance of the blue economy. It should not behave like a rogue state, hiding behind the feeble excuse that it cannot ratify Conventions because it is a federal state, as it has done. It is paying a price for opting out, because others are taking advantage of the weak governance structures to further their own interests. In particular, China is moving into areas of economic, political and military influence where Washington once took its domination for granted. The USA increasingly lacks the 'soft power' to develop a multilateral regulatory system needed to revive marine ecosystems.

Having ceased to be the imperial hegemon, the USA is discovering the deficiencies of weakened international institutions in preventing the next imperial power from behaving in the same way as it did. For instance, the 1959 Antarctic Treaty declared the predominantly blue continent of Antarctica to be a global commons 'for peaceful purposes only'. This was strengthened by the Madrid Protocol of 1991, which prohibits extractive mining and protects the continent for scientific research for the benefit of all countries.

Both the USA and China are signatories to the Treaty and Protocol. However, enforcement is through an inspection system of periodic visits to the research stations maintained by about thirty countries. These inspections are infrequent and incomplete. As of 2021, none of China's bases had been inspected since 2015, despite evidence that it is constructing infrastructure that could be used for military purposes as well as mineral exploitation. The USA has not conducted any inspections since 2011, hampered by a lack of functioning polar icebreakers. When the Treaty was being negotiated in 1959, John Foster Dulles, US Secretary of State, said the USA had an interest in keeping Antarctica 'in friendly hands'.[26] A better formulation would have been 'in neutral hands'. Now, Antarctica is becoming an area of increasing international tension as countries jockey for advantage ahead of 2048, when the Treaty expires and mineral exploitation may become possible.

Clearly, UNCLOS itself should be updated. The rule on access to 'surplus' fish must be rescinded; the MSY concept must be reinterpreted. Outside fishing, Article 76 of UNCLOS, which allows countries to claim an extended continental shelf, should be scrapped, to stop ocean grabbing.

The impasse in World Trade Organization talks on limiting fishery subsidies, which were supposed to conclude in 2020, is another example of the failure of global governance. Again, agreement requires consensus of all WTO members. One sticking point has been whether certain subsidies should be banned per se or allowed if they are not contributing to overfishing and, if the latter, how that should be defined. Another set of problems arises from the special and differential treatment given to developing countries, which is a feature of almost all WTO accords. China and Indonesia, among the world's most powerful fishing nations, have argued that they should benefit from these provisions. And some countries want a 'carve-out' for subsidies to small-scale artisanal fisheries, which raises issues of definition and sustainability. Other differences relate to monitoring, enforcement and sanctions for breaching the agreement. Meanwhile, behind the negotiators are commercial interests lobbying to keep their benefits and competitive edge intact.

More generally, perhaps the most urgent priority in governance of the blue economy is to respect the basic management rule of separating 'principals' from 'agents'. The former set rules and administer rules and regulations; the latter are supposed to operate according to the rules. When agents become principals, the management system is institutionally corrupted.

There is no business school in the world that does not understand and teach that basic principle, yet it is wilfully abused in the governance of global seafood. Industrial fisheries, aquaculture and the seafood industry in general have seen a process of conglomeration, in which thirteen multinational corporations have emerged as 'keystone actors', analogous to keystone species that have a profound and disproportionate effect on ecological communities and ecosystems.[27] These corporations obtain huge rentier incomes through economies of scale (falling costs as output rises) and economies of scope (falling costs by extending into related sectors). They can insulate themselves from economic shocks and, indeed, use such shocks to enlarge themselves by swallowing smaller, more vulnerable firms.

They dominate international bodies responsible for setting or influencing rules and implementing regulations. Thus, the International Seafood Sustainability Foundation was founded by Thai Union, the world's largest canned tuna producer and major shrimp farmer, and a subsidiary of Dongwon, a leading tuna producer. Dongwon and Japanese seafood giant Maruha Nichiro are represented through the Korean and Japanese fishery associations in the Organization for the Promotion of Responsible Tuna Fisheries.

The Global Aquaculture Alliance has as 'strategic partners' two Thai keystone actors and the Spanish giant Pescanova. And Norwegian mega-corporations Mowi (formerly Marine Harvest), Austevoll and Nutreco are active in the Aquaculture Stewardship Council, the Global Salmon Initiative and the Marine Ingredients Organization. Keeping companies off governance bodies is essential if effective independent gatekeepers are to emerge. At the very least, multi-stakeholder institutions should ensure counterbalancing representation with independent scientists, environmental groups and small-scale fishing organizations.

In this context, it is not surprising that the existing system of international regulation of fisheries is fragmented and disjointed. The governance of ocean fisheries has been largely delegated to the regional fisheries management organizations (RFMOs), some responsible for managing diverse species in a wide geographical area, some for just one specific prized species, typically a variety of tuna. RFMOs have been much criticized, deservedly, for putting the interests of commercial fisheries ahead of conservation and thereby allowing overfishing and even illegal fishing.

RFMOs covering individual high-value species have not had conspicuous success. For instance, the International Commission for the Conservation of Atlantic Tunas (ICCAT) has been dubbed by critics as the International Conspiracy to Catch All Tuna.[28] An expert review, ordered by its management, concluded that it was 'an international disgrace'. The Indian Ocean Tuna Commission, responsible for 'the worst managed yellowfin stock in the world',[29] apparently put off essential quota reductions until Indian Ocean rim nations did the same in their own waters. 'That's like saying, as long as you keep stealing my toys, I don't need to be honest either. It's unbelievable logic,' said Jessica Meeuwig, director of the Centre for Marine Futures at the University of Western Australia.[30]

In July 2020, the Western and Central Pacific Fisheries Commission, which is supposed to regulate the world's biggest tuna fishery, absolved fishing vessels using purse-seine nets from the obligation to carry a fisheries observer. These purse-seine nets, which can be two kilometres long, close like a purse around everything they scoop up, not just tuna. Removing monitors gives licensed fisheries free rein to fish beyond legal limits, kill bycatch, and trespass in waters reserved for local artisanal fishers. It is inexcusable.

Most regional fishery bodies have had too little money to combat illegal fishing. They do not know how many vessels are in their waters, as there is no comprehensive register or reliable global tracking system. Furthermore, RFMO rules bind only their members. And they are dominated by industrial fishing interests. They fail the basic rules for governing a commons.

Since industrial fisheries consistently fail to abide by sustainability rules, it is vital to have strong monitoring and deterrence. But both are widely absent. It is evident that the failings of RFMOs are linked to the power of industrial fisheries and the narrow elite in their orbit. Not only can they bribe and lobby relatively low-paid officials in RFMOs. They also operate 'revolving doors', a feature of rentier capitalism of all varieties. So, senior officials in RFMOs aspire to move into senior positions in industrial fisheries, while executives in industrial corporations take senior posts in RFMOs to advance their careers.

RFMOs must give more attention to protecting and strengthening local artisanal fisheries. Breaking the domination of a few industrial fisheries would help shift governance structures and priorities to conservation and reproduction rather than short-term profit maximization. And revolving doors might slow to a stop.

Then there is the seabed Area outside national jurisdiction, the subject of a gathering campaign to ban all extractive activity and to classify the Area as the common heritage of 'all life', rather than 'mankind' or 'humankind'. A mining ban would force corporations to find ways to reduce demand for metals and minerals and to recycle what has already been extracted and used. Currently, less than 1% of rare earths is recycled.[31] Unfortunately, as things stand, a mining ban looks unlikely. But any meaningful international agreement on a Mining Code must create an enforceable system with adequate resources and authority to deter and punish damage to blue ecosystems. Penalties should make rule-breaking punitively expensive.

Reaching an accord on the Conservation and Sustainable Use of Marine Biodiversity of Areas Beyond National Jurisdiction – aka the Global Ocean Treaty - remains enormously important for the future of the blue planet. It is crucial that any agreement treats the high seas as well as the Area as a global commons rather than a free-for-all. It also needs to state, and enforce, a strong precautionary principle, because much of what is unknown, unmeasured, unvalued and unappreciated exists in the deep seas outside the enclosed Exclusive Economic Zones.

Forging more functional global governance of the blue economy also requires overhauling or scrapping Investor-State Dispute Settlement (ISDS), an undemocratic mechanism of neoliberal rentier capitalism, which allows multinational corporations to sue governments if a change in policy threatens prospective future profits. A commitment to use ISDS has been included in over 2,600 international trade and investment agreements and more than a thousand cases have been brought under the system, often with judgment going in favour of corporations. Awards against governments can run into hundreds of millions, even billions, of dollars.[32]

For example, if an oil company is operating legally off a country's coast and the government subsequently introduces more stringent environmental standards, the company can demand compensation. This could be relevant to local action to restore or strengthen common rights, involving, say, recovery of seaspace or control over fish quotas or protection of reefs or mangrove swamps endangered by corporate activity. Two ocean-related cases indicate what can happen.

In Nova Scotia in 2007, Bilcon, a US concrete company, was denied permission to build a large basalt quarry and an adjoining marine terminal after a Canadian federal and provincial review panel concluded that the project would damage the marine environment and the local fishing community. The company won damages from Canada under the ISDS provisions in the North American Free Trade Agreement (NAFTA), for what was described as an 'opportunity lost'.[33] Though the damages of $7 million was far less than the $443 million claimed by Bilcon, the case was only settled in 2019 after years of legal action and cost the public much more than the eventual fine itself. The new United States-Mexico-Canada Agreement that has replaced the North American Free Trade Agreement abolishes ISDS between Canada and the USA but retains largely the same regime for other foreign investors.

The second example is ongoing. In 2020, a US marine exploration company sued the Mexican government for $3.5

billion for denying it an environment permit to mine the world's largest phosphate sand deposits in the Gulf of Ulloa.[34] The environmental review concluded that mining would threaten many sea species, including whales, dolphins, orcas, sea lions, sea turtles and seabirds. A tribunal judgment is expected in 2022. But this is a clear example of corporate muscle being exercised over the commons.

The UN's Commission on International Trade Law began work in 2020 on possible ISDS reforms, hastened by EU concern to enforce stricter controls over polluting fossil fuel power stations. ISDS is a powerful impediment to implementing policies to meet climate change targets.[35] Reform must ensure that policies to protect the environment, including the marine environment, as well as social objectives such as public health, are given immunity from corporate challenge.

A future for marine protected areas

Great hopes for reviving fish populations and ocean ecosystems are placed on marine protected areas (MPAs), where fishing and other exploitative activities are banned or restricted. MPAs have also been promoted by some RFMOs, such as the Commission for the Conservation of Antarctic Marine Living Resources. And the establishment of MPAs in the high seas, which requires some form of international governance to make it feasible, is being discussed in the Global Ocean Treaty negotiations. But while there is much to be applauded in their creation, existing MPAs have not been an unequivocal success. Most are not fully protected. And they can divert attention from other revival mechanisms. In the enthusiasm for conservation, it is easy to miss potential and actual limitations of MPAs, including possible threats to blue commons communities barred from access to traditional habitats by 'fortress conservation' approaches.

The only durable way of rescuing and reviving the blue economy is to rebuild blue commons communities, putting those closest to marine life largely in charge. If possible and practicable, the local commoners should have charge of management functions. For the most part, there are good grounds for being suspicious of public-private partnerships, since they tend to involve the public bearing the cost while a private firm takes the profits. But one successful model applied to national parks in Africa could be worth taking to MPAs.

There are over 8,000 protected areas in Africa and its surrounding waters. But as in Britain, they have been dubbed 'paper parks' for lack of effective enforcement. Many African countries lack adequate resources for protecting animals such as elephants and rhinoceros from sophisticated poaching gangs, which has led some governments to hand management of their parks to African Parks Network, an NGO set up in 2000. By 2020 it was managing nineteen parks, including the Bazaruto Archipelago National Park on the Mozambique coast. African Parks Network has had impressive success in preserving animals from poaching.[36] It is also contributing to community development, and has tapped into financial contributions from many sources, including the EU, the World Bank and major foundations.

In November 2020, the tiny, remote and scarcely inhabited island of Tristan da Cunha, a British overseas territory in the South Atlantic, announced that 90% of its sea area – almost 700,000 square kilometres, three times the size of Britain – would become an MPA, making it the fourth largest in the world. Without apparent irony, the chief executive of the Royal Society for the Protection of Birds described the new MPA as 'the jewel in the crown of UK marine protection', and Prime Minister Boris Johnson called on other nations to join Britain in the push to protect 30% of the world's oceans by 2030.[37]

Yet Britain is not protecting its own coastal waters. Almost all Britain's offshore MPAs are open to destructive activities, including bottom trawling. In frustration at government refusal to ban the practice, Greenpeace has begun sabotage action by dropping giant boulders onto the seabed in protected areas in the North Sea and the Channel, thereby blocking destructive trawling.[38] In 2021 the UK government announced a pilot scheme to designate five or more 'highly protected marine areas' where 'extractive, destructive and depositional uses' will be banned. However, waiting to see the results of pilots may also be an excuse to delay further a total ban on bottom trawling, dredging and other damaging fishing methods in MPAs. Let the boulders roll!

The Tristan da Cunha example also underscores the unfairness of UNCLOS. A tiny island of 250 inhabitants has almost as much 'territorial waters' as the People's Republic of China, and these waters are over 6,400 miles from Britain. The fact that this vast expanse of sea in the South Atlantic counts as 'British' at all is bizarre in the twenty-first century. There is also the little matter of what is meant by 'protection'. Currently, the UK has twelve coastguard vessels to protect all its seaspace against illegal or unregulated fishing.

Would any of these boats be able to reach Tristan da Cunha in time to catch an illegal fishery?

Undoubtedly the blue planet needs more and better MPAs, with much more financial and technological assistance in implementing what they are supposed to be and do. But the most important policy must be to empower local blue commoners to manage and monitor what happens within them. It is not primarily a matter of lack of finance.

Curbing private property rights

So far, we have seen how the governance of the seas must be reoriented to safeguard the commons, reduce corporate power and spread protected zones. The dismantling of rentier capitalism in the blue economy will inevitably be a piecemeal process, and should focus on rolling back the institutional mechanisms erected to advance neoliberalism in the sea. Effective action to revive the blue commons should involve taking the following urgent steps.

Countries should revise their fishing quota systems to limit the amount of fish quota any one fishery can accumulate and combine that with strict regulation of transfers of quota entitlements. There should be strict quota limits for foreign fisheries, including joint ventures, to respect and rebuild local commoners' rights and commitments. In effect, quotas should be decommodified, with transfers normally confined to within the local fishing community.

Reviving the blue commons would also be helped by jettisoning existing 'neocolonial' fishery access agreements, which have enabled industrial fishing powers to fish in developing-country waters for derisory payment and considerable cost to local artisanal fisheries. Their cheating character derives from the concept of maximum sustainable yield (MSY), the pseudo-scientific idea that there is a scientific measure of how much fish can be taken from a given area without risk of depletion.

In 1977, Peter Larkin, a leading marine biologist at the University of British Columbia, published an article in the *Transactions of the American Fisheries Society* entitled 'An epitaph for the concept of maximum sustained yield'. He argued that data on single fish populations were unreliable, and that a more holistic understanding of marine ecosystems was needed. This is known as the 'ecosystem-based approach'. There is much to like about it. But despite efforts to put it into practice, it has not displaced the MSY. It requires too much data to be practical. Sadly for Larkin, we must echo Mark Twain's comment that rumours of the death of MSY are much exaggerated.

Another champion of the ecosystem approach, Daniel Pauly (also from the University of British Columbia), has nevertheless conceded that the MSY is probably as good as it gets for fisheries management, provided it is applied for sustainable fishing. One issue is setting a global catch limit for fish populations in a region, given that they are made up of distinct communities. A global catch limit fails to recognize that this may allow intensive fishing within one community, less in another. However, Pauly and colleagues argue that the biggest mistake with MSY has been to use it as a *target* for optimal fishing. It should be considered a limit.

Most commercial fisheries would be within safe limits if the MSY were set at half the estimated fish population, allowing for good harvests while enabling fish populations to reproduce healthily. Yet fishery scientists often recommend an MSY of 60% to 70% of fish populations and lobbying by industrial fisheries can push the limit higher. From the perspective of advocates for small-scale fisheries, another problem arises. The MSY focuses on how much fish should be taken. But just as important is *how* they are fished. Tweaking application of the MSY obscures the reality that many industrial fishing methods are in themselves unsustainable. Local communities are best placed to apply limits in the interest of sustainable livelihoods and stable fish populations.

Stronger monitoring of industrial fishing practices is also essential. Every industrial fishery should have independent monitors on board, their number depending on the size of the vessel.[39] Monitoring and surveillance, backed by adequate resources, should be incorporated in any fishing access agreement or arrangement with foreign fisheries. While EU agreements have insisted on monitoring and surveillance, they have not provided enough finance for it, and European fleet owners, like others, have not allowed host country observers on board.[40] There should be known punitive sanctions against vessels refusing to allow onboard observers, including suspension of their licence to fish. The same should apply to those caught overfishing, or fishing in banned waters or with inappropriate equipment. For their part, African host countries should prioritize vessels that offload their catch in local ports, to give added value to local processing and to check on legality.

A much-discussed and much-praised alternative to quota-based fishery access agreements has evolved from an agreement in 2011 between eight Pacific island states, joined by the

Tokelau Islands, to set up a Vessel Day Scheme.[41] Previously, for access to the world's richest tuna fishing waters, home to half of all skipjack tuna, foreign fisheries were paying about 2.5% of the market value to the island states, or 5% of the declared catch.

The foreign industrial fishing vessels were using purse-seine nets and fish aggregating devices equipped with transponders and echo-sounders, enabling them to capture up to 300 tonnes in one haul of the net. But the technique also netted a large amount of bycatch, about one-fifth of the total catch, in the form of sharks, turtles and hundreds of other fish species, including unwanted juvenile bigeye tuna. The result was plummeting stocks of bigeye tuna, which as adult fish are highly sought after and fetch high prices.

Since 2011, the Vessel Day Scheme has required vessel owners to bid for each day they want to fish. With a current minimum of $8,000 a day, the charge now averages nearly $12,000. The group also banned the use of fish aggregating devices for three months a year to reduce bycatch of young bigeye. As a result, these states' revenue from the fishing grounds has risen tenfold and the population of bigeye tuna has stabilized. Kiribati's fishing revenue increased from $27 million in 2008 to $160 million in 2020, even though it decided to set aside 11% of its EEZ as the Phoenix Islands Protected Area, where all commercial fishing was banned. (In late 2021 the Kiribati government said it would relax the ban to increase fishing revenue. However, at the time of writing it was not clear whether the decision would survive strong opposition from conservation groups and UNESCO, which had classified the protected area as a World Heritage Site of Outstanding Universal Value.)

It remains an open question whether similar auction schemes should be applied elsewhere. In West Africa it would probably be a big improvement on current fishing access agreements and dubious joint ventures. However, it would require strict rules on fishing standards and the landing of all fish for certification. In the Pacific, the Vessel Day Scheme has not reduced total fishing effort, and the number of fish aggregating devices has grown in response to the three-month ban. The development of a secondary market for vessel day licences suggests that a longer-term trend to domination by a few industrial fisheries could be merely a matter of time.

Certification: overcoming contradictions

Much faith is attached to certification of sustainable seafood as a way of encouraging sustainable fishing practices. About 80% of the seafood now certified as sustainable is wild catch, the remainder being farmed.[42] But certification of aquaculture is growing faster. Five countries account for two-thirds of all certified seafood – Peru, the USA, Norway, Chile and Russia, in that order. Asia has lagged way behind the trend.

This form of civil governance came into the mainstream in 1995 when Unilever set up the Marine Stewardship Council (MSC) in alliance with WWF to operate a fisheries certification system. Unilever was then buying about a quarter of all groundfish (demersal bottom-dwelling fish including cod and haddock) sold globally for processing. No doubt, this made commercial sense for Unilever, enabling it to keep and win customers wanting sustainably managed fish. Confusingly, several other certification schemes have since emerged for wild and farmed fish, but the MSC retains a near-monopoly in what is really a *market* for sustainable seafood certification that favours industrial fisheries. In 2021 the 421 MSC-certified fisheries accounted for 14% of all global fish landings.[43]

Despite admirable intentions, the MSC has in practice marginalized vulnerable communities of small-scale fishers, particularly in developing countries, whose catches become unsustainable by default.[44] They never reach the threshold for size of fishery to be classifiable under the scheme. The MSC was established without any explicit social or community-oriented principles, criteria or indicators in its standard of sustainability, and so has given no weight to the need to support artisanal fisheries and blue commons communities.

Eco-labels and environmental accreditation standards are new forms of neoliberal governance, providing a market incentive – increased consumer demand – for desirable types of behaviour. The MSC judges the sustainability of individual fisheries based on twenty-eight performance indicators, on sustaining fish stocks, ecosystem impact and effective management, assessed by independent certifiers accredited to Assurance Services International. The assessment process, which takes roughly a year and a half, is paid for by the applicant fishery, and costs between $15,000 and $120,000, a hefty sum for small-scale fishers. In effect, the eco-label is a form of contrived competition, a way of setting up winners and losers by creating barriers to entry to the privileged segment of the seafood market. Eco-labelling is a way of stratifying the market.

As noted earlier, certification schemes are also susceptible to deliberate mislabelling of fish at every stage of the fishing process, from mislabelling at sea, particularly in transhipment and filleting, to sale in retail outlets and restaurants. Conservationists say the MSC certification process does not adequately account for bycatch, especially sharks and whales and other cetaceans entangled in fishing gear. For this reason, eco-labels are not a fool-proof quality control mechanism.

That said, could certification be extended to indicate that the fish in question have been caught in a local commons? If so, this could have a positive effect on artisanal fisheries. Consumer pressure could then raise the return to commons-based fisheries and lower it to industrial fisheries and aquaculture.

Can China become a gamekeeper?

Certification is only a modest tool to induce more sustainable seafood production, making consumers and producers feel better. But reform of other governance mechanisms too will have only limited effect if they are unable to check China's growing role in fuelling the crisis in fisheries and other spheres of the blue economy.

For the past two decades, through its vast, marauding long-distance fishing fleet, China has been the world's leading poacher. Can it turn itself into a primary gamekeeper? In 2020, the government announced tighter regulations over its distant-water fishing fleet in an encouraging sign that China was taking the threat to the world's marine life more seriously and responsibly. Whether these will be adequately enforced remains to be seen.

Size matters. As one US marine biologist responded, 'China is the country that will shape what the future of ocean health becomes . . . If China elects to govern its fisheries more sustainably, not only does China benefit, the world benefits. China can act fast – when it wishes to do so.'[45] But even if the new rules have a beneficial impact, they will not alter the fundamental threat posed by huge industrial fishing fleets.

China, like the rest of the world, must be persuaded to stop plundering and allow local communities to reclaim their commons. It must take its stewardship role more seriously and foster more gatekeepers to ensure sustainable rules are followed. We cannot be too optimistic at this moment. But that makes it even more important that all countries should strengthen their local artisanal blue commons, to keep rent-seekers at bay.

None of the existing international governance mechanisms is fit for purpose – UNCLOS, the ISA, RFMOs, the EU's CFP, MPAs, the certification schemes and so on – beyond which are the crimogenic tendencies of ocean exploitation, including corporate-state collusion and corruption. In that context, only a return to basics will offer a viable resolution to the crisis. This means erecting a commons-based governance system; it means immediate action to achieve the much-discussed and much-postponed rollback in fishing subsidies that entrench corporate fisheries and corporate interests in other aspects of the blue economy; and it means minimizing the role of global finance. It is clear what needs to be done. It is the will to do it that is lacking.

Reviving the Commons, Sharing Common-Wealth

The past few hundred years have been dubbed the Anthropocene, a period during which humans have sought to dominate and exploit nature rather than just coexist with it. In the oceans, a late target of conquest, the frenetic phase of the Anthropocene can be said to have started with the Great Acceleration after the Second World War, further intensified in the Blue Acceleration since the 1990s.

Paul Crutzen, the atmospheric chemist who popularized the idea of the Anthropocene, died in early 2021, at a time when the COVID-19 pandemic had intensified calls for the Anthropocene to be ended, at least in its current form. Our age looks more like the Age of Extinction, not only of millions of species in the natural world, but of humankind itself. Climate change threatens to make large swathes of the planet uninhabitable. And nature is gaining revenge for the destruction of animal habitats by humans, by triggering zoonotic pandemics. COVID-19 was already the fifth zoonotic pandemic of the twenty-first century.[1]

Meanwhile, the global economic system has morphed from the neoliberalism of the 1980s and 1990s into rentier capitalism. Financial and other international economic crises have long ceased to be 'black swans' – rare events with unpredictable consequences – but have become normal features of an unstable economic system. The combination of ecological and economic shocks and decay has generated what some call 'radical uncertainty', accompanied by lost resilience at both societal and individual levels. We are confronted by multiple unpredictable shocks and hazards with the potential to have devastating consequences.

Unlike risk and most forms of insecurity, uncertainty is about 'unknown unknowns', an inability to predict an adverse event or its consequences, or how to cope or recover from it. This is the context in which we should look to the commons and commoning to regain a sense of balance and resilience. We cannot do much quickly to overcome today's inherent uncertainty. But we can ameliorate it and build robustness (immunity) and resilience (ability to cope and recover) in the face of it.

A commons cushions individuals and communities against uncertainty. A blue commons would be more resilient than a blue economy based on industrialized accumulation, commodification and financialization. It is not being unduly romantic to claim that localized communities tend to operate under norms of reproduction, conservation and informal social protection. And vernacular knowledge handed down from generation to generation reproduces a flexible, adaptive set of responses to threatening hazards, shocks and uncertainty.

A commons nurtures and depends on certain structural forms of 'inefficiency'. In managing marine fishing grounds, for example, any system based on private property rights will generate negative 'externalities' because owners prioritize their individual advantage over the wider effects of their activities. By contrast, a commons system, if properly designed, is likely to have positive externalities, in that individual or group actions have broader benefits for the whole community.

What are the principles that should guide policies and actions to revive the blue commons? And what income distribution system would be an equitable means of strengthening the commons and blue degrowth?

From blue growth to blue commoning

The commons are not resources to be exploited and depleted, but expressions of a way of living, of sharing and of reproduction. In the case of the natural commons, they are an expression of balance between humans and the rest of nature, not about exploitation of nature by humans. There is an implicit recognition that everything depends on everything else.

On their own, words like 'degrowth' and 'sustainability' are ambivalent. If taken to mean simply producing fewer things, they do not alter the human-centred logic. The focus must be on reviving commoning, in the form of reproduction, preservation and sharing. This must include care for the vocabulary that we use, and the images it conveys. For example, most of the literature on the blue economy refers to 'fisheries' and 'fish stocks', as if marine life belonged to humankind and as if the sole interest of communities linked to the sea was generating income from extracting fish as 'seafood'. That is why it is preferable to refer to 'fish populations', analogous to human populations. We would be worried if politicians started to refer to 'human stocks'.

Blue growth is inherently destructive, since it relies on

the structures and mechanisms of rentier capitalism that are incompatible with claims of sustainability and inclusion. Instead, we should adopt a paradigm based on reviving the blue commons that promotes small-scale production, small-scale fishing, small-scale aquaculture (or mutualized fish farming), small-scale local tourist providers, small-scale cruises, and so on. This is not romanticizing. It is a call for the bias to change, combating the presumption that industrial-scale production backed by international finance is the most efficient and thus the most productive way to go.

The commons should be seen, potentially, as a zone of 'thrivability', not just sustainability, that can encourage adaptation to changing external forces, including deteriorating ecosystems. In that context, 'small' should be interpreted in terms of localized communities of commoners, such that all commoners know who else is in their community and who is responsible for its wellbeing, including the stewards, gatekeepers, knowledge providers, and those in charge of distributing the shares of resources and the gains from the commons.

Reviving commons traditions and ethos means being more animist and less dualistic in our attitude towards nature. To be animist, as Jason Hickel has reminded us, is to recognize our interconnectedness with nature, our interdependency, whereas the dualistic perspective, which he traces to the likes of René Descartes and Francis Bacon, regards humans as having a mission to subjugate nature and make it serve humanity's interests.[2] This is not a call for a return to a more primitive way of living, but rather to see ourselves as part of nature, rejecting the conceit of 'natural capital'.

There are numerous little examples of what could be done.

In Canada, Vancouver-based Organic Ocean Seafood (OOS) has worked with the University of Guelph in Toronto to authenticate fish using DNA samples. Many of the fish supplied to OOS are caught by First Nation communities in what the company's co-founder has described as 'a happy partnership based on shared values of conservation and environmental stewardship'.[3]

For nearly one hundred years, First Nations were largely banned from commercial fishing in the big rivers in British Columbia. They are now creating a 'narrative of reconciliation' with the salmon, in the process generating a trust-based organic supply chain that augurs well for a commons production and reproduction system. Regrettably, other companies have shown no interest in voluntary DNA testing, and the Canadian Food Inspection Agency has been disinclined to make it mandatory, even though it has used DNA identification itself to document the extensive seafood mislabelling in Canada.

A rarely acknowledged advantage of a blue commons over a private property rights regime relates to voluntary compliance with rules, particularly rules of conservation. Commoners who develop and impose their own rules are more likely to respect them. By contrast, monitoring and policing fishery practices by outside agencies is costly and administratively complex, as fishing takes place over large areas, by many boats, day and night, throughout the year.

Very few fisheries are adequately monitored, even in rich OECD countries. The UK has just twelve boats equipped and designated for the purpose to cover its entire coastal waters. Even with aerial support, monitoring is likely to be weak. One response would be to raise the penalties for breaking the rules, so increasing the risk cost. But this could encourage more devious ways of cheating. As with other forms of unlawful behaviour, the best deterrent is being caught.

In a blue commons, the community as a whole can develop and enforce norms based on trust, moral suasion, culture and fear of excommunication.[4] The risk of reputational damage is considerable, since failure to respect community norms can result in lingering disapprobation. But there is also a dynamic between rules set from the outside and their legitimation within blue commons. If they are not perceived as fair or sensible, blue commoners can connive collectively to undermine their effectiveness.

Of course, willingness to adhere to rules depends on recognition of the longer-term communal benefits if everybody abides by them. One way of resurrecting commons fishing is to institute an 'access rights regime' that gives local commoners control of fishing areas and their fish populations. The UN Environment Programme, FAO and other multilateral bodies could promote these more effectively. In the spirit if not the letter of a commons, 'territorial use rights fisheries' (TURFs) give limited access to an area of enclosed seabed to small-scale fisheries and coastal communities. One review identified over 1,000 TURFs in forty-one countries.[5] In some countries they are long-established and are enshrined in fisheries legislation. In South Africa, for example, fishing communities are allocated priority rights to fish in demarcated fishing zones. Although they are far from being a panacea, TURFs have an additional advantage because rules on fishing practices, type of gear, and limits on fish catches and size can be adapted to local conditions.

TURFs have been most entrenched in Japan, where they date back to the feudal era and ancient guilds formed in the sixteenth century.[6] Ad hoc user rights were given legal status as TURFs in the Fishery Law of 1901, and the guilds were transformed into fishing cooperative associations by the Fishery Cooperative Law of 1948. Under this system, the government operates as the steward, allocating exclusive access rights to the fishing cooperatives and leaving them to manage themselves, subject to a total allowable catch limit.

Traditionally organized around coastal fishing communities, the cooperatives act like well-functioning commons; they can limit fishing, constrain competition, institute measures to restore fish populations and so on. Under the law, the cooperative cannot reject eligible individuals, who must be working fishers, living locally and engaging in a minimum annual number of days fishing. That last criterion means, in practice, that aspiring new members must begin by working for an incumbent fisherman.

Even with a sensible total allowable catch, left to themselves vessels will typically go to the most fertile fishing spots in the TURF demarcated area, which can result in overfishing. Some cooperatives eliminate this problem by rotating access to fishing grounds, so that over the year and seasons all fishers have opportunities in good and bad spots. Some go further in pooling the income and then distributing the proceeds, which supports effort coordination. Most set up monitoring procedures, often using peer pressure, with sanctions for rule-breakers including confiscation of fish catches and prohibition of fishing. They also have collective activities to regenerate the ocean forests of kelp and seaweed that provide habitats and breeding areas for many species of fish and other marine creatures. And a number of cooperatives coordinate marketing and have brand labels analogous to eco-labels.

The Japanese TURF system is a commons system that has stood the test of time. The pooling procedures and flexible rules on access and effort restrict 'the race to fish', while the incentive to shirk in a pooling system is combated by peer and reputational pressure, and the existence of sanctions. It is to be hoped that this commons ethos will survive a trend in recent years towards consolidation of local cooperative associations into prefecture-wide ones, which critics claim has disempowered local small-scale fishers and failed to improve their livelihoods.[7]

TURF systems are, if properly managed, more equitable and ecologically sustainable than systems such as individual transferable quotas (ITQs) based on private property rights. They point the way towards viable forms of commons. The big question is how to secure for the community the material security that will make a commons both feasible and desirable.

Principles of blue common-wealth

So far, the focus has been on commoning as shared activity geared to reproduction and shared access to common pool resources. But a healthy commons also requires respect for what might be called common-wealth principles. This involves a different form of individualism than implied in neoliberal thinking; it fosters individual flourishing within communal solidarity, the essence of what Aristotle called *philia*, convivial friendship. Besides ideas of cooperativism, guild socialism and the 'mutual aid' or anarchism of Peter Kropotkin (1842–1921), this perspective is linked to the influential idea of *buen vivir*.[8] The Andean concept of *sumak kawsay* from which it is derived signifies collective harmony between human beings and nature, emphasizing community rights over individual property rights, and a resolute opposition to commodification and 'natural capital'. Also related are the African ethos of *ubuntu* (particularly *eco-ubuntu*, its variant in South Africa) and the Korean principle of *hongik ingan*, spreading benefits by spreading community, on which Korea was founded in 2333 BC.

The commons at best celebrates individual freedom but not in the libertarian sense. Rather, it combines the notions of 'liberal' and 'republican' freedom. Liberal freedom is the freedom to be moral, the freedom to make decisions because one believes they are right, not out of necessity or because some paternalistic authority dictates what to do. Republican freedom means being free from *potential* domination by figures or institutions in positions of unaccountable authority. This leads to some foundational commons principles.

THE RIGHT-TO-SUBSISTENCE PRINCIPLE

In a commons, every commoner should have the inalienable right to subsistence. In England, the Charter of the Forest of 1217 established the principle that everybody has the right to subsistence in the commons, stating that every 'free man' had the right to access commons resources to work, to eat and to provide shelter. The Charter also required reparations for individuals and social groups if actions to restrict the commons compromised the right to subsistence. In various forms, this right – an economic human right – has been restated over the ages.

Some have interpreted the principle as a 'common property right', claiming that only if subsistence for all is achieved and guaranteed can private property rights be allowed. This idea is supported in the classic defence of individual private property rights by the seventeenth-century philosopher John Locke. Modern libertarians and neoliberals have taken only the pronouncements from Locke that contribute to their claim that private property rights are sacrosanct. But they have ignored his three caveats, known as the 'Lockean provisos'.

First, Locke said, an individual may appropriate land or resources from the commons only if 'enough and as good' is left for others to obtain their subsistence. This implies a *prior* right to subsistence in the commons before individual property rights can be justified. Denying that prior right by neglect, encroachment, enclosure or privatization of the commons is illegitimate. Locke understood that where land is scarce relative to the population, appropriation should be restricted. As he put it, very precisely, 'where there is plenty of people under government, who have money and commerce, no one can inclose or appropriate any part, without the consent of all his fellow commoners.'[9]

Locke's second caveat, known as 'the sustenance proviso', essentially states that those who become private owners of land or resources have a moral duty to provide those without private property with enough to avoid 'extreme want'. This reinforces the priority that should be given to the right of subsistence. Because this is a *right*, it does not require commoners to behave in certain ways, unlike many of to-day's welfare benefit programmes.

The third caveat, known as 'the spoilage proviso', states that a property owner – and Locke meant landowners in the main – should not 'ingross as much as he will' from the commons but only as much as he can make practical use of. The word 'ingross' became important in the Tudor period, a time of extensive enclosure of the commons. It referred to one of three ways by which the commons were enclosed, the others being 'regrating' and 'forestalling'. Ingrossing (or engrossing) referred to monopolizing ownership or control; regrating meant purchasing a commodity for resale; forestalling meant withholding a commodity from the market in order to push up the price. All of these are hallmarks of global rentier capitalism and financialization.

If we accept the right to subsistence in the commons as a fundamental principle of common justice, then we can justify demanding compensation and reparations for blue commoners, as for any group of commoners, for the encroachment, spoilage, enclosure or privatization of commons resources that imperil that right to subsistence. This is the starting point for proposals elaborated later in this chapter for a Commons Fund and common dividends.

THE RIGHT-TO-HABITAT PRINCIPLE

The right to subsistence can be distinguished from a right to the commons itself. Commoners have always valued places, or spaces, as part of their heritage. A common habitat is a social commons; it is not just a place in which to reside but also an imagined or 'mapped out' community in which to live in the surrounding environment – to work, to care, to common, to leisure in the ancient Greek sense of *schole*, as in participating, learning and acting.

This may be called the 'right to habitat' principle, the right to live in a commons and the right to preserve what has been built up and handed down to its inhabitants. There is a rich vein of social thinking around 'the right to the city', a term attributed to Henri Lefebvre who used it in an article in 1968 and which was later refined by David Harvey.[10] Lefebvre depicted the city as 'an oeuvre', a work in progress shaped by its members. The right to the city is the right 'to habitat and to inhabit. The right to the oeuvre, to participation and appropriation (clearly distinct from the right to property).'[11]

A marine commons, such as a fishing community, will also have its shape, its physical character, its moods, its in-built reciprocities between those who have grown up in it. It is not about private property; it is about use value triumphing over exchange value, about social organization of production, distribution and protection, not about capitalistic profit maximization. Life has a rhythm, a way of doing things and of not doing things. Similarly, a mangrove habitat will exist not as a resource but as a social organization, with its rituals and traditions.

When an outside commercial interest, such as a large fishing trawler, enters the waters of a community habitat, it is not just taking the fish, it is disrupting the habitat. When a fish farm is constructed in a mangrove swamp, it is not just occupying part of a commons, it is disrupting the habitat. When a luxury hotel is built on a sandy beach, it is not just privatizing a piece of the seashore. And when economists or others talk about the need to 'value nature', they ignore the vital notion of habitat. You cannot put a market value on a habitat as a community.

The right to habitat is more than a right to access community resources or services; it is a right to change ourselves and the locale through commoning. It is a common right, not an individual property right. And there is absolutely no reason to restrict this to cities. It is about spatial justice and is therefore about the legitimate transformation of communities by and for commoners, not for profit or by external interests. It is grounded in commoning as a social practice. The habitat should be off-limits to commodification or privatization.

If this principle is abused, as it certainly has been, there should be compensation for the commoners adversely affected. Thus, if a pristine beach is privatized, depriving the local community of a time-honoured landscape, a source of leisure and access to marine resources, the commoners should be compensated.

THE SOCIAL MEMORY PRINCIPLE

In designing a commons strategy, it is obviously important to establish mechanisms to ensure the legitimacy and continuity of the commons and to combat any erosion from neglect or external corrosion. A commons and traditions of commoning have always required acceptance by a community for some considerable time. Recall that in medieval England, for hundreds of years, an area or practice was accepted as a commons if it had existed as such for as long as anybody living could recall. This was gradually formalized, until the Limitation Act in 1623 set the time limit, unchanged today, at twenty years.

Other countries and communities may have different informal or formal rules of inherited legitimacy. But the twenty-year rule seems adequate as a guide for legitimating a commons and commoning in any blue commons. It offers a buffer against encroachment, enclosure, privatization and, most of all, any form of colonization. So, in a blue commons, the management system must operate with respect to social memory.

THE PRECAUTIONARY PRINCIPLE

The next vital challenge is to prevent unnecessary risks in the face of uncertainty, and to establish mechanisms to monitor the impact of proposed changes. Long used in environmental and other risk assessments, the precautionary principle requires policymakers and investors to err on the side of caution when thinking about actions that might entail serious or unknown ecological and health risks. That should mean forgoing altogether an activity such as deep-sea mining. Although recent years have seen a welcome commitment to the precautionary principle in international agreements and international reports, in practice growth has tended to win out over caution.

A blue commons approach would give the precautionary principle a high priority, especially as the harm would probably be felt by the community or its ecological basis. If scientific knowledge is limited, as is usually the case, or if there is discordance between scientific knowledge and vernacular or commons knowledge acquired over the generations, then real efforts should be made to minimize the risks and uncertainty before proceeding. And the risks should be extended beyond what is conventionally considered as the natural environment to the commons as a functioning socio-ecosystem.

The precautionary principle requires individuals in decision-making positions to take precautionary measures to reduce the probability of harm in the face of uncertainty. It places the burden of proof or evidence on those wishing to change or innovate. It requires decision-makers to explore alternatives to what might be harmful actions. And it requires respect for public, transparent participation in decision-making.

THE INTERGENERATIONAL EQUITY PRINCIPLE

It has always been understood that whatever is regarded as the commons should be protected for posterity, and that each generation has a duty to pass on at least the equal of what it inherits. But it is not easy to translate this into a practical set of rules. In 1977, economist John Hartwick formalized the principle in what became known as the Hartwick Rule of Intergenerational Equity. This stated that society should invest enough of the rental income derived from extraction, and the use of exhaustible, and thus naturally scarce, resources so that future generations would benefit as much as today's. As the World Bank put it, 'The Hartwick Rule holds that consumption can be maintained – the definition of sustainable development – if the rents from non-renewable resources are continuously invested rather than used for consumption.'[12]

Scant respect has been paid to this principle in the pursuit of growth in the blue economy, partly because of a persistent, and convenient, presumption that the seas' resources were inexhaustible. While that is wrong, some resources taken from the sea, such as fish and seaweed, are renewable, at least in principle, rather than exhaustible like minerals. But since they are common pool resources, those taking commercial advantage still owe compensation to the commoners of today and tomorrow.

THE PUBLIC TRUST DOCTRINE PRINCIPLE

If something in nature is converted into a resource for human use, the state becomes the trustee, charged with acting on behalf of all the commoners. As already noted, this is an accepted common-law legal principle that derives from Justinian law developed in the Roman Empire, but civil law countries have an equivalent concept of 'the public domain'.

The idea of a public trust took practical form in twelfth-century England when trusts were set up to manage and protect estates while the owner was away to take part in the Crusades. The trusts distinguished between the beneficial owner of the property and the trustee, who was required to serve the owner's long-term interests. Legally, the person who manages the assets has a fiduciary duty of complete loyalty to the owner, just as lawyers do to their clients today. As such, trustees differ from politicians, who can and should listen to many points of view.

This perspective led to the idea of 'the common heritage of mankind' associated with Arvid Pardo in 1967, and the related idea of a 'planetary trust', which includes not just the seas and oceans but Antarctica, the Arctic, the moon and outer space. The classic statement of this was made by Edith Weiss:

> This planetary trust obligates each generation to preserve
> the diversity of the resource base and to pass the planet to

future generations in no worse condition than it receives it. Thus, the present generation serves both as a trustee for future generations and as a beneficiary of the trust. In fulfilling our role as planetary trustees, we can draw on the law of trusts, a body of distilled teachings concerning intergenerational cooperation and conflict, to help resolve the challenges confronting our global heritage.[13]

Weiss added the important caveat that present generations also owe a fiduciary duty to other members of their own generation. One aspect of the public trust doctrine relates to the legal *positive duty* to protect the environment. Here we may recall the common-law precedent established in 1299 in the case brought by Juliana the Washerwoman described in Chapter 3. It established a principle that has never been overturned.

Trustees cannot do whatever they wish with the perceived resources. Under common law, states must act towards natural resources, such as minerals under the sea, as trustees, not as owners or proprietors. In a case in the United States in 2017, the Supreme Court of Pennsylvania ruled that, since state parks and forests, including the oil and gas they contained, were owned by the state, the state must act as trustee, with loyalty towards the beneficiaries (the commoners), prudence in management and impartiality towards the commoners. Crucially, it also ruled that the proceeds of natural resources could not be used by the state government as its own funds.

Pennsylvania's Constitution Section 27 sets out the public trust doctrine nicely: 'The people have a right to clean air, pure water, and to the preservation of natural, scenic, historic, and aesthetic values of the environment. Pennsylvania's public natural resources are the common property of all the people including generations yet to come. As trustee of these resources, the Commonwealth shall conserve and maintain them for the benefit of all the people.'

The principled legal position is for the institutions of common law to have a positive duty to defend the commons and thus to respect the public trust doctrine. There should be a presumption that common rights have priority over private property rights. The common law system should act as custodian of the blue commons, as of any other commons.

There are several subsidiary elements of the public trust doctrine. Not only does it require the state to maintain the capital value of any natural resources that are converted into commodities, but it also requires a commitment to conserve the natural inheritance in general, imposing a duty against waste and a duty to restore natural resources damaged by extractive activity. The state therefore has a duty to conserve the environment affected by economic activity. This surely rules out ecological 'credit' or 'offset' schemes of any kind, such as creating or maintaining a coral reef as payment for destroying or damaging another, or abstaining from industrial fishing in one protected area in return for more intensive fishing in another.

The public trust doctrine also requires the free and prior informed consent of the commoners to any commercial or other intrusion into a commons environment that risks damaging or reducing its perceived value to the local communities. And they should be fully compensated if any damage is done. Thus, the public trust doctrine imposes the duty of the legal system to uphold the rights of communities and their ability to withstand pressure from powerful commercial interests. Failure to do so can have devastating consequences for local communities and the 'thrivability' of the commons and commoning.

THE DELIBERATIVE DEMOCRACY PRINCIPLE

In a market economy, particularly one oriented to rentier capitalism, the minority with market power will opt for short-term profiteering. In a commons community, economic decisions made communally will tend towards deliberative democracy, holding rent-seeking in check because a majority will wish to reproduce the common pool resources. This has been supported by an interesting experiment involving an 'intergenerational game' designed to test what conditions best support conservation of resources for future generations.[14] The experiment showed that if decisions were left to individuals, even a small minority could quickly exhaust resources by taking as much as they could for themselves, leaving nothing for generations to come. However, if decisions were made through democratic voting, as should be the case in a commons, the majority could set extraction rules to ensure resources would be handed intact (or replenished) to the succeeding generations.

For this to happen, the experimenters noted, decisions voted by the majority of 'cooperators with the future' must be binding on everyone, to restrain potential 'defectors' and reassure 'conditional cooperators' that their efforts will not be futile. Conditional cooperators are more motivated to contribute to a public good if they see or can depend on others doing the same, and they tend to make up a sizable proportion of any community.[15] So, the state must create and preserve structures of deliberative democracy in order to support a sustainable commons, enabling local communities to manage a resource system by their own rules.

Although this is compatible with what in the European Union is called 'the principle of subsidiarity', that decisions should be delegated to the lowest level of technical competence where possible, this is not a call for total self-rule for every local community. This is because there are complex layers of commons, from tiny specialist communities to the level of the state and then the 'global commons'. But at every level there must be respect for stewardship, the public trust doctrine and other commons principles.

Commoners, with most to lose from whatever decisions are made, must have the primary votes compared with any 'outsider'. In another set of deliberative democracy experiments, individuals subjected to external pressure or psychological influence were less likely to vote for principles of social justice and compassion than those who deliberated with members of their community. This has been tested in various countries by independent researchers.[16] And the experiments demonstrate that people are more likely to vote in favour of equal basic security for all members of their community if they have spent time discussing options. A commons without mechanisms for deliberative democracy is unlikely to remain a commons for very long.

Of course, respect for deliberative democracy will not always lead to optimum outcomes, even if every commoner is provided with the same full information. For example, Climate Assembly UK, a citizens' assembly on how to meet the UK's target of net zero greenhouse gas emissions by 2050, compressed a vast array of issues and proposals into six weekend meetings of 108 randomly chosen individuals. One of the many conclusions was that 95% were in favour of more offshore wind energy, partly it seems because that 'would be out of sight'. The participants should have been asked whether they would support more offshore wind farms given uncertainty about the ecological impact and whether the sites selected were optimal. Deliberative democracy must be linked to a model of the commons as a whole.

A blue commons distribution system

For a commons to be thrivable, the community must have adequate incomes and an ability to raise living standards, without jeopardizing the commons or veering back to the pursuit of GDP growth. With the above set of ethical guidelines in mind, the following proposals rest on three distributional claims.

First, based on the recognition of common-wealth, all forms of rentier income and common-wealth should be shared, by being recycled in some equitable way. Recall that rentier incomes stem from contrived scarcity created by private riches (the Lauderdale Paradox) and from institutions, regulations, fiscal policies and other measures that governments and international bodies have put in place, not on the merits or efforts of individual recipients. So, if rentier incomes are to be captured for the commons, we need to look at all the resources that are part of the commons heritage, comprising the natural, social, civil, cultural and knowledge commons.[17]

For instance, why financiers today make much more money than their predecessors is largely due to the ideologically driven financial market liberalization of the 1980s and 1990s.[18] Why Big Tech has spawned a plutocracy of multi-billionaires and generated unaccountable global monopolies is largely due to the globalization of the US intellectual property rights regime in the 1990s. Why fishing conglomerates are so dominant in marine fishing is largely due to lavish subsidies and weakened states obliged to enter one-sided fishery access agreements or questionable joint ventures.

Second, those imposing costs that imperil the commons, such as pollution and damage to ecosystems, should pay, on the 'polluter pays' principle. At the very least, polluters should be required to pay the equivalent of the advantage they gain from it, so as to induce them to stop. There is obviously a difficulty in defining and valuing the cost of pollution or ecological damage, as shown by attempts to value nature. Still, if the pollution persists, the cost imposed is not high enough. There may be extenuating circumstances, but the justification for imposing a lesser cost should be made transparent, to show why 'less is enough'.

The third claim is that the income and wealth of all of us are mainly due to the efforts, achievements and luck of the many generations before us, rather than individual merit or even hard work. We should all have a fair share of that public wealth, as equal commoners. As a matter of common justice, everybody in society has an equal right to the inherited commons, which we can picture as a cascading set of demands, from global to local.

This was well put by Herbert Simon, a Nobel Prize-winning economist, in 2000:

> If we are very generous with ourselves, we might claim that we 'earned' as much as one fifth of our present wealth. The rest is patrimony associated with being a member of an enormously productive social system, which has accumulated a vast store of physical capital and an even larger store of intellectual capital.[19]

Or as the immensely wealthy Warren Buffett, the 'Oracle of Omaha' and over the years perhaps the world's most successful investor, said honestly: 'I personally think that society is responsible for a very significant portion of what I've earned.'[20]

Blue Commons Funds

The world is in the grip of rentier capitalism. In almost every country, the share of income going to capital, or owners of assets, is rising relative to the share going to people who rely on labour, work and commoning. Without strong countervailing measures to reverse rising income inequality, there will be explosive social unrest as well as growing immiseration and economic insecurity. To combat rentier capitalism, and in line with commons principles and common justice, countries should establish Blue Commons Capital Funds, focusing on the rentier income gained from the blue economy and the plunder of the blue commons and its resources.

Many governments, including Britain's, have treated public revenue derived from natural resources, such as minerals, oil and gas, as windfall gains and used them to cover budgetary spending and/or cut income and wealth taxes. This blatantly disregards the intergenerational equity principle. A Blue Commons Fund would respect both that principle and the public trust doctrine. It would be a variant of a public trust, tasked with preserving assets and their value in the interests of beneficiaries. And there are several existing commons funds from which to draw inspiration, with those of Alaska and Norway in the lead. Norway especially has set a global standard in respect for the principles of common-wealth and in establishing a governance structure on which the proposed Blue Commons Funds could be modelled.

On 23 December 1969, Philips Petroleum informed the Norwegian government that it had discovered a very large oilfield in the country's North Sea continental shelf. It proved to be first of several, which made Norway one of the world's leading oil producers for several decades. Unlike Britain, in whose North Sea areas large oil discoveries were also made around that time, the Norwegian government took an ownership stake in North Sea oil production and assets in awarding production licences to private companies as well as allocating production zones to the state-owned company Statoil. Once revenue began to flow, the Norwegian government used the proceeds to cut public debt and then invested the rental income in a special national fund.

The Petroleum Fund of Norway, a national sovereign wealth fund, was established in the early 1990s and the first revenues were transferred to it in 1996. Today, it is the world's biggest sovereign wealth fund, with assets of over $1.1 trillion. Renamed the Government Pension Fund Global (though it is not primarily a pension fund), it was described by *The Economist* 'as perhaps the most impressive example of long-term thinking by any Western government'.[21] Respecting the Hartwick Rule, the Fund protects its capital while distributing money annually, the total distributed being determined by the annual return on its investments averaged over the previous five years.

The Fund has a designated investment policy. It invests exclusively outside Norway, in four classes of assets – equities, bonds, physical property and renewable energy infrastructure. Today it has investments in over 9,000 companies and controls over 1% of all shares listed on global stock markets. It has also invested many billions of dollars in government debt and has a huge portfolio of properties, including part of Regent Street in London, and Fifth Avenue and Times Square in New York. As part of its ethical investment strategy, it aims to put pressure on invested companies to prevent ocean pollution and damage to ocean ecosystems, including overfishing.

The Fund's investment strategy helped to avoid the worst consequences of 'Dutch disease', first identified when large gas reserves were found off the coast of the Netherlands. Foreign investment in the sector and surging gas exports increased demand for the Dutch guilder and pushed up the exchange rate. This made other sectors of the economy less internationally competitive, leading to a decline in manufacturing and a rise in unemployment. By channelling revenue into a capital fund and investing abroad, Norway was able to contain the exchange-rate effect, while the revenue went largely to finance public services.

The UK, by contrast, fell into the resource trap. The

government awarded North Sea oil production licences at risibly low prices, failed to take ownership stakes in production and assets, and privatized the state-owned oil company BNOC, leaving tax royalties as its only source of revenue. Then it treated its sudden income from North Sea oil as a windfall gain that was squandered on tax cuts and welfare benefits for the rising number of unemployed. Between the end of the 1970s and 2015, oil companies paid the UK Treasury about £330 billion in taxes. Existing generations gained directly. But it all went on current expenditure, leaving nothing for subsequent generations. It was probably the worst economic mistake ever made by a modern British government (perhaps to be surpassed by Brexit). Norway has gained twice as much revenue from every barrel of North Sea oil.[22]

While the Norwegian Fund has flourished, the Alaska Permanent Fund has run into rocky waters. Established in 1976, it was built up through levies (royalties) on the offshore oil industry, which accounts for nearly a third of the oil used in the United States. At the end of each year from 1982 onwards, the Fund has paid a dividend to every legal resident of Alaska, the amount depending on its investment performance over the previous five years.[23]

At the end of 2020, the Fund was worth over $70 billion, a third more than Alaska's GDP. For years, its portfolio of investments earned annual returns of nearly 10%, enough to pay an annual dividend of up to $2,000 to all Alaskans.[24] But its popularity has made it susceptible to cynical political manipulation. In 2016, faced with falling oil revenue and with no revenue from income or sales taxes, which had been abolished by a Republican-dominated legislature, Alaska's governor was desperate to fill a gaping budget hole. He cut the dividend for 2016 and the two subsequent years, using the money saved to fund state services. This proved so unpopular that he was forced to withdraw from his 2018 re-election campaign.

His elected successor played super-populist by promising not only to restore the dividend but to increase it, in effect to unsustainable levels. In office, he proposed to pay for this by slashing public services, which ran into stiff opposition. As of end-2021 the political wrangling was continuing, but the lesson is clear. The governance of such a fund must be kept out of party politics, as the Norwegians have managed to do.

Other interesting if flawed examples of something close to Blue Trust Funds have been established by six of the smaller Pacific island states –Nauru, Palau, the Federated States of Micronesia, the Marshall Islands, Kiribati and Tuvalu – which have been mainly used to provide budget finance.

Kiribati's Revenue Equalisation Reserve Fund, set up in 1956 by the British colonial administration, was initially built up from tax revenue, or mining royalties, from guano (phosphate) reserves. After these were depleted, the Fund was topped up with revenue from fishing licence fees. It was very profitable, reaching 800% of GDP by 2000. But poor investment decisions and excessive withdrawals by the government for current public spending soon halved the Fund's capital value.

Nauru established a phosphate-based fund in the 1970s intended to provide a continuing revenue stream after the mines were exhausted. But its government also splurged the money on current expenditure, exhausting the fund and eventually leaving the economy dependent on payments for hosting an

Australian refugee processing centre. The Tuvalu Trust Fund, created in 1987 with government and foreign donor contributions, has become increasingly reliant on fishing licence fees. This and other trust funds in the Pacific island states have all invested in foreign financial assets, and the returns used for current budgetary expenditures. Thus, they have not satisfied the intergenerational equity principle.

The Shetland Charitable Trust, set up for Scotland's Shetland Islands in the mid-1970s, is another trust fund variant. The local council negotiated with oil companies operating in the North Sea to give the community 'disturbance payments', which were deposited in the Trust managed by the council. In 2003, the Trust became independent, operating as a 'permanent' fund expected to distribute the returns on its investments but keeping the capital intact.

By 2018, the Trust had distributed £300 million for the benefit of the small population of the Shetland Islands, including funding schemes intended to reduce inequality and improve living standards. Perhaps the money could have been spent more widely and equitably, but the scheme's local popularity shows how a quasi-commons fund can work to share capital.

Among several examples of trust funds in the United States, perhaps the most relevant to the proposal for a Blue Commons Fund is the Texas School Fund, set up as far back as 1854 to help finance Texan public schools. Later the Fund was granted control of half the state's land and the mineral rights that remained under state ownership. In 1953, the Fund gained income from coastal 'submerged lands' extending three miles offshore, after the US Congress passed the

Submerged Lands Act, which relinquished to coastal states all rights to US navigable waters within state boundaries. In 1960 Texas won an extension of its waters to 'three marine leagues', 10.3 miles, beyond the coast because that had been its boundary in 1845 when it joined the Union. Since then, the Fund has received earnings from beaches, bays, estuaries and 'submerged land' in the Gulf of Mexico, where drilling rights and royalties have provided considerable revenue. The Fund today is thriving, although it fails to respect common justice principles, as it only benefits students.

Also relevant to a Blue Commons Fund is a proposal for Community Land Trusts linked to the idea of reparations for slavery in the United States and the never-fulfilled promise that freed slaves would be granted 'forty acres and a mule'. Moving more land into such trusts, it is suggested, would make it easier for African Americans to gain access to land for farming, housing and other purposes that would be a springboard for increased income and wealth.[25] Community land trusts might be a vehicle for coastal (and other) communities to reclaim or consolidate their traditional lands as commons.

A Blue Commons Fund could be a stand-alone fund or integrated into a more general Commons Fund at national or even international level. In what follows, however, the focus is on how to build a Blue Commons Fund from levies on exploitation of resources in the blue economy.

Building a Blue Commons Fund

A Blue Commons Fund must necessarily be built from scratch, and governments may need to make an initial transfer to get it started. But from then onwards, it should be built up with revenues from a set of levies, or taxes, on economic rents gained from use of the commons. Some levies would be costs imposed on polluters and destroyers of common resources, thus having the double appeal of combating ecological harm and reducing the advantages gained by 'accumulation by dispossession', that is, gains from taking from the commons. If levies have the desired effect in deterring incursions into the commons, fund revenues will be reduced – but by that time the fund should have accumulated sufficient capital to be self-sustaining – and levies on renewable resources will continue.

The term 'levy' is preferred to 'tax' in this context, to convey the idea that all will benefit from recycling revenue raised from levies on activities that deny or damage the commons. By contrast, 'taxes' are seen as going to the government to spend on its priorities, for the benefit of those it chooses, and can be a source of resentment and resistance.

One major revenue source for any Commons Fund should be a Carbon Levy, a tax on carbon dioxide emissions that are causing dangerous climate change and warming and acidifying the oceans. According to the IMF, only about a fifth of global emissions are covered by pricing programmes and the global average price is a lowly $3 a ton, compared to the $75 a ton it estimates is needed to keep global warming below 2°C.[26] Set at a suitably high level, a carbon levy would in effect transform the atmosphere from an open access resource into a regulated commons. And the proceeds should go into a Commons Fund, because the cost of global warming is borne by all commoners, and more so by low-income groups.[27]

A high carbon tax would have additional benefits in curbing pollution from burning fossil fuels, estimated to cause well over eight million premature deaths globally every year, accounting for a staggering one in five of all deaths.[28] Fine particle pollution from fossil fuels is associated with heart disease, respiratory ailments and even loss of eyesight, and hits low-income communities disproportionately hard. According to a joint IMF/OECD report, the overall benefits of a high carbon price, which also include reduction in traffic congestion and accidents, far outweigh the cost to industry and consumers in almost every country, especially in coal-reliant countries such as China, India and South Africa.[29]

Carbon taxes have been opposed on two grounds – they tend to slow economic growth, as measured by GDP, and they are regressive – although less regressive than energy efficiency standards, on one estimate, because richer households can afford the higher cost of more efficient vehicles and appliances.[30] Recycling the revenue raised by the tax, as Canada has done in the form of a 'carbon dividend' and as the proposed Commons Fund would do as a common dividend, reverses the regressive effect. Poorer households, which tend to spend less on energy than richer ones, receive more in dividend than they pay in higher energy costs, while richer households receive less. As for the potential effect in slowing GDP growth, this can be regarded as a favourable feature in itself.

Sweden has set the lead with what is easily the highest carbon tax in the world, equivalent to over $120 per tonne in 2020 from about $23 per tonne when first introduced in 1991. It is applied to all sectors, including fisheries. There and elsewhere, the tax has been shown to be effective and efficient in reducing emissions.[31] Of course, it is not an ecological panacea. By itself a carbon levy will probably have only a modest positive effect in reducing emissions overall.[32] Other policies are needed. But it could make an important difference in deterring destructive fishing practices and, potentially, deep-sea mining.

A carbon tax combined with removal of fuel subsidies would make longlining, dredging, bottom trawling and beam trawling prohibitively expensive. In EU waters, these seemingly hyper-efficient fishing techniques use about seven times as much fuel per kilo of fish caught as 'passive gear' fishing used by small-scale fisheries. One reason is that much of the fuel consumption of industrial fisheries is used for subsidiary activities, such as fish processing on board and refrigeration.

Sensible carbon taxation would give some cost advantage to local small-scale fisheries and the local population involved in processing the fish on land. Moreover, the removal of fuel subsidies alone would make most distant-water fishing uneconomic, and with a carbon levy in addition even more so, which would reduce the pressure on fish populations around developing countries. And a carbon levy applied to all carbon emissions by fisheries, not just fuel, would further penalize bottom trawling and dredging, which release as much carbon as air travel by disturbing seabed sediment, an important source of carbon storage.[33] The levy should not, however, be a substitute for a ban on bottom trawling in sensitive areas. That is needed more than ever.

Maritime shipping has long used the dirtiest fuels in the world – called 'bunkering fuels' – which are a major source of pollution. In 2015, fifteen of the world's largest ships emitted as much nitrogen oxide and sulphur oxide as the world's 760 million cars.[34] The impact of this pollution on the health of people and wildlife justifies levies on dirty fuel use, in addition to a carbon levy. In 2021 the European Union led the way in announcing that maritime fuel would be taxed for the first time, while its emissions trading scheme would be expanded to cover journeys by ship within the EU and half the journeys outside it.

High fuel costs would also give added impetus to moves already underway in shipping to reduce fossil fuel use and increase use of renewable energy technologies. This would be a better mechanism than the subsidies for renewable energy sometimes proposed, which like all subsidies will tend to reward those who would have made the change anyway (deadweight effects) and provide no incentive to others to reduce fuel consumption.

In addition, there should be a Cruise Liner Levy. These monstrous vessels pollute the water and the surrounding air where they dock, causing severe health problems, ecological destruction and habitat degradation. They may sit in harbours for days, all the while keeping their engines going. While they should be regulated much more stringently, all cruise liners should be required to pay a levy based on ship size and fuel use during the time they spend in national waters.

The number of ports around the world has multiplied. Often privatized, they are profitable for the corporations that own them. But the local population pays the price in pollution of the air and water, noise and disturbance, justifying a Port Use Levy. Compensation for commoners should come indirectly from levies on total income generated by the ports and paid into the Blue Commons Fund.

What other levies should be sources of finance for the

Fund? For many countries, the most lucrative would be a levy on exploitation of minerals, oil, gas and related assets in and around the sea. Ownership should be retained by the state, acting as steward for the commons, and royalties should be levied so that the capital value is not lost.

Another obvious source of revenue for the Blue Commons Fund is a Resource Use Levy. Fishing powers have been paying shockingly low fees for access to fishing grounds, in the range of 2–5% of the nominal value of fish catches. Raising this to about 20%, if not more, would have the advantage of generating serious revenue for the Blue Commons Fund and would also encourage local fishers relative to foreign long-distance fleets.

Fish aggregating devices are intensifying overfishing and contributing to the 'race to extinction' of fish populations. Banning them for parts of the year, as the Pacific islands' Vessel Day Scheme does, is a sensible way of reducing bycatch and helping fish populations to reproduce. Although FADs reduce the cost and effort of fishing by reducing fuel costs and labour time and effort, they accelerate the taking of common pool resources, for which local commoners should be compensated. A high FAD Levy should be imposed on their use, while monitoring and regulation should be strengthened in the interest of conserving fish populations.

Next, there should be a Fish Levy on all commercial fish catches. All fishing vessels above twenty metres should be obliged to carry independent monitors on their fishing excursions, which would improve the recording of fish catches. There might be an argument for the cost of monitoring to be paid from the Fund, provided the revenue raised from penalties were also deposited in it. If the monitoring is suc-cessful in reducing overfishing or damaging activities, the commons will be strengthened. So, blue commoners will have a long-term interest in making the system work effect-ively. The Fish Levy should apply to all fishery vessels but should be higher on long-distance vessels allowed into a country's EEZ.

One particularly harmful consequence of industrial fish-ing in the waters of most fishing countries is the scourge of substantial bycatch, including sea mammals, turtles and sea-birds. Some analysts propose the payment of 'bycatch reduc-tion' subsidies.[35] But this could encourage taking bycatch, so as to reduce it later. A better policy would be a formal ban on deliberate bycatch coupled with a Bycatch Levy on incidental bycatch, with the revenue going into the Fund. Higher levies could be imposed on fishing companies using practices likely to result in bycatch such as shrimp trawls and tuna longlines, to incentivize a switch to other methods.[36]

Since bycatch is a renewable blue resource, part of the revenue from any levy should be used for renewing the marine life hurt by bycatch, ideally channelled to blue com-moner communities best able to achieve the reproduction objective. A group of US-based tuna companies has volun-tarily begun investing $1 a tonne of longline-caught tuna into community-based turtle conservation projects in the Pacific, with early positive and cost-effective outcomes for coastal communities as well as turtles.[37] And one study has suggest-ed that a 12% levy on the value of all tuna caught would pay for conserving 20–30% of the world's oceans,[38] though a levy designed to reduce bycatch directly would be preferable.

Next, a levy should be put on the damage imposed by industrial aquaculture firms on the environment and surrounding communities. Recall that up to 40% of the full cost of industrial salmon farming is not borne by the corporations, but by society. If that would result in higher prices for consumers, so be it. But such a levy would put pressure on companies to reduce those externalities. Meanwhile, it would contribute nicely to the Blue Commons Fund.

Moving into less familiar territory, noise pollution is now an acknowledged threat to ocean ecosystems, compounding the damage from overfishing, pollution and the climate crisis.[39] Human activity is causing a cacophony of noise under the sea surface from ship engines and propellers, the building and operation of oil rigs, prospecting for deep-sea mining, military sonar and seismic survey detonations, and the construction of vast wind farms. While more rigorous regulations are needed to limit noise in the sea, a Noise Pollution Levy should also be imposed as an incentive to find ways of reducing it.

And what about the skyline along the coast? Numerous beautiful seascapes are blighted by unsightly billboards and neon lights. While we might wish to regulate or ban them altogether, meanwhile they should be subject to levies. A Billboard Levy, based on size and location, would make a small contribution to the Fund's revenue and help to deter intrusive advertising.

Perhaps more controversial would be a Rentier Capitalism Levy. In the rentier capitalism era, almost all industries have become increasingly concentrated in the hands of a few major corporations. This has enabled them to increase the markup of prices over production costs and gain from economies of scale and scope. One study that looked at 70,000 firms across 134 countries estimated that average markups had risen by 50% between 1980 and 2016.[40]

The blue economy has seen extraordinary conglomeration. By 2021, globally, the ten largest corporations accounted for 93% of all revenue generated by cruise tourism, 85% of all revenue from container shipping, 82% from port activities, 67% from shipbuilding and repairs, 51% from offshore oil and gas, 48% from offshore wind, 18% from marine equipment and construction, and 15% from seafood.[41] Given the scale of the global seafood industry, even that last figure indicates massive corporate control.

Market concentration can be conceived as a negative externality similar to pollution. Companies do their utmost to maximize profits and shift costs and harms to others. These harms include higher prices paid by consumers, lower wages, and often loss of innovation. Thinking along those lines, a Market Concentration Levy would be analogous to an atmospheric pollution fee. A levy proportional to market share – starting, say, when a company captures 20% of a market – would be one way to do that.[42] Imposing a cost would raise a barrier to concentration and monopolization. Reduced concentration would mean less revenue for the Fund. But consumers and the market economy would gain.

Proposals by others for Commons Funds include a Common Heritage Fund for Future Generations, a single global fund which would be financed by a 1% import tax on the total value of world trade. The fund's capital would be used to support efforts to preserve the living conditions of future generations.[43] This proposal derives from one put forward by Nepal at the Geneva session of UNCLOS in 1978, to establish a fund for the 'equitable and graduated sharing of benefits' from mineral exploitation to benefit all countries, especially the poor and landlocked.[44] Nepal proposed a 15% tax on mineral extraction activities within EEZs, as well as distribution of royalties collected by the International Seabed Authority from extraction in the Area, the seabed beyond national jurisdiction.

Blue Commons Fund investment strategy

How should a Blue Commons Fund manage its finances? To respect the intergenerational equity principle, it must act as an investment fund trying to maintain the value of its capital. And it must respect commons-based principles if it is to be compatible with the blue commons.

The rules applied by the Norwegian Pension Fund Global are a good starting point. Answerable to the Ministry of Finance but governed independently, it is required to invest mainly in moderate-risk bonds and equities, and only in foreign assets, not domestic firms. Since 2007 it has increased the proportion of its portfolio invested in equities from 40% to 70%, becoming the largest owner of equities in the world. In 2019, it reported a 20% return, its second highest after 2009. Its outgoing chief executive said that Norway had moved from being 'an oil nation to an oil fund nation'.[45]

Similarly, a Blue Commons Fund should be separate from any branch of government, to insulate it from possible political pressure, especially to prevent fund resources being drawn down for current public spending. All such wealth funds should be assigned a straight financial objective: long-run maximization of risk-adjusted returns on invested capital. Fund managers should not be made responsible for other rules, which should be set by democratic processes outside the fund.

Again, the Norwegian Fund provides a model. The government sets ethical guidelines, which are endorsed by parliament. The Ministry of Finance appoints an independent five-member Council of Ethics, which can recommend exclusion of companies from the universe of stocks in which the Fund may invest. The criteria for exclusion include firms involved in the production of nuclear weapons and cluster bombs, those responsible for gross violations of human rights and those inflicting severe environmental damage. A list of excluded companies, and firms under observation, is published by Norway's central bank, the Fund's asset manager, which makes the final decision.

This governance structure raises concerns that could be more problematic elsewhere. It would be politically and democratically safer if parliament, rather than the Ministry of Finance, appointed the Council of Ethics. And if the central bank is the final arbiter of which companies are excluded, it becomes the de facto decision-maker on ethical matters better left to those responsible for ethical issues. There is also a potential conflict between maximizing returns and a responsible sustainable investment strategy. Norges Bank squares this circle by arguing that companies that violate human rights or damage the environment are not only unethical but unacceptably risky investments. It also sets out expectations for companies it invests in, on children's rights, climate change, water management, human rights, tax and transparency, anti-corruption and ocean conservation. And it is making investments in companies developing environmentally friendly technologies.

Still, the Fund has come in for criticism for maintaining investments in firms with dubious human rights or environmental records. A Blue Commons Fund should adhere more strictly to the public trust doctrine principle of a positive duty to protect the commons, by weighting investment towards ethical companies. While this could lower the overall return on investment, it would be less of a constraint as the fund grew. To guard against public pressure for higher short-term returns, a Blue Commons Fund should be constitutionally required to make investments that respect the common-wealth principles.

A capital fund investing in global equity markets might expect to earn an average annual rate of return of close to 7%. The Norwegian Fund has been earning an average of 6.5%, reduced to 4.7% net of management costs. Moreover, since a Commons Fund would have an assured flow of revenue from the various levies, this would lower the interest rate it would have to pay on any borrowing to invest in the international equity market. Borrowing at a low long-term interest rate, which in 2021 was close to zero for countries with high investment-grade ratings, would enable the Fund to achieve a return similar to that of the Norwegian Fund. Size matters, and the assured access to revenue from activities in the future would help stabilize the fund and strengthen its distributive capability.

Blue common dividends

> Whether believers or not, we are agreed today that the
> earth is essentially a shared inheritance, whose fruits are
> meant to benefit everyone.
> — Pope Francis, 2021

What should be done with the proceeds of the Blue Commons Fund? We should start by recognizing that, just as the wealth and income of all of us comes mainly from the common-wealth bequeathed by past generations, so the levies that go into the Commons Fund are derived from that common-wealth.

The Fund's first statutory responsibility should be to act as a steward or trustee to preserve the capital value of the resources, and do so in a way that respects the Hartwick Rule of Intergenerational Equity. It can make investments to achieve that aim, which should increase the Fund's capital value. It can then distribute the surplus as common dividends to the commoners deserving compensation for loss of the commons. The only equitable way to do that is via equal common dividends, paid as a basic income. This should become an economic right. Referring to the payments as common dividends has the advantage of suggesting a 'property right', rather than a transfer, which is more likely to win public acceptance. As a general rule, the rich do not like to argue against property rights.

The Fund should treat revenue from the common pool resources – its 'assets' – according to whether they count as exhaustible, renewable (replenishable) or non-exhaustible.

Extraction of exhaustible assets, such as oil or minerals, diminishes the capital value of a national asset. So, to respect the Hartwick Rule, only the annual net return on investment of revenue from exhaustible resources should be recycled as dividends, a rule the Norwegian Fund follows.

Fish and other marine life taken for consumption, for food or other purposes, are replenishable resources. The amount that can be distributed as dividends would then be the amount raised by whatever levy is imposed *minus* what is required to replenish and preserve the resource, respecting the precautionary principle in particular.

Finally, there are non-exhaustible resources, such as the air, wind and, in some places, water. In those cases, the full levy revenue could be distributed as dividends. In practice, the boundary between replenishable and non-exhaustible resources will often be blurred. If, for instance, a port pollutes the air and water used by commoners, there should be pollution levies on the owners and users of the port, and a regulatory obligation to rectify the damage. The one without the other would not be good enough.

What are the arguments for distributing the returns to Fund investments as equal common dividends? Taking the carbon levy as an example, research in the USA and elsewhere has shown that a carbon tax is a highly efficient way to curb greenhouse gas emissions. However, by itself it increases inequality because poorer people spend a higher proportion of their income on fuel. Recycling the revenue from a carbon levy in the form of equal dividends is the optimal way of making it progressive.[46] This is because richer people use more energy in absolute terms; the richest quintile of the population accounts for ten times as much carbon use as the poorest quintile. It has been estimated that the revenue from a carbon tax alone would be enough to pay a significant basic income to everybody.[47]

To take another example, most existing fishing quota systems are inequitable and defective. Those given a quota are effectively given a rental income that in principle belongs to every citizen equally. Thus Iceland's fishing law begins by stating, 'The exploitable marine stocks of the Icelandic fishing banks are the common property of the Icelandic nation.' If so, every Icelandic resident citizen should be treated as an equal beneficiary. It is not for the government to choose who should benefit more or less. The government is or should be the steward or trustee for current and future commoners.

Blue Commons Funds can be justified as instruments both of ecological justice and of common justice. Common pool resources, including marine life and ecosystems, do not belong to any individual and do not belong to *Homo sapiens*. If those resources are turned into private property, the beneficiaries should compensate not only all commoners but also nature itself. While part of the rent derived from taking from the commons should go to the commoners who have thereby been deprived of the revenue or capital value of the commons, some should also go towards renewing the value of the depleted asset/resource.

Moreover, Exclusive Economic Zones have converted over a third of the world's sea surface area into zones for privatization and profit-making. Ceasing to be 'the common heritage of humanity', EEZs were a huge deduction from what could have become the world's blue commons. As a matter of common justice, all commoners should receive an equal share of income gained from commercial use of whatever is treated as a resource in a country's EEZ.

A requirement to compensate for destructive activities does not mean they should be approved or given 'a licence to pollute'. There is also a danger that compensation payments could persuade locals to drop opposition to damaging projects. In Lamu, Kenya, a big port development will destroy traditional fishing grounds but the promise of cash payments in compensation has meant resistance has found little traction. A difficulty with a Blue Commons Fund partially financed from deep-sea mining is the compelling argument for leaving seabed mineral resources well alone. In addition, once allowed, today's commoners might press for rapid extraction to boost the Fund's coffers and pay-outs, negating the intergenerational equity principle.

It could be argued that Blue Commons Funds should only be financed from payments derived from renewables or sustainable uses of the blue commons, which leads back to the discussion about 'degrowth'. However, a ban on all mining is likely to be too purist for many countries, so a fallback position would be to insist on stringent conditions, including independent prior assessments of the social costs and benefits as well as the ecological ones.

Another issue relates to 'adjacency rights'. Should those living and working in communities adjacent to the sea receive more than others? They are more directly affected by commercial depletion of marine life, various forms of environmental pollution, disruption of community life and degradation of habitat. So there is a case for local commoners to benefit more than others from a Blue Commons Fund, if that can be done fairly and transparently.

A small example of how a commons dividend system could work relates to Korea's foundational ethos of *hongik ingan*, or spreading benefit by spreading community. It expresses a historically grounded wisdom that Koreans should be re-teaching the world in our era of unbridled individualism and consumption-driven notions of individual 'success'.

It conveys the sense of not just sharing in the benefits of production but sharing in the preservation and reproduction of community, social participation and relationships in and with nature. It captures the essence of the commons beautifully. And it relates to the deep understanding of the connectedness of humanity and nature, its inherent reciprocities and mutual dependencies first articulated by Alexander von Humboldt in the early nineteenth century.

The ethos of *hongik ingan* was severely tested by the Japanese occupation between 1910 and 1945, during which most land in village communities was effectively enclosed. Korea had a model of the commons stretching back into its history, the idea of *hyanghak* (village contracts) that subsumed individuals in their communities through assigned roles, without assigning absolute ownership. The Japanese occupiers destroyed those contracts but could not erase Korean history. What they did do, sadly, was set the scene for growing inequalities, individual greed and selfishness, and concentration of private wealth.

Now is the time to recover the ethos of *hongik ingan* and *hyanghak* in a synthesis based on reviving the commons as a societal ecological model. And, as the saying goes, 'every journey starts with a single step'. Take the experience of South

Korea's Janggo Island, a small island with a community of about 200 residents.[48] Its main product is the sea cucumber, considered a delicacy in China, but also popular throughout East Asia. In 1983, the village's newly elected head persuaded the residents to stop renting out the fishing grounds to fish farmers, who were paying a very low rent, and to reclaim the fishing grounds and the profits for the community.

In 1993 the island launched a dividend programme to share out equally all profits from the sea cucumbers. The community's common interest in the fishing grounds promptly improved the quality of management. By 2019, each household was receiving a basic income of eleven million won (about $10,000) a year for doing a minimal amount of commoning work in helping to harvest the sea cucumbers. As sea cucumbers grow on their own, residents need only sow the 'seeds' and then harvest them.

In addition, learning from the experience, the commoners have also come to share the income from collecting clams, a classic form of commoning practised in some other parts of the world. As a result, the household basic income has risen to twenty million won. The commons have been revived and there is stable income equality, unlike in other islands, where large income gaps exist between those employed in the aquaculture industry and those who are not.

This is a small, enlightened example of what a commons could be like, if only mechanisms for common security were adapted to local common pool resources. There is no reason why it could not be emulated on a much larger scale around the world.

*

The proposed Blue Commons Funds should have three distinct elements or objectives, following a famous rule of thumb stated by Jan Tinbergen, an early winner of the Nobel Prize in Economics, that the number of policy instruments should equal the number of policy objectives. Its fundraising should aim to reverse the loss of the commons while improving the environment, which should determine what levies should be introduced. Its investment policy should aim to promote ecologically sustainable development. And its distributional policy should aim to reduce inequality and increase basic economic security. In addition, blue common dividends would be an incentive to preserve the commons as commons, by showing that this would bring material benefits as well as social and environmental ones.

The world will not make progress in protecting the blue economy or the blue commons through endless international summits and conferences, where governments sign up to platitudes and high-sounding commitments. Action is needed. Governments and organizations will only change course if we put more pressure on them to do so. Of course, extra pressure by itself will not suffice either. Real progress will come only if we can agree on a vision of a thrivable blue commons, a viable alternative to a growth-oriented way of living, one that offers a prescription for reversing the rush to extinction guaranteed by rentier capitalism in the sea as on the land. A blue commons is feasible, if there is an income distribution system to ensure that those in it have living standards that are good, dignifying and emancipatory. We can recover abundance and ecological balance. But there is no time to lose.

Notes

PREFACE

1. For a magisterial account, see D. Abulafia, *The Boundless Sea: A Human History of the Oceans* (London: Allen Lane, 2019).

2. 'Ocean benefits increasingly undermined by human activity, UN assessment reveals', UN News, 25 April 2021.

3. J. Vidal, '"Tip of the iceberg": Is our destruction of nature responsible for Covid-19?', *Guardian*, 18 March 2020; H. Watts, '"Promiscuous treatment of nature" will lead to more pandemics – scientists', *Guardian*, 7 May 2020.

4. 'Factsheet: People and oceans', The Ocean Conference, United Nations, New York, 5–9 June 2017.

5. European Environment Agency, *State of Nature in the EU: Results from Reporting Under the Nature Directives 2013–2018*, EEA report no.10/2020 (Luxembourg: Publications Office of the European Union, 2020).

6. F. Gell, 'The Blue Planet effect: The plastic revolution is just the start', *Guardian*, 25 March 2019.

7. In the USA, the *Blue Planet* and other BBC documentaries are far less popular than elsewhere. According to Alex Barasch, Attenborough is considered too boring, and his documentaries are dubbed over by celebrities. The most popular US wildlife documentaries are typically anthropomorphic, depicting animals with human-like personalities. US wildlife documentaries, such as *March of the Penguins*, reinforce conservative Christian values, rather than raise concern about the negative impact of human industry or climate change. A. Barasch, 'Blue Planet II captivated audiences abroad. Why didn't America care?', *Slate*, 13 March 2018.

8. S. Jiang, 'UK's Theresa May tries box-set diplomacy on China's Xi Jinping with "Blue Planet II"', CNN, 1 February 2018.

9. K. McVeigh, 'Public grasps threat to ocean even as leaders fail to meet targets, poll finds', *Guardian*, 8 June 2021.

10. G. Standing, *Plunder of the Commons: A Manifesto for Sharing Public Wealth* (London: Penguin, 2019).

11. 'Rachel Carson biography', US Fish and Wildlife Service, available at: https://www.fws.gov/refuge/rachel_carson/about/rachelcarson.html

12. R. Carson, *The Sea around Us* (Oxford: Oxford University Press, 1951), pp.121–2.

CHAPTER 1: WHO OWNS THE SEA?

1. H. Grotius, *The Freedom of the Seas*, translated from the revised Latin edition of 1633 by Ralph Van Deman Magoffin (New York: Oxford University Press, 1916), p.21.

2. S. Macinko and D.W. Bromley, 'Property and fisheries for the twenty-first century: Seeking coherence from legal and economic doctrine', *Vermont Law Review* 26, 2016, pp.623–61.

3. P. Holm, 'World War II and the "Great Acceleration" of North Atlantic fisheries', *Global Environment* 10(10), January 2012, pp.66–91.

4. L. Nahuelhual et al., 'Is there a blue transition underway?', *Fish and Fisheries*, 31 January 2019, p.4 [pp.1–12].

5. There was a poignant aftermath of the cod wars in Britain. In 2012, the British government gave £1,000 compensatory payments to 2,500 fishermen who had lost their jobs as a result of the agreements, mainly in Grimsby, Hull and Fleetwood.

6. United Nations, *United Nations Convention on the Law of the Sea* (New York: UN Division for Ocean Affairs and the Law of the Sea, 1982), p.43.

7. Address by Arvid Pardo to the First Committee, 1515th Meeting, UN General Assembly 22nd Session, New York, 1 November 1967.

8. A. Vanaik, 'The UNCLOS isn't perfect, and it's time we acknowledge that', *The Wire*, 27 July 2020.

9. FAO, *The State of World Fisheries and Aquaculture 2020: Sustainability in Action* (Rome: Food and Agriculture Organization, 2020).

10. 'Felonious fishing: The outlaw sea', *The Economist*, 24 October 2020, pp.52–4.

11. V.W.Y Lam et al., 'Projected change in global fisheries revenues under climate change', *Scientific Reports* 6, Article 32607, 2016.

12. FAO, 2020, op. cit.

13. D. Pauly and D. Zeller, 'Catch reconstructions reveal that global marine fisheries catches are higher than reported and declining', *Nature Communications* 7, Article 10244, January 2016.

14. C. Roberts, *The Unnatural History of the Sea – The Past and Future of Humanity and Fishing* (London: Island Press, 2007), p.128.

15. R. Myers and B. Worm, 'Extinction, survival or recovery of large predatory fishes', *Proceedings of the National Association of Sciences* 360, 2005, pp.13–20.

16. G. Readfearn, 'Will sharks survive? Scientists fear for ocean's apex predators without more protection', *Guardian*, 30 January 2021.

17. M. Taylor, 'Krill fishing poses serious threat to Antarctic ecosystem, report warns', *Guardian*, 13 March 2018.

18. M.W. Beck et al., 'Oyster reefs at risk and recommendations for conservation, restoration, and management', *BioScience* 61(2), February 2011, pp.107–116.

19. T. van Dooren, *Flight Ways: Life and Loss at the Edge of Extinction* (New York: Columbia University Press, 2014).

20. S. Altherr and N. Hodgins, *Small Cetaceans, Big Problems: A Global Review of the Impacts of Hunting on Small Whales, Dolphins and Porpoises* (Pro Wildlife (Germany), Animal Welfare Institute (Washington, DC), Whale and Dolphin Conservation (UK), 2018).

21. N. Hodgins, 'Small cetaceans, big problems', *Ecological Citizen* 3(2), 27 November 2019.

22. O. Millman, 'North Atlantic whales shrinking due to fishing gear entanglements', *Guardian*, 3 June 2021.

23. Myers and Worm, 'Extinction, survival or recovery of large predatory fishes', 2005, op. cit.

24. E. Anyanova, 'Rescuing the inexhaustible: The issue of fisheries subsidies in the international trade policy', *Journal of International Commercial Law and Technology* 3(3), 2008, pp.147–56.

25. T. Danson, *Oceans: Our Endangered Ocean and What We Can Do About It* (New York: Rodale, 2011), p.104.

26. K.J. Mengerink et al., 'A call for deep-ocean stewardship', *Science* 344(6185), 16 May 2014, pp.696–8.

27. FAO, *The State of World Fisheries and Aquaculture 2020*, 2020, op. cit.

28. I. Urbina, *The Outlaw Ocean: Journeys Across the Last Untamed Frontier* (New York: Knopf, 2019), p.65.

29. Danson, *Oceans*, 2011, op. cit., p.82.

30. T.J. Pitcher and W.W.L. Cheung, 'Fisheries: Hope or despair?', *Marine Pollution Bulletin* 74, 2013, p.510 [pp.506–16]; D.J. McCauley et al., 'Marine defaunation: Animal loss in the global ocean', *Science* 347(6219), 16 January 2015, 1255641.

31. WWF, *The World's Forgotten Fishes* (Gland, Switzerland: WWF International, 2021).

32. World Fish Migration Foundation, *Living Planet Index for Migratory Freshwater Fish – Technical Report* (Groningen, The Netherlands: World Fish Migration Foundation, 2020); D. Carrington, 'Migratory river fish populations plunge 76% in past 50 years', *Guardian*, 27 July 2020.

33. R. Diaz, 'World Fish Migration Day 2020', World Association of Zoos and Aquariums (WAZA), 18 February 2020.

34. P.H. Tyedmers, R. Watson and D. Pauly, 'Fueling global fishing fleets', *Ambio* 34(8), December 2005, pp.634–8.

35. J.D.K. Wilson, *Fuel and financial savings for operation of small-scale fishing vessels*, FAO Fisheries Technical Paper 383 (Rome: Food and Agriculture Organization, 1999).

36. G. Dyer, 'Chinese algae spreads to tourist resorts', *Financial Times*, 12 July 2008.

37. J. Hance, 'Lethal algae blooms – an ecosystem out of balance', *Guardian*, 4 January 2020.

38. See, for example, S.K. Moore et al., 'An index of fisheries closures due to harmful algal blooms and a framework for identifying vulnerable fishing communities', *Marine Policy* 110, December 2019, 103543.

39. K.S. Jayaraman, 'Dead zone found in Bay of Bengal', *Nature India*, December 2016.

40. J. Abraham, 'Our oceans broke heat records in 2018 and the consequences are catastrophic', *Guardian*, 16 January 2020.

41. K. Evelyn, 'Huge "hot blob" in Pacific Ocean killed nearly a million seabirds', *Guardian*, 16 January 2020.

42. 'The oceans are increasingly bearing the brunt of global warming', *The Economist*, 26 September 2019.

43. R. Syal, 'Licence to krill: The destructive demand for a "better" fish oil', *Guardian*, 7 September 2021.

44. R. Unsworth et al., 'Seagrass meadows shrank by 92% in UK waters – restoring them could absorb carbon emissions and boost fish', The Conversation, 4 March 2021.

45. 'Seagrass – secret weapon in the fight against global heating', United Nations Environment Programme, 1 November 2019.

46. M.D. Aronsohn, 'How will the ocean carbon cycle evolve in the future? New project aims to find out', Columbia Climate School, 28 September 2020.

47. On the emissions, see J.-P. Gattuso et al., 'Contrasting futures for ocean and society from different anthropogenic CO_2 emissions scenarios', *Science* 349(6243), 3 July 2015.

48. K.J. Kroeker et al., 'Impacts of ocean acidification on marine organisms: Quantifying sensitivities and interaction with warming', *Global Change Biology* 19, 2013, pp.1884–96; A. Mitchell, D.J. Booth and I. Nagelkerken, 'Ocean warming and acidification degrade shoaling performance and lateralization of novel tropical-temperate fish shoals', *Global Change Biology*, 17 December 2021.

49. D. Narita and K. Rehdanz, 'Economic impact of ocean acidification on shellfish production in Europe', *Journal of Environmental Planning and Management* 60, 2017, pp.500–518.

50. Pitcher and Cheung, 'Fisheries: Hope or despair?', 2013, op. cit.

51. R.A. Watson et al., 'Global marine yield halved as fishing intensity redoubles', *Fish and Fisheries* 14(4), December 2013, pp.493–503.

52. IPCC, *Special Report on the Ocean and Cryosphere in a Changing Climate* (Geneva: Intergovernmental Panel on Climate Change, 2019).

53. M.A. Cisneros-Mata et al., 'Fisheries governance in the face of climate change: Assessment of policy reform implications for Mexican fisheries', *PLoS One* 14(10), 2 October 2019.

54. V.W.Y. Lam et al., 'Projected change in global fisheries revenues under climate change', *Scientific Reports* 6, Article 32607, 2016.

55. C.D. Golden et al., 'Fall in fish catch threatens human health', *Nature* 534(7607), 16 June 2016, pp.317–20.

56. A. Armand and I.K. Taveras, 'Harming the ocean impacts children in low- and middle-income countries', CEPR, 11 April 2021.

57. N. Melia, K. Haines and E. Hawkins, *Future of the Sea: Implications from Opening Arctic Sea Routes* (London: Government Office for Science, July 2017).

58. P. Ryan et al., 'Rapid increase in Asian bottles in the South Atlantic Ocean indicates major debris inputs from ships', *Proceedings of the National Academy of Sciences of the USA* 116(42), 15 October 2019, pp.20892–97. See also 'Marine pollution: A message in some bottles', *The Economist*, 5 October 2019, p.87.

59. R. Thomas, 'Plastic rafting: The invasive species hitching a ride on ocean litter', *Guardian*, 14 June 2021.

60. F. Harvey, 'Plastic waste entering oceans expected to triple in 20 years', *Guardian*, 23 July 2020.

61. F. Harvey, 'Plastic pollution in Atlantic at least 10 times worse than thought', *Guardian*, 18 August 2020.

62. Harvey, 'Plastic waste entering oceans expected to triple in 20 years', 2020, op. cit.

63. S. Casey, 'Garbage in, garbage out', *Conservation Magazine* 11, 2010, pp.13–19.

64. P. Greenfield, 'Call for drone users and jetskiers to keep away from marine wildlife', *Guardian*, 31 December 2019.

65. C. Pekow, 'While the rest of the world tackles plastics disposal, the US resists', Mongabay, 18 May 2021.

66. C. Roberts, *Reef Life: An Underwater Memoir* (London: Profile Books, 2019).

67. IPCC, *Special Report on the Ocean and Cryosphere in a Changing Climate*, 2019, op. cit.

68. E. Crist, 'Restoring the living ocean: The time is now', *Ecological Citizen* 3(Supplement A), 12 November 2019, p.29.

69. G. Vince, 'Why there is hope that the world's coral reefs can be saved', *The Observer*, 18 October 2020.

70. Australian law states that there must be conclusive scientific evidence that a pesticide is unsafe before it can be removed from use. Other countries stipulate that a pesticide must be proven safe before it can be sold. J. Brodie and M. Landos, 'Pesticides in Queensland and Great Barrier Reef waterways – potential impacts on aquatic ecosystems and the failure of national management', *Estuarine, Coastal and Shelf Science* 230, 2019, 106447.

71. 'No longer in the pink', *The Economist*, 26 October 2019, p.16.

72. 'Name that dune', *The Economist*, 14 September 2019, p.71.

73. M. Marschke et al., 'Roving bandits and looted coastlines: How the global appetite for sand is fuelling a crisis', The Conversation, 3 May 2020.

74. S. Knott, 'Ghana working to save eroding coastlines', VOANEWS.com, 12 October 2020.

75. E. Mcleod et al., 'A blueprint for blue carbon: Toward an improved understanding of the role of vegetated coastal habitats in sequestering CO_2', *Frontiers in Ecology and the Environment* 9(552), 2011, pp.552–60.

76. 'Save the swamp', *The Economist*, 25 May 2019, p.43.

77. G.V. Frisk, 'Noiseonomics: The relationship between ambient noise levels in the sea and global economic trends', *Scientific Reports* 2, Article 437, 2012; A. Standing, 'Big scale mining vs small-scale fishing: Concerns from East Africa', CAPE/CFFA, 23 January 2015.

78. A.D. Hawkins and M. Picciulin, 'The importance of underwater sounds to gadoid fishes', *Journal of the Acoustical Society of America* 146(3536), 2019.

79. 'Does military sonar kill marine wildlife?', *Scientific American*, 10 June 2009.

80. Local Peace Economy, 'Whales could save the world's climate, unless the military destroys them first', Counterpunch, 16 December 2021.

81. H. Dempsey and A. Kazmin, 'Sri Lanka faces ecological disaster as burning container ship starts to sink', *Financial Times*, 2 June 2021.

82. H. Partow et al., *X-Press Pearl Maritime Disaster – Sri Lanka*, Report of the UN Environmental Advisory Mission (UNEP – UN Environment Programme, and OCHA – UN Office for the Coordination of Humanitarian Affairs, July 2021).

83. Telesetsky, 2014, op. cit., p.953.

84. This section draws from an excellent study by Guillaume Vuillemey. G. Vuillemey, 'Evading corporate responsibilities: Evidence from the shipping industry', CEPR Discussion Paper No. DP15291, September 2020.

85. World Bank, *Container Terminal Concessions – Making the Most of Ports in West Africa* (Washington, DC: World Bank, 16 June 2017).

86. 'Tower grab', *The Economist*, 31 August 2019, p.58.

87. E. Apostolopoulou, 'How China's Belt and Road Initiative is changing cities – and threatening communities', The Conversation, 2 February 2021.

88. See, for example, P. Mason, *Tourism Impacts, Planning and Management* (Oxford, UK: Butterworth-Heinemann, 2003).

89. A. Giuffrida, 'Italy bans cruise ships from Venice lagoon after Unesco threat', *Guardian*, 13 July 2021.

90. T. McVeigh, 'As British tourists take to the seas, giant cruise ship flotillas spread pollution misery', *The Observer*, 8 January 2017, p.10.

91. A. Chrisafis, '"I don't want ships to kill me": Marseille fights cruise liner pollution', *Guardian*, 6 July 2018.

92. G.P. Gobbi, L. Di Liberto and F. Barnaba, 'Impact of port emissions on EU-regulated and non-regulated air quality indicators: The case of Civitavecchia (Italy)', *Science of the Total Environment* 719, 1 June 2020, 134984.

93. F. Harvey, 'Campaigners criticise global deal on carbon emissions from shipping', *Guardian*, 23 October 2020.

94. Speech on 8 August 1973, published as A. Pardo, 'A statement on the future Law of the Sea in light of current trends in negotiations', *Ocean Development and International Law* 1(4), 1974, p.324. Pardo actually said: 'There would still exist some marine plants, some floating seaweed, a few migratory species of fish and sea mammals and some manganese nodules outside the area under coastal State sovereignty of exclusive jurisdiction.'

95. G. Hardin, 'The tragedy of the commons', *Science* 162(3859), December 1968, pp.1243–48.

96. R. Hannesson, *The Privatization of the Oceans* (Cambridge, MA: MIT Press, 2004), p.24.

97. L.A. Nielsen, 'The evolution of fisheries management', MFR Paper 1226, December 1976, p.15 [pp.15–23].

98. Crist, 2019, op. cit., p.34.

99. M. Kurlansky, *World Without Fish: How Kids Can Help Save the Oceans* (New York: Workman, 2011).

CHAPTER 2: THE SIRENS OF 'BLUE GROWTH'

1. The structures and mechanisms of rentier capitalism are elaborated elsewhere. G. Standing, *The Corruption of Capitalism: Why Rentiers Thrive and Work Does Not Pay* (London: Biteback, 2016).

2. E. Griswold, 'How "Silent Spring" ignited the environmental movement', *New York Times Magazine*, 21 September 2012.

3. P.R. Ehrlich, *The Population Bomb* (Sierra Club & Ballantine Books, 1968).

4. G. Hardin, 'The tragedy of the commons', *Science* 162(3859), December 1968, pp.1243–48.

5. D.H. Meadows, D.L Meadows, J. Randers and W.W. Behrens, *The Limits to Growth* (Universe, 1972).

6. US Congress, *Energy Reorganization Act of 1973: Hearings, Ninety-third Congress, First Session, on H.R. 11510* (US Government Printing Office, 1973), p. 248.

7. L. Tulloch and D. Neilson, 'The neoliberalisation of sustainability', Citizenship, March 2014.

8. President Bill Clinton later signed the Convention on Biological Diversity, but it was never ratified by the US Senate. The USA eventually joined the Desertification Convention in 2001.

9. B. Unmüßig, W. Sachs and T. Fatheuer, *Critique of the Green Economy: Toward Social and Environmental Equity*, Vol. 22 (English edition) in the Publication Series on Ecology edited by the Heinrich Böll Foundation, 2012.

10. W. Sachs, 'The sustainability debate in the security age', *Development* 4, 1995, p.28.

11. Reported in O. Tickell and N. Hildyard, 'Green dollars, green menace', *The Ecologist* 22(3), May/June 1992.

12. Lutzenberger was already in official hot water after describing as 'totally insane' a leaked internal note by Larry Summers, then chief economist

at the World Bank, suggesting that it made economic sense to dump toxic waste in poor countries because lives there were valued more cheaply. Summers claimed the memorandum was meant to be 'ironic'.

13. Tickell and Hildyard, 1992, op. cit.

14. Schmidheiny inherited an asbestos company, Eternit, from his father's industrial empire. He began to phase out the use of asbestos in favour of other fibres but sold his shares and exited the company in 1989.

15. S. Schmidheiny, *Changing Course: A Global Business Perspective on Development and the Environment* (MIT Press, 1992).

16. P. Chatterjee and M. Finger, *The Earth Brokers: Power, Politics and World Development* (Routledge, 1994).

17. Cited by P. Doran, '"The Earth Summit" (UNCED): Ecology as spectacle', *Paradigms* 7(1), September 1993, p.57.

18. M. Finger, 'How to read the UNCED process', *Eco-Currents* 2(2), May 1992.

19. P. Dauvergne and G. LeBaron (eds), *Protest Inc: The Corporatisation of Activism* (Bristol: Polity Press, 2014).

20. M. Strong, *Where on Earth Are We Going?* (Texere, 2001).

21. See, for example, D. Cassimon, M. Prowse and D. Essers, *The pitfalls and potential of debt-for-nature swaps: A US-Indonesian case study*, IOB Working Papers 2009.07, Institute of Development Policy (IOB), University of Antwerp, 2009.

22. For an early critique, see G. Standing, *Decent Workplaces, Self-Regulation and CSR: From Puff to Stuff?*, DESA Working Paper No.62 (New York: UN Department of Economic and Social Affairs, 2007)

23. M. Khor, 'The battle for WSSD's endorsement', Global Policy Forum, 2 October 2002.

24. UNEP, *Towards a Green Economy: Pathways to Sustainable Development and Poverty Eradication – A Synthesis for Policy Makers*, (Nairobi and Geneva: United Nations Environment Programme, 2011), p.10.

25. P. Krugman, 'Errors and emissions', *New York Times*, 18 September 2014.

26. UNEP, *Green Economy in a Blue World: Synthesis Report* (Nairobi and Geneva: United Nations Environment Programme, 2012).

27. European Environment Agency, *Blue Growth Opportunities for Marine and Maritime Sustainable Growth*, COM (2012) Final (Brussels: European Commission, 2012).

28. UNEP, 'Blue Economy Concept Paper', United Nations, mimeo, 2012.

29. See, for instance, FAO, 'FAO contribution to part 1 of the report of the secretary-general on oceans and the law of the sea', Food and Agriculture

Organization, 28 January 2015; World Bank, *Oceans, Fisheries and Coastal Economies* (Washington, DC: World Bank, 2016).

30. Cited in M. Barbesgaard, 'Blue growth: Saviour or ocean grabbing?', *Journal of Peasant Studies* 45(1), 2018, pp.130–49.

31. G. Monbiot, 'Johnson's pledges on the environment are worthless. Worse is how cynical they are', *Guardian*, 30 September 2020.

32. See, for instance, K. Johnson and G. Dalton, *Building Industries at Sea: 'Blue Growth' and the New Maritime Economy* (River Publishers, 2018); UNECA, *Africa's Blue Economy: A Policy Handbook* (Addis Ababa: UN Economic Commission for Africa, 2016); O. Hoegh-Guldberg et al., *Reviving the Ocean Economy: The Case for Action - 2015* (Gland, Switzerland: WWF, 2015); P.G. Patil, J. Virdin, S.M. Diez, J. Roberts and A. Singh, *Toward a Blue Economy: A Promise for Sustainable Growth in the Caribbean* (Washington, DC: World Bank, 2016).

33. B.M. Campbell et al., 'Reducing risks to food security from climate change', *Global Food Security* 11, 2016, pp.34–43.

34. European Environment Agency, 2012, op. cit.

35. Patil et al., 2016, op. cit.

36. OECD, *The Ocean Economy in 2030* (Paris: OECD, 2016).

37. O. Hoegh-Guldberg et al., 2015, op. cit.

38. UNCTAD, *The Oceans Economy: Opportunities and Challenges for Small Island Developing States* (Geneva: UNCTAD, 2014).

39. Smithers, *The Future of Marine Biotechnology to 2025* (Akron, Ohio: Smithers, 2015).

40. African Union, *Agenda 2063: The Africa We Want* (Addis Ababa: African Union Commission, 2015).

41. African Union, *Africa Blue Economy Strategy* (Nairobi: African Union, 2019).

42. W.S. Jevons, *The Coal Question: An Enquiry Concerning the Progress of the Nation, and the Probable Exhaustion of Our Coal-Mines* (London: Macmillan, 1865); B. Czech, 'If Rome is burning, why are we fiddling?', *Conservation Biology* 20(6), 2006, pp.1563–65.

43. C.E. Boyd, 'Assessing the carbon footprint of agriculture', Global Aquaculture Alliance, 2 September 2013.

44. M. Deiye, A. Herman and T. Kula, 'Seabed mining in the Pacific is environmentally, economically vital', Press release, 8 June 2020, republished at https://www.opesoceani.com/

45. C.M. Duarte, I.J. Losada, I.E. Hendriks, I. Mazarrasa and N. Marbà, 'The role of coastal plant communities for climate change mitigation and adaptation', *Nature Climate Change* 3, 2013, pp.961–68.

46. R. Chami, T. Cosimano, C. Fullenkamp and S. Oztosun, 'Nature's solution to climate change', *Finance & Development* 56(4), December 2019.

47. R. Arnason, 'Property rights as a means of economic organization', in R. Shotton (ed.), *Use of Property Rights in Fisheries Management: Proceedings of the FishRights99 Conference*, FAO Fisheries Technical Paper 404/1 (Rome: Food and Agriculture Organization, 2000), p.14.

48. H.S. Gordon, 'The economic theory of a common property resource: The fishery', *Journal of Political Economy* 62(2), 1954, pp.124–42; A. Scott, 'The fishery: The objectives of sole ownership', *Journal of Political Economy* 63(2), 1955, pp.116–54; Hardin, 1968, op. cit. Hardin's article has become the standard reference because it was published at a time when the ideology of neoliberalism was in ascendancy and libertarians were searching for rationales in favour of privatization.

49. Gordon, 1954, op. cit., p.124.

50. P.A. Neher, R. Arnason and N. Mollett (eds), *Rights Based Fishing* (Dordrecht: Kluwer Academic Publishers, 1989), p.3.

51. World Bank, *The Sunken Billions: The Economic Justification for Fisheries Reform* (Washington, DC: World Bank, 2009).

52. Ibid., p.50.

53. World Bank, *Agriculture for Development: World Development Report 2008* (Washington, DC: World Bank, 2007), p.138.

54. *Principles for Responsible Agricultural Investment that Respects Rights, Livelihoods and Resources* (FAO, IFAD, UNCTAD and World Bank, 2010).

55. O. de Schutter, 'How not to think of land grabbing: Three critiques of large-scale investments in farmland', *Journal of Peasant Studies* 38, 2011, p.275 [pp.249–79].

56. FIAN International, Focus on the Global South, Rede Social and La Via Campesina, 'Why we oppose the principles for responsible agricultural investment', viacapesina.org, October 2010.

57. FAO, *Voluntary Guidelines on the Responsible Governance of Tenure of Land, Fisheries and Forests in the Context of National Food Security* (Rome: Food and Agriculture Organization, 2012).

58. World Bank, *Rising Global Interest in Farmland: Can It Yield Sustainable and Equitable Benefits?* (Washington, DC: World Bank, 2011).

59. W. Anseeuw and G.M Baldinelli, *Uneven Ground: Land Inequality at the Heart of Unequal Societies* (International Land Coalition and Oxfam, 2020).

60. European Commission, WWF, International Sustainability Unit and European Investment Bank, *Introducing the Sustainable Blue Economy Finance Principles*, 2018.

61. G.A. Epstein (ed.), *Financialization and the World Economy* (Cheltenham, UK: Edward Elgar, 2005), p.3.

62. Office for National Statistics, 'Transforming the UK financial accounts: Flow of funds', ONS, 26 November 2019.

63. See, for example, C. Arsenault, 'Financial speculation on food hurting world's hungry – UN', Reuters, 8 June 2015.

64. N. Boston, 'Trading the oceans: The brave "new" world of seafood futures contracts', *Ocean and Coastal Law Journal* 18(2), 2012, Article 4.

65. International Marine Mitigation Bank website: http://www.immb.us

66. R. Watson, 'The world's banks must start to value nature and stop paying for its destruction', *Guardian*, 28 October 2020.

67. P. Dasgupta, *The Economics of Biodiversity: The Dasgupta Review* (London: HM Treasury, February 2021).

68. P. Dasgupta, 'The nature of economic development and the economic development of nature', *Economic and Political Weekly* 48(51), 21 December 2013.

69. As discussed by David Pilling in D. Pilling, *The Growth Delusion: The Wealth and Well-Being of Nations* (London: Bloomsbury, 2018), pp.221–26.

70. World Bank, *The Changing Wealth of Nations: Measuring Sustainable Development in the New Millennium* (Washington, DC: World Bank, 2011).

71. G.-M. Lange, Q. Wodon and K. Carey, *The Changing Wealth of Nations: Building a Sustainable Future* (Washington, DC: World Bank, 2018), p.4.

72. MEA, *Ecosystems and Human Well-Being* (Washington, DC: Millennium Ecosystem Assessment, 2005).

73. S. Engel, S. Pagiola and S. Wunder, 'Designing payments for environmental services in theory and practice: An overview of the issues', *Ecological Economics* 65(4), May 2008, p.664.

74. R. Muradian et al., 'Payments for ecosystem services and the fatal attraction of win-win solutions', *Conservation Letters*, 2013, pp.1–6.

75. UNEP, 2011, op. cit., p.4.

76. UNCTAD, *World Investment Report: Investing in the SDGs: An Action Plan* (Geneva: UNCTAD, 2014).

77. F. Huwyler, J. Käppeli, K. Serafimova, E. Swanson and J. Tobin, *Conservation Finance: Moving Beyond Donor Funding Toward an Investor-Driven Approach* (Credit Suisse, WWF and McKinsey & Company, 2014).

78. UNEP, 2011, op. cit.

79. Environmental Defense Fund, The Prince of Wales' International Sustainability Unit and 50in10, *Towards Investment in Sustainable Fisheries: A Framework for Financing the Transition* (2014).

80. Encourage Capital, *Investing for Sustainable Global Fisheries* (Encourage Capital, Bloomberg Philanthropies and the Rockefeller Foundation, 2016).

81. Credit Suisse, 'The tides are turning, why the blue economy matters', Credit Suisse, 19 June 2018.

82. S. Cunningham and A.E. Neiland, 'African fisheries development aid', in D.R. Leal (ed.), *The Political Economy of Natural Resource Use: Lessons for Fisheries Reform* (Washington, DC: World Bank, 2010).

83. Blended Finance Taskforce, 'Mobilising capital for the oceans: Investor round-table at the WB/IMF Spring Meetings with Rare and the IDB', 1 May 2019.

84. Climate Bonds Initiative, *2019 Green Bond Market Summary*, Climate Bonds Initiative, February 2020.

85. Climate Bonds Initiative, *Bonds and Climate Change: The State of the Market 2017*, Climate Bonds Initiative, 2017, p.3.

86. A technical guideline for blue bonds has been drawn up by N. Roth, T. Thiele and M. von Unger in *Blue Bonds: Financing Resilience of Coastal Ecosystems* (Gland, Switzerland: International Union for the Conservation of Nature, March 2019).

87. See Mowi, 'First ever green bond issue from a seafood company', Press release, 24 January 2020.

88. See World Bank, 'World Bank and Credit Suisse partner to focus attention on sustainable use of oceans and coastal areas – the "Blue Economy"', Press release, 21 November 2019.

89. 'Debt relief for dolphins', *The Economist*, 7 September 2016.

90. The Nature Conservancy, 'Blue Bonds: An audacious plan to save the world's oceans', nature.org, 15 April 2019.

91. 'Belize shows the growing potential of debt-for-nature swaps', *The Economist*, 13 November 2021.

92. A. Valencia, 'Ecuador to expand Galapagos marine reserve, president says', Reuters, 1 November 2021.

93. J.-B. Jouffray et al., 'The Blue Acceleration: The trajectory of human expansion into the ocean', *One Earth* 2, 24 January 2020.

CHAPTER 3: THE BLUE COMMONS

1. P.T. Carbajal, S. Troncoso and A.M. Utratel, 'Commons: How the art of co-operation is the only way out of this crisis', Greenpeace International, 20 May 2020.

2. M. Pirie, 'Catch of today: A ten point plan for British fishing', Adam Smith Institute Briefing Paper, August 2016.

3. P. Booth, 'A post-Brexit alternative to the Common Fisheries Policy', Institute for Economic Affairs, 15 August 2016.

4. For a discussion of the evolution of this rule, see G. Standing, *Plunder of the Commons: A Manifesto for Sharing Public Wealth* (London: Penguin, 2019), pp.40–42.

5. Y. Benkler and H. Nissenbaum, 'Commons-based peer production and virtue', *Journal of Political Philosophy* 14(4), 2006, pp.394–419.

6. B. Berg, '"They're owned by all Alaskans": Salmon free-for-all draws throngs', *Guardian*, 20 August 2020.

7. For a first-hand account, see A. Weymouth, *Kings of the Yukon: An Alaskan River Journey* (London: Penguin, 2019).

8. A. Matel, '"Bringing beaches back to life": The First Nations restoring ancient clam gardens', *Guardian*, 23 September 2020.

9. S. Harper et al., 'Women and fisheries: Contribution to food security and local economies', *Marine Policy* 39(1), May 2013, pp.56–63; S. Harper, 'Contributions by women to fisheries economies', *Coastal Management* 45(2), February 2017, pp.91–106; M.D. Chapman, 'Women's fishing in Oceania', *Human Ecology* 15, 1987, pp.267–88; N. Weeratunge, K.A. Snyder and C.P. Sze, 'Gleaner, fisher, trader, processor: Understanding gendered employment in fisheries and aquaculture', *Fish and Fisheries* 11(4), December 2010, pp.405–20.

10. D. McGregor, 'Coming full circle: Indigenous knowledge, environment, and our future', *American Indian Quarterly* 28(3), 2004, pp.385–410.

11. K.L. Thompson, T.C. Lantz and N.C. Ban, 'A review of indigenous knowledge and participation in environmental monitoring', *Ecology and Society* 25(2): 10, 2020.

12. A. Longhurst, *The Mismanagement of Marine Fisheries* (Cambridge: Cambridge University Press, 2010).

13. The idea was addressed in a famous book by biologist and pioneer of biodiversity Edward Wilson, which includes a short devastating criticism of modern economics and its fetish with growth. E.O. Wilson, *Consilience: The Unity of Knowledge* (London: Little Brown, 1998), pp.324–6.

14. A.J. Reid et al., '"Two-Eyed Seeing": An indigenous framework to transform fisheries research and management', *Fish and Fisheries* 22(2), March 2021, pp.243–61.

15. Bessen Consulting Services, 'Evaluation of investment in the Dugong and Marine Turtle Project: Towards community capacity and biodiversity outcomes', Australian Government Land and Coasts Team and North Australian Indigenous Land and Sea Management Alliance (NAILSMA), December 2008.

16. C.R. Menzies and C.F. Butler, 'Returning to selective fishing through indigenous fisheries knowledge: The example of K'moda, Gitxaała Territory', *American Indian Quarterly* 31(3), 2007, pp.441–64.

17. S.N. Sethi, J.K. Sundaray, A. Panigrahi and S. Chand, 'Prediction and management of natural disasters through indigenous technical knowledge, with special reference to fisheries', *Indian Journal of Traditional Knowledge* 10(1), January 2011, pp.167–72; L. Hiwasaki, E. Luna and S.R. Syamsidik, *Local and Indigenous Knowledge for Community Resilience: Hydro-meteorological Disaster Risk Reduction and Climate Change Adaptation in Coastal and Small Island Communities* (Jakarta: UNESCO, 2014).

18. F. Berkes, *Sacred Ecology* (London: Routledge, fourth edition, 2018).

19. See, for instance, E. Schlager and E. Ostrom, 'Property-rights regimes and natural resources: A conceptual analysis', *Land Economics* 68, 1992, pp.249–62.

20. Elinor Ostrom gave particular emphasis to conventions of use. See, e.g., E. Ostrom, *Governing the Commons: The Evolution of Institutions for Collective Action* (Cambridge: Cambridge University Press, 1990).

21. J.M. Acheson, 'Variations in traditional inshore fishing rights in Maine lobstering communities', in R. Andersen (ed.) *North Atlantic Maritime Cultures: Anthropological Essays on Changing Adaptations* (Berlin: De Gruyter, 1979).

22. N. Matsue, T. Daw and L. Garrett, 'Women fish traders on the Kenyan coast: Livelihoods, bargaining power and participation in management', *Coastal Management* 42, 2014, pp.531–54.

23. This differs from Anne-Marie Slaughter's use of the two terms. A.M. Slaughter, *A New World Order* (Princeton, NJ: Princeton University Press, 2004).

24. B. Freedman and E. Shirley, 'England and the public trust doctrine', *Journal of Planning & Environment Law* 8, 2014, pp.839–48.

25. M. Willers and E. Shirley, 'The public trust doctrine's role in post-Brexit Britain', Garden Court Chambers, 31 March 2017.

26. https://www.ourchildrenstrust.org/juliana-v-us

27. G. Redfearn, 'Australian government to appeal ruling that it must protect children from climate harm', *Guardian*, 9 July 2021.

28. J. Bateman, 'Why climate lawsuits are surging', BBC.com, 8 December 2021.

29. 'Bachelet hails landmark recognition that having a healthy environment is a human right', Press release, UN Office of the High Commissioner for Human Rights, 8 October 2021.

30. R.H. Tawney, *The Acquisitive Society* (London: Bell and Sons, 1921), p.80.

31. On 'social memory' and 'social forgetting', see Standing, 2019, op. cit., pp.51–3.

32. Ibid.

33. For examples, N. Barnes, 'Implementing the provisions of the Nunavut claim: Re-capturing the resource', *Journal of Environmental Law and Practice* 12, 2003, pp.141–201; M. Bavinck et al., 'The impact of coastal grabbing on community conservation – a global reconnaissance', *Maritime Studies* 16: 8, 2017.

34. F. Obeng-Odoom, 'Property in the commons: Origins and paradigms', *Review of Radical Political Economics*, June 2015, p.5.

35. 'Title and ownership: Whose land?', *The Economist*, 12 September 2020, p.16.

36. C.D. Stone, 'Too many fishing boats, too few fish: Can trade laws trim subsidies and restore the balance in global fisheries?', *Ecology Law Quarterly* 24(505), 1997, pp.505–44.

37. P. Foley, C. Mather and B. Neis, 'Governing enclosure for coastal communities: Social embeddedness in a Canadian shrimp fishery', *Marine Policy* 61, 2015, pp.390–400.

38. A. Ghosh and A.S. Lobo, 'Bay of Bengal: Depleted fish stocks and huge dead zone signal tipping point', *Guardian*, 31 January 2017.

39. R.T. Naylor, 'Afishionados', in R.T. Naylor, *Crass Struggle: Greed, Glitz and Gluttony in a Wanna-Have World* (Quebec: McGill-Queen's University Press, 2011), pp.259–87.

40. P. Yeung and C. Dotto, 'Boom in seahorse poaching spells bust for Italy's coastal habitats', *Guardian*, 9 December 2018.

41. This draws on P.K. Nayak and F. Berkes, 'Commonization and decommonization: Understanding the processes of change in the Chilika Lagoon, India', *Conservation and Society* 9(2), 2011, pp.132–45.

42. Ibid.

43. T.T.T. Huong and F. Berkes, 'Diversity of resource use and property rights in Tam Giang Lagoon, Vietnam', *International Journal of the Commons* 5(1), 2011, pp.130–49.

44. M.T. Leopardi Mello, '"Property" rights and the ways of protecting entitlements – an interdisciplinary approach', *Revista de Economia Contemporânea* 20(3), 2016, pp.430–57.

45. Food and Agriculture Organization, 'Small-scale fisheries', fao.org [accessed February 2021].

46. S. Harper, C. Grubb, M. Stiles and U.R. Sumaila, 'Contributions by women to fisheries economies: Insights from five maritime countries', *Coastal Management* 45(2), 2017.

47. D. Pauly and D. Zeller, 'Catch reconstructions reveal that global marine fisheries catches are higher than reported and declining', *Nature Communications* 7: 10244, January 2016.

48. World Bank, Food and Agriculture Organization, and WorldFish, *Hidden Harvests: The Global Contribution of Capture Fisheries*, Economic and Sector Work Report No. 66469-GLB (Washington, DC: World Bank, 2012). Also see A.M. Cisneros-Montemayor and U.R. Sumaila, 'A global estimate of benefits from ecosystem-based marine recreation: Potential impacts and implications for management', *Journal of Bioeconomics* 12(3), October 2010, pp.245–68.

49. G. Monbiot, 'Anglers are our allies against unsustainable industrial fishing', *Guardian*, 24 January 2014.

50. For an earlier analysis, see A. Standing, 'Is blue growth compatible with securing small-scale fisheries?', Coalition for Fair Fisheries Arrangements, October 2019.

51. See G. Standing, *A Precariat Charter: From Denizens to Citizens* (London: Bloomsbury, 2014).

52. B. Neimark, S. Mahanty, W. Dressler and C. Hicks, 'Not *just* participation: The rise of the eco-precariat in the green economy', *Antipode* 52(2), March 2020, pp.496–521.

53. J.V. Catano, 'Reality TV and real work in the fishing industry', Working Class Perspectives, October 2020.

CHAPTER 4: FISHERIES: THE TRAGEDY OF DECOMMONING

1. Cited in R. McKie, 'Bottom trawling: How to empty the seas in just 150 years', *Guardian*, 10 February 2014.

2. P.H. Tyedmers, R. Watson and D. Pauly, 'Fueling global fishing fleets', *Ambio* 34(8), December 2005, pp.634–8.

3. J.D.K. Wilson, *Fuel and financial savings for operation of small-scale fishing vessels*, FAO Fisheries Technical Paper 383 (Rome: Food and Agriculture Organization, 1999).

4. P.M. Miyake et al., *Recent developments in the tuna industry: Stocks, fisheries, management, processing, trade and markets*, FAO Fisheries and Aquaculture Technical Paper 543 (Rome: Food and Agriculture Organization, 2010).

5. There is also difficulty in defining what constitutes a 'fishery'. The FAO Fisheries Glossary has two definitions. First, it is 'an activity leading to harvesting of fish', which can include aquaculture. Second, it is 'a unit determined by an authority engaged in raising and/or harvesting fish'. In the second case, it could be defined by reference to people involved, species of fish, areas of water or seabed, method of fishing, class of boats and purpose of the activities.

6. P. Holm, 'World War II and the "Great Acceleration" of North Atlantic fisheries', *Global Environment* 10(10), January 2012, pp.66–91.

7. See, for example, M. Weber, *From Abundance to Scarcity: A History of US Marine Fisheries Policy* (Washington, DC: Island Press, 2002).

8. C. Finley and N. Oreskes, 'Maximum sustained yield: A policy disguised as science', *ICES Journal of Marine Science* 70, 2013, pp.245–50; M.C. Finley, 'The tragedy of enclosure: Fish, fisheries science and US foreign policy, 1920–1960', PhD dissertation, University of California, San Diego, 2007.

9. C. Finley, 'The industrialisation of commercial fishing, 1930–2016', *Oxford Research Encyclopaedia of Environmental Science*, November 2016, p.6.

10. R. McKie, 2004, op. cit.

11. F. Le Manach et al., 'European Union's public fishing access agreements in developing countries', *PLoS ONE* 8, 2013, e79899.

12. See G. Standing, *Work after Globalization* (Cheltenham: Elgar, 2009), p.211.

13. O. Iheduru, 'The political economy of Euro-African fishing agreements', *Journal of Developing Areas* 30(1), 1995, pp.63–90.

14. A. Thorpe and E. Bennett, 'Globalization and the sustainability of world fisheries: A view from Latin America', *Marine Resource Economics* 16, 2001, pp.143–64.

15. R. Thorp and G. Betram, *Peru: 1890–1977* (New York: Columbia University Press, 1978).

16. FAO, *Production of fish meal and oil*, Fisheries Technical Paper 142 (Rome: Food and Agriculture Organization, 1986).

17. J. Kurien, *The Blessing of the Commons: Small-Scale Fisheries, Community Property Rights and Coastal Natural Assets* (New Delhi: Centre for Science and Environment, 2007), p.9.

18. Cited in G. Bernacesk, *Improving Fisheries Development Projects in Africa* (Nairobi: International Development Research Centre, 1991).

19. E. Bennet, 'The challenges of managing small scale fisheries in West Africa', in CEMARE, *The Management of Conflict in Tropical Fisheries* (Portsmouth: University of Portsmouth, 2002).

20. HKL & Associates, *Impact of Structural Adjustment Policies on the Fisheries Sector in Developing Countries* (Ottawa: International Development Research Centre and Canada International Development Agency, 1992).

21. D. Belhabib et al., 'Lots of boats and fewer fishes: A preliminary catch reconstruction for Senegal, 1950–2010', Working Paper Series, Fisheries Centre, University of British Columbia, 2013.

22. H. Josupeit, *A survey of external assistance to the fisheries sector in developing countries*, FAO Fisheries Circular 755 (Rome: Food and Agriculture Organization, 1987).

23. R. Hicks, *Trends and Impacts in Fisheries Development Assistance* (Washington, DC: World Bank, 2007).

24. B. Hersoug, 'Limits to aid: Some considerations of fisheries development aid projects', in I. Tvedten and B. Hersoug (eds), *Fishing for Development* (Stockholm: Scandinavian Institute for African Studies, 1992).

25. D. Rojat, S. Rajaosafara and C. Chaboud, 'Co-management of the shrimp fishery in Madagascar', IIFET 2004 Japan Proceedings, International Institute of Fisheries Economics and Trade, Oregon State University, 2004.

26. Tvedten and Hersoug, 1992, op. cit.

27. J. Kurien, 'Technical assistance projects and socio-economic change: Norwegian intervention in Kerala's fisheries development', *Economic and Political Weekly* 20(25/26), 1985.

28. A.M. Klausen, 'Technical assistance and social conflict: A case study from the Indo-Norwegian fishing project in Kerala, south India', *Journal of Peace Research* 1(1), 1964, pp.5–19.

29. G. Morgan and D. Staples, 'The history of industrial marine fisheries in South East Asia', FAO Regional Office for Asia and the Pacific, Bangkok, 2006.

30. C. Bailey, 'The political economy of marine fisheries development in Indonesia', *Indonesia* 46, October 1988, pp.25–38.

31. G.R. Morgan and D.J. Staples, *The History of Industrial Marine Fisheries in Southeast Asia*, RAP Publication 2006/12 (Bangkok: Food and Agriculture Organization of the United Nations, Regional Office for Asia and the Pacific, 2006).

32. 'GEF-6 Program framework document' for the Coastal Fisheries Initiative, 2015. https://worldfishers.org/wp-content/uploads/2015/11/GEF-CFI-Framework-document.pdf

33. J.C. Cárdenas and P.I. Melillanca, *Chilled Out*, Samudra Report No.76, May 2017.

34. A.A. Ibarra, C. Reid and A. Thorpe, 'Neo-liberalism and its impact on overfishing and overcapitalisation in the marine fisheries of Chile, Mexico and Peru', *Food Policy* 25, 2000, pp.599–622.

35. A. Guy, 'Loved to death: How pirate fishing decimates Chile's favorite fish', Oceana, 25 October 2018.

36. Cited in S. Mantesso, 'China's "dark" fishing fleets are plundering the world's oceans', ABC News, 18 December 2020.

37. I. Urbina, 'How China's expanding fishing fleet is depleting the world's oceans', Yale Environment 360, 17 August 2020.

38. M. Gutiérrez et al., *China's Distant-Water Fishing Fleet: Scale, Impact and Governance* (London: Overseas Development Institute, June 2020).

39. R. Kang, 'China's distant water fishing fleet growing unsustainably', *China Dialogue*, 6 December 2016.

40. C. Pala, 'China's monster fishing fleet', *Foreign Policy*, 30 November 2020.

41. W. Saumweber and T. Loft, 'Distant-water fishing along China's maritime silk road', Stephenson Ocean Security Project, 31 July 2020.

42. Fisheries Solutions Center, *2016 Rights-based Management Map*. Available at: https://fisherysolutioncenter.edf.org/map

43. See, e.g., R.Q. Grafton et al., 'Incentive-based approaches to sustainable fisheries', *Canadian Journal of Fisheries and Aquatic Sciences* 63(3), 2006, pp.699–710; J. Lubchenco et al., 'The right incentives enable ocean sustainability successes and provide hope for the future', *Proceedings of the National Academy of Sciences* 113, December 2016, pp.14507–14. A contrary view is that quotas are a form of usufruct – the right to use and gain the profits from a resource belonging to another, in this case the state. Because the resource, the fish, does not 'belong' to the rights holder,

the incentive to invest in the resource for the long term is reduced. See A. Rieser, 'Property rights and ecosystem management in US fisheries: Contracting for the commons', *Ecology Law Quarterly* 24(1), 1997, pp.813–32.

44. See, e.g., L. Pfeiffer and T. Gratz, 'The effects of rights-based fisheries management on risk taking and fishing safety', *Proceedings of the National Academy of Sciences* 113, 2016, pp.2615–20.

45. See, e.g., R. Arnason, 'Property rights in fisheries: How much can individual transferable quotas accomplish?', *Review of Environmental Economic Policy* 6, 2012, pp.217–36.

46. R. Arnason, 'Property rights as a means of economic organization' in R. Shotton (ed.), *Use of Property Rights in Fisheries Management*, FAO Fisheries Technical Paper 401/1 (Rome: Food and Agriculture Organization, 2000).

47. C. Costello, S. Gaines and J. Lynham, 'Can catch shares prevent fisheries collapse?', *Science* 321 (5896), 19 September 2008, pp.1678–81.

48. 'A rising tide', *The Economist*, 18 September 2008.

49. Ibid.

50. P. Copes, 'Adverse impacts of individual quota systems on conservation and fish harvest productivity', Discussion Paper No. 00–2, Institute of Fisheries Analysis, Simon Fraser University, British Columbia, 2000.

51. S.B. Longo, R. Clausen and B. Clark, *The Tragedy of the Commodity: Oceans, Fisheries and Aquaculture* (New Brunswick: Rutgers University Press, 2015), p.61.

52. For a review of critical studies, see P. Copes and S. Charles, 'Socioeconomics of individual transferable quotas and community-based fishery management', *Agricultural and Resources Economics Review* 33(2), September 2016, pp.171–81.

53. Longo et al., 2015, op. cit.; see also J. Olson, 'Understanding and contextualising social impacts from the privatization of fisheries: An overview', *Ocean and Coastal Management* 54(5), 2011, pp.353–63.

54. J.E. Host, 'Captains of Finance: An enquiry into market-based fisheries management', PhD dissertation, University of Copenhagen, 2013; M. Isaacs, 'Individual transferable quotas, poverty alleviation and challenges for small-country fisheries policy in South Africa', MAST 10(2), 2011, pp.63–84.

55. K. Benediktsson and A. Karlsdóttir, 'Iceland: Crisis and regional development – thanks for all the fish?', *European Urban and Regional Studies* 18(2), 2011, pp.228–35.

56. D.N. Edwards, 'The rise of the investor class in the British Columbia Pacific halibut fishery', Working Paper 2019-01, Institute for the Oceans and Fisheries, University of British Columbia, 2019.

57. Ibid., p.12.

58. N. Rahaim, 'California's confidential fishing rights leave millions of dollars in mystery', *Monterey County Weekly*, 7 July 2016.

59. World Trade Organization, 'WTO members edge closer to fisheries subsidies agreement', Press release, 15 July 2021.

60. FAO, *Marine fisheries and the Law of the Sea: A decade of change*, FAO Fisheries and Aquaculture Technical Paper 853 (Rome: Food and Agriculture Organization, 1992).

61. M. Fugazza and T. Ok, *Fish and fisheries products: From subsidies to non-tariff measures*, UNCTAD Research Paper No.34 (Geneva: United Nations Conference on Trade and Development, 2019).

62. U.R. Sumaila et al., 'Updated estimates and analysis of global fisheries subsidies', *Marine Policy* 109: 103695, 2019.

63. See a series of papers from the University of British Columbia: U.R. Sumaila et al., 'Global fishery subsidies: An updated estimate', *Marine Policy* 69, 2016, pp.189–93; U.R. Sumaila et al., 'A bottom up re-estimation of global fisheries subsidies', *Journal of Bioeconomics* 12, 2010, pp.201–25.

64. S. Cullis-Suzuki and D. Pauly, 'Marine protected area costs as "beneficial" fisheries subsidies: A global evaluation', *Coast Management* 38(2), 2010, pp.113–21.

65. E. Sala et al., 'The economics of fishing the high seas', *Science Advances* 4(6), 1 June 2018.

66. T.G. Mallory, 'Fishery subsidies in China: Quantitative and qualitative assessment of policy coherence and effectiveness', *Marine Policy* 68, 2016, pp.74–82.

67. R. Sharp and U.R. Sumaila, 'Quantification of US marine fisheries subsidies', *North American Journal of Fish Management* 20, 2009, pp.18–32.

68. E. Lindebo, 'Role of subsidies in EU fleet capacity management', *Marine Resource Economics* 20(4), 2005, pp.445–60.

69. G.R. Munro and U.R. Sumaila, 'The impact of subsidies upon fisheries management and sustainability: The case of the North Atlantic', *Fish and Fisheries* 3(4), 2002, pp.233–50.

70. D. Squires, R. Clarke and V. Chan, 'Subsidies, public goods and external benefits in fisheries', *Marine Policy* 45, 2014, pp.222–7.

71. N. Roy et al., 'Unemployment insurance and the length of the fishing season', IIFET Proceedings, Conference of the International Institute of Fisheries Economics and Trade, Paris, 1992.

72. A. Schuhbauer et al., 'How subsidies affect the economic viability of small-scale fisheries', *Marine Policy* 82, 2017, pp.114–21.

73. J. Jacquet and D. Pauly, 'Funding priorities: Big barriers to small-scale fisheries', *Conservation Biology* 22(4), 2008, pp.832–5.

74. A. Schuhbauer and U.R. Sumaila, 'Economic viability and small-scale fisheries – a review', *Ecological Economics* 124, April 2016, pp.69–75.

75. G. Porter, 'Fisheries subsidies and overfishing: Towards a structured discussion', paper for UNEP Fisheries Workshop, UN Environment Programme, Geneva, Switzerland, 12 February 2001.

76. 'What's the catch?', *The Economist*, 4 January 2020, p.53.

77. Interview in S. Gibbens, 'High seas fishing isn't just destructive – it's unprofitable', *National Geographic*, June 2018.

78. E. Sala et al., 'The economics of fishing the high seas', 2018, op. cit.

79. D. Pauly and D. Zeller, 'Catch reconstructions reveal that global marine fisheries catches are higher than reported and declining', *Nature Communications* 7: 10244, January 2016.

80. M.S. Yeo, 'Natural resource subsidies', World Trade Organization, Geneva, 2010.

81. E.Y. Mohammed, D. Steinbach and P. Steele, 'Fiscal reforms for sustainable marine fisheries governance: Delivering the SDGs and ensuring no one is left behind', *Marine Policy* 93, 2018, pp.262–70.

82. Ibid., p.266.

83. Le Manach et al., 2013, op. cit.

84. J. Alder and U.R. Sumaila, 'Western Africa: A fish basket of Europe past and present', *Journal of Environment and Development* 13(2), June 2004, pp.156–78.

85. A.F. Johnson et al., 'The European Union's fishing activity outside of European waters and the Sustainable Development Goals', *Fish and Fisheries*, 20 January 2021.

86. Le Manach et al., 2013, op. cit., p.6.

87. A. Standing, 'Are the EU's fisheries agreements helping to develop African fisheries?', CFFA paper, 27 October 2016.

88. A few years ago, André initiated legal proceedings against the European Commission as it kept its evaluations of these agreements confidential. It worked, and subsequently all documents were made public. However, when they were classified as 'confidential', they were far more candid

and useful. As soon as they were made public, they were turned into public relations documents. It was clear that the Commission listed payments for Sustainable Fisheries Partnership Agreements as part of their Overseas Development Aid, which is wrong. When this was raised in a letter, the Commission changed their reporting. The payments are a subsidy, not ODA.

89. Although the documents were treated with strict confidentiality, there were some that were shared by the consultants employed by DG-MARE with other fisheries researchers. Many of the consultants regarded the confidentiality as absurd.

90. André co-hosted a seminar on transparency in fisheries with Isabella Lövin in December 2012.

91. D.J. McCauley et al., 'Wealthy countries dominate industrial fishing', *Science Advances* 4(8), 2018.

92. L. Van der Voo, *The Fish Market: Inside the Big Money Battle for the Ocean and Your Dinner Plate* (New York: St Martin's Press, 2016).

93. L. Barratt, 'Western banks provide billions for firms driving tuna species to collapse', Greenpeace *Unearthed*, 28 September 2020.

94. J. Rattle, *A Case Study on the Management of Yellowfin Tuna by the Indian Ocean Tuna Commission* (London: Blue Marine Foundation, June 2019).

95. Barratt, 2020, op. cit.

96. P. Love, *Fisheries: While Stocks Last?* (Paris: OECD, 2010), p.81.

97. K. Pistor, 'Limited liability is causing unlimited harm', *Social Europe*, 11 February 2020.

98. T. Seaman, 'Could Blackstone go fishing for deals with new $22bn-plus fund?', Undercurrent News, 18 April 2019.

99. 'Alantra-backed Union Martin partners with Mauritanian fishing company SMPI', Private Equity Wire, 5 December 2019.

100. Seaman, 2019, op. cit.

101. K. Basu, 'Reeling in investments in sustainable fisheries', GreenBiz, 6 July 2018.

102. J.-B. Jouffray et al., 'Leverage points in the financial sector for seafood sustainability', *Science Advances*, 2 October 2019.

103. T. Danson, *Oceans: Our Endangered Ocean and What We Can Do About It* (New York: Rodale, 2011); A. Keledjian et al., *Wasted Catch: Unsolved Problems in US Fisheries* (Washington, DC: Oceana, March 2014).

104. Commission for Environment Cooperation, *CFP Reform: The Discard Ban* (Brussels: European Commission, 2011).

105. See, inter alia, W.W.L. Cheung, 'The future of fishes and fisheries in the changing oceans', *Journal of Fish Biology* 92(3), March 2018, pp.790–803.

106. M.L. Pinsky et al., 'Preparing ocean governance for species on the move', *Science* 360(6394), 15 June 2018, pp.1189–91.

107. A. Norton, 'It is time to control fishing on the high seas to protect the life of the ocean and coastal people who depend on it', International Institute for Environment and Development blog, 8 June 2019.

108. S. McLaughlin Mitchell and B.C. Prins, 'Beyond territorial contiguity: Issues at stake in democratic militarized interstate disputes', *International Studies Quarterly* 43(1), March 1999, pp.169–83.

109. K. Pierre-Louis, 'Warming waters, moving fish: How climate change is reshaping Iceland', *New York Times*, 29 November 2019.

110. 'Agreed record of conclusions of fisheries consultations between the European Union, the Faroe Islands and Norway on the management of mackerel in the North-East Atlantic for 2020', London, 17 October 2019.

111. Pierre-Louis, 2019, op. cit.

112. Pinsky et al., 2018, op. cit.

113. R. Hannesson, *The Privatization of the Oceans* (Cambridge, MA: MIT Press, 2004), p.42.

114. R. Caddell, 'Precautionary management and the development of future fishing opportunities: The international regulation of new and exploratory fisheries', *International Journal of Marine and Coastal Law* 33(1), March 2018, pp.199–260.

115. J. Lubchenco and K. Grorud-Colvert, 'Making waves: The science and politics of ocean protection', *Science* 350(6259), 2015, pp.382–3.

116. J. Briggs, 'How much of the ocean is really protected in 2020', Pew Bertarelli Ocean Legacy Paper, 7 July 2020.

117. E. Sala et al., 'Assessing real progress towards effective ocean protection', *Marine Policy* 91, May 2018, pp.11–13.

118. P. Evans, 'Are marine protected areas helping marine mammals and birds? Maybe, but more can be done', The Conversation, 16 December 2021.

119. K. Evans, '"We used to be leaders": The collapse of New Zealand's landmark ocean park', *Guardian*, 11 March 2020.

120. 'Whose fish are they anyway', *The Economist*, 8 May 2021, p.43.

121. G. Monbiot, 'Johnson's pledges on the environment are worthless. Worse is how cynical they are', *Guardian*, 30 September 2020.

122. K. McVeigh, 'Revealed: 97% of UK offshore marine parks subject to destructive fishing', *Guardian*, 9 October 2020.

123. D. Carrington, 'Supertrawlers "making a mockery" of UK's protected seas', *Guardian*, 11 June 2020.

124. F. Harvey, 'Supertrawlers ramp up activity in UK protected waters during lockdown', *Guardian*, 13 August 2020.

125. Ibid.

126. S.A. Lester et al., 'Biological effects within no-take marine reserves: A global synthesis', *Marine Ecology Progress Series* 384, 2009, pp.33–46. Note that the study found that not all species recover in such reserves.

127. Cited in D. Carrington, 'England names 27 new marine conservation zones', *Guardian*, 21 November 2013.

128. M. Dureuil et al., 'Elevated trawling inside protected areas undermines conservation outcomes in a global fishing hot spot', *Science* 362(6421), 21 December 2018.

129. K. McVeigh, 'Auditors slam EU for "marine protected areas" that fail to protect ocean', *Guardian*, 3 December 2020.

130. 'How can we encourage nations to come together to protect the high seas', *Prospect*, 16 March 2020.

131. R.B. Cabral et al., 'A global network of marine protected areas for food', *PNAS*, October 2020.

132. E. Sala et al., 'Protecting the global ocean for biodiversity, food and climate', *Nature*, 17 March 2021.

133. H. Österblum et al., 'Transnational corporations as "keystone actors" in marine ecosystems', *PLoS ONE* 10(5), 27 May 2015.

134. N. Degnarain, 'Satellites reveal Japan's Mauritius base for Africa fishing operations', *Forbes*, 14 December 2020.

135. A study of 70,000 firms in 134 countries found that average mark-ups of prices over costs have risen sixfold since the 1980s. J. De Loecker and J. Eeckhout, *Global market power*, Working Paper 24768 (Cambridge, MA: National Bureau of Economic Research, June 2018).

136. A. Pusceddu et al., 'Chronic and intensive bottom trawling impairs deep-sea biodiversity and ecosystem functioning', *Proceedings of the National Academy of Sciences* 111, 2014, pp.8861–6; M.R. Clark et al., 'The impacts of deep-sea fisheries on benthic communities: A review', *Journal of Marine Science* 73 (supplement), 2015, pp.151–69.

CHAPTER 5: COMMERCIAL FISHING:
CRIME UNDER OTHER NAMES

1. Cited in J. Hamilton-Paterson, *Seven Tenths: The Sea and its Thresholds* (London: Faber and Faber, 1992), p.213.

2. 'TRAFFIC warns of European eel trafficking surge as fishing season gets underway', TRAFFIC press release, 15 November 2019.

3. R. Tillman and M. Indergaard, *Pump and Dump: The Rancid Rules of the New Economy* (New Brunswick: Rutgers University Press, 2005), pp.26–7.

4. R. Tillman, 'Reputations and corporate malfeasance: Collusive networks in financial statement fraud', *Crime, Law and Social Change* 51, 2009, pp. 365–82.

5. R. Kramer, R. Michalowski and D. Kauzlarich, 'The origins and development of the concept and theory of state-corporate crime', *Crime & Delinquency* 48, 2002, pp.263–82.

6. J. Henley, 'Bribery allegations over fishing rights rock Iceland and Namibia', *Guardian*, 15 November 2019.

7. B. Gorez, *Illegal Fishing in Guinea: Stealing Fish, Stealing Lives* (Brussels: Coalition for Fair Fisheries Arrangements (CFFA), 2010); V.M. Kaczynski and D.L. Fluharty, 'European policies in West Africa: Who benefits from fisheries agreements?', *Marine Policy* 26, 2002, pp.75–93.

8. This paragraph draws on N. Degnarain, 'Satellites reveal Japan's Mauritius base for Africa fishing operations', *Forbes*, 14 December 2020.

9. L. Lambrechts, 'Stranded for months due to Covid-19, Mauritian fishers are now stuck between polluted waters and insufficient support', Coalition for Fair Fisheries Arrangements (CFFA), 23 November 2020.

10. J. Alder and U.R. Sumaila, 'Western Africa: A fish basket of Europe past and present', *Journal of Environment & Development* 13, 2004, pp.156–78.

11. D. Belhabib et al., 'Euros vs Yuan: Comparing European and Chinese fishing access in West Africa', *PLoS One* 10(3), 20 March 2015.

12. FAO, *A third assessment of global marine fisheries discards* (Rome: Food and Agriculture Organization, 2018).

13. S.M. Mwikya, *Fisheries Access Agreements: Trade and Development Issues* (Geneva: International Centre for Trade and Sustainable Development (ICTSD), April 2006).

14. J. Virdin et al., 'West Africa's coastal bottom trawl fishery: Initial examination of a trade in fishing services', *Marine Policy* 100, 2019, pp. 288–97.

15. M. Rauchholz, 'Resources, boundaries and governance: What future for marine resource in Micronesia?', in E. Fache and S. Pauwels (eds),

Fisheries in the Pacific: The Challenges of Governance and Sustainability (Marseille: pacific-credo Publications, 2016).

16. The European Commission's Directorate-General for Maritime Affairs and Fisheries (DG MARE) issued a press release on this in 2009 entitled 'Is Europe really giving Senegal a raw deal?'.

17. B. Gorez, 'Investment and transparency in EU-Africa fisheries relations: What about joint ventures?', Coalition for Fair Fisheries Arrangements (CFFA), Brussels, 28 July 2020.

18. Environmental Justice Foundation, *China's Hidden Fleet in West Africa: A Spotlight on Illegal Practices Within Ghana's Industrial Trawl Sector* (London: Environmental Justice Foundation, 2018).

19. C.C. Schmidt, 'Identifying current and emerging fisheries trade issues', *Biores* 9(2), March 2015.

20. S. Leahy, 'Revealed: Seafood fraud happening on a vast global scale', *Guardian*, 15 March 2021.

21. This section draws in part on R.T. Naylor, *Crass Struggle: Greed, Glitz, and Gluttony in a Wanna-Have World* (Montreal: McGill-Queen's University Press, 2011), p.266.

22. J. Patinkin, 'Somali fishermen struggle to compete with foreign vessels', VOA News, 20 May 2018.

23. G. Petrossian and R. Clarke, 'Explaining and controlling illegal fishing', *British Journal of Criminology* 4(1), 2014, pp.73–90.

24. G. Pramod et al., 'Estimates of illegal and unreported fish in seafood imports to the USA', *Marine Policy* 48, 2014, pp.102-5.

25. P. Ganapathiraju, T.J. Pitcher and G. Mantha, 'Estimates of illegal and unreported seafood imports to Japan', *Marine Policy* 108, October 2019.

26. P. Love, *Fisheries: While Stocks Last?* (Paris: OECD, 2010), p.64.

27. J. Cusack, 'Intelligence briefing – Illegal unregulated & unreported fishing by FCN', Financial Crime News, 30 September 2019.

28. D. Pauly and D. Zeller, 'Catch reconstructions reveal that global marine fisheries catches are higher than reported and declining', *Nature Communications* 7: 10244, January 2016.

29. A. Telesetsky, 'Laundering fish in the global undercurrents: Illegal, Unreported and Unregulated fishing and transnational organized crime', *Ecology Law Quarterly* 41, 2014, pp.943-44.

30. National Intelligence Council, *Global Implications of Illegal, Unreported and Unregulated (IUU) Fishing* (Washington, DC: Office of the Director of National Intelligence, September 2016).

31. Pauly and Zeller, 2016, op. cit.

32. U.R. Sumaila et al., 'Illicit trade in marine fish catch and its effects on ecosystems and people worldwide', *Science Advances* 6(9), 26 February 2020.

33. A. Standing, 'Goodies and baddies: IUU fishing as state-corporate crime, not "organised crime"', Coalition for Fair Fisheries Arrangements (CFFA), 7 October 2014.

34. J.G. Odom, 'Europe's double standard for China's overfishing', *European Journal of International Law*, 16 April 2020.

35. G. Hosch, 'China bottom of illegal fishing index', China Dialogue Ocean, 16 April 2019.

36. Telesetsky, 2014, op. cit., p.947 *et passim*.

37. T. Woody, 'China is key to closing ports to illegally caught fish', Maritime Executive, 25 October 2019.

38. 'Monsters of the deep', *The Economist*, 24 October 2020, p.14.

39. 'Felonious fishing: The outlaw sea', *The Economist*, 24 October 2020, pp.52–4.

40. A. Sundstrom, 'Covenants with broken swords: Corruption and law enforcement of the commons', Working Paper Series 2014:10, University of Gothenburg, 2014; A. Standing, 'Corruption and industrial fishing in Africa', U4 Issue 2008:7, Anti-Corruption Resource Centre and Christian Michelsen Institute, Bergen, 2008.

41. A. Standing, 'Making transparency work in Africa's marine fisheries', U4 Issue 2011:11, Anti-Corruption Resource Centre and Christian Michelsen Institute, Bergen, 2011.

42. J. Pena-Torres, 'The political economy of fishing regulation: The case of Chile', *Marine Resources Economics* 12(4), 1997, pp.253–80.

43. S. Singleton, 'Co-operation or capture? The paradox of co-management and community participation in natural resource management and environmental policymaking', *Environmental Politics* 9(2), June 2000.

44. M. Bavinck, 'Understanding fisheries conflicts in the South – A legal pluralist perspective', *Society and Natural Resources* 18(9), 2005, pp.805–20.

45. S. Ponte and L. van Sittert, 'The chimera of redistribution in post-apartheid South Africa: "Black Economic Empowerment" (BEE) in industrial fisheries', *African Affairs* 106(424), 2007, pp.437–62; H. Melber, 'Of big fish and small fry: The fishing industry in Namibia', *Review of African Political Economy* 30(95), 2003, pp.142–49; M. Rey and J. Grobler, 'Spain's hake appetite threatens Namibia's most important fish', *The Namibian*, 7 October 2011; A. Standing, 2008, op. cit.

46. L. Buur, with O. Baloi and C. Tembe, 'Mozambique synthesis analysis: Between pockets of efficiency and elite capture', DIIS Working Paper 2012:01, Danish Institute for International Studies, 2012.

47. L. Nhachote, 'Mozambique's "Mr Guebusiness"', *Mail and Guardian*, 6 January 2012.

48. Buur et al., 2012, op. cit.

49. E. Havice, 'The structure of tuna access agreements in the Western and Central Pacific Ocean: Lessons for Vessel Day Scheme planning', *Marine Policy* 34(5), 2010, pp.979–87.

50. M. Tsamenyi and Q. Hanich, 'Managing fisheries and corruption in the Pacific Islands region', *Marine Policy* 33(2), 2009, pp.386–92.

51. K. Mfodwo, *Negotiating Equitable Fisheries Access Agreements* (Dakar: International Union for the Conservation of Nature, 2008).

52. C. Nunns, 'China's Poly Group: The most important company you've probably never heard of', The World, 25 February 2013.

53. Rey and Grobler, 2011, op. cit.

54. R. Tillman, 'Making the rules and breaking the rules: The political origins of corporate corruption in the new economy', *Crime, Law and Social Change* 51, 2009, pp.73–86; S. Tombs, 'State-corporate symbiosis in the production of crime and harm', *Journal of State Crime* 1(2), 2012, pp.170–95.

55. E. Havice and L. Campling, 'Shifting tides in the Western Central Pacific Ocean tuna fishery: The political economy of regulation and industry responses', *Global Environmental Politics* 10(1), 2010, pp.89–114.

56. L. Griggs and G. Lutgen, 'Veil over the nets: Unraveling corporate liability for IUU fishing offences', *Marine Policy* 31(2), 2007, pp.159–68.

57. S. Sloan, *Ocean Bankruptcy: World Fisheries on the Brink of Disaster* (Guildford, CT: Lyons Press, 2003).

58. J. Rattle, *A Case Study on the Management of Yellowfin Tuna by the Indian Ocean Tuna Commission* (London: Blue Marine Foundation, June 2019).

59. M. Mereghetti, 'EU finds Spain guilty of excess tuna catch in Indian Ocean', Undercurrent News, 29 October 2019.

60. E. Tribiloustova, *Fisheries Industry Profile – Russia* (Rome: Food and Agriculture Organization, 2005).

61. J. Cohen, 'Russia's new scramble for Africa', *Wall Street Journal*, 11 November 2011.

62. The following is largely drawn from A. Standing, 'Mirage of pirates: State-corporate crime in West Africa's fisheries', *State Crime Journal* 4(2), 2015, pp.175–97, and Greenpeace, *The Plunder of a Nation's Birthright:*

The Fishing License Scandal – a Drama in Five Acts (Johannesburg: Greenpeace Africa, 2012).

63.   United Nations Environment Programme, *Integrated Assessment of Trade Liberalization and Trade-related Policies: A Country Study on the Fisheries Sector in Senegal* (Geneva: UNEP, 2002).

64.   M. Lossa, P. Niang and A. Polack, *Selfish Europe* (Johannesburg: ActionAid, 2008), p.6.

65.   Marine Resources Assessment Group, *Estimation of the Cost of Illegal Fishing in West Africa* (London: Marine Resources Assessment Group, 2010).

66.   S. Faye, 'Senegal. Dispute over foreign fishing permits hots up', InterPress Service, 16 April 2011.

67.   D. Recalde, 'Senegalese and Russian army pact may bring about fisheries deal', Fish Information Services, 18 September 2007.

68.   Personal communication, International Union for the Conservation of Nature (IUCN), Bissau, June 2011.

69.   G. Allix, 'The risks of Senegal's David and Goliath battle over fishing rights', *Le Monde*, 14 July 2011.

70.   C. Pala, 'Senegal's leader urged to save sardinella', InterPress Service, 15 April 2013.

71.   T. Jean-Matthew, 'Russia to grant free scholarships in exchange for fishing access', *NewsAfrica Review*, 11 December 2012.

72.   S. Diouf, 'Senegal sardinella fishery should be reserved for the artisanal fishing sector', Coalition for Fair Fisheries Arrangements (CFFA), Brussels, 2014.

73.   T. Mallory, 'China's distant water fishing industry: Evolving policies and implications', *Marine Policy* 38, 2013, pp.99–108.

74.   Belhabib et al., 2015, op. cit.

75.   A. Cheriff, *La Convention Poly-Hondone Fishery – Mauritanie* (Nouakchott: Pêchecops, 2011).

76.   André visited the Poly HonDon factory in 2018 as part of research for the Fisheries Transparency Initiative. He gained access to the factory by being mistaken as a government official, although his camera was confiscated at the gate. Having met the manager to discuss local investment, he was promptly escorted out of the facility.

77.   Jeune Afrique Business, 'Poly-Hondone Pelagic Fishery Co accused of failing to meet obligations of $100m contract in Mauritania', *Jeune Afrique*, 24 July 2020.

78.   Nunns, 2013, op. cit.

79. M. Godfrey, 'New data indicate big jump in China distant-water catch', *Seafood Source*, 18 August 2020.

80. Amnesty International, 'People's Republic of China sustaining conflict and human rights abuses: The flow of arms accelerates', Press release, Amnesty International, 2016.

81. T. Ng, 'Beijing slams US sanctions on Chinese companies', *South China Morning Post*, 12 February 2013.

82. H. Hang Zhou and K. Seibel, 'Maritime insecurity in the Gulf of Guinea: A greater role for China?', China Brief 15(1), Jamestown Foundation, Washington DC, 2015.

83. 'Chinese Poly Technologies partners with Denel to build naval vessels for South Africa', *Defense World*, 21 September 2016.

84. T. Rabenasolo, 'A closer look at AMDP's blue economy project', *Manila*, 6 June 2019.

85. H. Ning, 'Madagascar rocked by fishing deal that never was', *China Dialogue Ocean*, 17 October 2019.

86. B. Gorez, 'Small scale fisheries at risk: Madagascar signs destructive fishing agreements with Chinese investors', Coalition for Fair Fisheries Agreements (CFFA), Brussels, 17 November 2020.

87. K. McVeigh and K. Kargbo, '"Catastrophic": Sierra Leone sells rainforest for Chinese harbour', *Guardian*, 17 May 2021; 'Hook, line and sinker', *The Economist*, 21 August 2021, p.39.

88. Environmental Justice Foundation, 'New trawlers arrive from China as Ghana's fisheries teeter on brink of collapse', Environmental Justice Foundation, London, 27 May 2020.

89. J. Wall, 'China plans $200 million fishery industrial park 100 miles from Australia', *Maritime Executive*, 9 December 2020.

90. M. Faa, 'Why PNG's Daru would "reluctantly" support a $204 million Chinese fishing plant on Australia's doorstep', *Pacific Beat*, 17 December 2020.

91. I. Urbina, 'The deadly secret of China's illegal fishing armada', NBC News, 22 July 2020.

92. D. Collyns, '"It's terrifying": Can anyone stop China's vast armada of fishing boats?', *Guardian*, 25 August 2020.

93. E. Fitt, 'China tightens sustainability rules for its notorious fishing fleet', Mongabay, 19 August 2020.

94. Ibid.

95. R. Syal, '"Aphrodisiac" of the ocean: How sea cucumbers became gold for organised crime', *Guardian*, 12 April 2021.

96. L. Pressly, '"Cocaine of the sea" threatens critically endangered vaquita', BBC News, 13 May 2021.

97. J. Feltham, L. Capdepon, S. Stoner and O. Swaak-Goldman, *Giant Clam Shells, Ivory, and Organised Crime: Analysis of a Potential New Nexus* (The Hague: Wildlife Justice Commission, October 2021).

98. Naylor, 2011, op. cit., p.267.

99. M. Gianni and W. Simpson, *The Changing Nature of High Seas Fishing: How Flags of Convenience Provide Cover for Illegal, Unreported and Unregulated Fishing* (Australian Government, Department of Agriculture, Fisheries and Forestry, International Transport Workers Federation, and WWF International, 2005).

100. M. Gutiérrez et al., *China's Distant-Water Fishing Fleet: Scale, Impact and Governance* (London: Overseas Development Institute, June 2020).

101. T.G. Mallory, 'China's distant water fishing industry: Evolving policies and implications', *Marine Policy* 38, 2013, pp.99–108.

102. 'Ensuring better control of the EU's external fishing fleet: Reflagging by EU fishing vessels – the need for stricter standards', Environmental Justice Foundation, Oceana, Pew Charitable Trusts and WWF, September 2016.

103. For a detailed account, see T. Seaman and J. Smith, 'Amid allegations of huge fraud, report says Ngs pocketed $158m from Pacific Andes', Undercurrent News, 2 May 2019.

104. E. Tallaksen, 'China Fishery takes $55m hit on Lafayette, fishing vessels, buys Peruvian vessel', Undercurrent News, 3 January 2014.

105. R. Messick, 'No more Mozambiques! No more hidden debts', Global Anticorruption Blog, 10 July 2019.

106. 'Mozambique and the "tuna bond" scandal', Spotlight on Corruption, 24 February 2021.

107. B. Korby, P. Burkhardt and L. Pronina, 'Mozambique's fishy $850m bond issue doubles its naval forces', *Business Day*, 14 November 2013.

108. 'Investing in frontier markets: Fishy tale', *The Economist*, 23 November 2013.

109. This section draws on, and takes examples from, A. Standing, 'One of the greatest barriers to sustainable fisheries? The role of fishing agents in Africa', Coalition for Fair Fisheries Agreements (CFFA), Brussels, 14 September 2017.

110. Ibid.

111. 'IOTC head "forced to resign" amid links to videotaped executions', Undercurrent News, 9 December 2015; T. McKinnel, J. Lee and D. Salmon,

Made in Taiwan: Government Failure and Illegal, Abusive and Criminal Fisheries (Taipei: Greenpeace East Asia, April 2016).

112. V. Cogliati-Bantz, 'Introductory note to the M/V "VIRGINIA G" case (Panama/Guinea-Bissau) (ITLOS)', *International Legal Materials* 53(6), 2014, pp.1161–226.

113. T. Bruckner, 'Liar's poker in Africa: How hidden agendas drive the politics of fish in Mauritania', HuffPost, 25 August 2015; A. Daniels, '"Fish are vanishing" – Senegal's devastated coastline', BBC, 1 November 2018.

114. Standing, 2017, op. cit.

115. Ibid.

116. The World Bank's evaluation report for Ghana is available at: http://documents1.worldbank.org/curated/en/866911554409721545/pdf/Ghana-Under-the-First-Phase-of-the-West-Africa-Regional-Fisheries-Program-Project.pdf

117. See, for example, OECD, *Combatting Illegal, Unreported and Unregulated Fishing: Where Countries Stand and Where Efforts Should Concentrate in the Future* (Paris: OECD, December 2018).

118. H. Österblom, 'Catching up on fisheries crime', *Conservation Biology* 28(3), January 2014, pp.877–9.

119. Tillman, 2009, op. cit.

CHAPTER 6: THE EUROPEAN UNION'S COMMON FISHERIES POLICY . . . AND BREXIT

1. Cited in C. Wilkins, 'British fishermen battle "codfathers", quotas – and Brexit delay', *France 24*, 30 October 2019.

2. M. Hadjimichael, 'A call for a blue degrowth: Unravelling the European Union's fisheries and maritime policies', *Marine Policy* 94, August 2018, pp.158–64.

3. *Facts and Figures on the Common Fisheries Policy: Basic Statistical Data – 2020 Edition* (Luxembourg: European Union, 2020).

4. G. Carpenter, R. Kleijnans, S. Villasante and B.C. O'Leary, 'Landing the blame: The influence of EU member states on quota setting', *Marine Policy* 64, February 2016, pp.9–15; F. Harvey, 'EU set to miss targets on sustainability after agreeing fishing quotas', *Guardian*, 17 December 2020.

5. Cited in LIFE, *Fishy Business: Fish POs in the EU* (Bristol: Low Impact Fishers of Europe, 2017), p.22.

6. E. Fahey, *Overkill: The Euphoric Rush to Industrialise Ireland's Sea Fisheries and its Unravelling Sequel* (Amazon, 2013).

7. LIFE, 2017, op. cit., p.23.

8. Ibid., p.25.

9. 'The costs of IUU fishing to the EU', Pew Environment Group, Brussels, November 2008.

10. D. Symes and J. Phillipson, 'Whatever became of social objectives in fisheries policy?', *Fisheries Research* 95, 2009, pp.1–5.

11. Marine Management Organisation, *UK Sea Fisheries Statistics 2019* (Newcastle, UK: MMO, 2020).

12. D. Boffey, 'Catches, quotas and communities: The key fisheries issues at stake', *Guardian*, 17 October 2020.

13. P. Sim, 'Brexit: Why is everyone talking about fishing?', BBC News, 28 November 2018.

14. 'Brexit shellfish threat: No deal Brexit shellfish warning', *Fishing News*, 30 July 2018.

15. R.H. Thurstan, S. Brockington and C.M. Roberts, 'The effects of 118 years of industrial fishing on UK bottom trawl fisheries', *Nature Communications* 1(2), 4 May 2010.

16. Marine Stewardship Council, 'North Sea cod certified as sustainable', Press release, 19 July 2017.

17. R. Cook, 'North Sea cod should never have been labelled sustainable in the first place', The Conversation, 26 September 2019.

18. A. Topping, 'Haddock from UK waters removed from sustainable seafood list', *Guardian*, 17 March 2017.

19. K. McVeigh, 'UK fishing licences for bottom-trawling could be unlawful, says Oceana', *Guardian*, 17 December 2021.

20. What made the claim more offensive was that Nigel Farage, a prominent leader of the Leave campaign and former MEP, was a member of the European Parliament's fisheries committee and so must have known how the CFP operated. However, he apparently only turned up twice.

21. G. Carpenter and R. Kleinjans, *Who Gets to Fish?* (London: New Economics Foundation, 2015).

22. T. Appleby, Y. van de Werf and C. Williams, 'The management of the UK's public fisheries: A large squatting claim?', Working Paper, University of West of England, Bristol, January 2016.

23. T. Appleby, E. Cardwell and J. Pettipher, 'Fishing rights, property rights, human rights: The problem of legal lock-in in UK fisheries', *Elementa: Science of the Anthropocene* 6(40), 2018.

24. E. Cardwell, 'Invisible fishermen: The rise and fall of the UK small boat fleet', in K. Schriewer and T. Højrup (eds), *European Fisheries at a Tipping Point* (Murcia: Editum – Ediciones de la Universidad de Murcia, 2012).

25. Cited in Appleby et al., 2018, op. cit., p.4.

26. Ibid., p.5.

27. LIFE, 2017, op. cit., pp.28–9.

28. Select Committee on Agriculture, Minutes of Evidence, Examination of witnesses, 20 May 1999.

29. Cited in C. Dowler, 'Privatising the seas: How the UK turns fishing rights into a commodity', Greenpeace Unearthed, 7 March 2019, p.7.

30. Ibid.

31. M. McClenaghan and C. Boros, 'Big fish quota barons squeeze out small-scale fishermen', Greenpeace Unearthed, 20 May 2016.

32. Cited in F. Harvey, 'Spanish fisheries receive some of the biggest fines in UK maritime history', *Guardian*, 26 July 2012.

33. M. McClenaghan, 'Investigation: Government inspections of fishing fleet plummet amidst cuts', Greenpeace Unearthed, 30 May 2016.

34. Cited in Dowler, 2019, op. cit.

35. G. Carpenter, *The Accidental Privatisation of Marine Life: How the Way We Manage Our Fisheries is Undermining Our Chances of Sustainability* (London: New Economics Foundation, October 2019).

36. McClenaghan and Boros, 2016, op. cit.

37. Ibid.

38. Ibid.

39. 'Master and owner ordered to pay over £102,000 for illegal mackerel catch', Press release, Marine Management Organisation, 10 March 2015.

40. Cited in D. Sabbagh, 'Four navy ships to help protect fishing waters in case of no-deal Brexit', *Guardian*, 11 December 2020.

41. J. Lichfield, 'A "Brexit bonanza" for UK fishing? That's a fishy tale with an unhappy ending', *Guardian*, 31 August 2019.

42. L. O'Carroll, 'Brexit: Failure to secure UK-Norway fishing deal a "disaster" for sector', *Guardian*, 1 May 2021.

43. S. Morris, '"I shouldn't be out there in gales": Brixham fishers take Brexit hit', *Guardian*, 1 March 2021.

44. Appleby et al., 2018, op. cit., p.2.

CHAPTER 7: AQUACULTURE: SAVIOUR OR THREAT?

1. FAO, *The State of World Fisheries and Aquaculture 2020: Sustainability in Action* (Rome: Food and Agriculture Organization, 2020).

2. Such shrimp must, under US regulations, be washed in chlorine bleach to kill bugs. This could become a slipped-in feature of any British-US trade deal. C. Clover, *The End of the Line: How Overfishing is Changing the World and What We Eat* (London: Ebury Press, 2005), p.252.

3. *Facts and Figures on the Common Fisheries Policy – 2020 Edition* (Luxembourg: European Union, 2020).

4. L. Nahuelhual et al., 'Is there a blue transition underway?', *Fish and Fisheries* 20(3), May 2019, pp.584–95.

5. R. Gentry et al., 'Mapping the global potential for marine aquaculture', *Nature Ecology and Evolution* 1, 14 August 2017, pp.1317–24.

6. L. Cao et al., 'China's aquaculture and the world's wild fisheries', *Science* 347, 2015, pp.133–5.

7. O. Torrissen et al., 'Atlantic salmon (*Salmo salar*): The "super-chicken" of the sea?', *Reviews in Fisheries Science* 19(3), 2011, pp.257–78.

8. L. Chim and T. Pickering, 'Feed for aquaculture', Presentation at the SPC/IFREMER seminar on Fish Waste Utilization, Noumea, New Caledonia, 11 June 2012; J. Shepherd, 'Aquaculture: Are the criticisms justified? Feeding fish to fish', *World Agriculture* 3(2), 2012, pp.11–18.

9. K.I. Stergiou, A.C. Tsikliras and D. Pauly, 'Farming up Mediterranean food webs', *Conservation Biology* 23(1), 2008, pp.230–32.

10. B. Belton, S. Bush and D.C. Little, 'Not just for the wealthy: Rethinking farmed fish consumption in the Global South', *Global Fish Security* 16, 2018, pp.85-92.

11. See, for example, the interview with Edward Allison in I. Evans, 'Fish fight: Is aquaculture feeding the people who need it most?', Oceans Deeply, 30 March 2018.

12. M. Feijoo, 'Young Norwegian firm aims to become the largest aquaculture group in Africa', Undercurrent News, 11 November 2019.

13. S. Oirere, 'East Africa fish farming project supports food security, mitigates climate change', Seafood Source, 20 November 2019.

14. E.K. Okai, 'Africa's tilapia farmers rise to Chinese challenge', The Fish Site, 18 January 2019.

15. Ibid.

16. Gentry et al., 2017, op. cit.

17. World Bank, *Fish to 2030: Prospects for Fisheries and Aquaculture* (Washington, DC: World Bank, December 2013).

18. CFFA, 'Replacing fisheries and decarbonizing the sector? We should not expect it from industrial fisheries', Coalition for Fair Fisheries Position Paper, Brussels, 26 October 2020.

19. T. Ward and B. Phillips (eds), *Seafood Ecolabelling: Principles and Practice* (Oxford: Blackwell, 2008); R.E. Brummett (ed.), *Aquaculture Technology in Developing Countries* (Abingdon, UK: Routledge, 2013).

20. M. Allsopp, D. Santillo and C. Dorey, 'Sustainability in aquaculture: Present problems and sustainable solutions', *Ocean Yearbook* 27, 2013, p.292 [pp.291–322].

21. F. Murray, J. Bostock and D. Fletcher, 'Review of recirculation aquaculture system technologies and their commercial application', Report prepared for Highlands and Islands Enterprise, University of Stirling, UK, 2014.

22. Cited in J.K. Bourne, 'How to farm a better fish', *National Geographic*, June 2014.

23. L. Poppick, 'The future of fish farming may be indoors', *Scientific American*, 17 September 2018.

24. O. Morrison, 'AquaMaof fishes new markets after $230 million investment', Food Navigator, 10 July 2019.

25. M. Kurlansky, *Salmon: A Fish, the Earth and the History of a Common Fate* (London: Oneworld, 2020).

26. Malcolm Beveridge, branch head of FAO's aquaculture division, cited in P. Tullis, 'How ocean aquaculture could feed the entire world – and save wild fish', Oceans Deeply, 16 August 2017.

27. P. Love, *Fisheries: While Stocks Last?* (Paris: OECD, 2010), p.58.

28. Bourne, 2014, op. cit.

29. Just Economics, *Dead Loss: The High Cost of Poor Salmon Farming Practices* (London: Just Economics, February 2021).

30. F. Harvey, 'Global salmon farming harming marine life and costing billions in damage', *Guardian*, 11 February 2021.

31. Allsopp, Santillo and Dorey, 2013, op. cit., pp.316–17.

32. A. Welz, 'How aquaculture is threatening the native fish species of Africa', Yale Environment 360, 30 October 2017.

33. L. Dabbadie et al., 'Effects of climate change on aquaculture: Drivers, impacts and policies', in M. Barange et al. (eds), *Impacts of Climate Change on Fisheries and Aquaculture: Synthesis of Current Knowledge, Adaptation and Mitigation Options*, FAO Fisheries and Aquaculture Technical Paper 627 (Rome: Food and Agriculture Organization, 2018), Chapter 20,

pp.449–63. Also see N. Handisyde, T.C. Telfer and L.G. Ross, 'Vulnerability of aquaculture-related livelihoods to changing climate at the global scale', *Fish and Fisheries* 18(3), 2017, pp.466–488.

34. 'Salmon advocates challenge approval of Washington net pen aquaculture', Press release, Center for Biological Diversity, 11 February 2020.

35. M.C.M. Beveridge et al., 'Climate change and aquaculture: Interactions with fisheries and agriculture', in Barange et al., 2018, op. cit., Chapter 22, pp.491–500.

36. M. Karim et al., 'Asset or liability? Aquaculture in a natural disaster-prone area', *Ocean and Coastal Management* 96, 2014, pp.188–97.

37. Nahuelhual et al., 2019, op. cit., p.8.

38. J. Franco et al., *The Global Ocean Grab: A Primer* (Amsterdam: Transnational Institute (TNI), 2014), pp.33–4.

39. FAO, 2020, op. cit.

40. A. Standing, 'European industries must disinvest in West Africa's booming fishmeal and fish oil sector', Coalition for Fair Fisheries Arrangements, 10 December 2019.

41. Changing Markets Foundation and Greenpeace Africa, *Feeding a Monster: How European Aquaculture and Animalfeed Industries are Stealing Food from West African Communities* (Utrecht: Changing Markets Foundation, and Nairobi: Greenpeace Africa, June 2021).

42. Greenpeace, *A Waste of Fish: Food Security Under Threat From the Fishmeal and Fish Oil Industry in West Africa* (Amsterdam: Greenpeace International, June 2019).

43. B. Öztürk, 'Some notes on the Turkish fishing fleet in the Islamic Republic of Mauritania', *Journal of the Black Sea/Mediterranean Environment* 23(1), 2017, pp.88-91.

44. For further detail on the Mauritanian situation, see A. Standing, 'The growth of fishmeal production in Mauritania: The implications for regional food security', Coalition for Fair Fisheries Arrangements, 23 February 2017.

45. Greenpeace, 2019, op. cit.

46. Personal communication to André Standing from Ad Corten, October 2019. Corten has been a member of the working group and is the EU's technical expert on joint committee meetings with the government of Mauritania.

47. FAO Working Group on the Assessment of Small Pelagic Fish off Northwest Africa, Banjul, The Gambia, 26 June–1 July 2018.

48. FAO, *Report of the FAO Working Group on the Assessment of Small Pelagic Fish off Northwest Africa*, Casablanca, Morocco, 8–13 July 2019, FAO Fisheries and Aquaculture Report (Rome: Food and Agriculture Organization, 2020).

49. H. Summers, 'Chinese fishmeal plants leave fishermen in the Gambia all at sea', *Guardian*, 20 March 2019.

50. For information on the FIP: https://fisheryprogress.org/fip-profile/mauritania-small-pelagics-purse-seine

51. Sustainable Fisheries Partnership, 'The seafood industry guide to FIPs', April 2014.

52. André Standing, through the Coalition for Fair Fisheries Arrangements, was involved in this exchange.

53. Allsopp et al., 2013, op. cit., p.295.

54. M.L. Pinsky et al., 'Unexpected patterns of fisheries collapse in the world's oceans', *Proceedings of the National Academy of Sciences of the United States of America* 108(20), 2011, pp.8317–22.

55. C.I. Nwoye, 'Barcelona or die', Quartz Africa, 27 February 2020.

56. Ibid.

57. A.M. Ellison, 'Managing mangroves with benthic biodiversity in mind: Moving beyond roving banditry', *Journal of Sea Research* 59(1–2), February 2008, pp.2–15.

58. B.A. Polidoro et al., 'The loss of species: Mangrove extinction risk and geographic areas of global concern', *PLoS ONE* 5(4), 2010.

59. B.G. Paul and C.R. Vogl, 'Impacts of shrimp farming in Bangladesh: Challenges and alternatives', *Ocean and Coastal Management* 54, 2011, pp.201–11.

60. G. Pallares, 'Governing mangroves: From Tanzania to Indonesia', CIFOR Forests News, 12 October 2017.

61. Cited in K. Evans, 'Protecting Tanzania's mangroves', CIFOR Forests News, 1 February 2017.

62. Tullis, 2017, op. cit.

63. K. McVeigh, 'Blue carbon: The hidden CO_2 sink that pioneers say could save the planet', *Guardian*, 4 November 2021.

64. The Nature Conservancy and Encourage Capital, *Towards a Blue Revolution: Catalyzing Private Investment in Sustainable Aquaculture Production Systems*, 2019. The Nature Conservancy is a non-profit group and Encourage Capital is a New York-based impact investment firm.

65. Public Citizen, *Fishy Currency: How International Finance Institutions Fund Shrimp Farms* (Washington, DC: Public Citizen, April 2005).

66. M. Skladany and C.K. Harris, 'On global pond: International development and commodity chains in the shrimp industry', in P. McMichael (ed.), *Food and Agrarian Orders in the World Economy* (Westport, CT: Greenwood Press, 1995), pp.169–91.

67. B. Johns, 'Bechtel reaps rewards from Thai projects', JOC.com, 1 June 1993.

68. R. Cordes, 'Why dealmakers are getting hooked on aquaculture', The Street, 8 February 2016.

69. D. Gibson, 'Mowi paid high price for full fjord control in latest acquisition, say analysts', Undercurrent News, 23 July 2019.

70. L. Burwood-Taylor, 'Fish 2.0: Bridging the gap between investors and aquaculture', Agfunder News, 4 August 2015.

71. Cited in M. Godfrey, 'Financing aquaculture: The cash is there, but information is lacking', Seafood Source, 18 July 2018.

72. Spheric Research, *Aquaculture Frontiers, Part 5: Financing Aquaculture's Potential*, December 2019.

73. Cited in K. Basu, 'Financing the aquaculture revolution', Conservation Finance Network, 15 April 2019.

CHAPTER 8: COMMODIFYING THE SEA: THE MINING JUGGERNAUT

1. UNEP, 'Wealth in the oceans: Deep sea mining on the horizon?', UN Environment Programme, 2014.

2. K.J. Mengerink et al., 'A call for deep-ocean stewardship', *Science* 344 (6185), May 2014, p.696 [pp.696–8].

3. C. Digges, 'Ten years after the Deepwater Horizon, new spills seem imminent', Bellona, 24 April 2020.

4. S. Laville, 'Oil firm aims to extend Dorset coast drilling despite marine life risk', *Guardian*, 14 February 2019.

5. B. Tian et al., 'Drivers, trends and potential impacts of long-term coastal reclamation in China from 1985 to 2010', *Estuarine, Coastal and Shelf Science* 170, January 2016, pp.83–90.

6. E. Jones et al., 'The state of desalination and brine production: A global outlook', *Science of the Total Environment* 657(20), January 2019, pp.1343–56.

7. European Commission, *Seabed Mining* (Strasbourg: European Commission, 2019); UNECA, *Africa's Blue Economy: A Policy Handbook* (Addis Ababa: UN Economic Commission for Africa, 2016).

8.   STF Analytics, *Submarine Telecoms Industry Report*, Issue 7, 2018–19.

9.   ECORYS, *Blue Growth: Scenarios and Drivers for Sustainable Growth from the Oceans, Seas and Coasts* (Rotterdam: ECORYS, 2012).

10.   Address by Arvid Pardo to the First Committee, 1515th Meeting, UN General Assembly 22nd Session, New York, 1 November 1967, para. 91.

11.   T.R. Bromund, J.J. Carafano and B.D. Schaefer, '7 reasons U.S. should not ratify UN Convention on the Law of the Sea', Heritage Foundation, Washington DC, 4 June 2018.

12.   J.B. Jouffray et al., 'The Blue Acceleration: The trajectory of human expansion into the ocean', *One Earth* 2, 24 January 2020, pp.43–54.

13.   S. Ali et al., 'Mineral supply for sustainable development requires resource governance', *Nature* 543, 2017, pp.367–72.

14.   G.M. Woodwell, 'Curb deep-sea mining now', *Nature* 471, 2011.

15.   L.M. Wedding et al., 'Managing mining of the deep seabed', *Science* 349, 2015, pp.144–5; IUCN, 'Draft mining regulations insufficient to protect the deep sea – IUCN report', Press release, 16 July 2018.

16.   R. Wolfrum, 'Common heritage of mankind', in R. Wolfrum (ed.), *Max-Planck Encyclopaedia of Public International Law Online* (Oxford: Oxford University Press, 2009).

17.   L. Casson et al., *Deep Trouble: The Murky World of the Deep Sea Mining Industry* (Amsterdam: Greenpeace International, December 2020).

18.   For a comprehensive analysis of the payment mechanisms underpinning ISA's licence system, see K. Van Nyen et al., 'The development of a payment regime for deep sea mining activities in the Area through stakeholder participation', *International Journal of Marine and Coastal Law* 34(4), November 2019, pp.571–602. One is tempted to add that nature and marine life are not among the stakeholders.

19.   J. Watts, 'Deep-sea "gold rush": Secretive plans to carve up the seabed decried', *Guardian*, 9 December 2020.

20.   A. Vanaik, 'The UNCLOS isn't perfect, and it's time we acknowledge that', *The Wire*, 27 July 2020.

21.   Mengerink et al., 2014, op. cit., p.696.

22.   H. Scales, *The Brilliant Abyss: True Tales of Exploring the Deep Sea, Discovering Hidden Life and Selling the Seabed* (London: Bloomsbury, 2021).

23.   A. Gilbert et al., 'The world's next energy bonanza', *Foreign Policy*, 8 January 2020.

24.   'Deep sea mining could transform the globe', *The Economist*, 6 December 2017.

25. Y. Kato, 'Deep-sea mud in the Pacific Ocean as a new mineral resource for rare earth elements', Pacific Economic Cooperation Council, 2017. Available at https://is.gd/knne2T

26. 'The scramble for commodities: Mission critical', *The Economist*, 3 April 2021, pp.59–61.

27. D. Batker and R. Schmidt, 'Environmental and social benchmarking analysis of the Nautilus Minerals Inc. Solwara 1 Project', Earth Economics, May 2015.

28. D. Carrington, 'Is deep sea mining vital for a greener future – even if it destroys ecosystems?', *Guardian*, 4 June 2017.

29. M.D. Gerst and T.E. Graedel, 'In-use stocks of metals: Status and implications', *Environmental Science and Technology* 42, 2008, pp.7038–45.

30. C. Church and L. Wuennenberg, *Sustainability and Second Life: The Case for Cobalt and Lithium Recycling* (Winnipeg: International Institute for Sustainable Development, March 2019).

31. C.L. Van Dover et al., 'Biodiversity loss from deep-sea mining', *Nature Geoscience* 10(7), 2017, p.464.

32. O. Hefferman, 'Seabed mining is coming – bringing mineral riches and fears of epic extinctions', *Nature* 571, 21 July 2019, pp.465–8.

33. L. Casson et al., *In Deep Water: The Emerging Threat of Deep Sea Mining* (Amsterdam: Greenpeace International, June 2019).

34. S.Cooley, C.Robbins and K.Browne, 'Considering the Deep Sea as a source of minerals and rare elements', Ocean and Climate Discussion Series, Ocean Conservancy, June 2020.

35. P. Howard et al., *An Assessment of the Risks and Impacts of Seabed Mining on Marine Ecosystems* (Cambridge: Flora and Fauna International, 2020). The study was linked to the ISA in Jamaica.

36. Cited in W.S. Hylton, 'History's largest mining operation is about to begin', *The Atlantic*, January/February 2020.

37. See, for example, B.N. Orcutt et al., 'Impacts of deep-sea mining on microbial ecosystem services', *Limnology and Oceanography* 65(7), July 2020, pp.1489–510.

38. H.J. Niner et al., 'Deep-sea mining with no net loss of biodiversity – an impossible aim', *Frontiers in Marine Science* 5, March 2018, p.53.

39. Van Dover et al., 2017, op. cit., pp.464–5.

40. Cited in Hylton, 2020, op. cit.

41. E.O. Wilson, *The Diversity of Life* (Cambridge, MA: Harvard University Press, 1999), p.243.

42. A. Blanchard et al., 'Harmful routines? Uncertainty in science and conflicting views on routine petroleum operations in Norway', *Marine Policy* 43, 2014, pp.313–20.

43. Hylton, 2020, op. cit.

44. R.E. Kim, 'Should deep seabed mining be allowed?', *Marine Policy* 82, 2017, pp.135.

45. Cited in Hylton, 2020, op. cit.

46. J. Childs, 'Greening the blue? Corporate strategies for legitimising deep sea mining', *Political Geography* 74, October 2019.

47. J. Childs, 'Performing "blue degrowth": Critiquing seabed mining in Papua New Guinea through creative practice', *Sustainability Science* 15, 2020, pp.117–29.

48. Cited in K. McVeigh, 'UK's deep-sea mining permits could be unlawful – Greenpeace', *Guardian*, 12 May 2021.

49. This section draws on A. Standing, 'How BP is drilling through one of the world's largest deep-water coral reefs', Coalition for Fair Fisheries Arrangements, Brussels, 25 August 2019.

50. https://www.bp.com/en/global/corporate/what-we-do/bp-worldwide/bp-in-mauritania.html

51. A. Thomas, 'Panorama investigates $10 billion BP "energy scandal" in Senegal', *Energy Voice*, 3 June 2019.

52. A. Ramos et al., 'Letter with regard to BP EIA', 12 November 2018. Available at: https://static1.squarespace.com/static/517fe876e4b03c6b86a4b81b/t/5d62c0931dd64900018a0fff/1566752917055/letter+with+regard+to+BP+EIA.pdf

53. A. Freiwald et al., *Cold-Water Coral Reefs: Out of Sight – No Longer Out of Mind* (London: UN Environment Programme World Conservation Monitoring Centre, 2004).

54. WWF, 'Norwegian coldwater coral protection: Setting an international example in marine conservation', Gift to the Earth 86, 11 June 2003.

55. J.C. Colman et al., 'Carbonate mounds off Mauritania, Northwest Africa: Status of deep-water corals and implications for management of fishing and oil exploration activities', in A. Freiwald and J.M. Roberts (eds), *Cold Water Corals and Ecosystems* (Berlin: Springer, 2005), pp.417–41.

56. A.L. Cypriano-Souza et al., 'Rare or cryptic? The first report of an Omura's whale (*Balaenoptera omurai*) in the South Atlantic Ocean', *Marine Mammal Science* 33(1), January 2017, pp.80–95.

57. H. Mohr, J. Pritchard and T. Lush, 'BP spill response plans severely flawed', NBC News, 9 June 2010.

58. World Bank, 'Supporting gas project negotiations and enhancing institutional capacities', World Bank Projects and Operations (P160652), n.d.: https://projects.worldbank.org/en/projects-operations/project-detail/P160652?lang=en; International Development Association, 'Project appraisal document on a proposed grant to the Islamic Republic of Mauritania for supporting gas project negotiations and enhancing institutional capacities', World Bank document PAD2423, 22 February 2018.

59. https://www.economics.ox.ac.uk/research-centre/oxford-centre-for-the-analysis-of-resource-rich-economies-oxcarre

60. K. Cremers, G. Wright and J. Rochette, 'UN discussions on marine genetic resources shape the future of marine biotechnology', IDDRI blog, 29 April 2020.

61. For a critical review, see G. Standing, *The Corruption of Capitalism: Why Rentiers Thrive and Work Does Not Pay* (London: Biteback, 2016; third edition, 2021).

62. R. Blasiak et al., 'Corporate control and global governance of marine genetic resources', *Science Advances* 4(6), 6 June 2018.

63. M. Verros et al., 'Who owns the ocean? Policy issues surrounding marine genetic resources', *Association for the Sciences of Limnology and Oceanography Bulletin*, May 2016, pp.29–35.

64. Cited in 'Governing the high seas: In deep water', *The Economist*, 24 February 2014.

65. M. Ruiz Muller, *Access to Genetic Resources and Benefit-sharing 25 years on: Progress and Challenges* (Geneva: International Centre for Trade and Sustainable Development, 2018).

66. S. Arnaud-Haond, J.M. Arrieta and C.M. Duarte, 'Marine biodiversity and gene patents', *Science* 331(6024), March 2011, pp.1521–22.

67. K. Gjerde et al. (eds), 'Area-based management tools in marine areas beyond national jurisdiction. A report of the IUCN Workshop 8–10 October 2019', International Union for the Conservation of Nature (IUCN), Gland, Switzerland, 2020.

68. T. Maloney, R. Phelan and N. Simmons, 'Saving the horseshoe crab: A synthetic alternative to horseshoe crab blood for endotoxin detection', *PLoS Biology* 16(10), October 2018.

69. Reuters, 'Crab blood to remain big pharma's standard as industry group rejects substitute', *Guardian*, 31 May 2020.

70. J.M. Arrieta, S. Arnaud-Haond and C.M. Duarte, 'What lies underneath: Conserving the oceans' genetic resources', *PNAS* 7(43), 26 October 2010.

71. T.J. Price, 'James Blyth – Britain's first modern wind power pioneer', *Wind Engineering* 29(3), May 2005, pp.191–200.

72. International Renewable Energy Agency, *Future of Wind: Deployment, Investment, Technology, Grid Integration and Socio-Economic Impacts* (Abu Dhabi: IREA, 2019).

73. P.D. Jensen, P. Purnell and A.P.M. Velenturf, 'Highlighting the need to embed circular economy in low carbon infrastructure decommissioning: The case of offshore wind', *Sustainable Production and Consumption* 24, 2020, pp.266–80.

74. 'A worrying windfall', *The Economist*, 20 January 2021, pp.37–9.

75. Cited in G. Marston, *The Incorporation of Continental Shelf Rights into United Kingdom Law* (Cambridge: Cambridge University Press, 2008).

76. G. Paton, 'Queen to make millions from wind farms auction', *The Times*, 14 October 2019.

77. J. Garside and J. Ambrose, 'Offshore wind auction could raise millions for Queen', *Guardian*, 17 July 2019.

78. C.A. Caine, 'The race to the water for offshore renewable energy: Assessing cumulative and in-combination impacts for offshore renewable energy developments', *Journal of Environmental Law* 32, 2020, pp.83–109.

79. C. Early, 'Can offshore wind development avoid harming nature?', *GTM* (Greentech Media, 11 January 2021).

80. J. Ambrose, 'Scottish seabed windfarm auction set to bring in £860m', *Guardian*, 24 March 2021.

81. 'Missing ingredients', *The Economist*, 12 June 2021, pp.16–18.

82. Cited in S. Ranganathan, 'Global commons', *European Journal of International Law* 27(3), 2016, p.707.

83. R. Danovaro et al., 'An ecosystem-based deep-ocean strategy', *Science* 355, 2017, p.453. [pp.452–4]

84. H. Scales, 'Halt the mineral rush', *New Scientist* 251(3344), 24 July 2021, p.23.

85. World Bank, 'Investors partner with World Bank to highlight vital role of ocean and fresh water resources', Press release, 25 November 2018.

CHAPTER 9: RESISTANCE AND REBELLION

1. S. Jentoft, 'Small-scale fisheries within maritime spatial planning: Knowledge integration and power', *Journal of Environmental Policy & Planning* 19(3), 2017, pp.266–78.
2. D. Harvey, *The New Imperialism* (Oxford: Oxford University Press, 2003).
3. A. Hornborg, J. Martinez Alier and J.R. McNeill (eds), *Rethinking Environmental History: World-System History and Global Environmental Change* (Lanham, MD: AltaMira, 2007); A. Hornborg, 'Towards an ecological theory of unequal exchange: Articulating world system theory and ecological economics', *Ecological Economics* 25(1), 1998, pp.127–36.
4. J.C. Ribot and N.L. Peluso, 'A theory of access', *Rural Sociology* 68(2), 2003, pp.153–81.
5. M. Bavinck et al., 'The impact of coastal grabbing on community conservation – a global reconnaissance', *Marine Studies* 16, 2017.
6. S. Stonich and C. Bailey, 'Resisting the blue revolution: Contending coalitions surrounding industrial shrimp farming', *Human Organisation* 59, 2000, pp.23–36.
7. J. Moore, 'The modern world-system as environmental history? Ecology and the rise of capitalism', *Theory and Society* 32, 2003, pp.307–77.
8. See, for example, M. Glaser and R. da Silva Oliveira, 'Prospects for the co-management of mangrove ecosystems on the North Brazilian coast: Whose rights, whose duties and whose priorities?', *Natural Resources Forum* 28(3), 2004, pp.224–33.
9. J.C. Scott, *The Art of Not Being Governed – An Anarchist History of Upland Southeast Asia* (New Haven and London: Yale University Press, 2009).
10. Cited in M. Bavinck, S. Jentoft and J. Scholtens, 'Fisheries as social struggle: A reinvigorated social science research agenda', *Marine Policy* 94, 2018, pp.46–52.
11. K. Lasslett, P. Green and D. Stanczak, 'The barbarism of indifference: Sabotage, resistance and state–corporate crime', *Theoretical Criminology* 19(4), 2015, pp.514–33.
12. J. Martinez-Alier, 'Ecological conflicts and valuation: Mangroves versus shrimps in the 1990s', *Environment and Planning C: Government and Policy* 19(5), 2001, pp.713–28.
13. S. Veuthey and J.-F. Gerber, 'Accumulation by dispossession in coastal Ecuador: Shrimp farming, local resistance and the gender structure of mobilisations', *Global Environmental Change* 22, 2012, pp.611–22.

14. G. Ghiglione, 'Underwater museum: How "Paolo the fisherman" made the Med's strangest sight', *Guardian*, 17 November 2020.

15. L. Cecco, 'Why were indigenous crews in Canada shot at with flares for fishing?', *Guardian*, 23 September 2020.

16. L. Cecco, '"We won": Indigenous group in Canada scoops up billion dollar seafood firm', *Guardian*, 12 November 2020.

17. See, for example, M. Bavinck and D. Johnson, 'Handling the legacy of the blue revolution in India – social justice and small-scale fisheries in a negative growth scenario', *American Fisheries Society Symposium* 49, 2008, pp.585–99.

18. Historically, British examples of this include the actions that led to Peterloo in 1819 and the miners' strike in the early 1980s.

19. This description draws on the excellent account by Joeri Scholtens, 'The elusive quest for access and collective action: North Sri Lankan fishers' thwarted struggles against a foreign trawler fleet', *International Journal of the Commons* 10(2), 2016, pp.929–52.

20. M.A. Schreiber, I. Wingren and S. Linke, 'Swimming upstream: Community economies for a different coastal rural development in Sweden', *Sustainability Science* 15, 2020, pp.63–73.

21. D. Symes and J. Philipson, 'Whatever became of social objectives in fisheries policy?', *Fisheries Research* 95(1), 2009, pp.1–5.

22. Schreiber et al., 2020, op. cit.

23. J.K. Gibson-Graham, 'Diverse economies: Performative practices for "other worlds"', *Progress in Human Geography* 32(5), 2008, p.613 [pp. 613–32].

24. L. Towers, 'Small-scale fishermen defeat trawler barons in court battle for fish', The Fish Site, 11 July 2013.

25. J. Kurien, 'Collective action in small-scale fisheries', in D. Kalikoski and N. Franz (eds), *Strengthening Organizations and Collective Action in Fisheries – a Way Forward in Implementing the Guidelines for Securing Sustainable Small-Scale Fisheries*, FAO Workshop 18–20 March 2013, Food and Agriculture Organization, Rome, pp.41–65; FAO Fisheries and Aquaculture Proceedings 32 (Rome: Food and Agriculture Organization, 2013).

26. F. Berkes, 'Commons in a multi-level world', *International Journal of the Commons* 2(1), 2008, pp.1–6.

27. Veuthey and Gerber, 2012, op. cit., pp.619–20.

28. L. Sarah, 'Coal-ravaged Indian fishers take to the Supreme Court', *Sierra*, 26 April 2019.

29. S. Dhar, 'The US Supreme Court judgment: A challenge to World Bank's unfettered immunity', Committee for the Abolition of Illegitimate Debt, 31 March 2019.

30. K. Fried and M. Jalal, 'Tata Mundra: NGOs worry as US court rules World Bank can't be sued for "damages"', Counterview, 31 August 2020.

31. M. Simons, 'Jam v. IFC – some questions and answers after the Supreme Court's ruling', EarthRights, 4 March 2019.

32. S. Dias, 'Jam v IFC before the D.C. District Court: Forget the floodgates, there won't even be a trickle', ejiltalk, 1 April 2020.

33. R. Freedman, 'UN immunity or impunity? A human rights based challenge', *European Journal of International Law* 25(1), 2014.

34. C. Arsenault, 'International court to prosecute environmental crimes in major shift', Reuters, 15 September 2016.

35. G. Vince, 'Why there is hope that the world's coral reefs can be saved', *Guardian*, 18 October 2020.

36. This paragraph is based on B. Logger and P. Weijnen, 'De quota worden duur betaald [The quotas are paid dearly]', *De Groene Amsterdammer*, No. 6, 10 February 2021.

37. G. Standing, *Work After Globalization: Building Occupational Citizenship* (Cheltenham, UK: Elgar, 2009).

38. B. Neimark et al., 'Not just participation: The rise of the eco-precariat in the green economy', *Antipode* 52(2), March 2020.

39. A.M. Song et al., 'Collateral damage? Small-scale fisheries in the global fight against IUU fishing', *Fish and Fisheries* 21(4), July 2020, pp.831–43.

40. D. Palmer, S. Fricska and B. Wehrmann, *Towards improved land governance*, FAO Land Tenure Working Paper 11 (Rome: Food and Agriculture Organization, September 2009).

41. IPC Working Group on Land, Forests, Water and Territory, *People's Manual on the Guidelines on Governance of Land, Fisheries and Forests: A Guide for Promotion, Implementation, Monitoring and Evaluation* (International Planning Committee for Food Sovereignty, 2016).

42. Rights and Resources Initiative, *Who Owns the World's Land? A Global Baseline of Formally Recognized Indigenous and Community Land Rights* (Washington, DC: Rights and Resources Initiative, 2015).

43. M.B. Barreto et al., 'People power under attack: A global analysis of threats to fundamental freedoms', CIVICUS, November 2018.

44. J. Garside and N. Watts, 'Environment reporters facing harassment and murder, study finds', *Guardian*, 17 June 2019.

CHAPTER 10: FROM BLUE GROWTH TO DEGROWTH

1. Cited in P. Greenfield, 'Call for drone users and jetskiers to keep away from marine wildlife', *Guardian*, 31 December 2019.

2. W. Nordhaus, 'To slow or not to slow: The economics of the greenhouse effect', *Economic Journal* 101(407), July 1991, pp.920–37; J. Hickel, 'The Nobel Prize for climate catastrophe', *Foreign Policy*, 6 December 2018.

3. M. Cummings, 'Cheers and roses from undergrads for Yale's latest Nobel laureate', Yale News, 8 October 2018.

4. P. Bresnihan, 'Revisiting neoliberalism in the oceans: Governmentality and the biopolitics of "improvement" in the Irish and European fisheries', *Economy and Planning A: Economy and Space* 51(1), 2019, pp.156–177.

5. 'Walmart Canada is first retailer to offer smoked salmon from Kitasoo/Xai'xais First Nation', Press release, Walmart Canada, 8 December 2021.

6. S.M. Borras et al., 'Land grabbing in Latin America and the Caribbean', *Journal of Peasant Studies* 38, 2012, pp.845–72.

7. I.M. Mas, 'The fishing footprint of a tourism-based economy: Displacing seafood consumption from local to distant waters in the Balearic Islands', *Journal of Political Ecology* 22(1), 2015, pp.211–38.

8. H. Schandl et al., 'Decoupling global environmental pressure and economic growth: Scenarios for energy use, materials use and carbon emissions', *Journal of Cleaner Production* 132, 2016, pp.45–56.

9. H. Daly and J. Farley, *Ecological Economics: Principles and Applications* (Washington, DC: Island Press, 2004).

10. http://www.onthehook.org.uk/

11. L. Barratt, 'Western banks provide billions in backing for firms driving tuna species to collapse', Greenpeace Unearthed, 28 September 2020.

12. Portfolio Earth, *Bankrolling Extinction: The Banking Sector's Role in the Global Biodiversity Crisis* (Portfolio Earth, October 2020).

13. Cited in D. Rushe, 'Green investing "is definitely not going to work", says ex-BlackRock executive', *Guardian*, 30 March 2021.

14. 'The perils of stakeholderism', *The Economist*, 19 September 2020, p.58.

15. 'Hot air: The green boom', *The Economist*, 22 May 2021, p.13.

16. A. Raghunandan and S. Rajgopal, 'Do socially responsible firms walk the talk?', mimeo, 1 April 2021.

17. 'It is not so easy being green', *The Economist*, 27 March 2021, pp.55–6.

18. 'The meaning of green', *The Economist*, 19 September 2020, p.62.

19. D. Elmalt, D. Igan and D. Kirti, 'Limits to private climate change mitigation', IMF Working Paper 2021/112, International Monetary Fund, Washington DC, 29 April 2021.

20. This is a variant of Sinn's 'green paradox', which says that fossil fuel companies will try to ramp up production and profits before environmental taxes and/or regulation start to bite. H.-W. Sinn, *The Green Paradox: A Supply-Side Approach to Global Warming* (Cambridge, MA: MIT Press, 2012).

21. A. Raval, 'A $140bn asset sale: The investors cashing in on Big Oil's push to net zero', *Financial Times*, 5 July 2021; M. Taylor and J. Ambrose, 'Foreign control of North Sea oil licences threatens UK's net zero goal', *Guardian*, 29 July 2021.

22. International Energy Agency, *Net Zero by 2050; A Roadmap for the Global Energy Sector* (Paris: IEA, May 2021, revised October 2021).

23. F. Harvey, P. Dobson and R. Edwards, 'Environmentalists warn of close ties between oil and gas sector and UK's North Sea regulator', *Guardian*, 17 September 2021.

24. '14 world leaders commit to 100 percent sustainable ocean management to solve global challenges; Call for more countries to join', Press release, High Level Panel for a Sustainable Ocean Economy, 12 February 2020.

25. R. Teiwaki, 'Access agreements in the South Pacific: Kiribati and the distant water fishing nations, 1979–86', *Marine Policy* 11(4), 1987, pp.273–84.

26. A.B. Gray, 'China's next geopolitical goal: Dominate Antarctica', *The National Interest*, 20 March 2021.

27. H. Österblom et al., 'Transnational corporations as "keystone actors" in marine ecosystems', *PLoS ONE* 10(5), 2015, e0127533.

28. Cited in 'In deep water', *The Economist*, 24 February 2014.

29. J. Rattle, *A Case Study on the Management of Yellowfin Tuna by the Indian Ocean Tuna Commission* (London: Blue Marine Foundation, June 2019).

30. Barratt, 2020, op. cit.

31. R.E. Kim, 'Should deep sea mining be allowed?', *Marine Policy* 82, 2017, pp.134–7.

32. For a fuller critique, see G. Standing, *The Corruption of Capitalism: Why Rentiers Thrive and Work Does Not Pay* (London: Biteback, 2016), pp.74–81.

33. P. Withers, 'Canada ordered to pay U.S. concrete company $7m in NAFTA case', CBC News, 25 February 2019.

34. 'Odyssey Marine Exploration files first memorial in Mexico NAFTA case', GlobalNewswire, 16 September 2020.

35. 'How some international treaties threaten the environment', *Guardian*, 5 October 2020.

36. 'Elephants' graveyard no more', *The Economist*, 24 October 2020, p.31.

37. Cited in K. McVeigh, 'Tiny Atlantic island takes giant leap towards protecting world's waters', *Guardian*, 13 November 2020.

38. H. Fearnley-Whittingstall, 'If the UK government won't stop industrial fishing from destroying our oceans, activists will', *Guardian*, 26 February 2021.

39. B.M. Barber, 'Monitoring the monitor: Evaluating CalPERS' activism', Center for Investor Welfare and Corporate Responsibility, Davis CA, 2006.

40. D. Belhabib et al., 'Euros vs. Yuan: Comparing European and Chinese fishing access in West Africa', *PLoS ONE* 10(3), 2015.

41. C. Pala, 'How eight Pacific Island States are saving the world's tuna', *Foreign Policy*, 5 March 2021.

42. J. Potts, A. Wilkings, M. Lynch and S. McFatridge, *State of Sustainability Initiatives Review: Standards and the Blue Economy* (Winnipeg: International Institute for Sustainable Development, 2016).

43. K. McVeigh, 'Blue ticked off: The controversy over the MSC fish "ecolabel"', *Guardian*, 26 July 2021.

44. S. Ponte, 'The Marine Stewardship Council (MSC) and the making of a market for "sustainable fish"', *Journal of Agrarian Change* 12(2–3), pp.300–316.

45. E. Fitt, 'China tightens sustainability rules for its notorious fishing fleet', Mongabay, 14 August 2020.

CHAPTER 11: REVIVING THE COMMONS, SHARING COMMON-WEALTH

1. The others were Severe Acute Respiratory Syndrome Coronavirus (SARS-CoV) in 2002, H1N1 influenza virus in 2009, Middle East Respiratory Syndrome Coronavirus (MERS-CoV) in 2012 and Ebola virus in 2013.

2. J. Hickel, *Less Is More: How Degrowth Will Save the World* (London: Windmill, 2020), p.32.

3. S. Leahy, 'Fish detectives: The sleuths using "e-DNA" to fight seafood fraud', *Guardian*, 16 March 2021.

4. A. Hatcher et al., 'Normative and social influences affecting compliance with fishery regulations', *Land Economics* 76(3), 2000, pp.448–61.

5. G. Auriemma et al., *A Global Assessment of Territorial Use Rights in Fisheries to Determine Variability in Success and Design* (Santa Barbara, CA: Bren School of Environmental Science and Management, 2014).

6. The description of Japan's TURF system draws on J.P. Cancino, H. Uchida and J. Wilen, 'TURFs and ITQs: Collective vs. individual decision making', *Marine Resource Economics* 22, 2007, pp.391–406.

7. A. Delaney, 'Japanese fishing cooperative associations: Governance in an era of consolidation', in S. Jentoft and R. Chuenpagdee (eds), *Interactive Governance for Small-Scale Fisheries: Global Reflections* (Cham, Switzerland: Springer, MARE Publication Series Vol.13, 2015), pp.263–80.

8. The leading scholar of *buen vivir* is Eduardo Gudynas. See, for a short review, E.Gudynas, 'Buen Vivir: Today's tomorrow', *Development* 54, December 2011, pp.441–7.

9. J. Locke, *Second Treatise of Government* (1690), Chapter 5, Sec. 35.

10. H. Lefebvre, 'The right to the city', in E. Kofman and E. Lebas (eds), *Writing on Cities* (Oxford: Blackwell, 1996), pp.63–181; D. Harvey, 'The right to the city', *New Left Review* 53, 2008, pp.23–40; D. Harvey, *Rebel Cities: From the Right to the City to the Urban Revolution* (London: Verso, 2012).

11. Lefebvre, 1996, op. cit., p.174.

12. World Bank, *The Changing Wealth of Nations: Measuring Sustainable Development in the New Millennium* (Washington, DC: World Bank, 2011), p.9.

13. E.B. Weiss, 'The planetary trust: Conservation and intergenerational equity', *Ecology Law Quarterly* 11(4), 1984, p.499 [pp.495–582].

14. O.P. Hauser et al., 'Cooperating with the future', *Nature* 511, 2014, pp.220–23.

15. U. Fischbacher et al., 'Are people conditionally cooperative? Evidence from a public goods experiment', *Economics Letters* 71(3), June 2001, pp.397–404.

16. N. Frohlich and J.A. Oppenheimer, *Choosing Justice: An Experimental Approach to Ethical Theory* (Berkeley, CA: University of California Press, 1992).

17. G. Standing, *Plunder of the Commons: A Manifesto for Sharing Public Wealth* (London: Penguin, 2019).

18. The themes underlying this paragraph are elaborated elsewhere. G. Standing, *The Corruption of Capitalism: Why Rentiers Thrive and Work Does Not Pay* (London: Biteback, 2016; third edition, 2021).

19. H. Simon, 'Herbert Simon's last public lecture: Public administration in today's world of organizations and markets', 2000, available at https://inst.eecs.berkeley.edu/~cs195/fa14/assets/pdfs/simon_last_lecture.pdf Simon gave two estimates of the share of US wealth attributable to co-inherited social capital, 80% and 90%.

20. J. Lowe, *Warren Buffett Speaks: Wit and Wisdom from the World's Greatest Investor* (Hoboken, NJ: John Wiley, 2007), p.212.

21. 'Norwegian blues', *The Economist*, 10 October 2015, p.68.

22. K. Myers and D. Manley, 'Did the UK miss out on £400 billion of oil revenue', resourcegovernance.org, 17 November 2015.

23. O. Goldsmith, 'The economic and social impacts of the Permanent Fund Dividend in Alaska', in K. Widerquist and M. Howard (eds), *Alaska's Permanent Fund Dividend* (New York: Palgrave Macmillan, 2012).

24. 'Free exchange: We the shareholders', *The Economist*, 22 September 2018, p.62.

25. D. Bollier, 'Black commons, community land trusts and reparations', Resilience, 22 July 2020.

26. I. Parry, 'Five things to know about carbon pricing', *Finance & Development*, September 2021.

27. D. Klenert and M. Fleurbaey, 'The social cost of carbon and inequality', Vox EU, 28 April 2021. Ideally, there should be a global Commons Fund since greenhouse gas emissions in one country affect the global climate.

28. K. Vohra et al., 'Global mortality from outdoor fine particle pollution generated by fossil fuel combustion: Results from GEOS-Chem', *Environmental Research* 195, April 2021.

29. IMF/OECD, 'Tax policy and climate change: IMF/OECD report for the G20 finance ministers and central bank governors', Italy, April 2021.

30. A. Levinson, 'Energy efficiency standards are more regressive than energy taxes: Theory and evidence', NBER Working Paper 22956, National Bureau of Economic Research, Cambridge MA, 2016.

31. A. Baranzini et al., 'Carbon pricing in climate policy: Seven reasons, complementary instruments, and political economy considerations', *Wiley Interdisciplinary Reviews: Climate Change* 8(4), 2017, e462.

32. E. Tvinnereim and M. Mehling, 'Carbon pricing and deep decarbonisation', *Energy Policy* 121, October 2018, pp.185–9; R.A. Rosen, 'Carbon taxes: A good idea but can they be effective?', Perspectives, Institute for New Economic Thinking, 28 June 2021.

33. E. Sala et al., 'Protecting the global ocean for biodiversity, food and climate', *Nature* 592, April 2021, pp.397–402.

34. E. Stratiotis, 'Fuel costs in ocean shipping', More Than Shipping, 22 January 2018.

35. M. Walsh, *Finance for Pacific Ocean Governance* (Pacific Ocean Finance Program, 2 October 2018).

36. H. Booth et al., 'Bycatch levies could reconcile trade-offs between blue growth and biodiversity conservation', *Nature Ecology & Evolution* 5, 2021, pp.715–25.

37. F. Pakiding et al., 'Community engagement: An integral component of a multifaceted conservation approach for the transboundary Western Pacific leatherback', *Frontiers in Marine Science*, 9 September 2020.

38. Booth et al., 2021, op. cit.

39. C.M. Duarte et al., 'The soundscape of the Anthropocene ocean', *Science* 371(6529), 5 February 2021; D. Carrington, 'Cacophony of human noise is hurting all marine life, scientists warn', *Guardian*, 4 February 2021.

40. J. De Loecker and J. Eeckhout, *Global Market Power*, NBER Working Paper 24768 (Cambridge MA: National Bureau of Economic Research, June 2018).

41. J. Virdin et al., 'The ocean 100: Transnational corporations in the ocean economy', *Science Advances* 7(3): eabc8041, 13 January 2021.

42. For this idea, thanks are due to Peter Barnes. In 1968, University of Chicago law professor Richard Posner (later a US appeals court judge) proposed a surtax of 20% on monopoly profits in excess of a fair rate of return to be determined by a government agency. At the time, the basic corporate income tax rate was 52%. Posner argued that 'the public would have the satisfaction of knowing that 72% (normal corporate income tax plus surtax) of any monopoly profits would be extracted from the monopolist and used for public purposes.' R.A. Posner, 'Natural monopoly and its regulation', *Stanford Law Review* 548, 1968, p. 640. As of 2021, the basic corporate tax rate is 21%. For a related proposal for a monopoly tax, see M. Jarsulic, E. Gurwitz and A. Schwartz, *Toward a Robust Competition Policy* (Washington, DC: Center for American Progress, 2019).

43. M. Szabo, 'A Common Heritage Fund for future generations', in I. González-Ricoy and A. Gosseries (eds), *Institutions for Future Generations* (Oxford: Oxford University Press, 2017), Chapter 12, pp.197–213.

44. W.C. Lynch, 'The Nepal proposal for a Common Heritage Fund: Panacea or pipedream', *California Western International Law Journal* 10, 1980, pp.25–52. Available at https://jak.ppke.hu/uploads/articles/1213437/file/OUPfuturegenerations.pdf

45. R. Milne, 'SWF head says Norway now "an oil fund nation"', *Financial Times*, 27 February 2020.

46. A. Fremstad and M. Paul, 'The impact of a carbon tax on inequality', *Ecological Economics* 104(9), September 2019, pp.2872–99.

47. J.K. Boyce, *The Case for Carbon Dividends* (Cambridge, UK: Polity Press, 2019), p. 60.

48. H.-j. Yoon, 'Sea cucumber fisheries as shared property of islanders: "Rediscovering rural basic income experiments"', *The Hankyoreh*, 24 February 2021.

Index

8F Investment Partners, 337